A SOCIOLOGY OF
Contemporary Cultural Change

A Sociology of
Contemporary Cultural Change

BERNICE MARTIN DISCARDED

St. Martin's Press · New York

ISBN 0-312-74058-1

Library of Congress Cataloging in Publication Data

Martin, Bernice.
   A sociology of contemporary cultural change.
   Includes bibliographical references
   1. Social change. I. Title.
HM 101.M26862 1981 303.4 81-83757
ISBN 0-312-74058-1   AACR2

For my mother, Edith Thompson, and in memory
of my father, Frederick William Thompson, of
Bury, Lancashire

Contents

Acknowledgements

The author and publishers are grateful to the following for permission to reproduce lengthy extracts from literary works:

Faber and Faber Ltd and Random House Inc. for selections from *W. H. Auden: Collected Poems*, edited by Edward Mendelson. Copyright © 1976 by Edward Mendelson, William Meredith and Monroe K. Spears, Executors of the Estate of W. H. Auden. Reprinted by permission of Random House, Inc. Faber and Faber Ltd and Random House Inc. for selections from *Forewords and Afterwords* by W. H. Auden, selected by Edward Mendelson. Copyright © 1973 by W. H. Auden. Reprinted by permission of Random House, Inc.

Faber and Faber Ltd for the extract from *Paul Bunyan* by W. H. Auden and for 'Elvis Presley' by Thom Gunn

Adrian Henri for his poem 'If you weren't you, who would you like to be?' © Adrian Henri 1967 from Penguin Modern Poets 10 (Penguin Books, © 1967). Used by permission of Deborah Rogers Ltd, London

Roger McGough for 'Let me die a youngman's death' © 1967 by Roger McGough from Penguin Modern Poets 10

Secker and Warburg Ltd and Random House Inc. for passages from Thomas Mann's *The Magic Mountain*, *Doctor Faustus* and *Royal Highness*

The following sources are also acknowledged for the illustrations in this book:

BBC Record 'Monty Python's Flying Circus' (REB 73) and Terry Gilliam (p. 93)

Gilbey Vintners Ltd (p. 114)

MCA Records (p. 171)

Morris Newcombe (p. 126)

© David Redfern; photo by Richard E. Aaron (p. 181)

Libuce Taylor (p. 219)

Trevor Thompson (p. 58)

Wings of Love, 1972 by Stephen Pearson (p. 244)

CHAPTER 1

Of Infinity and Ambiguity

In the last few decades the Western world has experienced a transformation in the assumptions and habitual practices which form the cultural bedrock of the daily lives of ordinary people. This book is about the re-making of a good deal of what we take for granted. The shift began as a sort of cultural revolution among a small minority of crusading radicals, and finished by altering some of our deepest – and therefore most customary and commonplace – habits and assumptions.

The analysis which I offer here is intended as an exercise in interpretive sociology – more art than science and with no claim to neutrality or objectivity on the issues with which it tangles. The narrative 'I' will appear as often as the impersonal and generalizing 'one'. In this first chapter my aim is to clarify both my style of approach and the opinions and values from which it derives.

I see the process of cultural change in the post-war decades as a continued working out of the principles of Romanticism which had rooted themselves in North American and Western European culture at the outset of the modern age. Like Max Weber, I am inclined to take culture seriously and to consider ideas, norms and values as powerful patterns which may facilitate, deflect, transmute and perhaps even preclude the development of possibilities which lie in the structural arrangements of societies. The Romanticism which is the main subject of my argument is an historically and culturally specific phenomenon. My analysis is not intended to apply outside the Western hemisphere for that reason. In Japan, for example – the one non-Western case with which I can claim a nodding acquaintance – the same structural potentialities of modernity exist without giving rise to cultural transformations of the kind with which I shall be concerned. The traditional cultural constellation of Japan filters modernity through a mesh which largely excludes Romantic individualism of the Western kind.

In fact, I base my case on Britain – or, more accurately, England – though I believe that it has a general validity for the modern Western world and, more specifically, for North America, Protestant northern Europe and Scandinavia, where individuality and Romanticism are part of the cultural foundations of modernity. Nevertheless, I have too much respect for historical and geographical specificities to assume that the processes which I can delineate for England are *exactly* paralleled, even in these broadly comparable societies: each case needs to be separately established and documented before reliable comparisons can be made.

The main agency of cultural change was an international movement involving the arts and the politics of a cosmopolitan intelligentsia. For this reason national cultural boundaries are less significant within the innovating movement than in the cultures which received its impact: the latter are national, regional and class cultures whose roots reach deep into the particular histories of place and people. At the heart of the radical movement which will be the focus of my attention is the so-called 'counter-culture' of the late 1960s. My argument is that it served as a dramatic embodiment of certain crucial Romantic values which in the subsequent decade became intimately woven into the fabric of our culture: what was shocking in 1968 is often too commonplace today to require comment.

My first task is to make clear what I see as these crucial principles of Romanticism, but I am reluctant to do this through misleadingly precise definitions. I propose to approach the problem more obliquely, through art forms which are part of modern culture's reflection on the Romantic movement. After all, a sociologist who approaches the topic finds it already well worked by artists, philosophers, scientists and folk *bricoleurs* who have been ready to take sides in the struggle between Romantic and Classical imperatives. The arts have already provided a stock of living images for much of what the academic seeks to analyse in the laboured prose of a would-be-rational approach. I have therefore adopted as guides two major modern writers whose œuvres are critiques of Romanticism at many different levels: the novelist Thomas Mann and the poet and essayist W. H. Auden. Both were European by birth and American by adoption, so they straddled the Old and New Worlds. Both in the end drew back from what they saw as the abyss to which the logic of unrestrained Romanticism leads. Neither was a 'natural' classicist; both felt strongly the pull of the Romantic. The ultimate preference for balance and boundary constituted an opting for the poise that comes from dynamic tension rather than a championship of static formalism.

Mann and Auden provide most of the metaphors from which my thinking has grown, and they – more particularly Auden – state my values more cogently and profoundly than I am able to do myself. Beneath my prosaic sociological text runs a subterranean poetic (and perhaps theological) text which will occasionally be allowed to break the surface. Indeed, I feel rather as Walter Benjamin is said to have felt: it would be possible to make my whole case through a judicious juxtaposition of quotations. Fragments of such an anthology appear at the head of each chapter.

The primary metaphor through which I propose to approach my topic is that of infinity and cosmic ambiguity. It was a peculiarly salient image for the new Romantics of the late 1960s. Before plundering the works of Mann and Auden, I want to begin with a sociologist who uses this and related metaphors to advance an argument which will be of central importance to us. The following is an extract from Peter Berger's discussion of the 'marginal experience'.

Every socially defined reality remains threatened by lurking 'irrealities'. Every socially constructed *nomos* must face the constant possibility of its collapse into anomy. Seen in the perspective of society, every *nomos* is an area of meaning carved out of a vast mass of meaninglessness, a small clearing of lucidity in a formless, dark, always ominous jungle. Seen in the perspective of the individual every *nomos* represents the bright 'dayside' of life, tenuously held onto against the sinister shadows of the 'night'. In both perspectives, every *nomos* is an edifice erected in the face of the potent and alien forces of chaos. This chaos must be kept at bay at all costs.[1]

Beyond the horizon of every *nomos*, every social and personal construction of a system of meaning by which we make sense of experience, there lies the abyss of meaninglessness: chaos, *anomie*, infinity. It has many designations. Man runs up against the abyss in a number of ways, but particularly when he encounters a 'marginal experience' which threatens the adequacy or integrity of his always precarious *nomos*. It might be a traumatic change of circumstances, like a bereavement, divorce or exile, which the *nomos* proves powerless to tame, to reduce to 'sense' and 'meaning'. But everyday life too contains chronic and recurring threats to nomic security in experiences of the margin – the margin between sleep and waking, the experience of dreams which are products of neither consciousness nor total unconsciousness, the edge of drunkenness or extreme fatigue, where the accustomed contours of reality and self become blurred or distorted. Berger's judgement on the abyss, the chaos beyond the margin where alternative realities or 'irrealities' lurk, is an almost unrelieved negative. He sees the human enterprise as essentially defensive even at its most creative ('This chaos must be kept at bay at all costs'). It is quite literally awe-ful and terrifying: man therefore erects boundaries between himself and this threatening chaos. He categorizes, typifies, defines, names, labels his world, in order to domesticate experience and to bring it under his control; *nomoi* are dykes against infinity and the ultimate ambiguity.

Raids on the abyss may take several forms. Wresting new knowledge and experience out of the formless chaos beyond the bounds of the defined world is a major objective of art and science: Western rationality and artistic creativity both set out into the abyss to tame and claim it. The mystical quest too is a way in which the finite creature attempts to embrace the infinite. In the Eastern tradition of immanentist theology it is typically characterized as the unity of the One with the All; in the Western (and especially the Christian) tradition of transcendental theology it is related to the mystery of the finite housing the divine spirit – the burning bush, the pillar of cloud or of fire and, ultimately, the doctrine of the Incarnation. It rests on that paradox which can 'see infinity in a grain of sand' or 'the deity shrunk into a span'. From one aspect the Romantic imperative is the attempt to universalize that mystical descent into the abyss or ascent to infinity. The sweet thrill of cosmic ambiguity, the engulfing chaos of 'lurking irrealities' is sought after rather than shunned precisely *because* it is a threat to nomic order and the limits and control which that entails. The marginal experience becomes the very stuff of Romantic ecstasy. Consider this passage from *The Magic Mountain*.

there must be a chemistry of the immaterial, there must be combinations of the insubstantial, out of which sprang the material – the atoms might represent protozoa of material, by their nature substance and still not yet quite substance. Yet arrived at the 'not even small', the measure slipped out of the hands; for 'not even small' meant much the same as 'enormously large'; and the step to the atom proved to be without exaggeration portentous in the highest degree. For at the very moment when one had assisted at the final division of matter, when one had divided it into the impossibly small, at that moment there suddenly appeared on the horizon the astronomical cosmos![2]

Hans Castorp, Thomas Mann's ordinary, tempted mortal, is fascinated by the abyss. In the passage quoted above he is contemplating nature but with an approach far distant from the hygienic and rational scepticism which we normally associate with twentieth-century science. With his celebrated irony Mann calls the chapter 'Research'. In it Hans Castorp uses science as a vehicle for exploring the dangerous but exciting world of chaos, indeterminacy, ambiguity. Human 'sense' is confounded where the infinitely small and the infinitely great are indistinguishable from each other, where non-matter imperceptibly becomes matter and the inorganic mysteriously transmutes, unnoticed and unexplained, into the organic. Hans Castorp wallows in boundlessness. He inverts Pascal's admission 'le silence éternel de ces espaces infinis m'effraie' and finds not fear but excitement. The whole novel, at one level, is the story of his dangerous flirtation with the infinite; the Zauberberg and House Berghof are an extended metaphor for the abyss.

Mann evokes the infinite through a myriad of metaphors. For instance, he gives us long disquisitions on time: he describes the way time repeated, in the daily rituals of the cure, makes every day the same day and thus merges with eternity, as it does if unbroken into metric units. Hans Castorp ceases to wear a watch so that time may be always this eternal time and thus also timelessness.

Again, Mann gives an ultimately negative verdict on the infinite, but he acknowledges the magnetic pull of the 'lurking irrealities' beyond the horizon of the bounded *nomos*. The pursuit of the infinite, the descent into the abyss, is a thrilling adventure which can free one from the bonds, rules, constrictions and duties of ordinary society. Mystical ecstasy, not rational control, is the object of that adventure. Mann represents the disease as offering the tubercular patients of House Berghof an excuse for claiming kinship with death. The abyss, the infinite, the ambiguous, is the kingdom of death. Hans Castorp, albeit uneasily and with a bad conscience, turns his back on duty, station, work and the decencies of 'flat-land' society to embrace this passive, sensuous, irrational ecstasy. Frau Chauchat, one of the major embodiments of his temptation, expresses its values in the slackness of her posture and her invariable and ill-mannered habit of allowing doors to slam behind her. On Walpurgis Night Hans Castorp irrevocably enters the kingdom of licence with Clavdia Chauchat. It is a 'marginal moment' in every sense, the last night before Frau Chauchat's departure; it is a 'sort of 29th of February', a festival which moves its participants beyond secular time and settled society. Hans Castorp's good angel, the Italian rationalist Herr Settembrini, constantly warns his 'delicate child' against the seductions of the abyss, against Lillith and Kundry. The maxim *placet experiri* is anathema to Settembrini. The daemonic, mystical world can only be kept at bay by reason, duty, self-discipline and respect for the bonds and boundaries of the 'real' world.

When the counter-culture of the 1960s embraced the dictum *placet experiri* it was invoking the Romantic injunction with which Mann and others had already grappled and in relation to which they had had to define themselves and their art.

Although Mann himself ultimately and self-consciously opts for the ethical rather than the aesthetic, the rational rather than the irrational, the bounded rather than the formless, the representatives of the Romantic principle are always (and appropriately) the more powerful and emotionally charged of his creations. The irony which he used to distance himself and his readers from their power and attraction was even seen by Mann himself as a fragile and fallible protection, though the only purely *aesthetic* weapon of defence available. His figures of hope (the threadbare pedagogue, Ludovico Settembrini and the pedantic philologist, Serenus Zeitblom Ph.D.), the Apollonian remnants of the European rationalist tradition, are small, shabby, pathetically fallible and self-contradictory, but they constitute the only chance of keeping the abyss at arm's length. Mann understands the power of the infinite because he has crossed the fatal boundary himself. His later works, particularly *Doctor Faustus*, are an expiation as well as a warning. Like Tiresias, he has seen and suffered all: he *is* Aschenbach, Hans Castorp, Adrian Leverkühn. But he is also Settembrini and Zeitblom. The Romantic counter-culture of the 1960s was misled by a generational *hubris* if it thought it had discovered the attractions of infinity and ambiguity for the first time. Some of its adepts misread Mann, assumed that he was speaking sympathetically to their condition (especially, perhaps, in *Death in Venice*); but in general it is easy to see why they preferred Hermann Hesse to Mann as their Germanic guide on the route to secular ecstasy.

Despite his messily bohemian life, W. H. Auden was never in danger of being mistaken for a guru of the counter-culture. Indeed, he lived long enough to satirize and excoriate it in some of his later (mostly minor) verse and criticism. Auden was a champion of structure and form not because his judgement on the infinite was negative but because he saw the structures of the finite world as the solid base of human reality and thus as the only vehicles through which the transcendent possibility could be experienced. Boundaries and limits are not so much fences designed to keep the infinite cosmically at bay as landmarks by which we know who and where we are. Consider this poem from 1968 alongside Hans Castorp's mystical musing on cosmic ambiguity.

[*Ode to Terminus*]

The High Priests of telescopes and cyclotrons
keep making pronouncements about happenings
            on scales too gigantic or dwarfish
            to be noticed by our native senses,

discoveries which, couched in the elegant
euphemisms of algebra, look innocent,
            harmless enough but, when translated
            into the vulgar anthropomorphic

tongue, will give no cause for hilarity
to gardeners or house-wives: if galaxies
            bolt like panicking mobs, if Mesons
            riot like fish in a feeding-frenzy,

it sounds too like Political History
to boost civil morale, too symbolic of
            the crimes and strikes and demonstrations
            we are supposed to gloat on at breakfast.

How trite, though, our fears beside the miracle
that we're here to shiver, that a Thingummy
        so addicted to lethal violence
        should have somehow secreted a placid

tump with exactly the right ingredients
to start and cocker Life, that heavenly
        freak for whose manage we shall have to
        give account at the Judgement, our Middle-

Earth, where Sun-Father to all appearances
moves by day from orient to occident
        and his light is felt as a friendly
        presence not a photonic bombardment,

where visibles do have a definite
outline they stick to, and are undoubtedly
        at rest or in motion, where lovers
        recognize each other by their surface,

where to all species except the talkative
have been allotted the niche and diet that
        become them. This whatever micro-
        biology may think, is the world we

really live in and that saves our sanity,
who know all too well how the most erudite
        mind behaves in the dark without a
        surround it is called on to interpret,

how, discarding rhythm, punctuation, metaphor,
it sinks into a drivelling monologue,
        too literal to see a joke or
        distinguish a penis from a pencil.

Venus and Mars are powers too natural
to temper our outlandish extravagance;
        You alone, Terminus the Mentor,
        can teach us how to alter our gestures.

God of walls, doors, and reticence, nemesis
overtakes the sacrilegious technocrat,
        but blessed is the City that thanks you
        for giving us games and grammar and metres.

By whose grace, also, every gathering
of two or three in confident amity
    repeats the pentecostal marvel,
      as each in each finds his right translator.

In this world our colossal immodesty
has plundered and poisoned, it is possible
    You still might save us, who by now have
    learned this: that scientists, to be truthful

must remind us to take all they say as a
tall story, that abhorred in the Heav'ns are all
    self-proclaimed poets, who, to wow an
    audience, utter some resonant lie.[3]

Here again is a meditation on infinity and the infinitesimal in nature as revealed by the 'High Priests' of twentieth-century nuclear physics and biochemistry, the sciences of space, time and life. For Auden sanity — and humility — require that we live in a world where contours, edges, boundaries, forms and definitions constitute the 'real', to place and root us. Anything else is 'colossal immodesty' and, in the most serious sense, a blasphemy or impiety.

The chaos of infinite possibility can become a world of meaning only through the institution of these specific forms and structures. Without the landmarks and limits sacred to Terminus, human identity and communication would both be impossible.

Auden's reverence for rule and form has little to do with slavish conformity; it is the prerequisite of pleasurable brigandage and rebellious exploration.

Without these prohibitive frontiers we should never know who we were or what we wanted. It is thanks to them that we know with whom to associate, make love, exchange recipes and jokes, go mountain climbing or sit side by side fishing from piers. It is thanks to them, too, that we know against whom to rebel. We *can* shock our parents by visiting the dives below the railroad tracks, we *can* amuse ourselves on what would otherwise have been a very dull evening indeed, in plotting to seize the post-office across the river.[4]

Equally, his obeisance to the 'God of walls, doors and reticence' does not imply a rejection of the infinite, the transcendent possibility. Time and again Auden celebrates the ecstatic moment in which infinity enters the finite human world. In love, sex, drunkenness, dreams, the boundaries dissolve as we experience self-transcendence. Indeed, in many ways Auden is the supreme poet of Berger's 'marginal experience'.

> Soul and body have no bounds;
> To lovers as they lie upon
> Her tolerant enchanted slope
> In their ordinary swoon,
> Grave and vision Venus sends
> Of supernatural sympathy.

But it is only a moment — framed by the ordinary reality inside which it exists:

> Certainly, Fidelity
> On the stroke of midnight pass
>
> ... Every farthing of the cost
> All the dreaded cards foretell,
> Shall be paid.

> Beauty, midnight, vision dies:

Yet the moment of Infinity leaves refreshment so that

> Eve and knocking heart may bless,
> Find our mortal world enough.[5]

In 'The Age of Anxiety' Auden describes a similar moment of ecstatic one-ness of four strangers in a wartime bar who fleetingly catch 'that state of prehistoric happiness' in which time and surroundings are forgotten in a 'rare community'. This is what he describes in 'Ode to Terminus' as 'the pentecostal marvel as each in each finds his right translator'. Yet that too is a passing moment, not a recipe for permanent ecstasy: it is provisional and fleeting — the protagonists soon enough rediscover their separateness, loneliness and habitual inadequacies — but it is real, not illlusory. Such moments of self-transcendence are the fuel on which we run. Yet if we try to prolong them, to universalize the ecstasy of boundarylessness, the result will be disaster — the drivelling monologue, the resonant lie, 'colossal immodesty'. Infinity for Auden is both a temptation (especially for the artist) and a redemptive possibility. Boundaries are important not merely because they hold the real in place but also because they are the locus of blessed as well as dangerous ambiguity. Images of night and dreams frequently carry this cargo.

> Now let the complex spirit dissolve in the darkness
> Where the Actual and the Possible are mysteriously
>   exchanged,
> For the saint must descend into Hell: that his order
>   may be tested by its disorder

> The hero return to the humble womb; that his will
> may be pacified and refreshed
> Dear children, trust the night and have faith in tomorrow
> That these hours of ambiguity and indecision may be also
>   the hours of healing.[6]

> Clear, unscaleable ahead
> Rise the Mountains of Instead
> From whose cold cascading streams
> None may drink except in dreams.[7]

Infinity is a redemptive Not Yet; the pursuit of the impossible is a necessary human goal, but the attempt to live entirely in the world of Instead is madness. Perhaps the clearest expression of his position lies in two great poems of the war years, 'For the Time Being' and 'The Sea and the Mirror'. In the first these themes are approached through religious imagery and, particularly, through Auden's exploration of the doctrine of the Incarnation. The key couplet is one he gives to the Wise Men:

> Love's possibilities of realization
> Require an Otherness that can say I.

Even the possibility of ecstatic fusion with other (in sex, mysticism or a drunken intimation of community) requires that we have a definite self to start with. So too in the incarnation itself. The positive, the infinite, the unconditional, the abstract was incarnated in the specific, the finite, the conditional, the personal:

> that which we could only passively fear as the
> incomprehensible I AM, henceforth we may love with
> comprehension that THOU ART.

Infinity enters the real, historical world and is contained in a human body, confined by the limits of the senses. It directly encounters dilemma and constraint and in so doing embodies the transcendence of those very limits: it redeems art from its debased narcissism and reason from an incestuous fixation on its own logic.

In 'The Sea and the Mirror', Auden's commentary on *The Tempest*, some of these ideas take secular form. In it Auden's defence and celebration of boundaries and the finite hinges on two important polarities: the one and the many; self and other. A prose section of the poem 'Caliban to the Audience' is based on a conceit in which Ariel and Caliban are complement and antithesis to each other: Caliban is the real and Ariel is the poetic; at the same time Caliban is I, finite, brute self, id, an earthy Eros or Cupid, while Ariel is other, unconfined, ethereal, omniscient spirit. If either steps outside its appropriate sphere, the result is chaos and confusion. The Muse of Poetry has her own kingdom, in which the rules are not those of the real, finite world on the other side of the footlights. She can play fast and loose with time, space, motive, sequence; she can create a symmetry that life seldom, and then only accidentally, produces, a world in which virtue and vice get their due reward. Caliban – the real and the self – is a guarantee of disorder if he is introduced into the Muse's well-ordered realm. He ruins the party and finishes by making a crude pass at the Muse herself.

The opposite boundary violation may have even more horrifying consequences.

Is it possible that, not content with inveigling Caliban into Ariel's kingdom, you have let loose Ariel in Caliban's? We note with alarm that when the other members of the final tableau were dismissed He was not returned to His arboreal confinement as He should have been. Where is he now? For if the intrusion of the real has disconcerted and incommoded the poetic, that is a mere bagatelle compared to the damage which the poetic would inflict if it ever succeeded in intruding upon the real. We want no Ariel here, breaking down our picket fences in the name of fraternity, seducing our wives in the name of romance, and robbing us of our sacred pecuniary deposits in the name of justice. Where is Ariel? What have you done with him? For we won't, we daren't leave until you give us a satisfactory answer.[8]

Auden himself, as a devoted marauder across the sacred boundaries, was adept at introducing Caliban into the realm of the Muse: why else is he so much a sociologist's poet? Yet the confusion of the poetic in the real has far more radical consequences: it troubled Auden all his life, long after he had apparently solved the problem of art and life in resolving his ambivalence towards Spain and socialism. It was this boundary violation which attracted the Romantic counter-culture of the 1960s even more than 'making passes at the Muse'. The desire to loose Ariel into the realm of Caliban is the source of the most crucial cultural shifts of the 1960s and 1970s.

The second set of images in 'Caliban to the Audience' is even more apposite to the cultural developments and dilemmas associated with the counter-culture. What, asks Caliban, would be the result if he or Ariel were to grant to any fortunate member of the audience the wishes they are respectively capable of fulfilling?

If Caliban (Cupid, I) were to transport them to the Eden of 'Pure Self' where they think they want to be, how would it feel to be free ultimately from the constraints of others?

... at long last you are, as you have asked to be, the only subject. ... You have indeed come all the way to the end of your bachelor's journey where Liberty stands with her hands behind her back, not caring, not minding *anything*. Confronted by a straight and snubbing stare to which mythology is bosh, surrounded by an infinite passivity and purely arithmetical disorder which is only open to perception, and with nowhere to go on to, your existence is indeed free at last to choose its own meaning, that is, to plunge headlong into despair, and fall through silence fathomless and dry, all fact your single drop, all value your pure alas.[9]

Alternatively, if Ariel (spirit) were to free them from the prison of self, to merge the One in the All in 'that Heaven of the Truly General Case', how would that be?: 'a nightmare which has all the wealth of exciting action and all the emotional poverty of an adventure story for boys, a state of perpetual emergency and everlasting improvization where all is need and change'. Everything in the real world is there, all its horrors, pleasures, excitements, but the self cannot connect with any specific cause or case.

Even the circumstances of the tender passion, the long-distance calls, the assignation at the aquarium, the farewell embrace under the fish-tail burner on the landing, are continually present, but since, each time it goes through its performance, it never knows whether it is saving a life, or obtaining secret information, or forgetting or spiting its real love, the heart feels nothing but a dull percussion of conceptual forboding. Everything, in short, suggests Mind but, surrounded by an infinite extension of the adolescent difficulty, a rising of the subjective and subjunctive to ever steeper, stormier heights, the panting, frozen, expressive gift has collapsed under the strain of its communicative anxiety, and contributes nothing by way of meaning but a series of staccato barks or a delirious gush of glossolalia.

Written in 1944, that last sentence in particular might stand as a chillingly accurate prophecy of some of the more self-defeating techniques employed in the 1960s' frenetic pursuit of total expressiveness in life and art.

In the end Auden, like Mann, stands for paradox. Human beings need to know who and where they are. We cannot love, communicate or hope without that primary necessity. Only through our specificity can we rise above that same specificity because that always 'requires an Otherness that can say I'. Without definitions, boundaries and margins we are incapable of apprehending even the possibility of the infinite, of self-transcendence, of Instead. Auden sees the infinite and ambiguous as in constant dynamic tension with the finite and defined: the former can find no expression except through the latter. The Romantic crusade periodically tries to unhinge the two halves of the paradox by eliminating the saving, Classical negation. When it succeeds it releases the terrors *and* the *ennui* of ultimate meaninglessness: it leads us into one or other of those two anti-Edens, Caliban's heaven of 'Pure Self' or Ariel's heaven of the 'Truly General Case'. For myself I desire neither. I stand with Auden 'Contra Blake':

> The Road of Excess
> leads more often than not, to
> The Slough of Despond.[10]

CHAPTER 2

The Expressive Revolution

Our earth in 1969
Is not the planet I call mine,
The world, I mean, that gives me strength
To hold off chaos at arm's length

My family ghosts I fought and routed,
Their values, though, I never doubted:
I thought their Protestant Work-Ethic
Both practical and sympathetic

Sex was, of course – it always is –
The most enticing of mysteries,
But news stands did not yet supply
Manichaean pornography

Though I suspect the term is crap,
If there is a Generation Gap
Who is to blame? Those, old or young,
Who will not learn their Mother-Tongue

Me alienated? Bosh! It's just
As a sworn citizen who must
skirmish with it that I feel
Most at home with what is Real

W. H. Auden: from 'Doggerel by a Senior Citizen' (for Robert Lederer), in
Collected Poems

He thanks God daily
that he was born and bred
a British Pharisee

He likes giving presents,
but finds it hard to forget
what each one cost

So obsessive a ritualist
a pleasant surprise
makes him cross

* * *

Without a watch
he would never know when
to feel hungry or horny.

W. H. Auden: from 'Profile', in *Collected Poems*

It was an evening of masks and freedom, an irresponsible hour, when the thou was in force, and by the power of magic and dreams, somehow had – full sway. And – it was also the eve of Clavdia's departure.

Thomas Mann: from *The Magic Mountain*

When Mynheer Peeperkorn asks Hans Castorp the awkward question (is he Clavdia Chauchat's lover?) the resourceful but honest young man replies with the words of the third quotation above. In them Mann characterizes perfectly the nature of those festivals of expressive licence with which society punctuates mundane reality. Like Auden's account of sexual fulfilment or the state of semi-intoxication in his poem 'The Age of Anxiety', it describes a framed moment in which some kind of experience of the infinite, the impossible, the unbounded, becomes both possible and real. These moments are, above all else, rituals of horizontal integration, fragments of brotherly equality snatched out of the divided reality of status and role differences. They employ the symbols of chaos and disorder in order to create the momentary experience of *common* order. At its most intense such a moment confers ecstasy, and at the minimum it lifts the normal limits, controls and structures in favour of unbuttoned relaxation. The masks go with the freedom because they conceal our social and role-bound selves, thus allowing an escape from such inhibiting structures as hierarchy, responsibility and decorum. The selves underneath the masks cannot be called to account tomorrow for the activities of tonight: the normal rules are suspended.

Now, Hans Castorp's sin was his attempt to remove the frame from around the expressive moment ('I have never named Clavdia but with the "thou" ') and allow infinity to overflow into mundane reality, transforming it into permanent, timeless, boundaryless experience – an infinity of expressive indulgence. As a preliminary characterization of those movements

which came to be known as the counter-culture, this sin of Hans Castorp's
will serve for the moment. The counter-culture of the 1960s was an attempt
to make all life into an evening of freedom when the 'thou' had full sway. It
wanted to dispense with the masks too, to integrate the self below the mask
with the freedom which the mask alone had hitherto conferred.

To Auden this was heresy. It was chaos overwhelming structure; it was
the irresponsible release of Ariel into the kingdom of Caliban, the subversion
of the real by the poetic, a Utopian but destructive romanticism, the aspiration to Eden which 'springs the trap of Hell'.[1] In 'Doggerel by a Senior
Citizen' he charts the erosion of the boundaries: the defeat of the Protestant
Ethic, the transformation of sex from a private mystery into a public
blasphemy, the debasement of language by the 'thou' principle of
spontaneity and informality which inexorably undermines the possibility of
complex communication, and much more besides. In 'Profile', a sort of self-
portrait from the mid-1960s, he offers a caricature of himself, emphasizing
in the verses I have quoted precisely the characteristics most anathematized
by the expressive counter-culture. If structure and boundary maintenance
become strong enough, then expressive pleasure – food, sex – can *only*
occur at unspontaneous, programmed times. The watch becomes a lethal
instrument, the police force and bureaucracy of structure.

All this stands in marked and deliberate contrast to the movements of the
1960s. At the heart of the counter-culture was a single-minded, often
fanatical onslaught on boundaries and structures, a crusade to release Ariel,
the infinite, expressive chaos into the everyday world. The centre was
serious, deadly serious, and involved group experiences of an intensity comparable with Hans Castorp's and a charismatic thrust that quickly made the
crusade audible and visible. Around the white-hot centre there grew up a
colourful but more trivial and heavily commercialized periphery. Malcolm
Bradbury, in his satirical novel *The History Man*,[2] catches the sight and
smell of this periphery perfectly in his creation of Howard Kirk. David
Caute's Stephen Bright[3] is another fictional satire on the counter-culturnik
as comic anti-hero and stylistic model for the colour-supplement version of
the sixties' authenticity trip.

If one looks only at the superficial, theatrical extravaganza of the decade,
the happenings, demonstrations, psychedelia and the rest, it is easy to
assume that the counter-culture was merely trivial, ephemeral, a minor
footnote in the margin of cultural history. From the viewpoint of the
counter-culture's pioneers, it looks like a failed revolution. The argument of
this book is that it was more significant than the first and less than the
second. The counter-culture was an index to a whole new cultural style, a set
of values, assumptions and ways of living which Talcott Parsons, with
uncharacteristic exaggeration, has called the 'Expressive Revolution'.[4] The
sixties were the transformation point. They exemplified for society at large,

in striking ways, processes which would expand the frames within which expressive possibilities were currently contained. By the mid-1970s many things which had seemed traumatic, shocking, revolutionary in the previous decade had been incorporated into mainstream culture. The pioneers of the 1960s had genuinely sought to remove the frames altogether, but in the event the consequences were less drastic. The frames stretched, sometimes a long way from their former contours, but they ultimately reasserted their nature as limits and margins.

Yet within the expanded frames culture had institutionalized much of what the counter-culture had stood for. If it ever was truly a *counter*-culture (this point will be discussed later), it had certainly ceased to be so by the mid-1970s because its most characteristic methods and messages had been appropriated by mainstream culture.

In later chapters I shall explore aspects of the 'sixties phenomenon' in different areas of culture – the arts, the Underground, pop music and certain of the expressive professions. In this chapter I want to concentrate on the nature of the social system in and on which the changes of the 1960s operated. The argument is that the counter-culture was a particularly colourful symptom, herald and agent of structural changes which were occurring in the fabric of advanced industrial societies. The sixties' aspiration to let the djinn out of the bottle was itself the product of social change.

Advanced industrial societies are materially prosperous and minutely differentiated in terms of the division of labour, the structure of social institutions and the distribution of social roles. This development contains a central problem and contradiction: it gives with one hand and takes away with the other. At its heart is a phenomenon which Durkheim above all understood and lamented, what in optimistic language he characterized as the organic solidarity of interdependence and, in a pessimistic version, as *anomie* or the solvent of all solidarity. What it gives is affluence and a new possibility of freedom and individuality; what it takes away is natural social rootedness and automatic structures of belonging. Material plenty releases both people and resources from the immediate disciplines of survival so that whole populations are enabled to discover layers of 'expressive' needs – self-discovery and self-fulfilment, richness of personality, variety and depth of relationships – as legitimate and at least half-feasible aims. So 'experience' can become a positive, sought-after value; and mere 'coping' with the exigencies of one's material and social situation is no longer enough.

At the same time structural differentiation specializes and fragments experience so that more and more people find their lives split into separate enclaves of partial and specialized role-playing inside large and often impersonal institutional structures. Little is left beyond the privatized sphere of family as a place where it is unequivocally legitimate to be an integrated person with full affective and expressive rights. The consequence of this contradiction is twofold. First, it focuses the perception and social vocabulary of expressive fulfilment on the private and the personal: the very idea of fulfilment comes to imply individualized and personalized experience; the expressive sphere itself thus holds up a mirror to the egoistic and anomic normality of modern society. Second, it implies a socially structured deafness and blindness to fulfilment based not on individual choice and free affect but on custom, security, tradition, limits and ascription. This deafness and blindness is not total but involves yet another contradiction. Modern society's most natural social resource is the association (Tönnies's *gesellschaft*). Expressive needs are thus pervasively 'organized' in voluntary and state-provided associations – from yoga clubs to the doctor's surgery. But *gesellschaft* is precisely a manifestation of the very specialization and fragmentation which makes expressive fulfilment both so urgent and so elusive. Thus the vocabulary of institutionalization *per se* becomes as suspect as it is pervasive: *gesellschaft*, bureaucracy, organization, structure can thus be anathematized, while at the same time a vision of a lost golden age or millennium around the corner can idealize purified community (Tönnies's *gemeinschaft*, Durkheim's 'mechanical solidarity') as the only acceptable form of the collective pole of experience to balance the privatized pole of personal expressiveness. Thus the pure collective and the pure individual form the dynamic duality inside the myth which drives the Expressive Revolution. In Auden's terms, it is the desire to be in the kingdom of pure self *and* the heaven of the 'Truly General Case' simultaneously, to combine perfect freedom and individuality with the unity of the one with the all.

Of course, these tendencies are very unevenly developed across the range of milieux which form modern society. Traditional and semi- or quasi-communal enclaves protected from the ravages (and benefits) of differentiation, mobility and fragmentation continue to exist in all social classes, and particularly among the 'respectable' working class. Moreover, by a further twist in its logic, differentiation enables a growing enclave in each society to specialize in expressive activities as a form of work while other enclaves specialize in the instrumental sphere. The arts, the mass media, the universities, the Churches and the caring professions are *par excellence* in the expressive category, while the commercial, industrial and technological spheres constitute the major arena of instrumental activities. Thus the Protestant ethic confronts its antithesis on the disputed boundary between expressive and instrumental worlds. Daniel Bell[5] has made much of this point. He argues that the techno-structure of advanced industrial societies generates an ideology which places a high value on rationality, calculation and efficiency, while the cultural sphere – what (following Parsons) I have above called the 'expressive enclave' – isolates an ideology of self-fulfilment, spontaneity and experiential richness. Thus the ideological trajectories of the differentiated subcultural spheres of industrial society pull in contradictory directions and institutionalize an unresolved tension at the centre of society (what Bell calls the 'cultural contradictions of capitalism').

I have deliberately left out so far all mention of the political sphere, which Bell treats as the third semi-autonomous, subcultural sphere and which, in my view, is the most difficult to make sense of. With echoes of an older and now much battered convergence hypothesis, Bell argues that the imperatives of the political sphere are equality and participation. My own immediate response is sceptical. It may be that Bell's formulation is suggestive but unsatisfactory precisely because politics is a sphere in which the instrumental and expressive imperatives confront each other, vying for supremacy. One consequence of the contest could be the adoption of some expressive *rhetoric* in capitalist (if not in state Communist) societies, whatever the nature of the political conflict.

In a discussion of the nature of modernism, Eisenstadt argues that from the time of its invention by Western European society modernism has always had two by now near-inextricable facets, one symbolic or ideological and the other technical/industrial.[6] Modernism in its first guise has always involved something analogous to a religious mission, in this case a Romantic ideology of individual rights, wider participation and self-determination (national and individual) and the acceptance of perpetual change as a way of life. It has exported these values to the populations of the Third World, along with tractors, penicillin and napalm. Thus for Eisenstadt the ideological/political components of modernism are precisely the precursors of the values of the Expressive Revolution: both are offshoots of the Enlightenment and of Romanticism, and both have a structural, but not a one-way-determinist, relation to the nature of industrialism and structural differentiation.

All this is by way of prelude to the vexed question of whether the Expressive Revolution is and was inevitably politically radical or even revolutionary. Certainly, in the 1960s the counter-culture was popularly seen as intrinsically leftist. But if we accept the argument so far about the nature and derivation of the Expressive Revolution we would need to demur on two grounds. First, the progeny of the Enlightenment and Romanticism are already provided with a full range of political positions consonant with expressive values ranging from bourgeois liberalism through Romantic revolution to ultra-individualist anarchism. Indeed, it takes only a slight effort of the imagination to see how a style of politics like Burkean conservatism could be presented as caring for whole, integrated persons and allowing them to get on with the important expressive things of life by taking politics out of the sphere of controversy. In a very serious sense the expressive value system is *a*political, concentrating as it does on the individual, experiential dimensions and mistrusting the wider institutional nexus as impersonal, distorting and coercive.

At another level, however, the forces which release expressive needs also widen the possibilities of political dissent. A greatly expanded cultural class specializing in expressive work roles becomes the repository of anti-materialist and anti- or non-instrumental values which thus, for that class, form the locus of the sacred. The cultural class is distanced and protected from the Puritan disciplines of the economic sphere and can afford Utopian perspectives which reject the compromises and opportunism of practical politics and economics. It is perfectly poised to espouse what Weber called *Wertrationalität* or an antinomian and charismatic pursuit of absolute ends, and to despise and attack *Zwekrationalität*, the functional rationality of means which dominates the economic sphere. Thus a vocal and eminently visible wing of the Expressive Revolution was and remains anti-capitalist and anti-bourgeois and embraces every radical position between Maoism and anarchism. Other factors have colluded with this tendency.

By the mid-twentieth century, the traditional political left, particularly in the organized labour movement, had tacitly accepted capitalism as a fact of life. They merely conducted an institutionalized wrangle over the relative shares which labour and capital should take of the growing national product or, at least as often, over the shares which should go to different segments of labour. On the other hand, the radical intelligentsia, particularly in continental Europe, saw this as a triumph of what Marx had called the 'fetishism of commodities', and they came to despair of the proletariat as the bearers of revolutionary salvation. In the twentieth century certain neo-Marxist thinkers therefore became convinced that the seeds of revolution could not germinate under a capitalist cultural hegemony. The term was Gramsci's, but the thesis that this hegemony was becoming more complete and all-embracing was developed in the inter-war period by the Frankfurt School of critical theory. Adorno and his collaborators devoted their efforts to finding a philosophical chink in this cultural hegemony which they called 'affirmative culture', so that it might be possible to protect a remnant, a margin, from total expropriation (a few intellectuals perhaps or later, for Marcuse and his followers, the student generation). So where the old Marxist–Leninist left had idolized the proletariat (at least as a rhetorical device), the post-war New Left, taking its cue from the Frankfurt School, came to despise the undermass, particularly as it noted that even mobility and privatization had failed to release the proletariat from the 'fetishism of commodities' but had bound it ever more securely in its consumer niche.

Adorno himself was never anything but contemptuous of the view that popular expressive activities – more sex, less authority, fewer taboos and the egalitarian's 'rib-digging' charade of proletarian manners – was anything more than an illusory release. The permissiveness which he first noted with distaste in the Germany of the 1930s was, in his view, just another emanation of capitalist cultural hegemony. It operated not to release men into individual freedom but to make the contours of personal life fit increasingly neatly into the imperatives of the economic order: man as a rootless psychic atom paralleled man as a mobile unit of labour power. Adorno's 'negative dialectic' was a sophisticated and essentially cerebral technique and had about it a good deal of Mann's and Auden's wit, irony and double and treble distancing: paradox was his native element. But Adorno was far from being the favourite guru of the 1960s. Herbert Marcuse[7] was a more important influence on the New Left, particularly in the British and American university campuses of the late sixties as the new radicals attempted to devise strategies which would break through the cultural hegemony and splinter the cages in which traditional socialization ('false consciousness') had imprisoned the average citizen. In fact, the New Left was preaching the very permissiveness which Adorno had been decrying for thirty years as all too system-congenial. Moreover, they were doing this in the name of the existentialist and subjectivist philosophies which he had subjected to a scathing critique. At its crudest the idea was that the shedding of sensual and cultural inhibitions would act as the necessary preliminary to political liberation; the route to socialism would pass through the kingdom of licence.

This response of the radical intelligentsia of the 1960s was a nice combination of the incestuous and the self-destructive. Their *raison d'être* was the things of the mind, but they became anti-cerebral, believing that bourgeois rationalism had polluted cerebration by making it the servant of capitalism. Yet at the same time they were specialists in the Word and came to regard the realm of words and meaning and, more broadly, that of the expressive and symbolic activities of the cultured elite (or counter-elite) as holding the key to everything – even revolution. Their characteristic strategy was the attempt to politicize culture, to use the armoury of expressiveness, especially Surrealism, Dada and other techniques derived from the avant-garde arts, as weapons of psychic subversion and revolutionary re-socialization. The tactic had some limited success in continental Europe, but was almost null in Britain and North America. Whether one regards the latter as hospitable Anglo-Saxon pluralisms or whether, with Marcuse, one deplores their pseudo-liberal skill in the art of 'repressive tolerance', the fact remains that these two cultures are quite distinct from European societies like France and Germany, where a political polarization on class lines has deeper roots. In continental Europe the politicization of culture made some headway, whereas in Britain and North America it seems rather to have resulted in the transformation of much middle-class radical and counter-cultural politics into a system of essentially symbolic action. Thus Frank Parkin,[8] in his study of the British CND movement, found it necessary to coin the term 'expressive politics' for those middle-class gestures of personal, moral purification which have little or no practical political consequence.

In brief then, my argument is that the values of the Expressive Revolution, the *placet experiri* of the 1960s, is not inextricable from the political left. The relationship is contingent, not essential. The left-wing intelligentsia, partly because of its impasse *vis-à-vis* the affluent proletariat and partly through a professional *hubris* that took the tools of its trade for the key to the universe, adopted the values and techniques of expressiveness and thus gave them a contingent but highly visible radical colouration. The counter-culture of the 1960s looked revolutionary in its first flowering (hence the 'counter') and indeed was experienced as such by many of its early innovators. The wider society too was initially convinced of the 'revolutionary' nature of the new phenomenon, both because of its evident outrage and because so many of the counter-culture's practitioners declared themselves revolutionary. Yet underneath the red clothing was a beast of a different colour, or perhaps a chameleon able to take on *any* political colouring. The general argument, then, is that the so-called counter-culture was advance warning of the much wider and less spectacular thrust of the Expressive Revolution into the whole hemisphere of personal/cultural activities in advanced industrial society. It was a specialist and exaggerated form of a phenomenon which is affecting all spheres of society, though to different extents and at different rates. What it 'countered' was not so much traditional cultural values as the contrasting hemisphere of instrumentality and power, work and politics. The counter-culture was historically continuous with the humanistic/expressive values of the traditional cultural elite, and merely pushed Romantic individualism to ever more extreme lengths in contra-distinction to the bureaucratic and bourgeois individualism[9] of the instrumental enclave. That bifurcation is increasingly an institutionalized feature of advanced industrial society.

Two particular social facts have contributed to the swift incorporation of the values of the expressive counter-culture into the mainstream of social life. The first is the fact that the social group which acted as the main carrier of the expressive values, even in its most revolutionary guise, was a cultural elite located close to the status, if not to the power centre of industrial society. The main home of the anti- or non-instrumental values of the counter-culture was and remains the upper middle class in the expressive professions – the arts, education (particularly higher education), the mass media and the caring professions and semi-professions. There is a high degree of self-recruitment in all these areas, particularly at the upper status level of each field, and while this cultural class is functionally distinct from the traditional political and industrial elite, it is linked to the power centre by strong ties of family and by common educational experience. It is, for example, a commonplace of post-1960s research that the academic and professional classes contributed a disproportionate share of their progeny to the counter-cultural student movement of the sixties. Any movement located quite so close to the centre is unlikely to suffer total repression: the power centre will accommodate where it can so as to stave off a split in the societal hub.

The second fact is associated with the normal processes of legitimation in complex societies. Shils offers a persuasive analysis of the tension between the 'sacred centre' and any geographical, status or cultural 'periphery' which challenges that centre or makes a bid for independence from its control.[10] A complementary thesis is offered by Kolakowski.[11] Shils argues that the media of communication in modern society make it easier for the centre to control or interfere with the idiosyncrasies of peripheries because these deviations or challenges are both more visible and more accessible to penetration. Peripheries attempt to infiltrate the centre, while the centre offers certain concessions in return for the periphery's relinquishing of its ambition of total autonomy. The result is an inter-penetration which systematically reduces the difference between the culture of centre and periphery respectively. Kolakowski suggests that one favourite means which the centre has always employed in the face of a revolutionary movement within the society is to deploy the style and techniques of that revolutionary movement against it. He calls this the Counter-Reformation offensive, on the model of the Roman Church's response to the German Reformation. Elements of both Shils's and Kolakowski's processes clearly occurred between the late 1960s and the mid-1970s, aided by the fact that the counter-cultural 'periphery' in question was no agglomeration of the dispossessed but rather a budding cultural elite. One of Shils's cardinal points is that the values and life-style of the group at the societal centre naturally partake of the quality of sacredness. The counter-cultural 'periphery' was in fact not so much a periphery as the rising generation of 'culture specialists' at the societal centre. Thus the privileged social locus of the new wave of expressive values was inherently likely to assist the diffusion of those values because of the radiation effect of the cultural 'sacred'.

Certainly, by the early 1970s the political and commercial centre, as well as the older generation of the cultural class itself, found that hints of 'authenticity' and expressiveness helped sales and strengthened images. By these means many of the motifs of counter-cultural protest in the 1960s were transformed into the normal vocabulary of symbolic expression and now serve to reinforce assumptions that modern man has the right to subjective experience of a range and quality which most societies in the history of the world would have regarded as Utopian or absurd. (Many, of course, would also have regarded it as very distasteful.)

It might be argued that the sixties were able to 'afford' an expressive extravaganza because it seemed to most Western people in that decade that a never-ending economic expansion and rise in standards of living was one of the givens of life in industrialized societies. In the 1970s and 1980s, the prospects of galloping inflation, unemployment and zero or negative rates of economic growth might be expected to call into doubt the assumption that expressive values were the luxury product of an already past prosperity and of a misplaced sense of economic security. Certainly, it would be plausible to argue that the end of effortless affluence might help to account for the partial rehabilitation of the values of the Protestant ethic in the 1970s – signalled, for example, by the conversion of many hippies into disciplined Jesus freaks, or by the rediscovery of the value of sequence and structure in education. But these are perhaps only natural corrective mechanisms that operate when the pendulum has swung too far for viable social organization: and there are counter-indications too.

First, the transformation of what in the 1960s were esoteric motifs of the counter-culture into widely accepted themes is too pervasive to be ignored or denied: political tactics of disruption, pioneered by yippies, hippies and the like, are now used as routine modes of pressure-group activity; photographic and narrative techniques of brokenness and ambiguity developed in the Underground currently feature in women's magazines and popular television programmes: Monty Python and the Goodies have brought surrealism into even the lower-middle-class parlour; the cultural representation of sexuality in all its forms is far more explicit; authority is seldom able to legitimate itself with the old vocabulary of authority *per se* but only by means of a populist and anti-hierarchical rhetoric; and so on. So much of what was counter-cultural in the 1960s is now an unnoticed and accepted part of the givens of the 1980s, like the nude pin-up girl in the daily newspaper (or the nude boy in *Cosmopolitan*), or the assumption that it is pure anachronism to expect children to defer to adults or to use respectful modes of formal address to their elders. The process has gone furthest in the middle-class expressive professions, but it has also affected general cultural assumptions and many aspects of leisure-time style, even among those whose working lives are dominated by the instrumental milieu. In particular, it has infiltrated deeply the cultural vocabulary of the media of mass communication. One may, of course, wonder how deep the transformation has been and whether isolated and specialist items of expressiveness have been inserted in peripheral, private and interstitial niches or used in mass culture for the same old purposes of profit and easy titillation. Yet a shift in cultural norms has undoubtedly occurred, and one needs to explain why things which the market would not take in the 1950s now form the staple fare of the mass-communications industry.

The second indication of the increased salience of expressive values is to be found in the instrumental sphere itself. Ideas which are now regarded as politically and economically realistic responses to, say, ecological pollution or inflation often began as the freaky notions of angry, way-out hippies, yippies and cranks in the 1960s – the campaign to conserve the world's energy and fuel resources, the extirpation of waste, the drive for individual families and localities to become self-sufficient in food and basic necessities, 'survival strategies', the 'simple life' as the solution to everything from early redundancy to the besetting diseases of twentieth-century urban life (obesity, cardiac arrest, stress, and so on). Politicians have to take account of the popularity of anti-bureaucratic and 'small is beautiful' values which have spread outwards from the counter-culture and now reinforce political claims for, say, devolution or the abandonment of high-rise flats as the natural policy in urban housing programmes. So while it may be true that the Expressive Revolution and its counter-cultural storm-troopers were in part at least products of industrialized affluence, expressive values do not automatically lose their cultural hold when relatively modest checks on the growth of that affluence make themselves felt. A traumatic world recession might be a different matter, but short of that, increments of expressive possibility do not in any simple way seem to depend on stockpiles of material goods in themselves; indeed, the emptiness of consumer materialism is one of the strong messages of the Expressive Revolution. Ironically, of course, it is a message which can be processed and packaged by the very consumer materialism it began by rejecting and can be used to sell anything from breakfast foods and cosmetics[12] to gardening tools, seeds and do-it-yourself equipment. Above all, of course, it is used to advertise get-away-from-twentieth-century-technology holidays – by jet plane.

In sum then, the gist of my thesis is that the extravagant counter-culture of the 1960s was largely a medium of cultural transmission and transformation. It drew attention to, and familiarized the wider society with, a range of expressive values, symbols and activities by showering them forth in their most extreme and dramatic form. The process of the 1970s has been to shift the various cultures and subcultures to accommodate an expansion of expressive possibility inside their various styles. This results in very different constellations from context to context and has set off a number of defensive movements which resist the wider value shift by focusing on particularly evocative symbols – from opposition to fluoridization and pornography (that is, symbolic pollution) to the rising conversion rate of neo-Puritan sects like Jehovah's Witnesses or the Moon Family. But though the movement to expressiveness is selective and uneven, it nevertheless has every appearance of being inexorable.

The most salient feature of the counter-culture of the 1960s was the symbolism of anti-structure. It was essentially a pitting of freedom and fluidity against form and structure. Sixties expressiveness was a long and concerted attack on boundaries, limits, certainties, conventions, taboos, roles, system, style, category, predictability, form, structure and ritual. It was the pursuit of ambiguity and the incarnation of uncertainty. Yet it was also its own opposite, and in this lay a fundamental dilemma. I argued earlier that the Expressive Revolution idealized not only the pure, self-defined and self-determining individual but also the purified collectivity, the perfect community. So the anti-structure and anti-ritual of its symbolic system was contradicted by a search for new, purified rituals and symbols of belonging to a collectivity which could transcend the specificities and limits of time, place and cultural milieu. One central theme of the analysis in subsequent chapters will therefore be the contradictory pull of structurelessness and re-ritualization in the symbolic behaviour of the innovators of the Expressive Revolution.

The picture is further complicated if one considers the scenario against which the counter-culture of the 1960s played out its symbolic tableaux. Structural differentiation was certainly making its inexorable way through the British social structure, bringing increments of specialization, mobility and privatization to new segments of society. Yet it was spreading unevenly and still left relatively untouched some 'traditional' enclaves, particularly among the upper working classes. Even more than these social changes, full employment and unprecedented general affluence were making the aspiration to new levels of expressive fulfilment more than a pipe dream for the normal citizen. Yet the frames within which these possibilities were experienced – family systems, class and regional cultures, institutional arrangements for recreation and collective activity, role sets and the like – mostly dated from a past in which expressive priorities were *not* the central imperatives. And it is as well to remember that a frame needs only the passing of one generation before it is inherited as 'traditional'. Some loosening of the older boundaries and structures was already occurring in post-war Britain, but an expansion of expressive possibilities was filtering down the status hierarchy only slowly and up to the 1960s had affected mainly the most obviously 'private' spheres, such as marriage, sexual relationships, parenthood, concepts of 'mental health' and the 'integrated personality' and patterns of personal leisure activity. But normal social life was still littered with the symbolism of belonging and of structure, demarcations (between kin and non-kin, friend and stranger, Us and Them, public and private, male and female, adult and child, authority and obedience, everyday and festive, work and leisure) which formed the grammar and syntax of living. Rhythms, rituals and ceremonials were woven into the fabric of social behaviour; language, dress, taste and the whole taken-for-granted pattern of being, especially in the more 'traditional' enclaves of British society, were presided over by Auden's god Terminus, whose 'blessed frontiers' articulated 'who' and 'where' we were. It was these frontiers which came under concerted attack from the counter-culture, and it is hardly surprising that the initial response of most of the conventional world was an outraged sense that its very being, its contours of self, were being assaulted. The rest of this book is about that assault and the various responses to it.

CHAPTER 3

Symbols, Codes and Culture

SOME THEORETICAL CONSIDERATIONS

> *Poets have learned us their myths,*
> *but just how did they take them?*
> *That's a stumper.*
>
> *When Norsemen heard thunder,*
> *did they seriously believe*
> *Thor was hammering?*
>
> *No, I'd say: I'd swear*
> *that men have always lounged in myths*
> *as Tall Stories,*
>
> *that their real earnest*
> *has been to grant excuses*
> *for ritual actions.*
>
> *Only in rites*
> *can we renounce our oddities*
> *and be truly entired.*
>
> *Not that all rites*
> *should be equally fonded:*
> *some are abominable.*
>
> *There's nothing the Crucified*
> *would like less*
> *than butchery to appease Him.*

W. H. Auden: from 'Archaeology', in *Collected Poems*

Before launching into a sociological interpretation of the symbolism of cultural radicalism, it seems prudent to present certain theoretical assumptions explicitly rather than allow them to remain implicit in my use of language. This chapter therefore is a theoretical note on issues, sources and influences on the sociology of culture.

Cultural phenomena, especially of a symbolic and mythic kind, are curiously resistant to being imprisoned in one unequivocal 'meaning'. They constantly escape from the boxes into which rational analysis tries to pack them: they have a Protean quality which seems to evade definitive translation into non-symbolic – that is, cold, unresonant, totally explicit, once-for-all-accurate – terms. Music, painting, dance, mime, ritual are all symbolic forms with their own 'vocabulary', which can be commented on, interpreted and extended via the medium of the word but can never be fully translated *into* words. Even verbal symbolism is very difficult to render *without remainder* in analytic language. What the reader apprehends in a flash would take pages to spell out in explanatory gloss, and even then one could not hope definitively to exhaust possible meanings and resonances. The disciplines of literary, music and art criticism are after all premised on the inexhaustibility of meaning and relevance in the cultural artifacts which form their subject matter.

Moreover, the symbolic significance of any object or behaviour does not rest only in the symbol itself and the rules of its medium or code (the poem/poetry; the painting/visual art, etc.) but in its context and in everything the present actor (reader, gallery visitor) brings to his apprehension of and response to the symbol. A Greek nationalist will look at the Elgin marbles in the British Museum through a different network of symbolic associations than will a visiting English schoolchild. One must recognize that culture is a receptacle for symbolic artifacts which, once historically created, can be and indeed inevitably are recharged over time with new permutations of symbolic meaning and relevance. A nice illustration of the point occurs in one of Borges's Delphic short stories, 'Pierre Menard, Author of the *Quixote*'. It is a fictional fragment of a commentary on the extraordinary feat of Menard, a twentieth-century Frenchman, in literally creating several pages of Cervantes' *Quixote* word for word. Borges writes

Cervantes' text and Menard's are verbally identical, but the second is almost infinitely richer. (More ambiguous, his detractors will say, but ambiguity is richness.)

It is a revelation to compare Menard's *Don Quixote* with Cervantes's. The latter for, example, wrote (Part One, chapter nine):

... truth, whose mother is history, rival of time, depository of deeds, witness of the past, exemplar and adviser to the present, and the future's counsellor.

Written in the seventeenth century, written by the 'lay genius' Cervantes, this enumeration is a mere rhetorical praise of history. Menard, on the other hand, writes:

... truth, whose mother is history, rival of time, depository of deeds, witness of the past, exemplar and adviser to the present, and the future's counsellor.

History, the *mother* of truth: the idea is astounding. Menard, a contemporary of William James, does not define history as an inquiry into reality but as its origin. Historical truth, for him, is not what has happened. The final phrases – *exemplar and adviser to the present, and the future's counsellor* – are brazenly pragmatic.

The contrast in style is also vivid. The archaic style of Menard – quite foreign, after all – suffers from a certain affectation. Not so that of his forerunner, who handles with ease the current Spanish of his time.[1]

This is an immensely rich and ironic passage, and not for nothing does Borges invoke Surrealism in the sentence before the extract I have quoted. Surrealism, pop art, the *Nouveau roman* and various other forms in the avant-garde arts all play on the resonances which re-contextualization can set up in familiar objects or art works. It is a point to which we will return in a later chapter.

Walter Benjamin, Talmudic and Cabbalist scholar as well as Marxist, probably had the most acute *feel* for the symbolic of all the Frankfurt School and clearly shared something of Borges's ironic but deeply serious playfulness in this field. Benjamin as I have remarked, is said to have had an ambition to write a book composed entirely of quotations – presumably as a way of saying something new by embedding commentary and interpretation implicitly in the fact of juxtaposition. He is certainly known to have believed that modern art works embody their own criticism,[2] in part at least through their contexts. He argued that any work of art achieves its ultimate value only when it is a ruin, when it remains as nothing more than the emanation of a philosophical position after the specificities of historical form, genre, fashion and an audience versed in their interpretation have all fallen away. Thus we must see symbolism as a layered, encrusted, continually re-contextualized phenomenon in which the layering and encrustation create ambiguity: but as Borges remarks, in a profound, throw-away line, 'ambiguity is richness'.

Paul Ricoeur is one of the philosophical analysts of symbolism who focuses on this fact of ambiguity. He works in a semiological tradition (of which more below) which treats symbols as a structured code, literally a sign language, yet he argues that even when the medium in question is a verbal one 'the symbolic is a milieu of expression for an extralinguistic reality.'[3] For this reason he refers to his own analysis of the symbolic as 'under the regime of the open state of the universe of signs', because analysis confined purely to the internal, strictly linguistic structure of the code would miss a crucial dimension. This is so because the symbolic is always characterized by 'double sense'. 'It is the *raison d'être* of symbolism to disclose the multiplicity of meaning out of the ambiguity of being.'

Auden makes the point with greater economy.

> What we have not named
> or beheld as a symbol
> escapes our notice.[4]

However slippery the medium of the symbolic may be, it is nevertheless a concretization of experience: it is a mode of apprehension which tames, or partly tames the abyss or the infinite by manifesting what would otherwise remain 'lurking irrealities'. And perhaps both the slipperiness and the power of symbolic life lies precisely in the fact that, unlike reason and strictly cognitive conceptualization, it does *not* wholly tame and domesticate the abyss of pure, unframed experience and potentiality, but only partly brings it under the regime of order and structure. At best, in Ricoeur's terms, it transforms the ambiguity of being into a multiplicity of meaning. So the symbolic both embodies and at the same time points beyond that framed and frozen embodiment.

All of this may very well help to explain why cultural phenomena which are suffused with mythic and symbolic elements have been a particular 'problem' for the social sciences. Sociology was born as a child of the Enlightenment, and most of its founding fathers, with the partial exception of Durkheim and Simmel, worked under the rationalist assumption that symbol, myth and religion were the wasting assets of a rapidly disappearing stage of social evolution. Anthropology, however, followed Durkheim, and even from its earlier Tylorian rationalist stage had always treated myth and symbol as important, in 'primitive' societies at least. By contrast, much sociology until very recently viewed these aspects of social life as anachronisms or mere epiphenomena. Inevitably then, theoretical insights in the study of culture and symbolism tend to arise more from the work of anthropologists than from that of sociologists, with the honourable exception of the sociology of religion which, following Durkheim and Weber, went on obstinately treating myth and symbol as interesting and even important when such a position was unfashionable.

The problem was a dual one. Crudely rationalistic and, even more, crudely quantitative 'scientific' sociology often found the symbolic an embarrassment unless it could be reduced to the statistical analysis of publics, the class basis of tastes, of religious beliefs, of political attitudes and the like. The idea that cultural and symbolic behaviour might have some central relevance to life and therefore to sociological theorizing, that it might be something more fundamental than a frill or an expression of something else 'more real', were assumptions equally foreign to vulgar positivist and vulgar Marxist prejudice. The slippery, Protean nature of the symbolic was the other half of the problem. Human beings engage in and respond to symbolic behaviour every day of their lives. We swim, as it were, in symbolic media like fish who never need to be taught how. Yet when we become analytic observers, the fisherman rather than the fish (to alter the metaphor a little), then the rational explanation, the definitive account of the nature and process of symbolic action, escapes through the holes of the net.

Currently the net most widely canvassed as likely to catch the slippery symbol is semiology, the science of signs. It stems partly from linguistics, with Saussure as its inspiration, partly from structuralist anthropology and partly from phenomenological philosophy. It urges us to treat symbolism as a language, a code, a system of signs. It has many attractive features: it stresses the internal connectedness of symbolic manifestations; it treats them as coherent patterns; it rejects the simplistic notion of their fundamental 'irrationality'; it points up classification as a crucial element in symbolic life; it emphasizes the importance of structure as against that of content in the articulation of human communication and culture.

However, it also involves certain problems, which make it less attractive than certain other perspectives for my needs. It isolates the structure of the symbol system as (to adapt Ricoeur's term) a 'closed universe' in which the analysis is essentially a formal account of the internal structural elements of the medium. Only with difficulty and, as it were, by sleight of hand can it be referred back to the *content* of the symbolic medium and, with even more difficulty, to society and social behaviour. I am persuaded by Dan Sperber's argument[5] that many of the most fruitful insights which have come from 'semiological' analyses of culture, and above all from Lévi-Strauss, are not strictly semiological at all. Such writers, Sperber argues, in practice refuse to treat symbolism as a hermetically sealed, internally consistent formal structure and smuggle in insights from quite other intellectual traditions, and not least from the hunches which arise from their being adept in the use and interpretation of symbols in their own cultures.

One might see much of the debate about the ways, if any, in which the symbol differs from the sign as an implicit recognition of this analytical and methodological difficulty. If a 'sign' is made up of 'signified' and 'signifier', what is it that the symbol as 'signifier' points to as 'signified'? The question is virtually unanswerable because of the ambiguity, multivocality and contextual variation of the symbol. This is the major reason why Ricoeur and others (Benjamin was a pioneer in this field) have attempted to graft phenomenology on to semiology in hermeneutic analysis. Ricoeur writes (to quote this time in full),

in hermeneutics there is no *clôture* of the universe of signs. Whereas the linguistic moves in the enclosure of a self-sufficient universe and never encounters anything but intransigent relations of mutual interpretation of signs (to employ the vocabulary of Charles Sanders Peirce), the hermeneutic is under the regime of the open state of the universe of signs.[6]

The weakness of hermeneutics, he goes on to point out, is that by rejecting *clôture* it 'escapes from a scientific treatment' and becomes plagued by 'the war of rival philosophic projects'. I do not intend to join the battle on the hermeneutic field but only want to point out the locale of both the conceptual difficulty and the fascination of the symbol. It is just at the point where it appears to escape scientific treatment that its essence lies. Ricoeur puts the point this way: 'but the weakness is its strength, because the place where language escapes from itself and us is also the place where language comes to itself: it is the place where language is *saying*.'[7] So again we have the ambiguity of the symbol: it is at its most eloquent precisely where it transcends the form and structure of its code of expression.

Sperber, despite his rejection of the semiological approach, nevertheless does not resort to vagueness or metaphysics. He sees symbolism as an essentially cognitive phenomenon, a form of knowledge. He makes a persuasive case. Symbolic knowledge, he argues, is not 'encyclopaedic' – not a knowledge of objects, acts, words and definitions – but yet a knowledge of the 'conceptual representations' that describe objects, acts and utterances. Symbols do not in a strict sense form codes; they do not 'mean' in the sense that X 'means' the number 5 and Y 'means' the number 12, say, when algebra codes the formal equivalences between a set of letters and a set of numbers. Unlike X and 5, symbols are not strictly substitutable and translatable into equivalent codes: the interpretations of symbols are not substitutes or translations but *extensions* and therefore, themselves symbolic. In Sperber's view, the symbolic mechanism essentially focuses attention and then through a process of evocation searches the memory for the repertoire of conceptual representations which fall into the same class as the symbolic stimulus which triggered the response. The process is cumulative and complex:

Each new evocation brings about a different reconstruction of old representations, weaves new links among them, integrates into the field of symbolism new information brought to it by daily life: the same rituals are enacted, but with new actors; the same myths are told, but in a changing universe, and to individuals whose social position, whose relationships with others and whose experience have changed.[8]

The social classifications which form part of this conceptual input to the process of evocation often have the apparent character of *bricolage*, in Lévi-Strauss's sense. They may be incomplete – polarities with only one half of a pair made explicit, fragmentary systems of oppositions, less a 'system' than an *ad hoc* collection of binary oppositions. More important still, argues Sperber, they operate on the basis of *implicit*, shared knowledge among the members of any cultural tradition: the gaps in the 'system' of classification are filled at the implicit level.[9] The social classifications of culture are therefore contingent and incomplete though not lacking *implicit* coherence:

moreover, they change constantly in use and re-use. Thomas Mann is very clear about the contingent and implicit nature of cultural classification. The young Zeitblom (the narrator) and Leverkühn are discussing music. They speak in turn:

'But the alternative', I threw in, 'to culture is barbarism.'

'Permit me,' said he. 'After all, barbarism is the opposite of culture only within the order of thought which it gives us. Outside of it the opposite may be something quite different, or no opposite at all.'[10]

Hence hermeneutics, with its warring philosophical projects.

Sperber's position is very attractive, though still at the stage of a prologue to a theory rather than that of a definitive theoretical framework. I would, however, underline certain points which I take from him, in particular his emphasis on the role of implicit knowledge and on the degree to which the symbolic escapes the more rigid semiological definitions of 'code'. Yet the term 'code' is hard to avoid. When I use it below I shall not mean the invariant formal structure of a sign system but something looser – and perhaps more metaphorical than precise. By 'symbolic code' I shall refer to the content of social classifications (that is, shared and partly implicit knowledge of the 'conceptual representations', in Sperber's sense, of objects, acts and utterances) and shall assume these classifications to be rather unfinished and full of gaps at least at the explicit level.

Sperber's stress on implicit knowledge is, of course, of a piece with symbolic interactionism (*sic*) and the milder varieties of phenomenological approach which have been influential in Western sociology in recent decades (thanks in part to an academic variant of counter-cultural subjectivism). The point seems to me to be one of the valuable contributions which these traditions have made to sociological understanding. It is a central and fruitful contention too in the work of Clifford Geertz. He argues for example that the analysis of culture must rest on 'thick description', that is, precisely that steeping in the nuances of meaning, significance and webs of symbolic interconnection so much of which resides at the level of implicit knowledge among the natural members of a culture but which may for a long time evade the outside observer.[11]

Geertz is one of the most eloquent and elegant exponents of the view of culture and symbolism which forms the groundwork of the present analysis. Like Sperber, and even more strikingly like Thomas Luckmann,[12] Peter Berger[13] and Kenneth Burke,[14] he starts from the premise that man is ineradicably symbolic in his activities and that the creation of order out of chaos and meaning out of flux is the crucial defining function of this activity. He writes:

The drive to make sense out of experience, to give it form and order, is evidently as real and as pressing as the more familiar biological needs. And this being so, it seems unnecessary to continue to interpret symbolic activities – religion, art, ideology – as nothing but thinly disguised expressions of something other than what they seem to be: attempts to provide orientation for an organism which cannot live in a world it is unable to understand. If symbols, to adapt a phrase of Kenneth Burke's, are strategies for encompassing situations, then we need to give more attention to how people define situations and how they go about coming to terms with them.[15]

This meshes well with Sperber's view of symbols as 'conceptual representations'.

Geertz, however, stresses another and equally important dimension of symbolism, that of motivation. The symbol calls forth if not quite 'meaning' at least conceptual orientation, but it also evokes and often well nigh *commands* appropriate emotions, motivation, feeling-tone, aura. This is sometimes precise but sometimes lies in the 'realm of the vaguely felt'. This 'aura effect' of the symbol is important both because it constitutes what I have symbolically (*sic*) referred to as the intimation of infinity and the abyss (thus escaping *precise* conceptualization and framing), and also because it operates at the level of implicit, unarticulated webs of connection and significance and of patterns of motivation. In his essay 'Religion as a Cultural System', clause 2 of Geertz's definition concerns the establishment by a system of symbols of 'powerful, pervasive and long-lasting moods and motivations in men'.[16] This is to treat cultural systems as having some overall coherence at the level of symbolic *content* and not only of structure. This coherence sets up patterns of mood and motivation through the 'thick' web of interlinked associations, classifications and injunctions, not only to *understand* and *connect* but also to *feel* and to *act*. Yet it is essential to keep sight of the ambiguity embedded even in the coherence. This ambiguity rests in the *imperfectly* conceptual elements in symbolic representations in the *implicit* nature of the knowledge on which they draw and in the 'aura effect' and the evoked motivations which, though powerful, may be imprecise and subconscious. Ambiguity and strategies for celebrating/coping with it will be central to the analysis below.

With this much of the ground if not cleared at least skimmed over, it may now be possible to present the main assumptions on which my substantive analysis of the symbol system of the counter-culture will be based. The exposition has two parts. The first takes the form of a set of propositions about the nature and role of cultural symbolism. The second is an outline of certain perspectives in the sociology and anthropology of religion which seem peculiarly apposite to any attempt to elucidate the cultural phenomena of the 1960s and their transmutation in the 1970s.

My first proposition is that man cannot be understood except as a symbol-using animal. Through symbolic activity he creates sense and order in his world. Man employs words, objects, images, gestures, and so on – the whole repertoire of the symbolic – both to pin down and to point beyond. The specific, finite and profane are employed to invoke the general, the infinite and the sacred. The profane instance can express the sacred generality: one woman can stand for the nature of Woman; one tragedy can both manifest and transfigure the universal character of loss and pain. This enterprise of culture is the indispensable condition of human-ness.

My second proposition is that human experience is inescapably precarious and ambiguous: we encounter very little which is unequivocally positive or negative. Most underdogs have an investment in some aspects of their state of life, and few of the privileged get by without some frustration and envy. The most crucial and universal ambiguity of all, however, is that of society itself. The group, the collective, is (as Durkheim has taught us) the *fons et origo* of all that is truly human, yet at the same time (as Freud among others has emphasized) it is also a prison, a control system, a mechanism for the suppression of whatever does not fit with the local and temporal pattern of things. This contradiction surely explains why Durkheim has two parts to his definition of the sacred: on the one hand, the sacred is the symbolic manifestation of the principle of group solidarity – positive and celebratory – and, on the other hand, it is 'things set apart and forbidden' – negative and controlling.

Thus the contradictions of social life rest on something deeper than the apparent universality of hierarchy and thus of exclusion and inequality (Kenneth Burke) or the specific inequities of capitalism (the Frankfurt and Neo-Marxist Schools). The contradiction and ambiguity inheres in the specific, temporal and finite nature of human life and experience. Even the most fortunate and fulfilled individual pays the price of his fulfilment in all the alternative experiences foregone for the sake of the one time and role-specific fulfilment (that is, the condition of finitude): for every profit and pleasure a lost opportunity. Hence everyone can be plausibly considered 'relatively deprived', not least because human systems of communication show us many things which we are not, as well as those that we are. As Auden wrote,

> Talkative, anxious
> Man can picture the Absent
> and Non-Existent.[17]

Proposition three is that this radical ambiguity of experience is both reflected in and amplified by symbolic communication. Man experiences ambiguity, searches to create order and certainty and does so with cultural tools which are themselves shot through with ambiguity. We have already noted the imperfectly conceptual nature of symbols, their 'aura effect', their capacity to evoke the 'realm of the vaguely felt', their often imprecise and implicit injunctions to emotion and motivation as well as to cognitive recollection and reconstruction. Yet ambiguity is not meaninglessness, and symbols could not act as media of communication and creators of order (however precarious) if they were not in some sense 'codes' which culture members could decipher and assume others could also follow. At one level, therefore, they must be treated as codes which follow certain rules and which rely on a knowledge – albeit largely implicit – of the shared praxis of social and conceptual classification. (I use 'praxis' rather than 'principles' here in acknowledgement of the fact, stressed by Sperber, that systematic uncovering of the implicit principles is seldom culturally institutionalized: the principles are normally embedded in practice.) In a loose rather than a strictly semiological sense then, symbols form codes, the rules and definitions of which are subject to constant change through use. At the simplest level the different media of symbolic communication are recognized in culture as specific forms; dance, music, poetry, painting, religion are treated as distinctive arts or spheres with forms, rules and structures that all competent members of the culture have no difficulty in recognizing and distinguishing from each other. We all know what a 'painting', a 'sculpture', a 'ballet', a 'symphony' is, at least in the most general sense, though we may also be aware that the forms and rules and perhaps even the classifications change: in the late sixties it was often difficult to decide whether a particular event was an art show, a poetry recital, a therapeutic or a theatrical encounter, a religious or secular event, but at least we had the cultural vocabulary to run through the question of within what range of things it might 'really' fall.

Because they are codes, systems of symbolism essentially operate in a language of dualities – a 'dialectic' to one school of thought, 'binary oppositions' to another. Each symbol by its very existence implies its own opposite or, more accurately, since virtually all symbols are multivocal, its opposites. Harmony implies discord, though the specific note combinations which fall under the two definitions change radically over time. The process of implying polarities is both fundamental and far from simple, even with verbal symbolism, because of multivocality or (at least) 'double sense'. We have already seen Thomas Mann playing with the problem in relation to civilization and barbarism. George Orwell provides an even more explicit illustration in his characterization of Newspeak in the novel *Nineteen Eighty-Four*.

It's a beautiful thing, the destruction of words. ... After all, what justification is there for a word which is simply the opposite of some other word? A word contains its opposite in itself. Take 'good', for instance. If you have a word like 'good', what need is there for a word like 'bad'? 'Ungood' will do just as well – better because it's an exact opposite, which the other is not. Or again, if you want a stronger version of 'good', what sense is there in having a whole string of vague useless words like 'excellent' and 'splendid' and all the rest of them? 'Plusgood' covers the meaning; or 'doubleplusgood' if you want something stronger still. ... In the end the whole notion of goodness and badness will be covered by only six words – in reality, only one word. . . . Don't you see that the whole aim of Newspeak is to narrow the range of thought? In the end we shall make thought crime literally impossible because there will be no words to express it.[18]

Thus eloquence and the possibilities of conceptual precision are embedded in the same ground as symbolic ambiguities – the *multiple* polarities of symbolic classification.

Symbolic polarities are legion, and their elucidation (and use) requires exactly what Geertz means by 'thick description' to chart the nuances: few symbol systems are as spare and as one-dimensional as Newspeak in the oppositions they imply. Following proposition two above, however, we should pay special attention to a set of polarities which will figure extensively in the substantive analysis in later chapters. These are society/individual, external/internal, structure/formlessness, order/disorder, control/freedom, boundaries/boundarylessness, hierarchy/ equality. Now, it is particularly important to note the parasitic nature of each half of any pair: it depends on its opposite number for its meaning. 'Freedom' as a concept and symbol can only make sense by contrast with 'control' or 'unfreedom'; 'equality' cannot be grasped except through an apprehension of 'inequality', and so on. Classification by its nature makes binary oppositions symbiotic, and thus one ineradicable ambiguity of symbol systems rests in that symbiosis.

If society or a social group employs symbols to celebrate and reinforce, let us say, the principle of hierarchy or order, it cannot help but draw attention to equality and disorder. Mostly, symbolic activity attempts to neutralize the potentially seductive power of the disfavoured half of a polarity by investing it with a heavy negative charge, but the technique is not automatically infallible: look at the effect in Milton's *Paradise Lost*, where Lucifer emerges for modern readers as more real and compelling than God.[19] Symbol systems are thus by their nature inescapably double-edged.

But this is not the last in-built ambiguity; let us take it further. One major function of symbol systems in all societies and groups is to legitimate, reinforce and celebrate the *status quo* – both the existence of the social *per se* and the particular disposition of roles, values, identities, privileges and so on in that place and time. But as I have argued above, society is always and everywhere a prison as well as a facility and is always inequitable in its distribution of burdens and advantages. So symbols of legitimation are always in danger of undermining themselves, of protesting too much and exposing their own implausibility. Consider the dual potential of any symbol of legitimation. It must reinforce the present system in all its imperfection by pointing towards a sacred, transcendent and purified model of that particular social pattern. The perfect symbol in its turn cannot fail to imply a judgement on the flawed actuality. Thus the symbol of, let us say, perfect authority – Christ Pantocrator, for instance – must carry a judgement on the temporal authority which it is validating.

Any symbol of legitimation is therefore in double danger. First, it must draw attention to the polar opposite in the classification system on which it relies for its own meaning (that is, it implies an alternative, inverted vision) and, second, it points up the imperfections where the present actuality and an ideal version of that actuality fail to coincide. In short, the same symbol simultaneously and necessarily masks and unmasks the reality.

For these reasons it seems to me fruitless to engage in a debate which conducts itself in an absolutist vocabulary – to argue the depth and extent of 'capitalist cultural hegemony' or to decide whether cultural expressions are 'really' manifestations of rebellion, status discontent, class-consciousness and the rest. Symbols are *endemically ambiguous* in at least three different ways and are seldom, if ever, 'really' only one thing – 'conformity' or 'rebellion'. Nevertheless, I do not wish to imply that the ambiguity is total or that contradictions are always held in equilibrium: far from it. The outcome (resolution would be too balanced and finished a word) of the tensions inherent in the employment of symbol systems raises a real sociological question; this, indeed, is a central issue in the study of social change. While I would hold that there must be some kind of 'elective affinity' between the pattern of social relations in a group or a society and its pattern of symbolic expression, I would not want to imply that a perfect correspondence exists between something that constitutes the 'objective interests' of a group or an individual and the symbol system through which identity and 'interest' are mediated. The alternatives offered to consciousness by the available stock of symbolic forms and the nature of the classification system are as much a part of the social experience of relative contentment or frustration as are material or 'objective interests'. The symbolic vocabulary through which we comprehend and experience our social world, including our 'interests', is not a frill on the top but a fundamental part of the inner structure of social life: culture is central, not peripheral, to sociological concerns.

Of course, the degree of contentment or frustration with present social reality is not a simple function of the nature of the symbol systems: to hold that would be as crass as to give automatic primacy to material conditions. Symbol systems constantly interact with features of the social world, such as the distribution of power and resources. For the moment, however, all that I want to assert is that frustration is never absent and contentment is never total in any society and that symbol systems express and amplify both the frustration and the contentment – but ambiguously. As well as celebrating and reinforcing existing arrangements, they coin symbols of despair, resignation and rebellion, images of hope and expectation, blueprints of forbidden or implausible alternative realities, Utopias of past or future, political ideologies, religious visions, artistic fantasies, scientific models. They do not exist in a vacuum but have to take institutional form: even in order to be communicated by a visionary to his audience of potential converts, they must find a medium of expression – that is, they must employ a pre-existing social resource. Their explicitness will vary with a number of factors, including the institutional distribution of power and resources and the nature of the existing symbolic alternatives.

Several consequences flow from this. First, almost anything can act as the symbolic focus of the multiple sources of frustration and strain which are endemic in all social systems, provided it can give the *experience* of hope and euphoria through the creation of an alternative sacred centre in the effervescent social solidarity of the out-group. The recent analysis of political movements – both those with clearly symbolic aims and those with apparently practical programmes – has shown that the experience of belonging to the movement becomes a major goal and reward for participants.[20] The ultimate paradox which we see in the counter-culture of the sixties is that an ideology based on the symbols of freedom, individualism and boundarylessness takes its existential strength from the experience of being a solidary out-group in opposition to 'square' or adult society.[21]

Second, I would draw attention to two particular features of the symbolism of alternative visions: the mechanisms of inversion and of escape. Because of the binary nature of classification systems, much the most likely alternative vision is a simple inversion of the legitimated sacred model. Melanesian cargo cults are good examples of such inversion, with their images of a Utopia in which black and white will change places and even colours. This, of course, is why successful revolutions so often look like the mirror image of the order that they overthrow. Yet because symbolic oppositions are multiple rather than single, as in Newspeak, the question of *which* binary opposite or cluster of polarities will be the focus of the inverted vision is hard to determine from the symbol system alone. What, for example, is the binary opposite of an unliberated woman? A liberated woman, certainly, but the images that invokes might range from earth-mother to self-sufficient Amazon – a range full of contradiction and diverse social blueprints. So inversion is a far from simple social and symbolic process and frequently produces unintended and contradictory consequences through the subterranean reverberations in these networks of multiple symbolic polarities.

A sub-variant of the technique of inversion is the attempt to exchange the categories of the sacred and the profane. Items which have been central to the sacred – the 'things set apart and forbidden', that is, tabooed because hallowed – are claimed for the profane sphere. Ironically, this normally means not a real exchange of categories but a re-definition of the sacred for the out-group as *transgression of* rather than respect for the taboo: the tabooed object or experience must become universally available where before it had been set aside and protected.

Escape is an equally important and equally ambiguous option. The most important symbolic escape routes are flights from society and structure into unmediated 'being'. This is what I have characterized above as the pursuit of infinity and/or the abyss. Adorno and the critical theorists refer to them as 'moments' of subjectivity which become atavistic because they cannot be accommodated by capitalism (for which I would read 'society'). Daniel Bell[22] makes a related point in his discussion of the pursuit of ecstasy through modern cultural forms. In ecstasy or the atavistic 'moment' man seems to escape society and the mediations of culture in an individual experience of transcendent intensity. The three sources of ecstasy to which I would draw particular attention are sexual orgasm, violence (particularly killing and/or dying) and mystical experience (which can be approximated through the chemical technology of drugs): the ancient description of mystical experience as *coincidentia oppositorum* (the fusion of all *senses*) makes the point perfectly. All three are ambiguous. In a sense they are escapes from society and structure into the subjective moment, but they are at the same time part of society's symbolic vocabulary and thus are in constant danger of being expropriated by the societal centre. They are harnessed, organized and bound in institutional forms – marriage, the armed forces, the religious order: and not for nothing do these particular societal structures so often form excellent examples of Goffman's 'total institutions'. The strongest electrical charge needs the thickest insulation. Society always seeks to convert these potent experiences into sacred symbols – again, literally, 'things set apart and forbidden' – so that their ecstasy potential can reinforce instead of negating the societal and the structured. Thus they become hotly contested symbolic resources, which can be employed on behalf of the sacred centre (family, state, Church) or can stand for the principle of disorder against order, the individual against the social, chaos against structure and so on. They are central foci in religion and the arts because of the intensity and range of their symbolic message. Above all other symbols they attract taboo-breaking symbolic activity. Clifford Geertz's penetrating analysis of cock fighting in Bali[23] is a perfect example of the process of ritualizing just the most powerful and tabooed forces (sexuality and animality) into a rigidly framed and codified sacred game.

Thomas Mann not only understood the point but made it central to much of his writing. In *The Magic Mountain* Naphta frequently couches his 'terroristic' defence of the medieval Church in just such terms. Sexuality plays the same symbolic role in Mann's novels. Marital sexuality and even conventional pre-marital congress with a peasant girl are perfectly 'healthy' for Zeitblom while the daemonic is symbolized by Esmeralda, the diseased whore. In *The Magic Mountain* it is, as we have seen, Clavdia Chauchat; in *Death in Venice* it is Aschenbach's Dionysiac passion for the boy Tadzio. The symbolic resources which carry the images of ecstasy and danger thus are found in the battle ranks both of order and of disorder just because of their potency.

Now, none of this seems to me to be peculiar to capitalist society: it is an entirely general phenomenon. Nevertheless, each societal type has its own distinctive mode of expropriating the symbols of ecstasy and disorder. As Adorno and his collaborators noted at length, the special technique of capitalist society is to convert the threat embodied in such symbols into a marketable commodity which then becomes an item of life-style which ties both its buyers and sellers the more firmly into the existing social system while providing them with an illusion or image of their escape from it. I would agree that the escape is mostly image rather than substance, but the ambiguity remains. The establishment at the very least has to ape the style of the periphery or to pretend to be aperiphery. Moreover, expropriation is not infallible: revolutions (cultural and political) and, even more often, minor shifts of consciousness and realignments of forces do occur.

Processes such as the one mentioned above are a direct consequence of the fact noted earlier that symbol systems, whether of the centre or of the periphery, must use the institutional forms which the social system of the particular time and place makes available. The message can therefore never be pure and contextless but always takes colour both from the abstract necessity of being institutionalized and from the specific features of its particular social milieu. One consequence of this has already been indicated. The cause of freedom must enclose and imprison itself in an institutional form; the message of individualism must be carried by a group structure; the opposition to boundaries must erect a new boundary between its adherents and the boundary-conscious structures outside in order to protect the open pattern inside. So the possibility of structurelessness is expressed as a structure; the aspiration to spontaneity takes the form of a group ritual. In order to acquire any social power an anti-symbol must take institutional form and thereby contradict its own inner meaning.[24] This, after all, is a process extensively illustrated in Weber's sociology of religion – the institutionalization of charisma is a perfect case in point.

The alternative strategy is, if anything, more self-defeating. It is what Kenneth Burke calls the principle of entelechy[25] – stripping the idea (or symbol) of all ambiguity and pushing it to the furthest point of its own logic. This must involve each symbolic item of a classification system in the impossible task of destroying its own *alter ego*. Disorder must become an absolute value which denies order *per se*; individualism must extirpate the collective principle totally; spontaneity and equality must be perfect and finally banish role, style, distance and hierarchy. The logic of this process is the destruction of the code itself, since each symbol depends for its intelligibility on its own negation. If the strategy is successful, the possibility of communication is destroyed. The preferred symbol becomes literally incomprehensible; language reverts to babel; music becomes meaningless noise. What usually happens, of course, is less drastic – there is simply an extension and amplification of the symbols of disorder and anti-structure, which then become the symbolic focus of belonging, the sacred language of identity for a new, purified community which stands over against unregenerate society, a new spiritual elite set apart from the children of darkness. Students of millenarianism will be familiar with the syndrome.

In his work on myth Mircea Eliade has noted the paradoxical process just outlined as the consequence of pursuing the entelechial principle to its conclusion. Eliade describes it as a typical 'myth of the elite'.[26] It may be worth closer scrutiny in the context of his general delineation of myth. Eliade argues that myth is a basic human resource, and he too conceives of it as a tool for creating order and sense. He writes:

Its function is to reveal models and, in so doing, to give meaning to the World and to human life. ... It is through myth ... that the ideas of *reality, value, transcendence* slowly dawn. Through myth, the World can be apprehended as a perfectly articulated, intelligible, and significant Cosmos. In telling how things were made, myth reveals by whom and why they were made and under what circumstances. All these 'revelations' involve man more or less directly, for they make up a Sacred History.[27]

For Eliade myth begins as symbolic narrative and evolves in the modern world into science, philosophy, theology, ideology, non-sacred history, literature and the rest. In short, it is 'de-mythicized' or, as Weber put it, 'de-mystified', 'dis-enchanted'. Yet, Eliade argues, the change is more apparent than real. Mythic thought is no mere 'survival of archaic mentality': 'certain aspects and functions of mythical thought are constituents of the human being.[28] Much of Eliade's work was the hunting out of the mythic in modern thought – in Marxism, in Freudianism, in modernized Christianity and in secular ideas, and the tracing of their tradition back to earlier models and above all to models of sacred history, myths of origin and myths of renewal. In a tantalizingly short passage in *Myth and Reality* he outlines an interpretation of myths in the modern mass media, noting phenomena like folk heroes, the perpetual war of good and evil and the 'worship' of fashion and success as a form of salvation, a way of transcending the mundane human condition through, for example, the 'cult of the sacred car'.

Even more suggestive, however, is Eliade's treatment of certain features of the avant-garde arts as characteristic 'myths of the elite'. The 'difficulty' of much modern music, art, literature (and, indeed, its apparent 'meaninglessness') he likens to the initiatory ordeals of archaic and traditional societies. One's 'understanding' of such difficult works sets one apart from the uninitiated mass and proclaims membership of an elite gnosis 'that has the advantage of being at once spiritual and secular in that it opposes both official values and the traditional churches'; he adds, in parenthesis, 'modern elites lean towards the left.'[29] At the same time the meaninglessness of avant-garde art acts as a myth of renewal. All traditional myths are cyclic, in Eliade's view. They involve regressions to chaos in order that a new creation may be born, just as Zeus followed Chronos or the New Jerusalem will replace the old, rising out of the disorder of Armageddon. Just so, says Eliade, in the arts: the 'reduction of "artistic Universes" to the primordial state of *materia prima*'[30] is the prelude to a renewal of the art form. Most important of all, avant-garde techniques in the arts and especially, he believed, in the modern novel constitute attempts to 'escape Time', to retreat from real time into sacred or mythic time, into infinity and the abyss – Hans Castorp's discarded watch again. These too are ideas to which we must return in chapter 5.

Eliade's approach straddles the philosophical/anthropological tradition in the study of symbols and the more directly sociological tradition of institutional and historical analysis: the two traditions overlap particularly in the analysis of millenarianism. So far in this discussion of theoretical approaches the social and institutional have been smuggled in through the back door, so to speak, while the primary focus has been symbol systems *in abstracto*. It is now appropriate to shift the focus and to look more directly at the social and institutional elements: in short, to move on from theories of symbolism to the sociology and anthropology of religion. Indeed, the fundamental framework out of which my initial interest in the counter-culture arose was that mixture of Durkheim and Weber which underlies the analysis of millenarianism, sectarianism and Utopian religious movements. The models and concepts in this field are sufficiently well known not to need extensive repetition here. My main intention is to acknowledge particular debts to writers whose terminology has fed into my perspective while recognizing that there are as many uncited who might have been equally valuable sources.

The tradition of millenarian and sectarian analysis has always attempted to relate the realm of ideas and symbols to that of social and institutional forms and forces. It has looked at the 'fit' between the two levels and has therefore often stressed the 'relatively deprived' social composition of the millenial group. We have already seen that the typical participants in the counter-culture cannot plausibly be described as absolutely deprived, and even the relative deprivation thesis has to be stretched to absurd lengths to encompass privileged middle-class youth and members of the artistic elite. The counter-culture looks more like one of Bryan Wilson's 'gnostic sects'[31] or like the pre-Reformation Brethren of the Free Spirit, than like a Cargo Cult or a traditional sect of the lower orders.

David Martin raised this point in his study of religious and secular pacifism in the 1920s and 1930s[32] which is the direct ancestor of the 1960s counter-culture. It clearly constitutes a millenarianism of the elite. In other ways it shares the obvious millenial features. The myth is one of destroying an old, evil order and inaugurating a New Age in which a perfected social system may emerge. As both Martin and Eliade (among others) have noted, the myth frequently invokes images of purification which seek to restore original innocence once the structures which are the source of evil have been removed. It sees history as moving to a culminating point in which sacred time may be restored after a final battle between the forces of light and of darkness. It is a pursuit of a Utopian vision of impossible perfection which gives the experience of hope and certainty through the generation of what Durkheim called the 'social *sui generis*' in the euphoric experience of group solidarity.

Such movements have an endemic tendency to shatter and, in particular, to split into a violent adventist and a passive quietist wing, the latter often promoting attempts to found alternative Utopian communities. Both developments are found in the counter-culture, from violent adventist groups like the Manson Family, urban guerrilla movements of a specifically political kind like the Weathermen, the Baader-Meinhof group (which incidentally arose out of a Lutheran theological radicalism) or the Japanese Red Army, through to the peaceable commune experiments which have left residual settlements as far apart as California and South Wales. Both wings face certain common problems. Ideology and organization combine to eliminate hierarchy and to institute equality, fraternity and liberty. This combination of goals sets up severe tensions, since the three principles are pulling at least partly in different directions. David Martin places this cental dilemma squarely in the antinomian tradition of proto-Protestantism. He sees the proponents of the counter-culture as both the heirs and the re-inventors of antinomianism.[33] We can now perhaps designate anti-nomianism as an ideology or theology which aspires to a social experience transcending form, structure and institution: it seeks the freedom and the spontaneous, uncoerced solidarity of the elect.

Martin argues that antinomian movements characteristically either dissolve in fission or become totalitarian institutions in which the absolute power of the charismatic Messiah figure can alone guarantee the equality of the rest of the saints; freedom then has to be redefined. This is the dilemma which will preoccupy much of the analysis which follows, since it involves tension both in and between symbol systems and organizational forms in the counter-culture. It is exacerbated by the other leg of the triangular tension, that between the group solidarity of the elite, the saints, the enlightened, and the principle of individualism and self-realization: the tension between spontaneous self and purified community. In short, the most crucial tensions in millennial movements, as in the counter-culture, are exactly those which Auden describes so graphically in 'Caliban to the Audience': they may be resolved by flight into the Eden of pure self or by the fusion of the one with the all, but either 'resolution' negates one of the originally precious principles which set up the tension in the first place. It is these tensions with which I am concerned.

The work of two contemporary anthropologists, Mary Douglas and Victor Turner, has been especially valuable in offering concepts through which these central tensions might be charted. Both have been particularly concerned with religious, ritual and symbolic behaviour, and both have explicitly, though very much in passing, related their conceptual schema to certain facets of the counter-culture.[34]

First, from Mary Douglas, 'group'/'grid' and 'ritual'/'zero structure'. Her basic premise is that symbolism and the pattern of social relationships tend to echo each other. Where a social milieu is characterized by a set pattern of social roles and the rhythmic repetition of tasks and activities, by roots and continuity, then the structure and rhythm will tend to be repeated in the cultural and symbolic vocabulary of the group. It will be ritualist and traditional, its cultural forms rich in allusive and economical symbols of the group's corporate identity, and it will be highly likely to use the metaphors of bodily control and the language of purity and pollution to emphasize its boundaries as protection against the potential encroachments and alien otherness of the rest of the social world. By contrast, where the life-style is individualistic, egocentric and competitive, the cultural vocabulary will be utilitarian and abstract rather than expressive, emotional and personalized. It will devalue ritual, metaphor and pure reinforcing repetition in favour of celebrations of individual distinctiveness and the articulation of definitions and distinctions.

Mary Douglas herself points to Basil Bernstein's linguistic concepts of 'elaborated' and 'restricted' codes[35] as lying behind her own dichotomy. The 'elaborated' code is paired with grid forms of symbolic expression and the 'restricted' code with group forms: she describes ritual as essentially a 'restricted' code. Maurice Bloch makes a related point when he argues that ritualized (and therefore stylized) forms of speech, dance and song are essentially modes of communicating traditional authority,[36] in other words, group symbolism in Douglas's sense. I shall argue later that even stylized speech, dance and song can carry messages of disorder as well as of traditional authority and mechanical solidarity.

There is something very important in this parallel between group and grid on the one hand and 'restricted' and 'elaborated' code on the other, but it is not yet fully clarified. Bernstein's own definition of 'restricted' code certainly contains strong overtones of what we have seen as the peculiar marks of symbolic communication – the resort to implicit, shared knowledge which is never stated in full, a residue of imprecise implication, a stock of economical representations which the members of a group can decode without full verbal explicitness. Yet Bernstein uses the term at least in part to indicate inadequate (and not just richly ambiguous) communication as compared with the precise distinctions and definitions and the complex grammar and syntax of the elaborated code. In Bernstein's own usage the elaborated code is *par excellence* the language of Western reason and science and of what I have above referred to as analytic or fully cognitive language,[37] it spells out meaning and discriminations in full and leaves little or nothing to the implicit dimension, to what Ricoeur calls the pressure of 'Desire', both features which are central in symbolic communication. As Mary Douglas interprets it, 'the elaborated code challenges its users to turn round on themselves and inspect their values.'[38] So are all symbols essentially sub-types of 'restricted' code? It has been suggested that the term 'elaborated' code should be used to refer only to linguistic codes of complete verbal explicitness, while the 'restricted' code should be divided into 'impoverished' and 'rich' sub-types.[39] An 'impoverised restricted' code could then designate a language pattern which pathologically inhibits communication, while a 'rich restricted' code would be patterns of (essentially symbolic) communication which effectively rely on implicit, shared knowledge. Perhaps this is less a re-classification of codes than of persons and social milieux, taking account of the existence of a category of conceptually hopelessly ill-equipped people who can employ neither 'elaborated' nor 'restricted' codes effectively and thus find that a distressingly large amount of experience remains at the level of meaningless or threatening 'lurking irrealities'; in short, people making only little, rudimentary and inflexible 'sense' and 'order' in the world. These again are issues which for the moment I can only raise and leave aside for further discussion later in this book. Certainly, the suggestion of some such paradoxical category as 'rich restricted' code has certain attractions – poetry and ritual seem to be essentially of this kind. Yet it is also clear that some terms are needed to differentiate between symbolic expressions of group solidarity on the one hand, whether mechanical or organic, and on the other hand of grid patterns – ego-based and extensively differentiated, but symbolic for all that. For this reason it seems wise to stay for the moment with Mary Douglas's own terms. In her usage group symbolism emphasizes the distinction between inside and outside, while grid symbolism expresses internal differentiation.

Mary Douglas argues that most social systems combine elements of the two patterns. Thus one can have strong group structures combined with weak or strong internal differentiation of the grid variety, or one can have a strong grid pattern varied, say, at the level of the family or a few predominantly 'expressive' institutional areas, by weak or restricted group elements. The latter seems to be increasingly characteristic of urban industrial societies. She produces a four-square diagram with a double axis to represent the various logical permutations of group and grid in a social pattern. The range runs from strong group plus strong grid, where ritual and symbol express control, belonging *and* internal differentiation, through to a position of weak group and weak grid, where symbols are diffuse, and control and belonging minimized and where ritual expressions of inside/outside and of role differentiation are virtually non-existent. This she sees as the 'conditions for effervescence', characterized by a preference for spontancity. 'The second case', she writes, 'provides the social conditions for a religion of ecstasy as distinct from a religion of control.'[40] This is the position of 'zero structure', and it has an immediate appeal as a label for much of the counter-culture. In conditions of zero structure social contacts become fleeting and tangential; bonds are weak or non-existent; and a free-floating, ill-defined pattern − or lack of pattern − is the norm. Such a case will produce a highly privatized and idiosyncratic symbolic language, personalized but vague and acutely anti-ritualistic except perhaps in emphasizing the sense of being part of an 'undifferentiated and insignificant mass'. Mary Douglas believes that zero structure can occur either among the deliberate drop-outs in an otherwise structured society or among the failures at the bottom of a harshly competitive grid system. This characterization of zero structure is a persuasive and attractive idea, but problematic if one looks a little closer.

First, there is the difficulty that ecstatic phenomena (religious and otherwise) do not confine themselves to conditions of what she calls 'lack of articulation in social structure'. In fact, however, she modifies her own case to argue that ecstasy is sought after and unfeared (casual?) in such cases but is regarded as 'dangerous' where social organization is highly structured and control is prized. This would tend to support my earlier argument that experiences carrying an ecstasy potential are strongly contested social resources which in highly structured situations ('total institutions' and so on) are bound in to the sacred centre whenever possible.

A more serious difficulty in the zero structure category concerns the contradictory tendency to re-create rituals expressing membership of an 'undifferentiated and insignificant mass'. Basil Bernstein has noted this paradox in various ways in his discussion of what he calls weak and strong classification and framing:[41] the context is mostly educational and linguistic but the point has a more general relevance. Where classification and framing are weakly articulated the natural consequence might well be expected to be either grave problems of communication (because without classification or with deeply ambiguous classification, codes of communication may break down) or accelerated creativity, since social interaction must articulate everything *de novo* in the absence of taken-for-granted underpinning. In practice, as Bernstein notes, situations of weak classification and framing, or of 'invisible' rather than 'visible' pedagogy[42] rely on unstated but shared ideologies which constitute an invisible (hidden, mystified, implicit) counter-classification to the one which the apparently weak surface classification denies. In short, weak classification and framing often has the character of taboo breaking. In the context of an educational institution it may have the effect of 'de-contextualizing' pupils (denial of their inherited classifications equalling an induction into *anomie*) while resting on an implicit common ideology among teachers into which the children are ultimately to be integrated, not least through common rituals of taboo (classification) breaking. Whether whole social systems can be found in which something like weak classification and framing or zero structure exists is an issue about which I remain open-minded. What is clear, however, is that in modern society milieux which apparently have these characteristics are *sub-cultures* whose vocabulary (social and symbolic) of weak classification, differentiation and control depends for its meaning and intelligibility on the context which juxtaposes it with a wider culture in which strong classification, differentiation and control are normal. In fact, weak classification is part of a broader system of classification in which weak/strong classification is one of the intelligible binary oppositions: weak and strong classification are symbiotic categories extracted from a larger symbolic code.

Weak classification – zero structure – may therefore be a transitional technique of re-socialization and/or the surface cover not for the *absence* of classification but for an *alternative* classification system and, with it, an alternative system of power and control. It looks less like zero structure than like an alternative group without internal grid differentiation.

There is a further related difficulty. This paradoxical but normal combination of attacks upon structure and ritual combined with the re-creation of rituals of the undifferentiated (but far from insignificant) mass (anti-ritual rituals) cannot make sense until one distinguishes between zero structure as an actual life pattern and zero structure as an ideological goal and rhetorical device – a metaphor for infinity/abyss rather than its existential reality. The metaphor, I believe, is far more frequent than the reality. Zero structure as a life pattern is very rarely found, particularly for whole aggregates of people, since its essence is pure *anomie*. It is notable that so non-viable a social ideal should have such symbolic potency and, moreover, in both a black and white form, so to speak. Zero structure was a Holy Grail to initiates of the counter-culture. At the same time it was anathema not merely to the 'square', structured, bureaucratic world against which it pitted itself but, more particularly, to a defensive, traditionalist element which focused its dislike of the specialized, fragmented and impersonal contemporary world by regarding 'zero structure' as a special disease of modernity, the daemon in the system. Martin Pawley's book *The Private Future*[43] is a good example of heavy rhetorical exaggeration and of very selective reading both of actual and of viable social patterns – in fact, of zero structure' as a negative rhetorical device.

Where zero structure seems to characterize a whole social milieu it is always paradoxical. Its techniques may be used to attack the boundaries and rituals of other men's structures, but new rituals simultaneously evolve to mark the boundaries between the new freedoms and the old structures. In short, it is the contradiction already noted, whereby symbols of anti-structure become a language by which one identifies one's own kind – Eliade's myth of the 'elite'.

The persistence and the nature of ritual will be a central theme in my discussion of the cultural developments of the 1960s and 1970s. Rituals operate so as to affirm common belonging, sometimes in the face of deep and inescapable conflict or fragmentation and sometimes as expressions of an existential reality of daily life. No prolonged academic analysis seems to convey the essence of ritual better or more succinctly than the passage from Auden's poem 'Archaeology', which opened this chapter. Whether the solidarity being affirmed is based on likeness (mechanical solidarity) or on interdependent differences (organic solidarity), whether it is an aspiration (for instance, multi-racial liturgies in southern Africa) or a reality (such as the exclusive sacrament of a sect or the common Sabbath meal on a kibbutz), ritual always performs the same miracle of symbolically banishing difference and distance and manifesting commonness. As Auden says:

> Only in rites
> can we renounce our oddities
> and be truly entired.

And certainly one (if not the only) function of myth and symbol is, as Auden puts it, 'to grant excuses for ritual actions'. So ritual is always a paradoxical combination: a taste of transcendence and an experience of belonging at the same time.

Victor Turner's work offers valuable insights into this crucial paradox, particularly through his concept of 'liminality' and his account of the deep, equivocal nature of rituals. Turner has been essentially concerned with the ritual process in all of his work. Rituals are organized around a dominant ritual symbol, he argues. This ritual symbol is multivocal and always has two poles, the ideological (or socio-moral) and the sensory (or organic) respectively. The ideological pole consists of a cluster of meanings (not unlike Sperber's 'conceptual representations') concerned with social and moral rules and principles of social organization and classification. The sensory pole involves basic, often crude or 'wild' feelings, sensations, expressive needs deriving from human physiology (the Freudian id). The ritual process brings about an exchange of properties between the two poles, flooding the ideological with emotional (and therefore motivational) elements and thus transforming coercive social control into felt desire.[44] An effective ritual, then, is a powerful paradox which moralizes the amoral affective and organic drives and infuses moral rules with natural emotions. This fusion is surely part of the key both to the illogical aura which powerful symbols carry and which defies translation into definable verbal 'meaning' and to Auden's sense that in rites we can be 'truly entired' — that is, completed.

Following Van Gennep, Turner distinguishes ceremonial (the pure, effervescent reinforcement of a static role system or social pattern) from ritual by reserving the latter term for a dynamic process: the movement from one role to another — single to married, child to adult, sick to healthy, outsider to insider, profane to sacred. Unlike the purely static ceremonial, a ritual process always involves a stage of liminality, literally of being on the threshold, in no-man's-land, between clear social identities. At the stage of liminality a ritual characteristically involves either taboo breaking (consonant with the smashing of the discarded category and identity and the mandatory entry into the realm of *anomie*) and/or extremely rich, multivocal symbols which embody a wide range of social possibilities, most of which will again be tabooed once the stage of liminality is over. But for a brief time liminality encompasses every possibility and potentiality. It is society's natural crucible for social experimentation.

The experience and the symbolism of liminality are very sharply distinguished from those of non-liminality. Outside the liminal point, society is profane, organized, differentiated, hierarchical, role-structured: this portion of society Turner calls 'societas'. The liminal experience, by contrast, embodies the opposite of all this societal structuring: the ritual participant inside liminality experiences pure, sacred, unmediated 'communitas'. Not only is everything possible, at least at the symbolic level, but there is an undifferentiated and ecstatic one-ness with the other liminal participants and often, through them, with humanity in the abstract. The typical expression of communitas in liminality is the symbolism of anti-structure, since structure is the mark of profane societas. Not for nothing is the cross the sign of the criminal as well as of salvation. The experience of communitas in both small-scale and more complex societies is particularly a feature of interstitial roles and life experiences (childbirth, pilgrimage, the secret society) and of effervescent movements born of rapid social and political change (revolutionary uprisings, millenarian movements and, again, the counter-culture). If a group has once experienced the ecstasy of pure, spontaneous integration, there is a great temptation to try to transform 'existential' communitas into 'normative' communitas. This, however, always involves routinization by rules and control and a clear loss of spontaneity: 'normative' communitas is always partial and contradictory, always a compromise with the exigencies and structures of *societas*. What better framework could one have for comprehending the conflicting tendencies inside counter-cultural commune experiments?

Turner further argues that in complex modern societies, where social experience is less uniformly structured and more specialized than in the face-to-face social systems which he had studied as an anthropologist, the functional equivalent of liminality is above all the arts. Once literacy and a rich vocabulary of visual, aural and dramatic expressions exist, then society has a permanently available, 'liminoid' resource in which all the tabooed, fantastic, possible and impossible dreams of humanity can be explored in blueprint. Science, the arts and philosophy thus become the major liminoid media of modern society, exploring creatively (and often abortively) the principles of existent and possible orders. Where else then would you expect to find the primary expression of both anti-structure and communitas than in the avant-garde arts and among the young, poised between the protected but dominated structures of childhood and the responsibilities of adult (and elite) roles?

It is interesting that Turner's position is, by implication, the diametric opposite of that of the Frankfurt School. In Turner's analysis one must see capitalism as a particularly extended case of the multiplication of liminoid possibilities: symbolic expressions of anti-structure and alternative visions are easily and widely available as part of the institutional network of society. To the Frankfurt School, this very availability is read as evidence of a hidden cultural hegemony which renders alternative visions impotent at source – Marcuse's 'repressive tolerance'. My view is that the liminoid possibility is neither determinatively potent nor wholly mystified by cultural hegemony but always rests as a time-bomb in the system, liable to explode if circumstances combine to light the fuse by shifting the ambiguity of the anti-structural symbols in one direction rather than another. Alternative visions are not automatically and inevitably either rendered system-compatible or extirpated: it remains a genuine matter for intellectual curiosity what society does with, to and through them.

As I have argued above, the most consistent mark of the 1960s' counter-culture was its onslaught on boundaries and taboos of all kinds – the pursuit of what I earlier called infinity/the abyss and which I can now, with slightly reduced metaphoric weight, call liminality. It is Eliade's cyclic regression to chaos as a prelude to a new creation; it is Martin's dilemma of antinomianism and Douglas's zero structure. Now, liminality is an inherently unstable and precarious condition. It entails embracing *anomie* for the sake of the expanded creative possibilities it can offer and for the experience of existential communitas – the pure brotherhood of the 'high', the drunk and the inspired. It involves the employment of multiple instead of single systems of symbolic classification so that items can express ever richer amalgams of meaning and resonance. But this seeking out of creative ambiguity, as we noted above, can result in the destruction of code and classification and, with it, all possibility of communication. Real and painful *anomie* without compensating alternative 'group' solidarity is always a risk.

Turner has one final point worth considering here, which echoes some of Eliade's ideas about the way in which myth functions to provide us with models. All cultures contain in their repertoire of myth and symbol certain compelling images, models and narrative sequences which social actors and particularly the charismatic figures tend to find themselves re-enacting[45] precisely because of the 'aura effect' of unanalysed symbolic, mythic and ritual motivational patterns. These may be models of the super-hero or of the martyr. Both play a major part in the cultural scenario which the counter-culture inherited and re-played: the invincible hero (Che Guevara, Chairman Mao); the martyr who suffers at the hands of the evil and powerful (Che again at a later time, Mick Jagger on a drug charge, *Oz* on trial for obscenity); the inspired – daemonically possessed artist (de Sade, Mailer, Warhol). To these essentially Western models they added (as had their predecessors of the 1920s and 1930s) the mystical Eastern guru figure. It was a potent but deeply contradictory mixture.

CHAPTER 4

The Kingdom of Terminus

RITUALIZATION AND LIMINALITY IN BRITISH SOCIAL LIFE

Minister. *Cursed is he that removeth his neighbour's landmark.*
Answer. *Amen.*

The Book of Common Prayer, 1662: from 'A Commination: or Denouncing
of God's Anger and Judgements Against Sinners'

*There has always been and always will be not only the vertical boundary, the
river on this side of which initiative and honesty stroll arm in arm wearing
sensible clothes, and beyond which is a savage elsewhere swarming with con-
tagious diseases, but also its horizontal counterpart, the railroad above which
houses stand in their own grounds, each equipped with a garage and a
beautiful woman, sometimes with several, and below which huddled shacks
provide a squeezing shelter to collarless herds who eat blancmange and have
never said anything witty. Make the case as special as you please: take the
tamest congregation or the wildest faction; take, say, a college. What river
and railroad did for the grosser instance, lawn and corridor do for the more
refined, dividing the tender who value from the tough who measure, the
superstitious who still sacrifice to causation from the heretics who have
already reduced the worship of truth to bare description, and so creating the
academic fields to be guarded with umbrella and learned periodical against
the trespass of any unqualified stranger not a whit less jealously than the
game preserve is protected from the poacher by the unamiable shot-gun. For
without these prohibitive frontiers we should never know who we were or
what we wanted.*

W. H. Auden: from 'Caliban to the Audience', Part III of 'The Sea and the
Mirror', in *Collected Poems*

My main thesis is a simple one. The social structure of Britain which
formed, as it were, the receiving culture for the symbolic messages of the
Expressive Revolution, was minutely structured by group and grid. It had its

framed and classified 'moments' of liminality, which were programmed into an otherwise structured system. But liminality as a total way of life, even as an aspiration – that is a life-style based on weak or non-existent classification, framing and control – was not an option for the average man and woman. Not only was it not a conceivable option but anyone else's rejection of conventional classification and framing was likely to provoke immediate unease, if not direct hostility, because, as Mary Douglas and W. H. Auden both make very clear, our selfhood is tied securely to the sacred boundaries and categories that define who and where we are. In a very real sense, therefore, the counter-culture was initially experienced by a great many people as a conspiracy to take away their defining landmarks.

If anything approximating liminality (zero structure, weak classification) existed as a way of life, it was located at the two extreme ends of the social spectrum: that is, among the professional upper middle classes, especially in the expressive professions and, at the other end, among the undermass, the slum dwellers, the multi-problem families, the lumpenproletariat.

Muriel Spark in a pithy little story, 'You Should Have Seen the Mess',[1] captures the essence of this phenomenon far more surely than any sociological investigation of class. Lorna, her narrator, is a superb distillation of the spirit of working-class respectability. She is glad she went to the secondary modern instead of the dusty old grammar school because 'it was only constructed the year before. Therefore it was much more hygienic than the grammar school.' Lorna has recently met people of an educated type and has had her eyes opened to the perpetual mess in which they live. Her local doctor and his wife insist that she call them Jim and Mavis instead of Dr and Mrs Darby. Their furniture is a muddle, much of it old and worn; their paintwork is chipped; and they put their children out to play in dirty clothes ('Mum always kept us spotless to go out to play and I do not like to say it but the Darby children frequently looked like the Leary family, which the Council evicted from our block as they were far from houseproud'). One day Mavis shocks Lorna to the core by shouting out of the window to her son 'John, stop peeing over the cabbages at once. Pee on the lawn.' Such a word would never pollute the lips of Lorna's Mum, and her little brother Trevor 'would never pass water outside, not even bathing in the sea'. Lorna takes up with a friend of the Darbys, Willy Morley, who is an artist. Willy is the archetypical bohemian: 'He would not change his shirt very often, or get new clothes but he went around like a tramp lending people money as I have seen with my own eyes.' One evening, as she contemplates her parents' neat council flat, done out regularly by Dad in primrose and white, she suddenly realizes that Willy is no use to her: 'I agree to equality, but as to me marrying Willy, as I said to Mavis, when I recall his place, and the good carpet gone greasy, not to mention the paint oozing out of the tubes, I think it would break my heart to sink so low.'

Muriel Spark's Lorna understands what many sociologists have missed – that the Darbys and the Learys – the bourgeois bohemians and the lumpenproletarians – are alike in their patterns of unstructured mess, and that both are anathema to the spirit of respectability.

In between these two status extremes lay respectable middle England, consisting of the commercial and bureaucratic middle classes, managers, representatives and so on, the new and expanding technical and semi-professional segment, the clerical and administrative lower middle classes, minor self-employed tradesmen, shopkeepers and the like, the bulk of the respectable working classes stretching from old crafts to new semi-skilled employments, and the rural equivalent of all these folk from farmer to labourer. This is the Kingdom of Auden's god Terminus who watches over 'walls, doors, and reticence' – in short, boundaries. Here people live highly structured and ritualized lives, permeated and punctuated by the ordinary, daily symbolism of outside/inside and of role and status demarcations. Muriel Spark's Lorna is a splendid example of the respectable upper-working-class girl of the 1950s, for whom control, order and respect for the proper boundaries are spiritual and psychological necessities. She cannot comprehend the meaning of upper-middle-class 'mess', where categories seem to be hoeplessly muddled and where nothing seems to match or fit into symmetrical patterns and neatly segregated roles and activities. She might have been created expressly to illustrate Mary Douglas's definition of dirt (that which pollutes) as 'matter out of place'.[2] Everything about the Darbys is 'matter out of place' to Lorna, from their clothes and language, their muddle of 'old-fashioned', 'worn-out' furniture and contemporary pictures, their unemptied ashtrays and broken toys in the living-room, to Mavis's having her baby in their double-bed at home instead of in the purpose-made 'hygienic', single hospital bed. The single re-assuring fact about bohemian Willy is that he doesn't violate the one understood sacred boundary ('he did not attempt to go to the full extent'), even though his housekeeping shows distressingly weak classification and framing. Muriel Spark's brilliant little story even illustrates (or very nearly) Basil Bernstein's favourite test for weak classification and framing – whether the lavatory door is ever locked.[3] Even this episode, however, shows weak rather than non-existent classification. Mrs Darby doesn't want her cabbages polluted – but this was only the 1950s not the 1960s.

The second part of my thesis is that although between the extremes of expressive bohemianism and slum disorganization the characteristic social and symbolic pattern is a mixture of group and grid, at the margin group is the more dominant of the two among the respectable working class, (especially in traditionalist and community-like enclaves), while grid is stronger among most of the middle classes. The new privatized worker is an awkward case, for there grid elements are quite strong, while the group principle with its symbolism of inside/outside does not seem so much to be lost as to have shrunk to the level of the nuclear family as the defining Us group.

The thesis may be simple but its documentation is far from easy because we simply do not possess systematic ethnographic data on British life-styles such as anthropologists would habitually collect for more exotic tribes. Mary Douglas, however, is very clear about the kind of material that would be relevant. For example, towards the end of *Natural Symbols*, she discusses Bernstein's categories of elaborated and restricted code in their wider, extra-linguistic sense and offers the following thumbnail sketch, which makes a good starting-point for our discussion.

The restricted code allows a person to perceive his identity as part of his immediate social world: personal and social integration are achieved together. Here we should expect to find symbols of the human body actively expressing the solidarity of the social body. The first thing that is striking about the English working class home is the attempt to provide privacy in spite of the difficulties of layout. The respect for the privacy of bodily functions corresponds to the respect for the distinction between social and private occasions; the back of the house is appropriately allocated to cooking, washing and excretory functions; the front parlour, distinguished from the living room–kitchen is functionless except for public, social representation. Space by no means wasted, it is the face of the house which speaks composedly and smiles for the rest of the body; from this room a person must rush if he bursts into tears. Certain families of the middle class tend to break down the barrier between public and private. They seek to live in public together in an unstructured, open room, expressing aptly (perhaps disastrously) their unstructured personal system of control. In such a family it must be difficult to assimilate the image of society and the house to the image of the body, and correspondingly more difficult, one suspects, for the individual to incorporate into his personal identity any symbolic structures integrating him with his own society.[4]

I want to extend Mary Douglas's little sketch, beginning from the material I know best, the working-class culture of the Lancashire cotton towns in which I grew up in the 1940s and 1950s. We were Auden's 'collarless herds who ate blancmange' (but only on Sundays and at birthday parties) and never said anything witty (unless it was already contained in a folk saying). I do not claim any specially privileged or 'typical' status for the cotton towns – indeed, today they are depressed and clearly atypical in many respects. I am aware that there are immense regional variations, that Wales and Scotland have distinctive patterns, that London is a patchwork of different traditions, that small market towns like Banbury and rural areas like Gosforth and Akenfield display yet another series of patterns. I simply know the ethnography of the Lancastrian working class from the inside, and although subjectivity and selective recall have their dangers, the lack of systematic, 'objectively' gathered material means that one must rely on tainted or fragmentary sources or refrain from speaking at all. It happens, moreover, that a number of recent publications have documented something of the culture of the Lancastrian working class in a way that conventional community studies largely fail to capture. For example. Robert Roberts's perceptive and beautifully written autobiographical accounts of Edwardian and inter-war Salford[5] mesh perfectly with my recollections of the same period, gathered from extended kin and from interviews and discussions at old peoples' clubs in my home town of Bury, which is eight miles from Salford.[6] Jeremy Seabrook's jaundiced but eloquent portrait of Blackburn in the 1960s[7] is still recognizably about the same cultural pattern familiar from my own childhood and adolescence. And finally, Geoff Pearson's little essay on 'Paki-bashing' in the mid-sixties in Accrington, his own home town, indicates that the cultural contours for the latest generations are not radically altered.[8] Taking urban Lancashire as my main focus, I will, wherever possible, point to parallels, contrasts (or lack of evidence) in other areas. The picture will be intentionally generalized (a typification if you like), though I recognize that there is a good deal of variation within as well as between class cultures.

The first point, which is quickly obvious to any casual visitor to working-class Lancashire, is that Mary Douglas's description of the typical house is correct. The front of the house is the family's face to the world. The traditional terraced house wears its curtains with the pattern facing the street and not the inside of the room. The important rule is that the curtains at all the windows should match each other and the colour scheme of the external paint-work rather than the interior decoration and furnishing of each room. Viola Klein quotes a striking example of this particular sense of propriety from a study of Radby in Nottinghamshire;

The elder Bonnington girl ... was genuinely *shocked* at something she noticed about Buckingham Palace when she went to London on a Works' trip. The front curtains at the Palace did not match, and it was a sign of *pretty sluttish* housekeeping in her opinion.[9]

It might be Lorna speaking.

The persistent association of respectability with symmetry, matching and public face is deeply embedded in working-class culture. In respectable households it is important that things should have proper and appointed places and that certain things which witness to the respectability of the family should be on display. Robert Roberts cites many such examples. Edwardian families who fell on hard times would pawn indispensable objects such as beds and tables before they would part with the chiffonier and its ornaments because these were always on show through the half-open front door and thus constituted the family's face. The front parlour, as Douglas notes, has the same function. My inverviewees were unanimous

The Kingdom of Terminus: the house presents the family face to the world.

when I asked them what the front room was for – 'For show and for courting. Nowt else.' The door was always closed to protect it from the intrusion of the workaday world. The same sensibility about showing a good face dictated the donkey stoning of the front step and the practice of scrubbing the pavement down to the kerb to the width of the front doorstep. Both these habits were gradually discontinued after the Second World War, but the principle is easily transferred to the garden, when one acquires one, or to windowsills filled with flowers, plants and ornaments, which keep prying eyes from seeing the family's private place inside the room while displaying a good face. I have observed an interesting double-bind in some working-class households since the comparative affluence of the post-war period. They want to obey the traditional imperative of keeping the inside of the home a private place for the family, but they also want to display the consumer durables that are the modern equivalent of the chiffonier. Some brazenly leave the curtains open and the lights on so that all the neighbours who will never be invited indoors can admire the display, but they do so when the family is in the kitchen or out at work. Once the space is being used for intimate family affairs, the outer curtains are closed: it must be a still life not a *tableau vivant* that the world sees.

Post-war improvements in the material standard of living enabled the working class to express its sense of order, symmetry and face in new ways, both inside and outside the house. Matching furniture is *de rigueur* – the three-piece suite, the bedroom suite and the dining suite form the backbone of the mass furniture trade. J. M. Mogey, in his study of the respectable working class in Barton (Oxford) comments on the importance of having 'matching' furniture.[10] The rise of do-it-yourself home improvement and interior decoration is another expression of the same phenomenon (Lorna's father does the kitchen in primrose and white). Cars are even more implicated in the public face than any of the interior domestic improvements because so often they must stand on the street, witnessing to the status, respectability and 'standards' of the family. Woe betide the family that leaves a broken or rusting car too long on the street: it will lose face as surely as if the garden (or the family grave in the local cemetery) were unkempt or the front windows streaked and grubby.

The distinction between the front and the back of the house does not end with the front acting as face. In my childhood it was as routine among the working classes, as at the 'big houses', that different categories of people came to the front and the back door. The insurance man, the rent collector and the clergy came to the front, as did formally visiting kin. Dustmen, tradesmen and canvassers came to the back through the yard. I knew many respectable housewives who regarded it as shocking to go out of their own front doors in anything other than Sunday-best clothes. If they were 'slipping an errand' in working overalls, they would use the back door, even if it made the journey half a street longer. An aunt of mine took the principle to extremes and would always go out of her back door and walk half-way round the block to donkey stone her own front doorstep and wash her flags.

As Mary Douglas notes, washing and excretion were always properly undertaken at the back of the house. And I have yet to come across a respectable working-class household in which lavatory and bathroom doors do not lock securely from the inside. Even before the days of running hot water and bathrooms, the working-class family went to a great deal of trouble to secure privacy for washing at the 'slop stone'. It was usually organized on a careful rota system, with one member standing guard on the door. The same went for the Friday bath in the tin tub, when either the slop house or the warmer living-room was taken over. Ritual and hierarchy structured all these activities and were designed to define and frame a time and space for these particularly intimate body functions so as to protect the privacy of the individual.

Despite the crowded space of the working-class home, contrivances to secure personal territory are well developed in other ways too. Particular chairs 'belong to' certain family members, especially mother and father. In the days of open coal fires the access to warmth was always carefully graded in a spatial and temporal hierarchy. Roberts describes[11] and my interviewees confirm the widespread habit of having pint pots, plates and chairs only for adults in many households, sometimes even as late as the Second World War. Father would sit and eat while the children stood around the table and received scraps and titbits according to their age and sex. This was no disorderly practice but a ritualized set of working-class table manners as strict in its own rules as middle-class etiquette. One rule which has persisted up to the present day is that only immediate kin are normally present at meals in working-class homes. Roberts emphasizes the privacy of eating[12] in terms that remind one of Clifford Geertz's description of the Balinese. Among the poorest respectable Edwardian families it was not unusual for the door to be locked during meal times, to keep the world out. Public face and private reality must be strictly separated, especially if one's standing and respectability are under pressure. It is also, of course, a classic case of Douglas's body symbolism of the group pattern: ingestion, excretion and sexuality are all dangerous activities because they violate the integrity of the body contours; thus they are hedged around by rituals designed to keep out the polluting and dangerous 'outside' by defining and protecting the boundary between 'inside' and 'outside.

Another telling illustration of the importance of this distinction relates to courting rituals. Until the 1930s a girl would not bring a young man into her parents' house until their marriage had been arranged. If he was 'hanging up his hat', it meant they were engaged: only kin and quasi-kin have a right to come inside.

The functional specialization of time and space has continued into the post-war period of greater material comfort. It can be seen for example in the working-class dislike of open-plan domestic architecture which Mogey comments on in his 'Barton' study.[13] For the respectable working class each small space must have its specific uses: the more such spaces exist in a home the higher the status of the family. It is ironic and instructive that Mogey's respondents were busy building partitions to divide up the L-shaped room in their new council houses to create a separate parlour while the middle classes of London were buying up the old working class cottages and tearing down all the interior walls to create *un*structured space.

The crux of the matter, of course, is that all these ritualizations in working-class culture are the basis of *order*. The Lancashire cotton towns on which I am here concentrating are the home of the first real industrial proletariat. There are some features which are regional quirks but the important thing is to recognize the common predicament of the urban industrial working classes – the need to create order and meaning in conditions of scarcity and in a context dominated by the nature of factory production. The factory system as it established itself in Lancashire for the first time required a disciplined and orderly workforce to match the rhythm and economy of machine manufacture. 'Saint Monday' and all the other irregular work and role patterns of pre-industrial artisan practice were replaced by a rigid timing, sequence and role allocation suited to the factory system. Working-class culture espoused a pattern of order at least in part out of necessity and consistency. Jeremy Seabrook, in his analysis of Blackburn in the 1960s, pushes the point too far, however, when he argues a mechanical transfer of the discipline and authoritarianism of the workplace on to the personality structure and home life of the cotton proletariat. Human beings are never *only* ciphers of system needs: they are conscious moral agents too.

Seabrook brings a set of values to his analysis which cause him to shudder in horror at a culture based on the sanctity of boundary and order. When he contemplates Blackburn he sees only a bitter picture of racism, emotional starvation and a pinched and gossip-ridden life. What Seabrook fails to recognize is that historically this culture of control offered the only hope of creating human dignity and a modicum of self-determination against all odds. Until very recently indeed, the price of relaxing any of the boundaries and controls was very high. It made the difference between respectability and degradation, between coping and debt, between survival and starvation, independence and the workhouse. The crucial difference between the rough and the respectable was that the rough refused the disciplines of boundary and control. Consequently, their homes were hovels in which chaos was signified by literal as well as symbolic dirt, their work was casual and irregular, their budgeting was a seesaw of excess followed by inevitable destitution. The rituals in the working-class culture of control were the foundations of such dignity and independence as they were able to wrest from a hard environment. The *control* was not merely external, societal coercion; it was the control which the individual could actively exercise over his own conditions of life. Those who would not or could not exercise this control were infinitely more coerced by circumstance than were those who embodied controls in their own life-style. The Protestant ethic may have been the precondition of entrepreneurial capital accumulation, but this distinctive proletarian culture of control was the prerequisite of the organized labour movement and of the perhaps uniquely British tradition of the inherent dignity of manual labour. The point is paradoxical and too easily overlooked.

The house and its internal layout is only one small aspect of this culture of order and control. Ritual and repetition are the organizing principles in every aspect of life. In my childhood it was still normal for the dietary pattern to follow an unvarying weekly cycle even in the most affluent working-class households. This weekly repetition seems to have been common throughout the north of England.[14] Household chores were ritualized too. Particular jobs were done regularly at a specific time on the same day of the week. Washing Monday, ironing Tuesday, baking Wednesday and Friday, shopping Saturday. Sheets were changed on Fridays, tops to bottoms, with a fresh top sheet and pillow case. Certain jobs were reserved for the males – often cleaning the windows and mending the clogs and shoes, on Saturday morning. In large families the children all had their own chores. My mother was the second youngest of a family of ten girls and one boy. They each had their own job to do, arranged in a strict hierarchy with the chores at the front of the house having a higher status than the ones concerned with the back. As the girls married (and that too was supposed to take place in strict hierarchy of seniority), so the next eldest took on the top chore and so on down the line.

Robert Roberts tells a number of stories which hinge on the moralization of these chore rituals – for example, public disapproval of housewives who did not wash on Monday. He repeats the street rhyme still current in my adolescence which embodied the rule. It concludes:

> Them as wash on Thursday are folk that wash for shame.
> Them as wash on Friday most likely wash in need.
> But them as wash on Saturday – they are sluts indeed.[15]

The old people I talked with often raised this issue and, without exception, believed that it was normal and natural to want to organize their time and chores on a rhythmic pattern, even if the actual pattern they now worked by was different from the one they had inherited. They described to me their own and their daughters' transmutation of the *idea* of pattern into much more varied actual patterns, which responded to new household appliances, affluence, the routines of old people's flats with shared vacuum cleaners and washing and drying rooms, and so on. Their sense of the need for order and rhythm was still very strong but by the 1970s many looked back on the old *invariable* rituals as 'daft, really, when you come to think about it'.

The continuing, though usually privatized ritualization of household chores is extensively documented for the whole British Isles by Ann Oakley.[16] Shopping takes on the same pattern. Marketing agencies have recognized the prevalence of brand loyalties. Furthermore, housewives tend to patronize particular shops and market traders at absolutely regular times, regular not just to the day but even to the hour, often, I have observed, ignoring weather conditions just to keep the pattern regular. Dennis, Henriques and Slaughter comment on this kind of regularity in the Yorkshire mining town they studied in the 1950s.[17] After her death in 1975 the highest praise that her neighbours could heap on one of my aunts was that 'You could tell the time by her.' This kind of routinization and the assessment of it as praiseworthy even survives the hyper- and supermarket revolution. The context alters and makes for individual variations, while the underlying structure of pattern and routine remains. In the same way dietary routinization has expanded its repertoire to accommodate the Chinese and Indian take-away alongside the fish and chip shop and the home freezer alongside market day, but the sense of the 'rightness' of regularity and repetition lies deep in the cultural code and helps to account for the well-documented persistence of regional and class nutritional patterns.[18]

Clothing follows similar rules. Roberts shows that before the First World War respectability meant having a change of clothes for the week-end. The Friday night bath preceded the change into non-work clothes and, if you were very lucky, a day and a half in shoes instead of clogs. The clogs had gone by my time but the distinction between working clothes and week-end clothes was important. Saturday clothes were usually out-of-date or handed-down Sunday clothes. Sunday clothes were replaced once a year for Whit Sunday, when everyone paraded in a complete new outfit and went to all the relatives to have a new penny (or more) put into the pocket 'to help it wear well'. Sunday clothes were worn for church and Sunday school, for formal visits to kin, for birthday parties, for the Whit. processions and for Christmas Day and New Year's Day. Clothing, like time and space, was strictly functionally divided. The clothes you wore declared what kind of activity you were engaged in. Post-war prosperity has swelled the wardrobe and, as with furniture, it has extended the possibilities of having matching combinations. It has also added whole new categories of clothes, especially holiday and party clothes, but it has not seriously eroded the principle of strict functional categorization in this important area of body imagery.

The rhymes and games of the street and the school playground are another ritualized resource of this culture. They had and have their due season: marbles, hopscotch and skipping come in proper sequence, just as the Church's liturgical calendar performs its ritual revolution. Skateboards, chopper bikes and expensive mechanical toys have expanded the options much more at the private, domestic level than in the communal street play of the children, in which the old rituals maintain themselves with remarkable vigour. It is important, too, that respectable families 'put the children out to play'; they do not 'let them run wild'. (Mogey again notes this among his 'Barton' families.)[19] Lorna's Mum 'always kept us spotless to go out to play'.

The differentiation between work and play generally receives elaborate emphasis. The week-end clothes are part of it, of course. Roberts recalls the frenzies of cleaning and polishing which preceded the week-end. Even if they had no Sunday clothes, the women would put on clean, starched white aprons; the protective covers came off the furniture; the best fender was put in the hearth; all the ornaments were taken out and dusted; and the family would gather for Sunday afternoon round the fire after the one good meal of the week. The sense of occasion, of celebration, of making all things clean and new which marked this precious leisure time was not different in essence in my experience up to the mid-1950s, although the white aprons and the blacking brush were obsolete by then. All leisure was minutely prepared for and marked out well in advance as a qualitatively different kind of time. It was the violation of the sanctity of hard-earned *leisure* rather than a Puritan Sabbatarianism that lay behind the heavy disapproval of 'unnecessary' and 'slovenly' cleaning and washing on Sunday. If one person violates the boundary, nobody's leisure seems safe.

The Friday or Saturday night out in the pub or club, or visiting relatives to play cards or, later, to watch television together all form part of this same ritualization of leisure. The key phrase describing such activities is: 'We *always* go (or do, or drink) so and so.' The repetition itself defines the sacred category. The same is true of holidays. In this too there is a normative pre- ference for repetition; families do not merely go to the same resort but patronize the same boarding-house year after year. The aunt of mine who was a living timepiece (Hans Castorp's watch again, of course) for more than fifty years alternated her holidays between Southport and Morcambe, with only the occasional aberration to Blackpool. She formed a long- standing nodding acquaintanceship not only with the boarding-house keepers but also with equally regular patrons who turned up, season after season, in the same place at the same week of the year. Nobody would have dreamed of extending the acquaintance into 'friendship' (not a working-class concept at all) outside the special context of the Wakes Week. The package holiday trade can document the continuation of this ritual repetition into the period of affluence, which has enabled the working-class holidaymaker to go further afield – to the Balearic Isles, to Yugoslavia and Ostend. It can also bear witness to the deep resistance to foreign food as 'muck'.

The pub – the term the 'local' makes the point in itself – displays a similar phenomenon. It has a stable clientele, which is at its maximum on Friday and Saturday night. The men go on their own during the week but often take their womenfolk along at weekends. Ship Street, Bethnal Green, Huddersfield and Ashton all conform to this pattern of repetition and predictability.[20] The same holds, as Roberts reports with more than a trace of irritation, of the practical jokes played on the newest recruits to the shop floor.[21] They are part of the guild secrets, rituals of initiation by humiliation known to all the adults and repeated without variation on generation after generation of young workers. Fetch a rubber hammer, some elbow grease, and so on. My younger brothers' experiences as raw apprentices in the 1950s might have come straight out of Roberts's pages.

Roberts is even more impatient with another instance of the love of repetition in this culture, the tendency to use 'sayings', to repeat stories and incidents word for word and at immense length until they are common property, to surround simple pieces of information with an enormous elaboration of the context, who (with genealogy), where, when and how, including much detail which might strike the outsider as immaterial to the story.[22] All these things seem to me central to the Lancashire working-class linguistic style. Indeed, I have often reflected that if Basil Bernstein had grown up in the cotton towns, he would have reversed the labels on his two language codes and concluded that every educationally mobile Lancastrian would make a prolific descriptive historian. I understand Roberts's impatience with the rigidity and I share his contempt for patronizing middle-class commentators who see these ritualized metaphorical practices as quaintly colourful and somehow vigorous in a Lawrentian way – that is mere sentimentality. The important point, surely, is that all these things are normal features of traditional oral culture. They are the mechanisms by which the lore of a people is preserved and extended without benefit of literacy. They fix what is known and understood; they form the body of symbolic representations from which myth and meaning are taken. The jingles of the TV commercials, the images of advertising, the catch-phrases of the comedy shows, the sit-coms and the soap operas and the gestures of the rock world have all supplemented the folk repertoire of sayings and symbols, but they still operate in essentially the way Roberts describes to supply a shared vocabulary, a 'restricted', code which defines the contours of both dream and reality. Where my maternal grandmother seemed to me to converse only in sybilline 'sayings', without any need for intrusive secular improvisation, I now hear conversations composed of short-hand evocations, the full resonance of which it is impossible to comprehend unless one is intimately familiar with the mannerisms of the stars of the mass media and the latest advertising gimmicks.

Sex, age and social status are minutely mapped by cultural boundary markers of which the stories, sayings and jokes are an important part: 'A whistling woman and a crowing hen will bring the Devil out of his den'; 'tha's fourteen now, owd enough to drink, smoke, swear and go out wi' girls' (the age oddly impervious to changes in the school-leaving age); and 'clogs should stick wi' clogs.' Seabrook's and Roberts's texts are both rich in examples of these role demarcations. Indeed, it is the one area which is exhaustively illustrated by all the community studies, those of market town, village and conurbation, and by all the studies of the family. The general outline is familiar and needs no reiteration here. I will therefore take up now only a few aspects, which are either neglected or which it is particularly important to clarify in view of the impact of the Expressive Revolution. The two most salient and most easily misunderstood of these features are sexuality and swearing.

There have been outsiders, often romantic radicals (see below, chapter 6) who like to see the working classes as sexually unrepressed, a race of Mellorses, Roberts, who knew the culture from the inside, sees the working classes as sexually inhibited, imprisoned in a culture of shame.[23] All the documentary evidence is on Roberts's side. Yet this trait too ought to be seen as a consistent part of a system of role and boundary demarcation rather than as a nonsensical and unnecessary piece of self-impoverishment. As Mary Douglas would be the first to recognize, where boundaries are rigid and sacred the act of crossing them, as in sexual intercourse, is a dangerous business, full of the risk of pollution by nameless evils and alien forces. This is surely the root of the old working-class horror of the homosexual; he who straddles such powerfully insulated categories is the embodiment of danger and pollution. In traditional working-class culture sexual knowledge was limited and furtive; complete nakedness, even before husband or wife, was rare and considered shameful; mothers told their daughters as little as possible. Psychic intimacy between the sexes, prolonged physical tenderness and sexual virtuosity seem not to have been either typical or encouraged, even if the equation of 'sex' with 'dirt' was perhaps less total than our aggressively hedonistic enlightenment might now lead us to suppose. Certainly, sex was emphatically *private*; that is why the parlour door was always shut and why even back street fornication was protected by the informal acknowledgement of territorial rights.

The studies of family and community show clearly that sex and gender roles are even now more rigidly demarcated among the working classes than among the middle classes. It is particularly interesting that this should be true of Lancashire, where women worked in the factories from the earliest days of the Industrial Revolution. Lancashire was and remains a matriarchal culture, not unlike that of Wilmott's and Young's picture of Bethnal Green, with the important exception that the Lancashire matriarch is more likely to control the purse, demanding and getting an unopened wage packet from husband and grown-up children alike. Yet this has never led to any serious blurring or inversion of the gender roles. Men and women traditionally lived highly segregated lives. Both inside and outside the mill women spent their time with other women and children, in the work group, the street claque and the home, while the men spent work and leisure time with other men on the shop floor, in their own street claque, in the pubs and clubs, the trade unions and Friendly Societies. Joint family leisure was confined to Sunday afternoon, high days and holidays. For the rest, life was divided by age and sex categories for every imaginable purpose. Most important, the content of all one's social roles had a sharp definition and an objective reality. Bernstein makes this the basis of his category, the 'positional family'.[24] Seabrook sums it up in these terms:

Traditionally, for the working class, relationships were prescriptive. The notion of kinship took precedence over any idea of personal and individual relationship. Certain roles, whether contracted voluntarily or by birth, demanded a fixed and determined behaviour, and people were judged according to their will and ability to live up to the duties and responses inherent in each role.[25]

The role categories and their attendant duties and identities were therefore embedded in all kinds of ritual formulae, both verbal and behavioural. One of the most fascinating of these role signals is swearing, and of all the community studies, only *Coal is our Life* treats it an any depth.[26] Swearing is one of the most minutely ritualized activities among the traditional working class and is far from being an indication of an uninhibited and vigorous libido or of contempt for convention and authority. It marks the edges of the various peer groups of age and sex. Co-swearing in a group is a mark of equality, companionship and solidarity: swearing will also be aimed aggressively at outsiders. Thus the same words can carry a message of comradeship, even tenderness, *and* of insult and humiliation, depending on context. Everyone knows the words and everyone knows the contexts in which they will be experienced as natural or shocking respectively. Men at work are expected to pepper their sentences with routinized obscenity and blasphemy, and even the most sanctimonious characters will find it hard to gain acceptance if they do not conform. Women and those from a higher status category who violate the protected boundary of the all-male group in the pub or betting shop or on the shop floor will be treated to aggressive swearing designed to shock and humiliate but women at a family party or in the pub legitimately at the weekend will be treated with 'respect'.[27]

Swearing among groups of women is common but decidedly milder in its scatological content. Among the respectable working classes swearing inside the family is either tabooed altogether, or kept at a very mild level or, more often, allowed in modified form and strictly according to a hierarchy of authority: father swears a little and justifies it with a 'saying' ('Don't do as I do, do as I say'); mother swears less; and the children are forbidden to swear altogether. Very young children who are just learning to talk are almost encouraged to swear for the amusement of adults, but a sharp cut-off point occurs around the age of four or five, when swearing begins to be treated as 'dirty' – inappropriate to the role and polluting to the family. Adolescence brings a new legitimacy to swearing, especially for boys – it acts as a mark of having grown up very much the same as confirmation or leaving school. Boys who never swear in adolescence will be seen as effeminate, but swearing is properly confined to the peer group and should not be brought inside the home. One of the refrains of the working-class mother to her teenage sons was always, 'I don't care what you do out there but I won't have it in *my* house.' The same went for smoking and sex, though by the late 1950s teenage smoking had begun openly to invade the home.

Violators of all these rituals of role lose face for themselves and their whole families, and our picture of this culture is not complete until we have examined more carefully the intersection of the vertical and the horizontal boundaries, for the distinctions with which we are concerned are not just between inside and outside, public and private, young and old, male and female, but also between status categories arranged in a minutely graded hierarchy. The distinction between rough and respectable has long been recognized as important in working-class history. Roberts gives us a more elaborated picture of the divisions within the respectable group into subtle status grades. Up above the 'no class' and 'low class' were minute variations by street and by family based on occupation, income, possession, inherited 'standards', public face, role performance and the like. Every public act and many private ones were tests of keeping face and performing to the standard expected of one's own category. Even the trades unions operated at least in part on the basis of these established status priorities, as indeed they still do, through the defence of wage differentials and the pursuit of a not entirely new instrumental militancy. A great deal of working-class history is misread if we mistake *category* identity for *class* solidarity.

Status boundaries probably need less illustration here than most of the other salient boundaries of working-class culture because historians and sociologists automatically collect material about them. Pubs, shops, streets, schools, churches, dance halls and the graded spaces of cinemas and football grounds were all organized on hierarchical principles so that one never need stray out of one's own status category. A nice instance which my Bury informants brought up on a number of occasions was the institution known as the Monkey Runs – almost the pre-war equivalent of youth culture. The social life of the unmarried largely took place on the streets where little groups of boys and girls strolled, chatted and picked each other up at week-ends. As my informants were quick to point out, courting (like everything else) went in status categories. You knew whether you had the right to go 'to t' top o' t' Street' (by the parish church in the town centre): that was for 'toffs' (the artisan elite). Union Square was for the 'middle class' (the middle of the respectable working class), while Princess Street was 'quite low really'. If you miscategorized yourself, it would do you no good – 'you just wouldn't get a chap or a lass.'

What is important and easily misunderstood about this hierarchical structure is that people usually knew their place and strove to keep to it. The display of the chiffoniers and later of the status-bearing household commodities is badly misconceived if it is seen as essentially an individualistic competition to outdo the rest: it witnesses to one's ascriptive category and is geared more to defending than to seeking to improve one's status. It was not seriously transmuted into a competition to better oneself until the mid-1950s, when affluence and a measure of privatization began slowly to affect the old system. In 1928, when my mother left school, she rashly proposed to my grandmother that it would be nice to work in a shop instead of going into the cotton mill like her older sisters. My grandmother was horrified and forbade any such thing: 'Our sort go int' mill.' It was less the social climbing than the violation of the 'natural' category that shocked her. It would be equally wrong to see this phenomenon as part of a slavishly deferential ideology. If moving up was unthinkable, so was taking a job (or a husband, or a house, and so on) below one that was appropriate to your 'natural' category. Ascriptive categories entail *rights*, and the culture of boundary and category defends those rights with all its energies because they are perceived as part of the natural *order*. Viola Klein, in her survey of traditional working-class life, glimpsed the essential point:

The psychological trait we have called 'striving after standards' is easily connected with a more general preference for well-defined situations. This preference manifests itself in social life as a preference for clearly defined, generally understood and rather rigidly maintained personal relations. In sociological language, the role structure is a simple one, allowing little choice or variation in behaviour.[28]

'Paki-bashing' in Accrington (or Brixton, or Walsall) and race prejudice in Blackburn (or Tottenham, or Bradford) in the 1960s make more sense if they are understood as manifestations of a culture which sanctifies boundaries and anathematizes mixed categories of all kinds. Each new element must be slotted into the strict pattern of vertical and horizontal bounds. One does not need to invoke either economic or psychological 'disturbance' to explain the treatment of Asians and blacks. It is all of a piece with the treatment of the Irish and Jews which Roberts describes:[29]

'outsiders' are put at the bottom of the hierarchy and subjected to purity/pollution rituals *no different in kind* from those which guard the other boundary markers in the culture. Ironically, the liberal mind tends to see ethnic prejudice as an inherently and qualitatively distinct phenomenon and therefore misses much of its meaning and function for the prejudiced group. No amount of education about ethnic minorities will make much difference until the receiving culture has begun to exemplify flexibility of classification and tolerance of ambiguity in its cultural code. Moreover, cultures of boundary and control which feel that they are under pressure from moral definitions which bear down on them from superior-status categories are likely to re-emphasize rather than abandon the sacred boundaries, and this goes for Asian sub-cultures in the 1970s[30] as much as for white working-class racists, since both are recalcitrant to liberal middle-class values and patterns. For the moment, the point that I want to establish is the fundamental identity of the symbolic processes which define and maintain both the vertical and the horizontal boundaries. Sexual and racial differentiation (and prejudice) are like status differentiation not because they are fundamentally 'class' phenomena, as some Marxist/liberationist theory claims, but because all three are cases of social definition and therefore of classification and framing.

I have described the traditional working-class life-style as a culture of control. The controls are both external in the sanctions that fall if one violates any of the sacred boundaries, and also internal because the whole sense of self develops through a vocabulary of clear categories, rules and roles. The realities of the working-class life-style have always seemed to me to discredit the old sociological chestnut that claims the working classes are characterized by the desire for 'immediate gratification', that they do not engage in forward planning or distant goals but opt for the hedonism of the moment. Here we have yet another legacy of middle-class sentimentality and incomprehension. Or could it be some kind of half-truth?

The culture of boundaries and control was always set against powerful temptations to break and erode the discipline on which it rested. The most intractable challenges came from drink and gambling. Roberts's auto-biography is the story of his mother's perpetual struggle to repair the depradations which his father's chronic drinking made on order and the self-sufficiency which depended on order. The problem was common and ineradicable, not least because the definition of masculinity and the solidarity of the male band was tied in with hard drinking and gambling. So women found themselves operating the characteristic double-bind of the symbol system, wanting their men to display their masculinity *and* hand over the wage packet. Role definition and control come into conflict here. My maternal grandmother was a splendid case in point. The respectability of her very large family was made possible by my grandfather's rigid teetotalism. He was a Methodist, non-practising and politically free-thinking but adamant against alcohol and swearing. My grandmother appreciated and respected him, and she knew, not least because she was constantly reminded of the fact by neighbours who used her as bank and pawn shop, that the family's good fortune (and the neighbour's loans) depended on not having a drinking man in the house. But over her Saturday jug of stout she would tease him mercilessly for his disciplined ways and would call him, half-affectionately, half-contemptuously, 'tha Methodistical owd bugger'. (Incidentally, he was quite literally a walking timepiece; he acted as knocker-up for the whole district.)

The precise historical origins of working-class drinking and gambling and the violence which often accompanied them are complex and uncertain. What matters for our purposes, however, is that these temptations to destroy through excess the financial and behavioural controls which the rest of the system so carefully institutionalized were themselves a structured part of working-class culture. In fact, they form central features of the repertoire of liminal possibilities. As we noted in chapter 3, societies normally frame these liminal moments, surround them with strict boundaries which mark off the liminal time and place from the non-liminal. So it was and is in working-class culture. The 'immediate gratification' which the middle-class observer has so often wrongly identified as a global characteristic of working-class culture, the sacramental swearing and the crude, aggressive sexuality of the male horde, the drinking and the violence, is a feature of the *liminal* moments in working-class life, as indeed is the equally misunderstood atmosphere of warmth and togetherness. It marks the brotherhood of 'communitas', set off against the rules, roles and categories of structured, mundane societas. Drink and gambling threaten the culture of control when they break out of the framed moment of communitas and try to universalize the liminal state.

In a period of poverty and hardship, such as the Edwardian era of Roberts's story, it is hardly surprising that many men and some women sought to stay inside the liminal cocoon even at the cost of destroying the meagre possibilities which structured societas had to offer. But the price was always high and the family of any addict of liminality would quickly find itself in the 'no class' or 'low class' category with no way out. Indeed, from Victorian descriptions of the 'dangerous and perishing classes', through Booth's and Rowntree's lowest levels of primary poverty (and much of the 'secondary poverty' which arose from poor budgeting (*sic*)), to contemporary descriptions of slum or problem families and the 'culture of poverty' (Muriel Spark's Learys), we find the lumpenproletariat distinguished by a culture of 'immediate gratification', loose or non-existent role and boundary differentiation and an absence of planning. The axial principles of liminality have eaten away the culture of control: the frames did not hold. This is Roberts's description of Ignatius's family, the Irish outcast prostitute's filthy and disorganized household;[31] it is Paneth's Branch Street[32] in the 1940s, and parts of Kerr's Ship Street[33] and Mogey's St Ebbs[34] in the 1950s. Viola Klein's reworking of all this material in her 1965 publication put into words what would have commanded wide assent at the time as according with common sense, that a culture based on immediate emotional response, in which no internalization of control occurs (from toilet training, to eating, to sex), is bound to produce damaged and inadequate personalities.[35] It is ironic that while psychiatry, social work and social psychology were premised on the self-evident nature of these 'truths' the movement we came to call the counter-culture was brewing up a concoction based on an exact inversion of these assumptions. Privileged bohemians like the Darbys and Willy Morley produced a generation of young crusaders preaching the superiority of what the respectable working class *knew* at first hand as the cultural norms of the 'no class' dregs. What respectable working-class family in 1968 could be expected to ignore the spectres of Ignatius and his kind when they took the first rhetorical impact of the Expressive Revolution?

The traditional pattern of framed liminality strictly limited the times and places where excess was appropriate and where role reversal, role expansion, horseplay, taboo breaking and celebration were planned for. The distinction between work and leisure is the starting-point – the rules of behaviour on the night out are already semi-liminal. The recurrent festivals are the real home of liminality, however – the Wakes Week, Whitsuntide with its new clothes and processions (now sadly obsolete), Christmas, New Year, weddings and funerals. All these are genuine rituals in a sense strict enough to meet Victor Turner's definition and are all sharply characterized by communitas and the symbolism of anti-structure. The funfairs and the vulgar postcards are important because they are precisely *un*like normal life – they break the normal taboos. On all these occasions everyone expects to do things which in other contexts they would find shocking. The wake after the funeral is the most vivid example, but there are many others; alcohol never comes into most houses (drinking is for pubs) but at Christmas it would not be respectable to fail to have a drink to offer visitors. Even non-drinkers are expected to take a glass at Christmas and weddings. Kissing, flirting, body contact and the like all have their place on 'evenings of masks and freedom'. Minor liminal moments include the works outings and birthday and pre-marriage 'footings' at the workplace, when the celebrant buys cakes and drinks all round and work is suspended in favour of alcoholically lubricated horseplay.

What is particularly interesting about these occasions is the degree to which the expected excesses are themselves routinized. Liminal role playing is pretty carefully programmed as a kind of inversion of workaday role playing. Though the experience of communitas is real enough, things are not as free-floating as all that: it is more like switching over the TV channel or changing to a new script; everyone knows his part in both channels and both scripts. The most striking single inversion is financial. Where careful budgeting is part of the workaday culture of control, the liminal times involve *mandatory* spending on a large scale. Working-class families would save up the whole year round for the conspicuous consumption at Christmas, the new clothes at Whit and the Wakes Week. Insurance policies were habitually taken out on a baby to cover his coming of age party or her wedding. There is very careful forward planning (or equally careful retrospective planning as it were through the loan club) to cover the necessary liminal excesses. Christmas in particular is very like the potlatch ceremonial. This characteristic is clearly not peculiar to Lancashire. Richard Hoggart, writing about his experience of the Yorkshire working class, calls these liminal occasions 'excursions into the Baroque',[36] Viola Klein calls it the 'Splash'[37] and the Ashton mining community referred to it as 'saving for a sunny day'.[38] The planning which goes into the preparation for these liminal festivities punctuates and thus gives order and meaning to the yearly round. It forms a kind of liturgical progression which feeds the sense of order by dividing time into defined and ritually bounded segments, each with a culminating goal.

Gambling, though deeply interwoven in working-class life, is less central to the pattern of liminal excess than is drink. Nevertheless, it always involves 'irrational' expenditure and a fantasy about an unlimited ability to spend when one's luck turns. Most working-class gambling is routinized and strictly limited − the weekly investment in a dream of winning the pools, small sums on the dogs, the horses, bingo. The chronic gambler is usually male, and the betting shop is not a place in which respectable working-class women are expected to be found. Yet the 'Flutter' is as regular as the 'Splash' in its more limited way. In the 1940s and 1950s virtually every housewife I knew put a little bet on the Derby and the Grand National through the (illegal) street bookies and their runners, even though regular betting would have ruined a woman's claim to respectability. It is characteristic of working-class culture to surround activities which involve taking risks with protective ritual practices − not just gambling but everything from the most trivial domestic superstitions (touching wood to make sure the cake rises) to the taboos and prohibitions which attend chronically dangerous occupations (the fisherman must not meet a woman or anyone whistling on his way to his ship). Again, these are framing devices in a culture of boundary and control.

A good deal of sociological literature on the working classes has taken off from David Lockwood's influential essay on working-class images of society.[39] Lockwood constructed three ideal types: traditional proletarian, deferential traditional, and privatized working class. These models have been stimulating as a heuristic device but they have also tended to obscure some of the aspects of continuity in the world view of the working classes, old and new, deferential and proletarian, even though Lockwood actually points out some of these continuities in his essay. They are *all* cultures of boundary and control incorporating protected and framed moments of liminality. It would not be difficult to re-work Lockwood's categories in terms of the different *placing* of the salient boundaries and the modes and degrees of ritualization of behaviour at the boundary for the three types. Although I have no serious quarrel with Lockwood's typology, I am less than happy with some of the attempts to use it in empirical research.[40] The fundamental ambiguity of so many features of the working-class culture of boundary and control is that they simultaneously embody hierarchy *and* solidarity. All three types live by classifying through vertical and horizontal boundaries. They differ in the value they attribute to membership of these various social categories but they are agreed in their unwillingness to straddle categories and cross boundaries. After all, the major finding of the affluent worker study was that the salient boundary between working and middle class had not been shifted even with the post-war affluence and the spread of the 'privatized' type among manual occupations.[41] That socially sacred boundary is still intact because is is minutely coded into the social classifications which underly all types of working-class and middle-class life-styles.

At the manual/non-manual border one of the most important characteristics which sets the traditional lower-middle-class life-style apart from that of the working class is the much more restricted role of liminal excess. The black-coated worker analysed by Lockwood, and the 'culture of the semi-detached' described by Ray Gosling[42] (see chapter 6), extends the disciplines of boundary and control even into the furthest corners of leisure time. Norms of rationality, consistency and moderation are applied across the board, and liminality is either excluded or kept within very rigid and moderate limits. Sometimes this is a legacy of Protestantism, though often it is secularized almost out of recognition by the late twentieth century.

Its counterpart in the traditional working class was the minority culture represented by my maternal grandfather and Roberts's mother. This was the self-conscious, self-educated and politically active minority. Sometimes it was individualistic and Liberal; often, later on, it was Labour and collectivist: it was the backbone of the trade union movement and the Workers' Educational Association. It produced creative renegades like Roberts. Internalized discipline, inculcated initially through an externally imposed culture of boundaries and control, can transmute through reflection into a set of norms consciously based on rationality and consistency. But what is really significant about this minority culture is that it exchanges the liminality of the bottle for the liminality of the book. Literacy brings with it a wider range of alternative realities than was ever dreamed of in the pub and the wake, and the strength of this liminality of the Word is that it has the capacity to become a critique of inherited categories and classifications. Then the boundaries can be perceived as contingent, not absolute; the specific instance can be distinguished from the underlying principle; the expressive enrichment that can come from straddling classifications and playing with ambiguity can be discovered and explored. But the re-thinking of rules, roles and categories remains at the level of escapism and fantasy unless the internalized culture of control has made available concrete skills which act as a passport into a *real* world of alternative possibilities.

Apart from the exclusion (or transmutation) of liminality, the other feature which distinguishes the lower-middle-class life-style is a more highly developed privatization and individuation. Lockwood's clerks keep themselves to themselves and define their status less in terms of the category to which they belong than in contrast to the category (manual workers) from which they set themselves apart. Where the typical working-class identity includes reference to 'our own sort' (that is, category identity or, in Douglas's term, group symbolism), that of the lower middle class is ego- or nuclear family-centred (that is, grid patterned or 'privatized'). The cultural vocabulary of both classes is that of boundary and control: the axial dichotomies in both cases are public/private, male/female, work/leisure, kin/non-kin, respectable/disreputable. Both take hierarchy and 'face' as important facts of life. At the margin, however, group is stronger among the working classes, both as a pattern of relationships and as a symbolic code, whereas grid is stronger for the lower middle class.

The middle classes proper are even less thoroughly researched than the clerical class or the petty bourgeoisie. Nevertheless, all the extant community studies indicate that the mainstream middle-class pattern is both more affluent on average and, in some important ways, marginally more flexible about the location and defence of boundaries. But it remains fundamentally a culture of order and control. Liminal excess, however, returns as part of the middle-class pattern and, as with the working-class liminal moments, tends to be associated with one-class occasions. A few interesting exceptions occur in deeply hierarchical contexts, such as the armed forces and the business firm, where liminal rituals of role reversal or momentary communitas (the Christmas dinner where officers serve the other ranks, the office party where managing director and office boy indulge in mandatory bonhomie) punctuate differentiated societas. Most of the pretexts for liminal excess among the middle classes parallel those of the working classes, though they are less likely to be exclusively kin-based activities.

Two distinctive marks of the middle-class life-style which affect the location and strength of boundaries are membership of formal and voluntary associations and the cult of friendship. The middle classes, unlike the working classes join formal associations – everything from churches to tennis clubs, discussion groups to yoga classes. Middle-class culture therefore accommodates many more differentiated nodes on its networks of social contact. The whole system is structured less by the system of kinship and primary ascriptive membership of categories than by voluntary extension and selection. Many of the associational contacts of the middle class, though voluntary, are as role-specific as the rigid role-based relationships of the working class. However, these fragmentary, role-specific contacts are supplemented by friendship – voluntary, multi-faceted, intimate relationships with persons who are not kin and who have no ready-made ascriptive claims on one. As we saw, friendship is not an important institution among the working classes, except for the all-male bond. Among the middle classes, however, friendship involves dining in each other's homes, going out together to concerts, theatres or cinemas, taking joint holidays and so on. Thus the intimate life of the middle classes is penetrated by voluntarily chosen others; ascriptive outsiders achieve insider status.

The middle-class home is therefore far less of a fortress manned against the intrusion of alien (non-kin) elements. The distinction between the 'face' of the home and its back or inside is correspondingly more blurred. The middle-class house can rearrange its internal elements, invert or muddle the functions and placing of 'back' and 'front' without any necessary incongruity or loss of face. Certainly, among the mainstream middle class, furniture and colour schemes should match, but curtains show their linings to the outside and the symmetry is expected inside a room rather than on the window 'face'. Indeed, the 'face' of the house seldom looks directly on to the public street. In this sense it is perhaps the garden which acts as the 'face', and the aspiration is to have the house as private as possible inside a protective garden surround. When the status of the family is to be displayed the audience will be invited inside. Thus the demarcation between inside and outside, public and private, is marginally less rigid, the boundaries a little more fluid than among the traditional working class.

The internal differentiation of the spaces and times of domestic life is well developed but more variable in its pattern, not least because hours of work themselves are more variable and more dependent on the choices of the individual worker than in most manual occupations. So meal times become moveable feasts, and the organization of chores more privatized and variable (and frequently not the direct responsibility of family members). The social networks and the symbolic boundaries are thus more complex and generally somewhat looser: they incorporate individual choice and variation and are less totally structured by pure ascription. Nevertheless, there is a well-developed sense of belonging to a status category, and a status striving no less marked than among the working classes, though the commodities and cultural traits which are considered as bearing high status are often distinct. Overall the grid principle of ego-based differentiation is stronger than the group principle. Yet boundaries, categories and classification are still the staple fare of this cultural vocabulary, and certain families, especially among the commercial and administrative middle classes, display a pattern no less rigid than that of the respectable working class. As Lewis and Maude summarized it: 'By and large, middle-class homes are distinguished by regularity, order and even ritual.' This remained true up to the 1960s, not just of Banbury and Woodford but even of most of Raymond Firth's Hampstead sample.[43]

The truly Bohemian middle class which pursues zero structure or permanent liminality has not yet come under the sociological microscope. One catches sight of it in biographies, and it dominates the novels of the 1960s and 1970s. It created and feeds off the progressive school movement, which began in the private sector. It is clearly a more viable option for the humanistic professional class, for artists of all kinds and for the elite in the mass media than for the commercial and bureaucratic class. It prefers unstructured or infinitely flexible space and time;[44] it rejects the special claims of 'face', mixes its roles and categories on principle, de-ritualizes its activities and attempts to deny the sacred distinctions between public and private, male and female and the rest. It produced Stephen Bright and Howard Kirk.

Such then are the crude contours of class culture on to which the expressive revolution broke in the late 1960s. Changes of a slow, fragmented but important kind had already altered some of the basic economic and social structures. Affluence had filtered down the status hierarchy enabling all classes to taste the possibilities of consumer hedonism. The celebratory elements in working-class liminality had always focused heavily on food, drink and spending: the time was ripe for these to spread outwards and soften the distinction between fasting and feasting. The development of the mass media meant that by the early 1960s most families had TV, radio and hi-fi recording equipment. Television in particular became a new focus for leisure and from then onwards must be regarded as the single most important source of the symbols and images both of order and continuity *and* of liminality. It took over where folk culture left off.[45] Sex roles had already undergone considerable modification by the late 1960s. The working classes remained more role-bound and ascriptive, but the ideal of sharing rather than of living segregated lives was fast softening (but not blurring) sexual and gender differentiation, at least at the level of personal relationships. Home-centredness was growing among the working classes, while the traditional communities were breaking up through population movements, immigration, housing policies, changes in industrial location and the rest. The 'privatized' worker formed an expanding category, growing with the new semi-skilled but well-paid occupations created by automation and the assembly line. The manual category itself was shrinking as a proportion of the occupation structure, while a new segment of clerical, administrative and service professions and semi-professions swelled the lower and middle reaches of the non-manual category. This new zone absorbed a large percentage of that one-third of each generation that moved up out of the manual working sector into which they were born.

Up to the late 1960s these structural changes had produced only slow modifications of the cultural pattern I have described above. Until the late 1960s they were experienced not as traumatic but mostly as gently beneficial and they had not yet seriously eroded the symbolic structuring of boundary and control, group and grid. Life had become a little more privatized, which for some (old people, housewives) entailed isolation, loneliness and a sense of futility, but at the same time most people were markedly more materially comfortable. Youth culture and the counter-culture were to prove powerful forces, switch mechanisms as it were, which radically shifted most of the old boundaries and expanded the frames. When the traumatic collision finally occurred in the late 1960s between the new imperatives of expressiveness and the old culture of order and control, it centred around symbols rather than around social structure.

The Bohemian children of the Expressive Revolution saw themselves as prophets called by history to free their fellow men from this repressive (and anachronistic) culture of control. They attacked all those sacred symbolic boundaries which embodied meaning and identity for all but a tiny minority of the expressive middle class. They wanted everyone to live like Muriel Spark's Willy Morley: Lorna was no longer a 'joy' but an implacable enemy. No wonder the 'square' world could initially see only Willy's dirty bottles and the 'good carpet gone greasy'. No wonder either that a few articulate movements of cultural defence sprang up from the heartlands of the culture of control. Mrs Whitehouse and the Festival of Light spoke the language of purity and pollution, the vocabulary of group symbolism and the sanctity of boundaries and order. Inevitably, many from all classes said a not always silent 'Amen', intuitively recognizing the sub-text of these movements as that Commination with which this chapter began – the invocation of Auden's god Terminus: 'Cursed is he that removeth his neighbour's landmark.'

CHAPTER 5

The Arts

ARIEL AND CALIBAN UNCONFINED

The Romantic Heritage

Is it possible that, not content with inveigling Caliban into Ariel's kingdom, you have also let Ariel loose in Caliban's?

W. H. Auden: from 'Caliban to the Audience', Part III of 'The Sea and the Mirror', in *Collected Poems*

The Marquis de Sade and Genet
Are highly thought of to-day.
But torture and treachery
Are not his kind of lechery,
So he's given his copies away.

W. H. Auden: from 'Marginalia' in *Collected Poems*

The avant-garde arts were the Pandora's box out of which came all the motifs and techniques of anti-structure which the counter-culture, the political Underground, the student revolutionaries and the expressive bohemians employed in their concerted attack upon the landmarks of the culture of boundary and control. In Auden's metaphor Ariel, the principle of poetry and the imagination, was loosed into the kingdom of Caliban, the world of profane reality, while Caliban, who represents both the real and the uncivilized id, had been allowed to disrupt the kingdom of Ariel, the realm of the Muse, of the ideal, of poetry and imagination. The real and the fantastic had been hopelessly confused: everything had become liminal.

The boundaries which suffered the sharpest attacks were those between the public and the private sphere, between decent and indecent, tabooed and available, sacred and profane, between art and ordinary life, good taste and vulgarity, between creator and creation, artist and observer, betweeen human and inhuman, male and female, animate and inanimate, man, animal and nature. The ideological rejection of control typically showed itself in a preference for randomness or chance over plan, for excess over balance, for the subjective over the objective mode, for the fantastic over the commonplace, for emotion over reason, for the ephemeral over the lasting, for immediacy over hard-won comprehension, for the purely personal or topical allusion over the historically rooted image. Structure, form and inherited assumptions were overturned or violated both at the level of subject-matter and over the issue of form and style itself. So far as subject-matter is concerned the taboos relating to sex, violence and good taste were the particular focus of a riotous iconoclasm – that of the Marquis de Sade and Genet, whose 'torture and treachery' were not Auden's 'kind of lechery'. So far as form and style are concerned, a great deal of ingenuity went into subverting, rejecting and replacing inherited forms in the interests both of expanding the possibilities of expression and of following the strict injunctions of taboo breaking.

Now none of this was new to the 1960s. It had all been happening in one way or another since about the end of the eighteenth century. The avant-garde of the 1960s was simply the latest product of that crucial break with tradition which occurred in all the arts at the onset of modernity, the period roughly coinciding with the French and Industrial Revolutions. The *enfants terribles* of the 1950s and 1960s were the legitimate heirs of the tradition of modernity which began with the Romantic movement. Hardly a single item or gesture of anti-structure which the counter-culture brandished in the 1960s was its own invention: Romanticism and its various modernist offshoots had already tried them all. All the late sixties generation contributed was a determination to push these techniques to their furthest limits and to have them noticed by a wider audience. In both aims the avant-garde succeeded, so much so, in fact, that its techniques quickly lost their exclusiveness and their shock value as mainstream culture adopted them for purposes as diverse as political campaigns, commercial advertising, pedagogic and liturgical innovation and forms of psycho-social therapy.

The Romantic movement was the crucible of all these changes in symbol systems, not only in the arts, but importantly in politics too, starting with the Romantic nationalisms of the nineteenth century. For the moment I want to pause to tease out some of the contradictions which are embedded in the Romantic enterprise in the arts. I argued earlier that culture generally and the specialist arts in particular always wear a double face. They affirm order and meaning while simultaneously offering alternative visions and intimations of transcendence, both of specific orders and even of order *per se*. The Romantic movement from its inception was the disorder/ecstasy face of Janus, while Classicism and traditionalism shared the task of showing the face of order and control. Expressive intensity and the representation or intimation of the transcendent possibility, the lurking irreality, are the Holy Grail of Romanticism: art becomes rather self-consciously an attempt to grasp the ungraspable, to represent ecstasy, to transfigure mundane reality. As I argued in chapter 3, such an enterprise, given the nature of symbol systems, tends to give rise to techniques for increasing expressive ambiguity, for violating the rules of given forms and structures and for emphasizing the forbidden or disfavoured extreme in the crucial polarities which code order/disorder, good/evil, licit/illicit in the symbolic languages of the time. Out of this come the techniques of boundary violation and the ideological rejection of control and structure which I indicated above. But these techniques are very diverse and in practice cannot all be employed at once. They involve a range of inner logics which lead in contradictory directions. Thus Romantic *techniques* can produce modes of expression which can look very Classical or even inexpressive as end-products. Conversely, the Romantic *intention* may often be best achieved by Classical techniques. In short, most of the modernist movements in the arts are logical and natural extensions of one or more of the welter of contradictions which formed the original Romantic movement. Many of them strike one as far from Romantic, and that is, first, because of this circular logic of many of the favourite aims and techniques of historic Romanticism which lead to their own opposites and, second, because the various branches of modernism were often explicitly developed in contradistinction to each other.

The Romantic attack on order leads in a variety of different directions. In all the arts from the late eighteenth century onwards a refusal to treat the rules as sacrosanct was part of an effective search for new and expanded expressive power. Ambiguity and the (selective) stretching or abandonment of rules gave us all the giants of late Romanticism and early modernism – Wagner, the Impressionists, Diaghilev, Joyce and Eliot. But to be fully effective rule violation needs an audience with a clear inner memory of the form and rules which are being violated, and beyond a certain point no code will stretch to more expressive ambiguity without cracking up altogether. By the twentieth century most artists were quite conscious of these formal problems and were aware that an impasse was looming. Romantic aspirations and techniques were threatening form itself and, with it, the possibility of communication. Often artists conceived of it as a struggle between Classical and Romantic principles. We should not be too surprised, however, to find that those who become the champions of neo-Classicism (say, Eliot or Stravinsky) are themselves expert rule breakers, taboo-violating innovators bringing in new materials (everyday language and the songs and speech of the street corner, for instance) and evolving new forms. Nor should we be surprised, conversely, if many who espouse the Romantic cause employ specific, formal, craft techniques to achieve their ends. In music, for example, the ultra-Romantics, Berlioz, Wagner and early Schoenberg, all fixed tempi, dynamic markings, ornamentation and so on with a precision which Classical and pre-Classical composers would never have dreamed of. (The point, of course, is that when the rules of the code can no longer be taken for granted composers cannot afford to allow performers to improvise, as Cavalli or Mozart did, and still be certain what kind of effect it will result in.)

The general problem bequeathed to twentieth-century artists is beautifully caught by Michael Tippett. In the extract below he is discussing the influence which Eliot had on him at a time when Tippett had consulted Eliot about the problems of verse drama in libretti.

Eliot stood for a certain set of aesthetics. . . . His whole aesthetic interested me because it was a part of the classical movement against the romantic world. I came into a period when the choices were between expressionism à la Shoenberg, or neo-classicism à la Stravinsky. Those really were the two divisions and you went one way or the other. I wasn't so conscious of it then as I am now, and I couldn't have formulated it as I do now, but I was moving away very strongly from the romanticism of my predecessors. I didn't get anything from either Elgar or Vaughan Williams except that I couldn't go that way and so I was in a kind of neo-classicism and this meant years and years of struggle with the question of classical form. Eliot was in the same boat. He made the sort of remark which got me round the corners. (Despite our classical ideals) we were nevertheless in a romantic period, which he defined in a special way. He simply said that the material we were dealing with was black material, which kept oozing out of the contours we gave it – as he considered it did in *Hamlet*, and as he considered it did in the Shakespearean sonnets, where the material was not eaten up completely by the form. The ideal, as we talked of it, was when this black material could be wrestled with and somehow contoured. This sort of insight was immensely valuable to me.

The more interesting figures to me personally, the people I feel I belong to, are figures in which both elements, the highly imaginative world and the formal world, are always interlocking. That would be Yeats, where everything is wrought out of a mixture of things, for example. Or Turner.[1]

I quote this long passage in full because it is such a perfect illustration of the way in which important elements of Romanticism lie inside the neo-Classicism of the twentieth-century arts. Eliot's metaphor is a wonderful expression of the 'lurking irrealities' which call the artist to reclaim them from the jungle of the not-yet-expressed: this 'black material' cannot be grasped or conveyed to others except through contouring and yet it is never 'eaten up completely by the form'.

Not all twentieth-century artists 'grappled with form' in the same Classical sense as Eliot and Tippett, and in all the arts the violation of inherited form ultimately produced a technical impasse which had to be faced. When this limit is reached, three alternative developments typically take place: the artist may break the code, create a new code, or engage his art in a debate on the nature of the code. Let us look briefly at these options in turn. First, there is the case where the ambiguities are pushed further and further until the form itself is destroyed. The destruction may be unintentional but in the most influential cases it was usually deliberate. Schoenberg's experiments with atonality were deliberate.[2] Dada deliberately embraced meaninglessness, incomprehensibility, the destruction of art itself, in a gesture which, with studied ambiguity, might be a joke, a revolutionary cry, a ritual of purification or a signal of in-group elitism. Dada is one of the most powerful influences – far more powerful than Marx, for instance – on the aims and techniques of the counter-culture of the 1960s in its recipes for the disruption and destruction of codes and in its equation of meaninglessness with ultimate meaning.

The second option is the re-creation of form and code. This is seldom a simple reinstatement of the code which has given way under the impact of excessive ambiguity and iconoclasm. The neo-Classicism of Stravinsky, Britten or Tippett is a different musical idiom from that of Mozart and Haydn. Moreover, radically new forms or codes may be created out of the dissolution of the old, such as Schoenberg's twelve-tone system which followed his experiments in atonality. This is the stage at which, time and again, we see the rediscovery of order as the prerequisite of creativity, communication, and aesthetic satisfaction. This stage sees not only Schoenberg's strict rules for the use of the tone row, but in painting, say, Cézanne's desire to preserve the flickering light of the Impressionists without, as Sir Ernst Gombrich puts it, 'leading to a loss of clarity and order'.[3] At this point we find a new objectivism, the return of what Mann calls 'naked convention', distortion, re-primitivization, abstraction and so on, as some of the solutions to the problem of form which the exhaustion or dissolution of the old style leaves in its wake.

The third option in a sense follows as a sub-section of the second, and it is peculiarly characteristic of the arts in the last few decades. In this case the subject-matter of the enterprise shifts so as to focus on the art form itself, which has been rendered equivocal by Romantic experiments in ambiguity. Literature and films, which are a play on the nature of narrative as such, are examples of this genre. Jorge Luis Borges is a good case in point. In visual art it appears as a kind of meditation on the nature of paint, brush strokes, canvas, stone and other textures and can again lead to both a minimalism and a primitivism of raw materials or to an abstraction of line and form. This development is one of the main sources of irony and of narcissism in the modern avant-garde. In any event, preoccupation with form has the effect of displacing the traditional subject-matter of the art in question, and especially the representation of human persons and their concerns, from the central focus. For this reason Malcolm Bradbury, among others, has called it a process of dehumanization.[4] It always has the effect of dissociating both artist and observer from direct involvement with the substantive subject (the representation of *human* reality or aspiration) by making the subject-matter no more than an excuse for an essentially cerebral meditation on, or experiment with, the nature of form itself. It can be an illuminating exercise in irony, as it is, for example, in Borges, whose play on the *machismo* legend serves to puncture by ironically celebrating the coercive Romanticism of that particular myth. Alternatively, it can become high (or low) camp, as in pop art, where no one knows whether the magnification of admass vulgarity is a wry comment on form or an excuse to enjoy its shiny, shallow content. Or again it may become the most cerebrally incestuous of all pursuits, a kind of in-group game played by pedants of form and structure, with all content evacuated.

At this point we encounter a further strange twist. Many of the practitioners in the avant-garde are well aware of the theorizing about their activities which takes place in academic circles. In particular, post-war artists have been very conscious of the developments in the social sciences and, in the last two decades, have often been both haunted and fascinated by the spectre of Structuralism peering over their shoulders. If the code has its own strict *structural* rules, may it be that the artist is just the tool of the code? He may think he is the speaker but perhaps he is really the spoken. Borges has several sharp and wry little tales with this import.[5] This suspicion has given a new impetus to the desire to smash the code because it can then seem, say to a writer/film-maker like Robbe-Grillet, that only when the code is utterly and finally shattered will any free and creative speech become possible. So Robbe-Grillet employs what has been called a 'counter-terror to the terrorism of language'.[6] But here we meet the same old irony. In what does his 'counter-terror' consist? It is just the usual techniques of anti-structural ambiguity (pornography, narrative uncertainty and so on), along with perhaps a standard narrative item repeated so often as to induce (or so seems to be hoped) a releasing sense of absurdity. So in some branches of the *nouveau roman* and in the 1960s' *nouvelle vague* in films we simply find a double layer of anti-structural symbolism deriving from this acute consciousness of the coercive order which underlies the code and form themselves. The alternative response to the recognition of the underlying structural autonomy of the art form is to celebrate its independence of the 'artist' and to treat art works as a kind of autonomous self-manifestation by the form itself, rather than as the creations of the artist's will and free choice. In action painting and certain kinds of free verse, for example, the materials are, as it were, allowed to dictate their own directions and use.

If the prolific modern 'isms' in the arts make it difficult to recognize the family face of Romanticism lurking under the contemporary make-up, the role of the artist himself will make the point abundantly clear. Art and the artist are both products of the modern world: Bohemia, that specialist realm of the liminal, simply did not exist in the pre-industrial era. In medieval Europe the artist was an artisan/craftsman or, if he worked with words or music, he may have been a cleric. In the eighteenth century he may often have been a gentleman. In any case he was integrated into a clearly marked system of status and patronage. Art did not exist as an autonomous, 'expressive' sphere but as a set of craft skills which found their unself-conscious place as an aspect of the traditional activities of the Church, court and city. The artist himself might be conformist or troublemaker in his personal capacity, but no special *éclat* attached to nonconformity. Gesualdo was a murderer and Purcell is said to have died of a chill caught when his wife locked him out after one of his many nights on the town, but their artistic reputations did not hinge on such matters. Handel may have suffered an acute anxiety neurosis and Michaelangelo may have been a homosexual, but Bach lived a model and orderly domestic and civic life, and Bernini was a pious Catholic and a devoted family man and citizen. The idea that the true artist is a rebel and a sufferer or that insanity and wildness are insepar-able from genius is a myth of Romanticism, and indeed one which many post-Romantics have endeavoured to live by. It is, if you like, one of the first instalments of the confusion of life and art in the Romantic canon: the craft techniques for achieving the expression of transcendence are played down, while the disordered life ceases to be a *metaphor* of creative ferment and acts as a kind of magical formula. So Byron and Berlioz, rather than Bach and Bernini, become ideal models of the artist.

At its extreme this myth can go so far as to value the bohemian life *itself as* the artistic creation. This position often appealed to the counter-culture of the 1960s, particularly since it entirely eliminated the distinction between life and art. Its clearest representative is perhaps the conceptual art movement, parodied, or perhaps just mercilessly reported, by Tom Wolfe in *The Painted Word*.[7] A straighter version of the syndrome is the subject matter of Patrick White's novel, *The Vivisector*.[8]

The original Romantic shift in the conception of the artist was not a simple product of disembodied ideology. It occurred in response to a radical alteration in the place and function of art. As the modern, highly-differentiated social system developed in the nineteenth century, so the arts, like so many other activities, took on the shape of specialist, semi-autonomous occupations. Artists ceased to be simply part of the entourage of court, Church and aristocracy and became producers for a free market. The art 'product' itself became differentiated as new subjects and objects of artistic endeavour became possible with the separation from its traditional patrons, whose needs had up to that point solely determined the object of the exercise. Art could now do anything, from self-expression, to social comment, to the prettification of the petit bourgeois home. In all this the artist was not merely enabled but virtually forced to specialize in the expressive function: it was the buyer who determined the use to which the art object would be put, not the artist himself. In this way the practitioners in all the arts became the core of what I earlier called the new cultural class, separated from the directly economic aspects of society and defined by their purely expressive *raison d'être*. In short, they became expert producers of liminal images, exactly as Turner argues.

Many commentators in different spheres have remarked on the way in which modernity elevates permanent change as a new sacred value. One of the most persuasive exponents of this view in the arts is Gombrich.[9] He argues that the late eighteenth century witnessed a crucial break with tradition in all the visual arts, including architecture. Up to this point, styles and techniques had certainly seen gradual alterations, not to fit some holistic 'spirit of the age', to be sure, but in response to concrete social changes and specific technical developments in form and practice. But style and function in art were not 'problems' until the onset of modernity, after the radical break. From that point onwards change and experiment became not only possible but favoured ends of artistic activity: traditionalism has never been sufficient since. So style as the taken-for-granted, inherited way of doing things, learned from a master and enshrined in common practice, gave way to a contest of styles in which innovation and 'originality' came to be valued for their own sakes. In part, of course, this positive attitude to change is a necessary reflection of and adjustment to the speed and persistence of change in social and technological matters which characterizes industrial society. In part, however, it is our old friend the Romantic preference for the transcendent over the finite, for taboo breaking over convention, for innovation over repetition. Either way, it serves to institutionalize the Romantic penchant for rejecting tradition and violating boundaries, rules and limits as the natural calling of the artist. The really creative artist must be constantly on the frontier, risking misunderstanding and ignorant rejection. *Epater le bourgeois* thus becomes the accepted creed.

This involves a number of problems which interact with each other but which for convenience of exposition I will take in turn. Let us first consider the problem of style. If the arts must be treated as codes of communication, systems of signs, then this fact involves not only the artist but his audience, since it must be capable of deciphering the code. Even deliberate nonsense or meaninglessness of the Dada variety cannot convey its message unless the audience can make the symbolic equation of meaninglessness with revolutionary gesture. The audience, then, must be to some extent 'literate' in the sign language. Gombrich makes this point with particular force in his discussion of Impressionist art.[10] What was new in the pictures of the French Impressionists was their faithful attempt to represent what the eye actually sees in different types of light. They were trying to eliminate from the actual canvas all the things which memory brings to our conventional perception of what we see and to paint only what the eye 'really' sees. Yet the first audiences were unable to appreciate or even to recognize this revolutionary accuracy because they 'saw' the pictures according to the conventions which had formed the basis of both painting and viewing pre-Impressionist works. A whole new way of seeing had to be evolved in order for eyes to see what, according to Manet and Monet, the human eye 'really' does see. In short, the whole code of seeing had to adjust itself to the new code of painting in order for any communication to occur at all.

Clearly, in a world in which styles are in constant flux and development the problem of how to 'see' (or 'hear', or 'read') becomes a permanent feature of artistic life. On the one hand this has a natural tendency to reinforce elitism among the avant-garde. Being different and confounding the philistine and the bourgeois become signs (if not the automatic guarantee) that one is on the right creative lines: as soon as the public adopts a new code it is time to find another. That is parody, of course, but a parody so widespread as to have become a universal joke. Eliade puts it in more neutral terms when he characterizes incomprehensibility, deliberate obscurity and the need for initiation into an abstruse style in the arts as a typical 'myth of the elite'. The difficulty as we have seen, however, is that impenetrability may not ultimately be very expressive and, further, that it becomes ever more difficult to apply *any* commonly accepted aesthetic standards to the avant-garde arts. Thus they often look like a game played between a very few initiates among the artistic fraternity and the elite representatives of arts patronage. Styles can then become a species of competitive, in-group comment on each other. At the same time, even though the constituency may be very small, it is necessary to spread an understanding of each code change simply in order to keep the in-group game going. So avant-garde artists can no longer be content with simply painting pictures, writing music or novels or putting on plays; they must constantly *explain themselves*. Thus they become entangled in theories, which arise as a kind of meta-art form.

Tom Wolfe makes great play with this point – indeed, it is the central issue in *The Painted Word*. While reading Hilton Kramer's review of an exhibition of seven Realist painters, Wolfe was 'jerked alert' by the following passage.

Realism does not lack its partisans, but it does rather conspicuously lack a persuasive theory. And given the nature of our intellectual commerce with works of art, to lack a persuasive theory is to lack something crucial – the means by which our experience of individual works is joined to our understanding of the values they signify.[11]

Wolfe indulges in an extended parody of the idea, seeing it as another example of the phoney and pretentious in Bohemia.

I read it again. It didn't say 'something helpful' or 'enriching' or even 'extremely valuable'. No, the word was *crucial.*

In short: frankly these days, without a theory to go with it, I can't see a painting.

Not 'seeing is believing' you ninny, but 'believing is seeing', for *Modern Art has become completely literary: the paintings and other works exist only to illustrate the text.*[12]

In Wolfe's view, the proper balance has been inverted: the art object first cannot be 'seen' without the theory and then comes to exist merely to illustrate a theory: the theory itself becomes the real art work. So much for that Romantic injunction to immediacy – 'one impulse from a vernal wood' and so on. Again we find a modernist inversion of Romanticism growing out of the faithful practice of a specific Romantic technique: the primacy of innovation destroys the possibility of untutored immediacy and subjective emotional response. It is also a case of the modernist option which focuses on form rather than substantive content (but, interestingly, not on form and code as *directly* employed but on form and code *transmuted into another medium*, that of the written word). The 1960s movement, art language, which to the uninitiated looks like somewhat incoherent fragments of a philosophy or a political programme, is perhaps the clearest illustration of the type. A very similar development occurred in avant-garde music in the 1960s. As notation, dynamics, instrumentation, sequence, tone, rhythm – in fact, every aspect of inherited musical form – came up for auction, the composer had to issue minute instructions as to how to decipher and perform his idiosyncratic score. Hence the published music typically consisted of a thick wedge of instruction manual for every thin sliver of composition.[13]

Tom Wolfe's case can be twisted the other way round, however. The pictures (or music) get simpler and barer while the legitimating theory gets more complex and rococo. It follows that once a new code has been learned, more and more of the attribution of meaning can be left to the observer. The observer is thus drawn progressively into the act of creation because what he reads into the apparently simple art work is the important thing. In this way the minimalism of a single brush stroke, or blob of primary colour, or isolated sound, can be experienced not as banal but as profound, rather like the stones in a Japanese Zen rock garden. Arthur Koestler makes an interesting case of this kind in his discussion of stylistic development in literature.[14] Like Gombrich, Koestler believes that styles have a natural sequence of development: he calls it the 'principle of infolding'. The image is of each style making a kind of loop back on itself before the line of development continues on to the next style. The idea is closely akin to Kenneth

Burke's 'principle of entelechy', the tendency for an idea to be stripped of all ambiguity and pushed to its own furthest logic. It also involves the Gombrichian argument that each style is premised on the solution to specific technical problems which arise from the multiple possibilities inside the last stylistic innovation. One complex of problems may have several different solutions, each of which will be pushed along its own separate logic. Thus, as Gombrich argues, the technical problems of painting posed by the Impressionist revolution led in three different stylistic directions: through Cézanne to Cubism, through Van Gogh to Expressionism and through Gauguin to Primitivism. Each was the result of the single-minded pursuit of one specific formal problem. One might make the same kind of case for twentieth-century music. Schoenberg pursued the problem of tonality while retaining most of the other formal elements in musical structure, while the neo-Classicists retained tonality and conducted their experiments on the other items of form, such as polyrhythms, multiple keys, new sequences of modulation, new uses of the various instruments and so on. The two schools sited their programming of expressive ambiguity in different areas of musical form.

Koestler makes the same sort of case in relation to literature. He believes that once a style is fully established, in order to avoid the tedium of repeating itself it can go in only two directions: it must either suffer exaggeration or be reduced to its own streamlined minimum. Given the high value that modern culture places on originality, every repetition brings only ennui – hence what he calls the 'law of diminishing returns'. Koestler sees the second of these options, the technique of streamlining or minimizing the constituent elements in the style, as the source of a recurrent tendency to leave more of the creative process to the audience/reader/consumer. It is a common stage in the development of a style. It leads to Burroughs and Beckett in literature.

Koestler's argument is important, but he perhaps neglects two matters. Often what we see is not so much an extension to the audience of a part in the creation of the art work but rather the artist's increased ability to rely on the audience's familiarity with the code. Even if it initially involves the publication of complex theoretical explanations, as with the twelve-tone system or action painting, once the code has been established, many things can begin to be left implicit and need not be spelled out in detail in the art work itself. The audience becomes used to a particular cueing system. The second point is that Koestler takes insufficient note of the fact that audience participation in the act of creation in other cases is an explicit technique of boundary violation in the avant-garde rather than the unconsidered consequence of a process of stylistic 'infolding'. When this occurs, the idea of the audience as co-creator can itself become a style and gives rise – precisely – to stylization. Artist and audience learn to play the game according to implicit rules by following precedent, from the cueing of other participants

and from a folk history of similar occasions. Thus the free theatre, the
happenings and the communal poetry readings of the sixties came to follow
a customary recipe. Even taboo violation and Dadaesque nonsense are apt
to fall into predictable, repeated patterns.

The high degree of stylistic differentiation in all the arts, and with it the
extension of competing codes – ways of 'seeing', 'hearing' and so on – has a
further consequence in the amplification of both ambiguity and irony. The
simultaneous currency of several codes means that any one art work may be
experienced through several code filters, as it were. In music, for example, a
piece may be 'heard' with both 'serial' and 'harmonic' ears. And when composers further experiment with oriental musical forms yet more ways of
'hearing' are brought in. The result may be either chaos and babel or expressive enrichment. Which of the two it is will hinge on a number of factors, not
least the degree to which the listener has shifted from a strictly classified
symbol system in which ambiguous items are troublesome, or has accepted
ambiguous categories and the simultaneous straddling of two or more
classificatory codes as expressive richness rather than pollution. In short, it
all depends on how one feels about landmarks.

In this way style in the twentieth-century arts has become a battleground
or market-place of ways of 'seeing' and 'hearing'. I use these two metaphors
intentionally. In so far as it is a battleground, style is a struggle between
would-be-exclusive schools. The antagonism between the neo-Classical and
the twelve-tone or serial school is a case in point, ultimately ameliorated by
Stravinsky's twelve-tone experiments on the one side and Berg's effortless
lyricism on the other. That battle is long over. But similar struggles between
absolutist positions occurred in all the arts, often around particular
charismatic figures such as Artaud, with his theatre of cruelty, or Steinberg
and his esoteric legitimations of pop art. In fact, the persistent phenomenon
of coteries in the arts illustrates the pull of the communitas element in
liminality as an accompaniment to the delight in symbols of anti-structure.
It also evidences that elitism on which Eliade and others have remarked.

The market-place metaphor also has certain merits. One of the consequences of the preference for innovation in the modern arts is that styles
have less and less staying power. The process of 'infolding' occurs at an
accelerating rate as Koestler's law of diminishing returns sets in for each
new style. What was peculiarly characteristic of the 1960s was that the
pursuit of the varied principles of anti-structure in all the arts took a fast,
final twist to reach the logical end of many roads at once. So the market was
flooded with new styles, all spinning swiftly to their briefly fashionable
climax. When this happens the aspiration to exclusiveness becomes absurd,
or at best heavily compromised, as the market (in this sense literally the
entrepreneurial popularizers) finds it necessary to be alert to catch the
newest, the latest, the coming style. In this situation, exclusiveness is just for

a fleeting moment, and ultimately the aspiration to permanence itself comes to be treated with suspicion as a sign of over-structuring. This is precisely the point at which pop art and pop music become the apotheosis (or, some would argue, the nadir) of their respective genres: art for the moment and for the masses. *Epater le bourgeois*, instead of producing an esoteric incomprehensibility, shocks by creating a camp copy of commercially popular styles. It is only distinguishable from the vulgarity of the real thing by its accompanying theory.

Here we encounter a further strange twist in the problem of interpreting what is going on in the avant-garde. We have examined the curious phenomenon that all the arts need a legitimating theory, indeed that the theory becomes almost more a work of art than the art works themselves. The Word is thus infiltrating arts whose essential codes are not verbal at all: language becomes the measure of all things. But pause a moment. We also have a distinguished scholar, George Steiner, arguing passionately that the late twentieth century is experiencing a culturally catastrophic *retreat* from the Word.[15] Literature has taken two easy steps from James Joyce to Marshall McLuhan. Joyce shaped words into a personal and idiosyncratic flow and fluidity. McLuhan pronounced the medium of the written word itself *passé* and rejoiced in the fact. The new technological media of twentieth-century communication, computer, television, film and so on, render the printed word an anachronism – slow, cerebral and essentially private (only one person can peruse a text at one time, while thousands can watch a film together). Whereas language was classically queen of the media – and the 'Word' the appropriate metaphor for the Second Person of the Trinity – today, Steiner believes, music is the archetype of art through its very abstraction and distance from the verbal.

Steiner is both right and wrong in his argument and each for important reasons. He is surely correct in noting the importance of abstraction in modern styles (we have already touched on a number of reasons for this), and in singling out music as the ideal case. He does not, however, take real account of the verbal theorizing which underpins the abstraction and is in its way an extension of the realm of the word. It is also part of a process by which artistic media are merging and inter-relating, since one of the many boundaries under attack from the neo-Romantic campaigns is the distinction between the various art forms themselves. One important object of the avant-garde in the progressive sixties was the multi-media experience to reintegrate the ultra-specialist arts. And if one did not know whether the happening was 'really' a political meeting, an art exhibition, dance, theatre, therapy or a rock festival, then all the better: 'Ambiguity is richness' as Borges remarked.

Steiner is right, however, on other grounds. The supreme importance of the Word and the aspiration to mass literacy is the mark of early bourgeois society, the era when the encyclopaedia of knowledge was the supreme achievement of civilization. Literacy is the crowning art of the Enlightenment and of a political and social system in which rationality, individual liberty and self-mastery were crucial to the culture of the creative classes. Steiner charts the flight from the Word in the twentieth century as the reduction of a rich verbal medium to a rudimentary state, first through the ideological preference for rudimentary states of consciousness (primitivism again in combination with anti-intellectualism), and second through the over-valuation of science as the supreme form of knowledge (abstraction again, but ultra-intellectual). Contradictory trends thus conspire together to erode and impoverish verbal culture, in Steiner's view.

Yet it may be that Steiner approaches one key fact at a tangent. Mathematics is certainly the model of logical, scientific argument and is at least as loftily abstract as music, but many of the most pressing aspects of the human condition do not easily lend themselves to being adequately encompassed by mathematical formulae, while they *can* find expression in words. In lamenting the loss of verbal richness Steiner perhaps forgets that what makes the Word suspect to many of the avant-garde in the twentieth century is not its capacity for expressive richness but the fact that it has been, *par excellence*, the medium of *cognitive rationality* and *bourgeois power*. Rational, internalized, individuated, conscious control of self and society has been exercised through language and above all through the written word. The Word is the basis of anything resembling cognitive adequacy: it is the lynchpin of the *high culture of control*. As such it was inevitably the most compromised medium of all in the eyes of the Romantic counter-culture. Steiner writes in a significant sentence: 'unless we can restore to the words in our newspapers, laws and political acts some measure of clarity and stringency of meaning, our lives will draw yet nearer to chaos.[16] The neo-Romantic pursuit of expressiveness is precisely the preference for chaos as richness, whereas for Steiner, richness is impossible without clarity and stringency. It is not surprising that he chose the title *After Babel* for a later collection of essays on these themes.[17]

One final consideration is relevant to understanding the general cultural slip towards Babel. Even mass literacy has never quite succeeded in making the written word the crucially important medium for the masses which it has been for the elite. Alongside the high culture of the Word, therefore, we need to consider what has been happening to popular culture. Roger Silverstone has argued[18] that many aspects of mass or popular culture are simple extensions of folk culture rather than radically new species of cultural form. Folk culture has always been a major source of all the unconsidered and customary attributions of meaning and rightness to existence and, therefore, of the conserving functions of culture. It codes and filters both what is taken for granted and also any new items which need to be integrated into old structures of meaning (like changes in the role of women) and updates the cultural *status quo* in a painless fashion. The technology of the twentieth century, the whole McLuhan universe, simply extends the realm of folk culture, and television above all takes over the old structures of folk narrative and song: the soap opera replaces the customary folk epic, and the advertising jingle supplements the folk saying. These modern media of communication are perfect for the purpose: they are all more immediate and collective and less cerebral and private than the written word; their content can pass through the senses without seriously engaging the intellectual filter which the written word always primarily requires before the other senses can be touched.

The problem, however, and the key to Steiner's distress, lies in the fact

With John Cleese, Michael Palin, Grahame Chapman, Eric Idle, Terry Jones, Carol Cleveland
from the BBC Television Series

Dali and Magritte invade the domestic hearth: Dadaesque nonsense and surrealist, anarchic juxtaposition became fare for popular television comedy in Monty Python's Flying Circus.

that the high culture of literacy in the mid-twentieth century has become hopelessly confused with folk culture. As we have seen, neo-Romantic movements in all the modern arts have explored the varied paths of liminality. They have assaulted all established boundaries, limits and taboos, one of which is the distinction between high art and mass or folk culture. What was really new in the 1960s was the very fast infiltration of the techniques of anti-structure into the realm of popular culture. This is the consequence, first, of the acceleration of cycles of stylistic change (Koestler's 'infolding') and, second, of the determined violation of the taboos against mixing vulgar commercialism with high art and confusing art with everyday life. Thus folk culture and the symbolic accompaniments and underpinnings of daily life are themselves flooded with the symbolism of liminality. No sooner has the coinage of anti-structure been struck among the avant-garde than it is passed through into the mass media and popular culture. Thus, for example, Dadaesque nonsense and surrealist, anarchic juxtaposition had become the staple fare of advertising and of family comedy by the late 1970s. Yet once anti-structure becomes a taken-for-granted style it changes its character and begins to display rules and predictable patterns – in fact, it loses its 'anti' prefix. In this way Romanticism first renders sacred and then popularizes anti-structure until it sweeps round in a perfect circle to become its own antithesis.

The Sixties: the Zenith of Anti-Structure

if you weren't you, who would you like to be?

Paul McCartney Gustav Mahler
Alfred Jarry John Coltrane
Charlie Mingus Claude Debussy
Wordsworth Monet Bach and Blake

Charlie Parker Pierre Bonnard
Leonardo Bessie Smith
Fidel Castro Jackson Pollock
Gaudi Milton Munch and Berg

Bela Bartok Henri Rousseau
Rauschenberg and Jasper Johns
Lucas Cranach Shostakovich
Kropotkin Ringo George and John

William Burroughs Francis Bacon
Dylan Thomas Luther King
H. P. Lovecraft T. S. Eliot
D. H. Lawrence Roland Kirk

Salvatore Giuliano
Andy Warhol Paul Cézanne
Kafka Camus Ensor Rothke
Jacques Prevert and Manfred Mann

Marx Dostoevsky
Bakunin Ray Bradbury
Miles Davis Trotsky
Stravinsky and Poe

Danilo Dolci Napoleon Solo
St John of the Cross and
The Marquis de Sade
Charles Rennie Mackintosh
Rimbaud Claes Oldenberg
Adrian Mitchell and Marcel Duchamp

James Joyce and Hemingway
Hitchcock and Bunuel
Donald McKinlay Thelonius Monk
Alfred, Lord Tennyson
Matthias Grunewald
Philip Jones Griffiths and Roger McGough

Guillaume Apollinaire
Cannonball Adderley
Rene Magritte
Hieronymus Bosch

Stephane Mallarmé and Alfred de Vigny
Ernst Mayakovsky and Nicolas de Stael
Hindemith Mick Jagger Dürer and Schwitters
Garcia Lorca
                    and
                         last of all
                                   me.

Adrian Henri: 'Me', in A. Henri, R. McGough and B. Patten, *Penguin
Modern Poets, vol. 10: The Mersey Sound*

Adrian Henri's poem (litany? genealogy?) is a very economical summary of
the sixties. It is made up of painters, writers, visionaries, revolutionaries and
musicians, pop, jazz and 'serious'. It is a catalogue of innovators, of Dada
and Surrealism in all the arts, with a nod to earlier prototypes. Categories
are mixed: Leonardo and Bessie Smith share a line; the arts and popular
culture are indiscriminately cheek by jowl; 'good' and 'bad' taste lie side by

side, barely even separated by grammar and punctuation; chronology is not acknowledged. But notice the ghost of form hovering there (perhaps represented by Bach?). There is metre and rhythm, though no rhyme, and there is maybe an echo of biblical tables of begetting, or of the hundred and forty and four who shall be saved. Note too the weight of implicit knowledge; all those names have to trigger a shared memory and understanding of multiple traditions. Without that knowledge who could say where one name ends and another begins, or which categories are being violated and mixed? That parasitic reliance of anti-structure on the very structures it is assaulting is the story of the sixties.

In this section I want to put some flesh on to the bones of the general arguments which have been advanced in the first half of this chapter by looking at what was happening in the arts in the sixties and early seventies. As I have already indicated, there were certain common themes in the arts, particularly the violation of the canons of good taste and the lingering taboos on the direct or extreme representation of sexuality and violence. The body symbolism of sexuality is a particularly potent device of anti-structure. All orifices become infinitely penetrable, and sex becomes public rather than private. This is an easy way of attacking the culture of boundary and control and simultaneously identifying one's own kind – the 'uptight' are patently not enlightened. All the arts employ both the pastoral idyll and the daemonic in relation to sex – sex as 'natural' lyricism, or sex as the route to salvation and enlightenment via the degradation of self and others. In literature, for example, it takes us from Lawrence through to Burroughs and Genet. There is a widespread use of sexual ambiguity and of what would have been regarded conventionally as perversions: indeed, a simple pastoral hedonism in association with sex is a far less widespread and less powerful symbol than its black, daemonic counterpart. Another barrier to fall is that between art and pornography, with consequences which still trouble English liberals and English law. This often involves the sanctification of violence and the explicit portrayal of much which had classically been inferred rather than directly displayed.

We have already noted the violation of good taste in some detail. The avant-garde of the sixties incorporated culturally despised forms such as advertising, *Grand Guignol*, the horror film and pop music. Thus 'camp' became an established element in the 'serious' arts, providing the opportunity for the superior sneer, sado-masochistic immolation in vulgarity and the key to the identity of fellow progressives all at the same time. The cult of the object also assists in eroding the distinction between art and life, art and the commonplace: the *nouveau roman* with its minute and seemingly random details of material objects, the film which lingers on incidental detail, décor or natural objects, the *objet trouvé* as sculpture and so on.

Religious and drug-induced mysticism is another powerful theme in all the arts, a very clear symbol of ecstasy and transcendence, especially when combined, as it frequently is, with either sexuality or violence. Every wave of bohemian anti-structure – the *fin de siècle*, and then the inter-war period – has rediscovered oriental religion for these purposes. The religious traditions of the East are convenient as a symbolic rejection of the inherited Judaeo-Christian culture of the west and particularly its Puritan strand. Moreover, oriental religions contain just that same bifurcation as the Romantic movement itself. Hinduism, in particular, and Buddhism by cultural extension contain both the monistic mysticism which culminates in the union of the One with the All and also subsidiary traditions which involve ritual cults of ecstasy through the daemonic. Pre-Christian paganism and the magico-relgious traditions of Africa and the Caribbean are almost as useful. The net result has been the ransacking of the world's religious traditions and their cultural artifacts to provide symbols of the rejection of bourgeois rationality, vehicles of mystical ecstasy and ritual foci of belonging for the avant-garde itself.

As well as these themes, which are common to all the arts, there are concerted attacks on structure and form in each separate sphere. I will begin with literature, since if Steiner's argument has any foundation, it is the art above all whose very existence is threatened. There remained from earlier in the century three particularly attractive models of extreme anti-structure for the sixties generation to rework. The first was Dada, leading on to Surrealism. These movements lie behind all the anarchic experiments in the visual arts and to some extent music (via Erik Satie) as well as literature. Tristan Tzara and his coterie created the original multi-media happenings around the period of the First World War: they made poetry from random syllables drawn from a hat, shocked and insulted their audiences, proclaimed the need to shoot all self-styled poets and artists, wrote manifestoes and repudiated them. For example, Tzara wrote: '*Order = disorder; me = non-me; affirmation = negation*; the supreme radiance of an absolute art. Absolute in purity of ordered cosmic chaos, eternal in its globule without time, without air, without light, without control ...'.[19] A decade later Michel Leiris, one of Bataille's coterie of Surrealists, wrote 'Masochism, sadism, almost all vices in fact, are only ways of feeling more human.'[20]

The second influential model in literature was provided by James Joyce's radical personalization of language. After Joyce grammar, syntax, narrative sequence, even the structure of words themselves were all fair game for attack or idiosyncratic distortion if a greater inward expressiveness could be achieved thereby. But it meant that Fowler's rules of linguistic usage were no longer held sacred except by letter writers to *The Times*, and that the more private the language and the more eccentric the stream of consciousness, the longer and more complex must the necessary critical glosses be. So the end of common grammatical rules meant the rise of theory as a 'meta-art' inseparable from literary works themselves.

The third, rather later model, itself much influenced by Dada, was the American Beat Generation of the thirties and forties. The scatalogical and deliberately shocking sexual explicitness, the contempt for the restrictions of given forms – grammar, good taste, the distinction between prose and poetry or between the novel, the documentary and the autobiography, and, above all, the ideological fusion of life and art. Not just Bohemia but the road, the hobo existence, the pure liminality of the bum, all this was held to be a vital and integral part of literary achievement. It was the Romantic myth of the artist at its most extreme. Of all the Beats, William Burroughs probably had the greatest influence on the sixties generation, particularly through the neo-Dada technique of the 'cut-up' which he popularized – the slicing up of books, manuscripts, newspapers or whatever and re-splicing the bits together with random and/or calculated anarchic intent.

In literature, probably more even than the other arts, the avant-garde violation of accepted form relies very heavily for its success on *not* destroying totally the reader's memory of the code and structure which are being bent, twisted or denied. Literature has always depended on the layered accumulation of meaning in words, images and linguistic forms: if these are all simply erased, neither Joycean private meaning nor Dadaesque and Beat shock value can be achieved since the shock (or expansion of consciousness) depends on the reader's *awareness* that something he has erstwhile taken for granted has been presented to him in a new guise. Thus the *more* successful the erosion of form, the *less* successful is the expressive enrichment. This became an acute problem in the sixties and early seventies. It was fashionable to reject grammar, 'correct' spelling and often all punctuation, to use exclusively lower-case letters, to leave pages unnumbered, to distribute words apparently randomly or decoratively on the page, to create uncertainty about whether the form was prose, poetry, fiction or documentary. All these techniques serve to blur boundaries and to undermine clarity and sequence, but they need readers who know what the rules are (or were) before the effects of their violation can be appreciated. Thus the old rejected form always remains as a necessary sub-text lying implicit beneath the surface text: anti-structure is parasitic on the covert retention of structure if it is to avoid sheer incomprehensibility.

A related phenomenon to that of the private language is the penchant for the exploration of essentially private states in literature and the relative neglect of (and even contempt for) issues and experiences which involve public behaviour. This reflects both the narcissistic individualism of Bohemia and the powerful Romantic sense that 'inner' reality is superior to objective or outer reality. Poetry and the so-called psychological novel particularly reflect this preoccupation and can give rise to new forms of deliberate ambiguity or indeterminacy. A favourite technique is to render a state of mind in language which embodies that condition: the reader is not to retain his distance but to be drawn directly into the state being described: in short, it is the printed word aspiring to the immediacy and the time-scale of film or television. When, as was frequent in the sixties, the states of mind which are regarded as worthy of literary exploration are those of neurosis, madness, hysteria, mystical ecstasy, violent catharsis and related abnormal/transcendent 'outsider' experiences, then incoherence in language, passionate chaos, is a central ingredient in the recipe. The example I like best, however, is one in which the author attempted to convey the essence of a senile ninety-four-year-old largely through blank pages.[21] When a book is an amalgam of several internal states corresponding to different moods or characters the result can be confusing and can erode narrative structure to the point of incomprehensibility. In these cases no clear narrative may emerge at all; the transition between perspectives, between different characters, between past and present, between 'real' and fantasy states may be left unmarked.

The principle of narrative indeterminacy is sometimes augmented by the author's refusal to give his characters a name, even to reveal their sex. All these techniques are, of course, part of the tendency to draw the reader into the act of creation. He may either wallow in indeterminacy or create his own 'story' out of the chaotic ambiguities offered by the writer. Even an author like John Fowles, who largely retains a Classical approach to the Word, despite his essentially Romantic themes, makes play with narrative uncertainty. The reader may even be left to choose his own ending to the story, as in *The French Lieutenant's Woman*.[22]

An element obvious enough to need minimal illustration is the taboo-breaking, sexual explicitness of sixties fashion. Lawrence, de Sade and the Beats all play their part as models and forerunners. As Auden remarked, de Sade enjoyed a vogue in the late sixties: he was republished, dramatized[23] and lionized. Similarly Burroughs, Miller and Kerouac. Jean Genet, with his antinomian theology of salvation through bestiality – a pure inversion of conventional moral categories – is a very important influence. Genet has sufficient aesthetic stature to act as the legitimating figure standing at the head of the avant-garde's Manichaean pornography brigade, making *L'Histoire d'O* and its kind required reading among the cultural vanguard.

The polymorphous perversity of the avant-garde's sexuality also encompasses another important theme, the ultimate oneness of man and nature, man and animal, man and object. It is an important paradox of the contemporary version of Romantic individualism that self-determination, the pursuit of one's own essence, leads all too often to a sense of hopelessly alienated isolation and the impossibility of relating to the Other. The supreme poet of this state is, of course, Beckett. Beckett's plays are real *rituals* of hermeticism, stylized representations of human isolation, which assert that common humanity consists in exactly this condition of uncommunicability. The only way out of the impasse of the universal *anomie and alienation* of extreme individualism is the assertion of unity between the One and the All. Thus the boundary between man and nature, man and animal falls, both sexually and in other ways. Indeed, some of the aesthetically most impressive products of the current generation of poets embrace this theme. Thom Gunn, in his collection of poems, *Moly*,[24] uses the image of the centaur to this effect. Ted Hughes returns again and again to mythic images of the fusion of nature and culture, man and animal, man and tree. This has powerful affinities with the neo-primitivism I remarked on earlier as one of Romanticism's later products.

Perhaps the most widely read author who treats the theme of unity between the One and the All is Hermann Hesse, whose novels were extensively translated into English in the sixties and who became a considerable cult figure. Hesse, of course, was a contemporary of Thomas Mann and a writer much more directly in the mainstream of German Romanticism. The themes of the counter-culture are all there in Hesse; *The Glass Bead Game*[25] in particular became almost a scripture and its vocabulary an infallible means of recognizing counter-culture 'insiders' during the late sixties. In *Klingsor's Last Summer*[26] Hesse produces a climax in which the painter creates a self-portrait which represents not only all men but all nature too, one object which can say everything – a recurrent ambition of the artists of the sixties, as we shall see. In Hesse's work the sense of societal decay and doom, the double option of escape and renewal either through totalitarian discipline of a neo-monastic kind or through amoral daemonic excess, the redundancy of the merely cerebral, the pathetic inadequacy of moderation, rationality and liberal humanitarianism all recommend him as a source book for the counter culture.

Resurrection through association with culturally 'low' forms of life was another popular literary technique of the sixties. It is the literary equivalent of pop art in many ways and is responsible for the reputation of someone, like Tom Wolfe, who uses all the most extravagant journalistic techniques – a kind of fusion of Joycean stream of consciousness and personalized language forms with admass vulgarity – in order to flay the 'phoney bohemians' and the commercial entrepreneurs of culture. In a sense, Wolfe is the ultimate achievement of camp, becoming a bestseller among precisely the groups he satirizes, trading on the capacity of the colour supplement progressives to relish the excoriation of their friends while mentally exempting themselves. It is a form of literature which, like pop art, wallows ambiguously in vulgarity and bad taste as part of its 'exposure' of that same vulgarity and pretentiousness. The circle of incestuous double-takes is endless.

Fusion with 'low life' has affected poetry too, and not just through the use of the language of the street and the office, as in Eliot and Auden. In the sixties the pop lyric and poetry merged, especially in what were known, following the popularity of the Beatles, as the Liverpool poets. This is what Steiner calls the 'voice of the megaphone and the read-in'.[27] Poetry is barely distinguishable from pop, political propaganda, the circus or a pub singsong; indeed, it was frequently part of the latter. The trend is certainly traceable to figures such as Whitman and Pound, but the sixties saw its culmination in the attempt to hand poetry back to the folk. McGough, Henri and Patten are examples of the genre. The contrary technique of anti-structure in poetry 'leads towards verse of a deepening privacy, experimentation and hermeticism',[28] to use Steiner's phrase. Steiner sees this as an attempt to preserve an aristocratic form from democratizing, philistine encroachments. It may well, in part, be just this, but it is also clearly a product of the narcissistic individualism which is a central thread of Romantic anti-structure and closely allied to experimental attacks on inherited form, on grammar, metre and publicly accessible metaphor and allusion. Like the alliance with working-class oral forms, it is an attempt to break out of what is regarded as a socially and spiritually constricting structure into a more fundamental mode of speech which can touch a universal level deeper than any culture-bound form. At its most extreme it is a desire to destroy and/or transcend an actual, specific language and, through incomprehensibility, to communicate at a pristine level not just with other members of one's own local language group but with all humanity.

A striking example of this kind of process moves us into the field of poetic drama (another boundary rendered uncertain). This is the collaborative creation of the poet Ted Hughes and the theatre director Peter Brook in *Orghast* which they presented at the 1972 Festival of Shiraz in Iran. 'Orghast' is the name of the new language created by Hughes as well as the play itself, though music and dance are as much a part of the experience as poetry and drama. Hughes and Brook wanted to reach beyond language. Tom Stoppard, himself a virtuoso of the word, commented: '*Orghast* aims to be a leveller of audiences by appealing not to semantic athleticism but to the instinctive recognition of a "mental state" within a sound.'[29] Brook and his team of actors tried out the effects of particular sounds on groups of nomads as part of the preparation for *Orghast*: the aim was primal, pre-Babel communication. The narrative backbone of *Orghast* was a cluster of myths: the Promethean myth, that first symbol of tragic individualism and independence, and a number of Manichaean sources. Again, we see a search for the primitive and fundamental in mythic narrative, but here it is combined with an attempt to arrive at perfect verbal communication which transcends the divisiveness of particular languages. Hughes wanted to uncover the basic connecting tissue of humanity and felt he had touched either a common tonal unconscious or a process of telepathy in his experiment. It is very important to note that the fundamental difference between printed literature and public drama is that the latter is communal and thus enables ritual – and communitas – to become an essential element in the experience. The use of other more immediately emotive arts like music and dance in a multi-media performance such as *Orghast* intensifies the ritual elements and minimizes the rational, intellectual response required. Stoppard remarked of his own experience of the play in Shiraz: 'If one knows too much the response is corrupted.' The conviction that knowledge distorts the response to the arts is a very frequent sixties belief and highly paradoxical in view of the enormous importance of the theoretical underpinning of most of the experiments of the time.

The assertion of common humanity, the All, and the attack on specific local identities and conventions are common themes in the theatre of the sixties. The distinctions between author, producer, actor and audience are all violated. Sometimes the audience becomes an integral part of the action, participating actively in the evolution of the drama which is anyway fluid and not fixed by a definite narrative or printed script. For example, in 1971 a performance at the Round House in London of the revolutionary events of 1789 by the Théatre du Soleil used the audience throughout as the Paris mob. The play (or experiment) by the Austrian dramatist Peter Handke, *Offending the Audience*,[30] does just that. The protection afforded by the audience's traditionally passive role is removed in order to reveal the deadening effect of roles and expectations and to replace them by spontaneous, living response, even if that response is authentically hostile. The British National Student Drama Festival of the late sixties and early seventies was a show-case of all the current symbols of theatrical anti-structure. A typical example was the 1972 entry of the West Midland College of Education, *The Audition*, which was simply four actresses being auditioned in the four corners of an arena. The programme note commented: 'Ideally, *The Audition* should be interminable, leaving an audience free to watch as much or as little as it wants.'

The Liquid Theatre probably takes the process furthest. The individual – is he client or audience? – is offered a range of sensory, tactile experiences, including dance, mime, touch, sight, smell, by the 'actors' (therapists? priests?). The stated purpose is to reintroduce him to his own body and to simple primal sense impressions which exist in their own right and not for any ulterior purpose. The aim is to elicit pure, context-less response to stimuli: primitivism and minimalism again. And again the same paradoxes crop up. The techniques of freeing the individual from his constricting roles and contexts look very ritualistic – 'Oh, taste and see!' – and the whole event is like a purification ceremony such as Mary Douglas attributes to the group pattern symbolizing a common belonging. And again the group in question is seen as all humanity. It is a variant on Romantic pastoralism: become as a little child and all will be well; 'Close your eyes: trust us.' The food on offer at Liquid Theatre is pure, organic, unpolluted by dubious twentieth-century technology and chemicals: 'You *are* what you eat.' A purification ritual here also eliminates the boundary between man and nature. Another inversion is that between public and private. Experiences of touch and intimacy which are conventionally restricted to the most private relationships are here made public and freely available. All human beings assert their unity by unrestricted touch: body contours are no longer the symbolic margin of the private individual but, as the name implies, liquid.

As well as such techniques, the same neo-Romantic themes preoccupied the theatre of the late sixties and early seventies as we noted in connection with printed literature. The outsider or deviant becomes a revered model; spontaneity is life and convention is death; violence and explicit sexuality are the means of asserting freedom and breaking taboos. So nudity, the depiction of sexual intercourse on the stage, brutally displayed criminality, insanity, cannibalism and so on become the stuff of the progressive theatre. Other taboos are broken by the pursuit of 'camp' and the incorporation of despised 'art' forms into progressive productions, especially *Grand Guignol* (as in *The Rocky Horror Show*) and pop music (in practically everything). By the time the same audiences are watching the musical of the life of Lenny Bruce and *Jesus Christ Superstar* the double-takes have gone beyond the possibilities of enumeration and no one knows who is having a giggle at whose expense. The whole avant-garde gamut has been trodden by the Living Theatre troup. Every de-structuring technique and every bohemian message, from Marxism-out-of-Brecht through surrealist anarchism to eastern mysticism, has been used by this group.

Many of the same themes can be traced in ballet. The audience may be involved in a number of ways. In one case they may be asked to guess what the dancers are miming; at other times they may be asked to suggest sub-jects for improvisation. Dance frequently draws in other media, experi-mental music and art displays (pictures, collages, sculptures). Narrative is often replaced by spontaneous response to stimuli, by improvisation, by the introduction of various elements of randomness. The roles of actor, choreographer and dancer merge. Ballet itself is transmuted into circus and charade: boundaries are not respected; art and life fuse. 'To breathe is a dance, a walk is a dance, typing is a dance, egg-beaters are dancers.'[31] The themes too echo the same preoccupations as we have seen in the theatre. Outsider figures are important, from Oscar Wilde, whose life story was danced at Sadlers Wells in 1972, to Genet, whose play *The Maids* was performed by the Royal Ballet in the same year. It seems to have been Genet's own suggestion that the title roles of the two sisters should be taken by male dancers to add an extra frisson of sexual perversity.

Because of its abstract quality music does not display the neo-Romantic themes in quite the same way as the literary arts. Indeed, it is noteworthy that whereas the high Romantics used the lyrics and libretti of vocal music as a major vehicle of verbal expression, this is hardly the case at all for the avant-garde musicians of the 1960s and early 1970s. Abstraction and pre-occupation with form and sound quality is highly characteristic of their vocal music – the use of the human voice for 'pure' tone, as in Dallapiccola, or sometimes the requirement for singers merely to breathe into micro-phones and not to vocalize at all. The neo-Romantic *verbal* message is more typically conveyed through those theoretical underpinnings we have already had cause to remark on, the composer's instructions on how to decipher his score and interpret his intentions. Sometimes part of the score itself becomes entirely verbal – the 'text score' – and often reads more like a Dada poem or a tract on meditation or a recipe for a surreal event than a set of musical in-structions. One section of Stockhausen's *Aus den sieben Tagen*, for example, reads:

for small ensemble
GOLD DUST
live completely alone for four days
without food
in complete silence, without much movement
sleep as little as possible
after four days, late at night,
without conversation beforehand
play single sounds
WITHOUT THINKING which you are playing
close your eyes
just listen.[32]

This is minimalism again, the jettisoning of all technique, memory, intellectualization, *all* form and structure: but it also looks very like a collec-tive ritual of meditation on the primal nature of sound and thus has affinities with *Orghast* and its like.

Dedications and titles, as well as texts and theories, carry the same neo-Romantic themes that we have seen in the literary arts. Henze devotes much of his work to the revolutionary masses; Nono, among others, features dedications to revolutionary poets and heroes; Bussotti even has an experi-mental piece with the title *La Passion selon Sade*; and so on.

The only avant-garde music which *sounds* like the high Romantics (Elgar, Strauss, Sibelius or Mahler), occurs on that margin of the art which deliberately courts confusion with pop or rock music. It would seem that melody in particular can be afforded only as long as one is valiantly embrac-ing vulgar rock: it is, if you like, a fair exchange of taboos. The distinction between 'pop' and 'serious' is, of course, one of the many boundaries under attack. The following extract from the sleeve of a 1969 LP by the Nice, *Five Bridges*, conveys something of the flavour of the fusion. Keith Emerson, who wrote the sleeve note, went on later to transcribe such melodious composers as Mussorgsky and Copeland in his progressive rock. Emerson wrote:

On a journey from the almost Utopian freedom of our music to the established orthodox music school I met Joseph Eger who was travelling in the opposite direction. . . .

Since that meeting we have on various occasions been catalysts in combining together music from our different backgrounds forming sometimes a fusion and other times a healthy conflict between the orchestra, representing possibly the establishment, and the trio, representing the non-establishment; ourselves having complete trust in a rebellious spirit and highly-developed, broadminded music brain whose reformed ideas in direction have been frowned upon, almost spat upon by so-called music critics.[33]

Emerson was a little mistaken about the 'established orthodox music schools', however. It is true they were not quite the riotous meccas of anti-structure that the art schools were, and to be sure most of the music students who were destined for performance and teaching rather than composition just went on practising instrumental technique for a disciplined six hours a day and ignored the counter-cultural spirit. But in quiet corners anti-structure was wreaking its expressive havoc on musical form. The twelve-tone revolution was *passé*: its own rules were being treated as taboos ripe for violation as 'pointillism' (the name, of course, borrowed from visual art after Seurat: another fusion of media) and 'integral serialism' developed out of two of the possibilities inhering in the original serial form. 'Pointillism' is an attempt to eliminate the distinction between vertical and horizontal, and 'integral serialism' is a rejection of the disciplines of the tone row which Schoenberg's radical successors such as Nono have identified as 'constraints and limitations' reminiscent of political totalitarianism. So again we encounter the drive against form in the interests of perfect liberation.

Fluidity, uncertainty, randomness and all kinds of improvisation are preferred to form of any kind. Composers reject not just the tempered scale but fixed, measurable tone and pitch, sometimes leaving the performer entirely free to choose tone and pitch, sometimes favouring an ambiguous and often pictorial indication of the rough type of sound required. The same thing happens to rhythm and dynamics. In the simplest case rhythm may be indicated by a notation in which the length of any note is suggested by the length of its tail. Alternatively, rhythm may be evolved in a group of musicians who are used to interpreting verbal, visual and other cues from each other or from a composer/leader — improvisation on the basis of implicit in-group understanding. At the other extreme rhythm and dynamics may be electronically programmed down to the millisecond. Not only electronic equipment but all sorts of other implements are used to make sounds: performers have been required to pour water, switch on radios, blow sirens and whistles, play tape recordings of all sorts of sounds from a heart beat to a steam train, either straight or artfully distorted. Any page selected at random from the avant-garde music magazine *Musics* will show where this leads. One issue, for instance, describes the musical event produced by a text score or script which calls for the cracking of 360 eggs in relation to random words and sounds.[34] 'Music' and everyday 'noise' are fused and confused together as the whole inherited structure of European music – tonality, harmony, key, sequence, melody, notation, dynamics, rhythm, specialist 'musical instruments' – comes to be treated as a constriction, the bars of the prison house.

The printed musical score reflects these radical shifts. Alongside the 'text score' which we have already noted, one also finds the 'graphic score', in which pictures and graphic representations of a wide variety are used to suggest sounds. Cathy Berberian has one piece, *Stripsody*, which is pure pop art – another fusion of media, of course. In addition we must take account of the 'concrete score', used for the juxtaposition on tape of sounds from life, and all the other electronic programmes in which not a ghost of a crochet or quaver is to be discerned. All are examples of the breakdown of the distinction between music and non-music. As Tzara's Dada manifesto said in 1918: 'order = disorder; me = non-me'.

Predictable sequence comes particularly under fire. Since the 1950s composers of the avant-garde, such as Boulez and Stockhausen, have sometimes indicated that the sections of their compositions need not be played in a fixed order or combination; thus time is no longer linear but circular or eternal. Chance and choice are given an ever larger part to play. Charles Ives, a natural New World musical non-conformist, and Erik Satie, who had direct contact with the Dada movement in France, were spiritual godfathers of all these developments. Both had used humour and chance in their music. Ives, for example, would write directions on his music such as: 'Play it at breakfast like...', 'Play it after breakfast like...', 'Play it after digging potatoes like....' By the 1960s, however, sophisticated technology could assist in the achievement of randomness. John Cage, doyen of the American avant-garde, took on the mantle of Ives and Satie and carried their anti-structure techniques to new lengths.[35] One well-known example of Cage's work will serve to illustrate several of these techniques. HPSCHD, a 'sound object' by Cage and Regiara Hiller, has been performed several times in London, including a Round House promenade concert. It requires seven harpsichords and between one and fifty-one computer-generated tapes. Any part may begin at any time; any soloist may play not only his own but anyone else's solo. The directions for the solos are anyway rather loose – for example, 'any kind of Mozart in any manner of your choice'. Members of the audience may take over a keyboard if they wish. This is a nice example because it depends on several forms and rules before it can offer any pleasure through their violation – the notion of 'one's own' solo, for example, and the memory of a Mozartian style.

More of the same paradoxes result from this kind of process, as we noted earlier in literature. There is the same attempt to arrive at a primitive universal through the rejection of inherited structure, the same ransacking of non-Western cultural traditions in the attempt to discard restrictive inherited forms and the same re-creation of group ritual when one starts out to create the conditions of total freedom. Cage is the perfect illustration of all this. In his early works in the fifties he used magical and ritual formulae from oriental cultures (and especially the *I Ching*) as a technique for freeing his Western-programmed imagination. This, however, involved both composer and performers in certain conscious choices in the selection and manipulation of the formulae. These remained too culturally tainted for Cage's idea of freedom, and he has, therefore, progressively replaced them by the mathematical (and thus purer) randomness of the computer. There is irony here too. Cage dislikes twentieth-century technology as part of the polluting and alienating complexity and impersonality of modern society: for choice he lives alone on wild fungi or watercress for long periods. But only that same twentieth-century apparatus can guarantee randomness and, therefore, real cultural freedom in his music. Again, the pursuit of the universal must transcend the local and culturally specific and so must dehumanize music.

Cage's use of silence is perhaps the most economical symbol of anti-structure in the whole avant-garde vocabulary. Silence is filled with the incidental sounds of life which *are* the primal music and rhythm of being. But equally silence is nothing: All and Nihil together. 'I have nothing to say and I am saying it and that is poetry,'[36] And music, too. Inside silence we are wholly free, everything is equally significant and man is joined to over-arching infinity. What more perfect musical expression than Cage's *Four Minutes Thirty Three Seconds*, in which a performer simply sits by the closed lid of a grand piano for the exact space of four minutes, thirty-three seconds. It is reminiscent of the all black and all white pictures of Cage's friend Robert Rauschenberg, the pop artist. Like so many of Cage's Dadaesque gestures, this ritual of collective silence leaves one uncertain about the balance of joke and seriousness, and the ambiguity is certainly intentional.

Ritual, magic words and formulae are often an end-product of avant-garde experiments in music. Perhaps the best known is Stockenhausen's *Stimmung*, a collective act of transcendental meditation which stems from the composers' jettisoning of all the old structures of European music. The parallels with *Orghast* are inescapable: the concern with the properties of 'pure' sound, the symbolization of the unity of mankind, primal, language-free communication, the submersion of the individual in the universal. At the other end of the scale, the unity of all men and all modes of expression can equally well be symbolically affirmed through camp. Folk, pop and advertising jingles can be incorporated as easily as their visual counterparts in pop art, and traditionally solemn occasions like concerts can be transformed into comically jolting, anarchic parties. John Cage excels at this too: his concerts in the late sixties and early seventies were much sought-after happenings.

We have already remarked on the way in which the anarchic violation of old forms transmutes into new-made ritual. In the case of the many composers who use non-Western music as their entrée into culturally untainted spheres, the subsequent re-ritualization and rediscovery of form is even more striking. They quickly discover that the Indian *raga* or the traditional rhythmic patterns of Indo-China are strict forms which have to be learned. An avant-garde composer like the American Steve Reich finds such patterns can only be employed on their own terms and only by musicians who are prepared to steep themselves in the forms, sequences and subtle cueing mechanisms that are a part of each specific non-Western tradition of musicianship. One frequent consequence of this, which also stems from the difficulties of idiosyncratic musical notation, is the tendency of particular composers to work with the same performers who thus form a kind of community: Reich has such a permanent group around him. This enables an implicit code of knowledge and practice to be built up in the group about what is required and how it can be signalled. It works on exactly the same principle as a jazz or rock combo: improvization and complex interaction become possible only if the members have a secure 'feel' for what can be taken for granted. So, again, anti-structure depends on group communitas for its effects.

The parallels between developments in the visual arts and music are naturally most striking in abstract art. Much geometric or non-objective art in the sixties starts with the same intentions as Cage or Berio in music, to free the artist from the constrictions of existing form. As the American minimalist sculptor, Don Judd, put it: 'My things are symmetrical because ... I wanted to get rid of any compositional effects.'[37] Geometric and mathematically precise shapes have a further merit, as the English painter Derek Southall explained in a television interview in 1972. He began by using palindromes and U curves on the grounds that a painting should 'include everything' and that such perfect symmetrical forms could be held to do just that. However, in the late sixties he moved on from geometric abstraction to follow Arp in to the new technique of action painting. Where Arp still used brushes to slap on the paint, Southall tipped large buckets of paint on to an enormous canvas, finding this a more satisfactory way of 'including everything'. He explained his philosophy (that wordy theorizing again):

We make our own world; it is not a fixed entity waiting to be perceived; so the painting is not a fixed entity; it merges with the world and so draws us in; consequently though each painting is specific and unique it also includes everything; the artist must try not to be wilful but 'to sense which way the painting wishes to go'; the artist must bring himself into tune with the materials he is using; the piece grows up itself; the artist mustn't 'tart it up' afterwards – come along with a little brush and put make-up on.[38]

This is the familiar theme of the absorption of the One in the All again: Hesse's Klingsor portrait. It is also the fusion of creator and creation (the painting *itself* has a 'will'), of art and life, of raw materials and form; in short, boundary violation.

The idea of art creating itself is a frequent sixties theme. Carl André's sculpture is a good case in point: his agglomerations of waste materials, the iron and bricks of London building sites, are 'natural' sculpture. The infamous Tate Gallery bricks are a typical example of the genre. Again, chance juxtapositions of objects of urban debris symbolize the identity of art and life as well as the self-creation of the objects. Destructible sculpture takes the point one step further. Objects – say, papier mâché tailor's dummies – are randomly placed in public space: some may be carried off to people's homes; children may dress up others; some may be broken or thrown into ponds. The 'art' is precisely this random fate, and the agents of creation are the home dressmaker or the children who do things with and to the found objects. So the distinctions between art and life, and between artist and audience, are eliminated; best of all, there is no permanent exhibit to be reified and mystified as art, so creation and destruction are equated too. The same is true of the visual-art component in the multi-media happenings of the sixties. By a particularly nice irony, this supreme expression of the superior value of the ephemeral over the permanent is enshrined in a volume of photographs edited by Adrian Henri[39] (our poet of the collective ego): each caption contains the phrase 'now destroyed'. It stands alongside the rest of the Thames and Hudson volumes as part of the acknowledged history of that specialist activity ART whose privileged existence it set out to refute.

Happenings (like Adrian Henri himself) are fusions of several art forms. The sixties movement art language is probably the best example of a deliberately uncategorizable art form. An exhibition by Conrad Atkinson which was displayed at the ICA in London in 1972 was made up entirely of documentary material relating somewhat imprecisely to an industrial dispute which, presumably, struck Atkinson as significant. The documents, letters, photographs, reports and census tables were left unfocused, as it were, to speak for themselves. Is it art, social science, propaganda, politics? It is impossible to answer because the question is absurd if one accepts the destruction of the separate categories. And again, the observer must create the meaning which the artist refuses to force upon him ready digested.

In producing pictures without frames the Impressionists were the first to break down the idea of the work of art as a clearly bounded object for permanent display, but they can hardly have anticipated the lengths to which their successors would go in violating that particular boundary. At one extreme Christo, the Bulgarian–American artist, may build a running fence over twenty-five miles of Californian farmland, or wrap part of the Australian coast, or drape an enormous curtain over a Colorado valley (he failed to get permission to drape the Reichstag in Berlin in 1977). The art object can then never be neatly packed and fixed on its owner's wall. Yet ironically, as with the happenings, photography provides a saleable and permanent record of such art events and books, films and exhibitions of Christo's work actually finance the projects themselves. The Conceptual Art movement at the other end of the spectrum deals not in the impossibly vast, as did Christo, but in the fleeting moment of experienced reality, the minute and the trivial. Here the art is the actual sensation – a dream, a meal, an act, a visual perception in the ordinary world – but again the irony is that the process of recording the momentary sensation takes the form of manuscripts, sketches or records. So the precious ephemerality is pickled in words and images and again can become an object of exchange, a piece of property.

The violation of the distinction between artist and observer takes many forms, some of which we have already encountered. It frequently goes along with the introduction of elements of chance and choice such as we have noted in music and literature. In 1972 an exhibition in Utrecht was devoted to the theme of Chance (Toeval) and included, for example, a 'one-day sculpture' of broken glass in which the audience was involved in making the object, and David Medella's *Stitch in Time*, a strip of cloth randomly embroidered by the visitors to the exhibition. Computer and video art frequently involves the spectator in making decisions and in taking part in the art experience. A London exhibition called 'Meta Filter' organized by Steve Willats in 1975 revolved around a word game played by two or more spectators working small computers and needing to interact minutely together. The Tate Gallery's 1976 'Video Show' included an exhibit by Brian Hoey which neatly turned the tables on the observers by throwing back their own images at themselves, while Roger Barnard went one step further by mingling the film of the viewers with images of absent or dead people, nicely confusing time categories as well as the distinction between observer and art object. Laser exhibitions such as the 'Holography Show' at the Royal Academy in 1977 can also play on the uncertainty of whether the observer is in the presence of a ghostly image or a real person or object: the laser is thus the perfect tool for creating ambiguity, this time not just between life and art but between reality and image.

In all these examples there is a heavy reliance on twentieth-century technology. In the visual arts we find that same ambivalence about technology which we have already seen in music. From Futurism and Cubism onwards, the machine has had a double face in visual art: it is the embodiment of impersonality and of our alienation, yet, at the same time, it is the instrument of new techniques of randomness. So technology is a source of symbols and of techniques of anti-structure. Not only computers but also plastics and modern materials, new printing processes and the facilities of mass production and the advertising industry are often used either to turn science back to primitive magic or, alternatively, to launch swingeing attacks on the society which lives by mass communication. A good deal of poster protest art, especially that concerned with ecology, involves the latter paradox – sophisticated technology attacking technology.

Another paradox which it is worthwhile underlining is the tendency for a particular anti-structural technique to become a fixed ritual. This is particularly true of minimalism. Thus an artist may find a formula – geometric, primitive, computerized, or like Christo's work, one involving costly engineering – and he will simply repeat that formula as his guarantee of free creativity, free, that is, from the weight of past form but not from ritual. Thus the American painter Barnett Newman has stuck for years to a renewal formula of one single 'zip', a jagged vertical stripe across a field of colour. The French artist Daniel Buren is perhaps an even more extreme ritualist. His paintings are vertical stripes exactly 8·7 centimetres wide in white and one other colour. In February 1972 a hoarding in Shaftesbury Avenue in London was rented to display one of his huge canvasses, which was unsigned and not labelled. Only those in the know could perceive it as an art work: the general public would not have known the difference between it and a fill-in hoarding cover. So only the *cognoscenti* could get any frisson of satisfaction from a gesture which symbolically removes the division between art and commercial objects.

The multi-media experience is peculiarly likely to reintroduce ritual as a side-effect of its boundary violation. Every such occasion has its ration of in-group communitas. An example which I particularly like was the abortive attempt of Los Angeles artist Newton Harrison to electrocute fish as part of his modern art work *Portable Fish Farm* at the Hayward Gallery in October 1971. Harrison's stated intention was to re-create the cycle of incubation, growth and harvest, to put on a display of the unity of a completed cycle paralleling the relations of colours and forms in a picture. The ritual killing and subsequent feast of catfish, shrimps and so on was prevented at the London exhibition by the intervention of one of Britain's authentic anarchic humourists, Spike Milligan. Milligan's sense of the interdependence of man and nature simply took a different form from Harrison's. But it was Milligan's intervention as a member of the audience which gave the exhibition its only memorable feature. Milligan's anarchy is in the mainstream of popular anti-structure in Britain: he has been a whole Dada movement for the family on the Clapham omnibus since the 1950s.

Of all the sixties movements the one which achieved the greatest *succès de scandale* and subsequently the most pervasive impact on popular culture was pop art. Like Spike Milligan, it was a direct inheritor of the tradition of Dada and Surrealism. Pop art offers us the whole anti-structure package: the breaking of taboos, the elevation of camp, the rejection of fixed form, the dislike of boundaries, roles, certainties of any kind, anarchic, mind-blowing humour, the use of violent motifs, of banality, of despised commercial images, materials and techniques, an investment in contradiction, fluidity and ambiguity. Duchamp and Dali, Breton, Aragon and their associates are obvious ancestors of a movement which in the sixties produced Claes Oldenberg's giant plastic French fries and ketchup, canvas medicine cupboard and sculpted fag-ends, Jim Dine's toothbrushes and tuxedos, Roy Lichtenstein's blown-up comic strips, Robert Rauschenberg's all black and all white paintings and Andy Warhol's soup cans from the psychedelic supermarket, his screenprinted car crashes, his Marilyns and his Jackies. Admass images and techniques are exaggerated in ways which may be celebration or critique; the banal, the shocking and the over-exposed are rendered even more so, perhaps to unsettle or to reinforce the taken-for-granted vulgarity from which they are spawned?

Warhol is not the most aesthetically impressive figure of the movement but he is the crucial one for our purposes, since he is *par excellence* the popularizer of all the most easily imitated techniques of anti-structure. He links the political Underground, the arts and the mass media. He claims that he wants immediate, unmediated response to his works; he refuses to clarify contradictory accounts of his early life not to protect his privacy but because uncertainty is better than certainty and, anyway, information is irrelevant to truth: 'Just look at the surface of my films and paintings and me, there I am. There's nothing behind it.'[40] Warhol can send his double, Alan Midgette, on a series of college lecture tours 'by Andy Warhol', or produce a novel which is simply the unpunctuated type-script of a taperecorded day in the life of transvestite actor Mario Montez with all the typing errors left in. Andy Warhol films like *Flesh* and *Trash* can be made without his ever being concerned in the project, and Brigid Polk can do all 'his' screen printing.

In Warhol's work sexual identities are left uncertain or are inverted (he can make Monroe look like a transvestite in his prints of her for example); sequence and narrative are discarded; time is distorted so that it resembles drug time or mythic time more than workaday time. Some of his films are a kind of minimalism without plot, narrative or form: *Eat, Haircut, Sleep* and *Kiss* depict exactly what the titles suggest, all the details of breathing, chewing, and so on. All the sexual taboos are broken too. *Blowjob* is simply a facial close-up of one man's orgasm; *Fuck* (in England, *Blue Film*) is just what it says, though conventionally heterosexual. Warhol's 'actors' play themselves – often homosexuals, prostitutes, and hustlers. Two very revealing comments by Warhol's disciple, Peter Gidal, may serve to bring out certain points to which I have persistently returned in this outline of anti-structural motifs and techniques in the arts, that is, the search for new rituals of common identity and the clear intention to subvert taken-for-granted assumptions about what the world is like and what it all means. Gidal writes: 'The hidden meanings, ideas and feelings evoked by simple acts (or simple things) bring back the ritualized aspect of modern life, the structures from which our backlog of modern experience emanates.'[41] We see again that sacramental primitivism or minimalism which crops up in all the arts. Of the eight-hour film of a man's night's sleep Gidal comments: 'Such facts have tremendous implications in terms of one's de-conditioning, awakening from bad habits, one's useless, demented, "sane" reactions to what is different.'[42] So again we find the psychic subversion of our existing catagorizations of reality as the aim of the exercise.

The 'art film' of the sixties exhibits all the same anti-structural tricks that we have noted not just in Warhol but in all the arts – the sexual explicitness, the use of violence, the narrative ambiguity, the slide into mythic time and the denial of sequence and certainty. Consider two archetypes of the genre. *L'Année Dernière à Marienbad* was probably the first film to make an impact at the very beginning of the 1960s, and it was followed by a wave of continental films based on ambiguity of narrative and time sequence. At the other end of our period, the early 1970s, *Last Tango in Paris* probably sums up the themes (as distinct from the techniques) of Romantic liminality. While it has a fairly clear structure and narrative, it is a film shot through with ambiguities of meaning and identity. Above all it centres on the doomed love affair of two people in an empty apartment (liminal space) who choose not to exchange names and personal histories but, in their timeless and role-less capsule, prefer to communicate by (pure, primal?) touch and by animal noises rather than words. Brando and Schneider are reputed to have 'played themselves' yet the end-product remains art not life, as Norman Mailer complains in his angry review:[43] the sex was simulated and real Schneider didn't shoot real Brando in the end. Although all the arts flirt with it, that final boundary between life and art is a major hurdle which few really want to destroy when they recognize the final, fatal and irreversible consequences of making Ariel and Caliban one and indivisible.

All these developments were the stuff of which the Expressive Revolution was made. Most of the techniques and preoccupations of the avant-garde had filtered into popular culture by the end of the 1970s. Nothing illustrates the fact more vividly than the overwhelming sense of *déjà vu* which the Hayward's definitive retrospective exhibition of Dada and Surrealism gave one in 1978. One had seen it all done so many times and so much more slickly in the colour supplements, the adverts and the television programmes: Dada had become a taken-for-granted part of our commercial world. How this happened is the story of the next few chapters, beginning with the counter-culture proper in the political Underground.

Surrealism is so easy to copy: comic incongruity is used for commercial purposes in this 1979 advertisement for vodka, part of a successful and decidedly surrealist campaign.

CHAPTER 6

The Underground

ON CIRCE'S ISLAND

*Liberation and development of the individual are not the key to our age, they
are not what our age demands. What it needs, what it wrestles after, what it
will create – is Terror. . . . We, when we sow the seeds of doubt deeper than
the most up-to-date and modish free thought has ever dreamed of doing, we
well know what we are about. Only out of radical scepsis, out of moral chaos,
can the Absolute spring, the anointed Terror of which the time has need.*

Thomas Mann: from *The Magic Mountain*

*Her Telepathic-Station transmits thought-waves
the second-rate, the bored, the disappointed,
and any of us when tired or uneasy
    are tuned to receive.*

*So, though unlisted in atlas or phone-book
Her Garden is easy to find. In no time
one reaches the gate over which is written
    large:* MAKE LOVE NOT WAR.

*Inside it is warm and still like a drowsy
September day, though the leaves show no sign of
turning. All around one notes the usual
    pinks and blues and reds,*

*a shade overemphasized. The rose-bushes
have no thorns. An invisible orchestra
plays the Great Masters: the technique is flawless,
    the rendering schmaltz.*

*Of Herself no sign. But just as the pilgrim
is starting to wonder 'Have I been hoaxed by
a myth?', he feels Her hand in his and hears Her
    murmuring:* At last!

With me, mistaught one, you shall learn the answers.
What is conscience but a nattering fish-wife,
the Tree of Knowledge but the splintered main-mast
    of the ship of Fools?

Consent, you poor alien, to my arms where
sequence is conquered, division abolished:
soon, soon, in the perfect orgasm, you shall, pet,
    be one with the All.

She does not brutalise Her victims (beasts could
bite or bolt), she simplifies them to flowers,
sessile fatalists who don't mind and only
    can talk to themselves.

All but a privileged Few, the elite She
guides to Her secret citadel, the Tower
Where a laugh is forbidden and DO HARM AS
    THOU WILT *is the Law.*

Dear little not-so-innocents, beware of
Old Grandmother Spider: rump Her endearments.
She's not quite as nice as She looks, nor you quite
    as tough as you think.

W. H. Auden: 'Circe', in *Collected Poems*

The political wing of the counter-culture of the 1960s came to be known popularly as the Underground. Despite its name, it was far from secret; indeed it was highly vocal and startlingly visible, and it is my contention that one of the major functions which it proved to have was that of displaying in colourful and arresting ways the anti-structural symbolism which the arts had forged. In fact, it is extremely difficult to draw a neat line between politics and the arts in the counter-culture, which is just what one would expect, of course, if my argument about boundary breaking has been correct so far. It is important to emphasize that the Underground is badly misconceived if it is seen as a simple emanation of political philosophies capable of division into definable ideological camps which can be accurately labelled 'Marxist', 'Trotskyite' and so on. We make more sense of the counter-culture if we see its political radicalism not as its only true base in some fundamentalist sense, but as one of many convenient symbols of anti-structure bearing no special ontological privilege just for being explicitly political. I will go further and say that the counter-culture owes more to Tzara, Dali and Burroughs than to Marx, Engels or Lenin. Even the most celebrated trick of all, Jerry Rubin's yippie ploy of putting up a pig for President against Richard Nixon, was a straight copy of what the Dadaists Grosz and Heartfield had done at an International Dada Fair in 1920, when they dressed up a pig in the uniform of a German officer.[1] Peter Gidal's book on pop art from which I quoted in the previous chapter sports a frontispiece in which the American yippie, Abbe Hoffman, exhorts his followers: 'Right now [we] must become Warhols.'[2] Marxism itself undergoes de-structuring at the hands of the alternative society. The hardline, Puritanical, organizationally rigid Old (Stalinist) Left gives way to the New (libertarian) Left, and the scriptures of the later Marx are neglected in favour of an existential reading of the Young Marx.

The political, then, should not be seen in isolation from the rest of the symbolism of anti-structure. Nevertheless, for convenience of exposition one must separate out the various elements, and this chapter will focus on the radical politics of the Underground. Much has already been written on this subject and is widely available.[3] My object is not just to repeat what is already well known but rather to argue a particular case, and this will involve being selective. My concern is with the direct impact of the Underground on conventional society and for that purpose I need to examine the popularizers of counter-cultural ideas in Britain, the figures who distributed the symbolism of anti-structure from the alternative society to the Kingdom of Terminus, that culture of control which I outlined in chapter 4. I have selected four writers whose influence spans the period from the late 1950s to the early 1970s, all of whom achieved extensive public exposure through the mass media. They are, in chronological order, Ray Gosling, Jeff Nuttall, Richard Neville and Mick Farren. They typify the style of radicalism of their successive generations and in their writings and actions illustrate both the increasing dominance of the symbolism of anti-structure and the permanently recurring and increasingly urgent tension between the logic of anti-structure and that of communitas in the counter-culture.

I argued above that the Romantic movement was the source of the symbolism of anti-structure in the arts. That movement, of course, had its political dimension, but it is pre-dated by an older radical tradition, that of religio-political antinomianism which has periodically both plagued and revitalized the Judaeo-Christian world since the time of earliest Hebrew prophets. Marx in some respects may stand in that distinguished line (as he and Engels recognized), but in Britain, as in America, the antinomian tradition passes more potently and directly through Protestant religious individualism and libertarianism, and its memory and echo is preserved in hymns, poetry and folk tradition. It stands behind and easily fuses with certain of the strands of the Romantic movement and is frequently re-invented by the intelligentsia, with whom it has a natural elective affinity. The intelligentsia receive it through Milton and Blake, and the masses through the periodic evangelical revivals, with their emphasis on 'heartwork' and their impatience with institutional forms.

The Underground displays all the classic marks of a millenarian movement: the belief that it stands poised on the narrow divide which separates history from its fruition; that there must be a final battle against the forces of Anti-Christ and the Children of Belial; that the members of the movement are the Elect, the Sons of Light, to whom revelation and salvation is given; that in the coming Kingdom perfection and total fulfilment will be realizable in the here-and-now. It clearly displays the usual bifurcation into an adventist or revolutionary and an introverted or passive wing, the one actively seeking to begin the Last Battle and the other waiting for God (or history) to perform it and, meanwhile, trying to create a protected enclave of the coming perfect kingdom among the Elect themselves. It shows too the characteristic dual potential for libertarian/antinomian or totalitarian development. The millennial movement typically regards the Elect as equal, often as divine in themselves. This can lead either to an amoral libertarianism in which anything the Elect choose to do is itself divine, or, on the other hand, to a supremely controlled perfectionism, often involving a warrior/priest/prophet-Messiah with the Elect placed under discipline for their part in the last struggle of Good against Evil. All of this is familiar and plausible enough as the bones of an analysis. What I want to pursue here are certain elements in the tension between the antinomian and the totalitarian pull. This is made clearer if we return to Victor Turner's idea of the symbiosis between anti-structure and communitas in the liminal phase of a ritual.

Turner, as we have seen, considers that mass movements in their earliest stages exemplify perfectly balanced liminality with the symbolism of anti-structure acting as the shared expression of 'existential communitas', or what Durkheim called the 'social *sui generis*'. There is no doubt that in many of the movements of the counter-culture of the 1960s there were genuine experiences of spontaneous communitas which brought heightened effervescence, euphoria, energy and creativity. It is equally clear, however, that the perfect balance does not hold for long any more than it does in mystical ecstasy or being romantically 'in love'. Beyond that initial stage all the old problems of routinization quickly set in. Pure liminality, in fact, is just a fleeting point of transition, and the attempt to turn all life into liminal ecstasy is doomed from the start. In the millennial movement a point is always reached at which a genuine conflict begins to be felt between the imperatives of anti-structure and those of communitas: self-expression and brotherhood are *not* inevitably compatible. In Turner's view, this is the stage at which typically 'existential communitas' gives way to 'normative communitas'; in other words, it is the point at which rules must be evolved in order to guarantee even a shadow of the mutual brotherhood which had initially been a spontaneous by-product of the social movement. What this essentially means is the *re-invention of social control*. The more extreme the doctrine of equality and brotherhood, the more complete must be the group control over its members in order to guard against the kind of egoism and individual privacy which erodes communal identity. The end-product of this development can be Charles Manson's Family, the Rev. Jim Jones's People's Temple, the Rev. Sun-Moon's Unification Church or a semi-secular commune such as Findhorn. Ironically, what we might call the 'brotherhood option' frequently involves a charismatic Messiah figure who can act as the embodiment of the 'sacred' for the group and be the source and legitimation of the rules which bind them together. Equality then comes to depend on authority.

The alternative option lies in the symbolism of anti-structure which pulls in a libertarian/antinomian direction. Here the insistence on individual self-determination and on the breaking of rules and boundaries as a sacred duty renders 'normative communitas' virtually impossible to achieve. The more fundamentalist the reading of anti-structural imperatives, the less it becomes possible to tolerate *any* rules, structures and continuities on which to build group cohesion. Hence, the high rate of failure in counter-cultural commune experiments and the general tendency to fission in the movements of the Underground. Yet the more communitas is treated as the first priority, the less the group can afford to allow the symbolism of anti-structure an unrestricted play, since its natural tendency is to attack the rules and structures of *all* groups and not only those of the conventional world. The typical compromise of the Underground was a contradictory combination of selective anti-structural rhetoric aimed at the boundaries and taboos of the unregenerate Kingdom of Terminus, together with a re-ritualization of the symbolic life of the group itself. Thus, for example, dress, gestures and vocabulary become signals of in-group recognition. But such compromises are always precarious. The antinomian possibility still lies hidden, only provisionally repressed, at the heart of the disciplined, radical sect (hence the often vicious and ruthless nature of social control and heresy hunting in such movements), while the totalitarian terror always lurks under the smiling libertarian exterior.

My first spokesman is Ray Gosling. Unlike Nuttall and Neville, his books are not bestsellers on railway station bookstalls, but Gosling is a well-established progressive journalist and a regular contributor to *The Guardian*, *The Times* and the BBC on both radio and television. He first achieved public notice in 1961 with a Fabian pamphlet, *Lady Albemarle's Boys*, which was (for the time) an impudent riposte to the establishment view about the state of modern youth. Gosling is a link between the constitutional radicalism of the fifties and the take-off into the sixties' politics of anti-structure. As has frequently been noted, it is the peace movement (and CND in particular) which marks the transition to the new-style radicalism of the sixties. Both Gosling and Nuttall are part of that transition and for both of them rock music, jazz and the arts, as well as CND, are an integral part of their political response.

Gosling was brought up in the heartlands of the culture of control – he calls it the 'world of the semi-detached'[3] He was an upper-working-class grammar-school boy with a long experience of marginality, of only half-belonging to that world of the semi-detached. At the age of twenty-three he published 'a sort of autobiography' after being 'discovered' as a writer by the then editor of *New Left Review*. In it he is very articulate about what led him to the Underground, the 'Youth thing', pop and real proles. Despite the style of hip-immediacy, he is perfectly lucid about the bones of his biography – a fact which marks him out as only incipiently counter-cultural, since sequence and causation are still held important. His mother was a schoolteacher and a country girl, his father a self-educated working man, very urban but with a front room full of books. It is one step up from Robert Roberts: a household on the ambiguous margins of the working class and the lower middle class. It contains the classic preconditions for educational mobility: respectability, a small family, a concern for schooling and 'getting on', and the books – that dangerously liminal resource – ready to hand. As Gosling describes himself, he was a chronic outsider throughout his childhood. He loved his mother's rural family but only felt at home in the city; he never belonged at school with either the 'real' working class or the 'real' middle class; he had years of illness with cancerous bones in one arm. It was a recipe for liminal individualism if you like. He hated school and all the pressure to succeed, the perpetual reminders that you were the 'cream'. He loathed the race for qualifications but loved books and words. The trouble with the books, however, was that they were part of an unacceptable package deal with school to get on, sell out and keep climbing. Yet he stayed at school and even spent a year at Leicester University, though he was rebelling all the time.

He sampled a wide range of manual jobs in school vacations and after leaving university, but above all he 'went on the town' – playing juke boxes, smoking, drinking, sitting around just looking at the streets and characters of the town, imaginatively identifying with the urban masses as his and his father's real brothers. He hitch-hiked along the arteries of the country to sample other cities and the society of the all-night 'caff' and the lorry drivers' pull-ups. But in all this dedicated search for the excitements *and* brotherhood of liminality he also joined the Catholic Church at the age of seventeen: Gosling always seems to have been conscious of wanting communitas as well as anti-structure. For two years after leaving university he organized or inspired a largely self-run youth club in Leicester. This was the basis of his riposte to the Albemarle Report. When the club broke up Gosling went Underground. He travelled, joined the Peace Movement, wrote a regular column for *Peace News* and embarked on what proved to be highly successful journalism.

In all Gosling's writing up to the present day the same preoccupations persist. His style is an artful intimation of spontaneity and real feeling; he believes in individuality and self-expression; he feels immediate sympathy with outsiders and protesters who don't, won't or can't fit, like the playwright Joe Orton, whose statement 'I'm glad I'm a weed, I couldn't bear to be arranged'[4] strikes deep chords of empathy in him. At the same time he has a nostalgia for the traditional proletariat to which he never really belonged; the world of the terraced house and the urban street still stands symbolically for that communitas and immediacy of which he was cheated in the world of the semi-detached. But Gosling does not ever take the principles of anti-structure to a self-defeating conclusion; he goes on recognizing the need for a modicum of inner discipline and structure if ever self-expression is to be achieved.

Violence, passion, change, immediacy and the personal are the most valued elements in experience – the opposite of what he calls 'all those terribly British things' for which the world of the semi-detached stands. Yet he remains 'terribly British', using nature and the working class as symbols of his passionate, Romantic desire for roots and belonging. The lumpenproletariat is a very economical symbol: it gives him the violence and the tribal brotherhood in one neat image. Moreover, for all his love of the liminal, he also wants these precious experiences 'hammered into concrete'. There is a tough individualism which wants to define the contours of self and which also loves words for their concreteness and permanence: one of the recurring motifs of Gosling's journalism is that 'words last'. So in the end it is the obsolete medium of the written word, not the new ephemeral culture of pop, 'caff' society and the Underground happening, that he chooses as the tool of his trade.

In other ways, too, he stops far short of the full dosage of anti-structure. He is as adamant as Auden about the sanctity of the distinction between public and private: He writes:

I may write about myself. I may 'expose' thoughts, actions, feelings, responses, but actual categorical definition for me ends at Religion. RC: Sex. M. I have read that Graham Greene is a bad Catholic, and I have heard that Cindy's no bloody good in bed. I don't know. I'm not interested. Only God can know about Graham Greene just as only Cindy's Lover can know about Cindy. These are things between two people exclusively, beyond the line of communication, outside any public area.[5]

The front room, religion and personal sexual relationships remain private for Gosling, and it is this private realm which enables him to retain his 'sense of perspective'.

Nevertheless, in the public realm Gosling seems to be a devoted violator of boundary and structure. He hates categories and glories in the arrogance of the arch-individualist:

We have to mix but it must be as two individuals, person to person. By all means set me apart, after all I'm in a class on me own; but don't, don't put me in a little box, as one of a caste, as one of a kind because I'm not. I'm like you. I'm on my own. I'm in a class all of my own. A class that consists of one person, just me.[6]

At the same time, by a paradox that has cropped up time and again in the arts, there is an equally passionate search for the ultimately all-embracing experience which says everything and joins all humanity in one. The schoolmaster who showed him how to read Shakespeare got through to him because 'for him the whole thing ran through from Langland through to the Organ Grinders' Journal, the latest Fabian Pamphlet and the *Sunday Express* serial. It all mattered. It was all in.'[7] Anything that matters must live up to the boast of the *News of the World*: 'All human life is here': it must contain *everything*, 'what it feels like, what it was, what it is to be a human being, to be born'.[8]

This was part of the appeal of rock 'n' roll. It was all there, all human emotions dramatized and glorified. Pop society was the one place where the young could escape from the dead hand of the culture of the semi-detached and rise to direct feeling. For Gosling himself enlightenment came through simple category inversion: 'What was scruffy became dignity and what was naughty became a way of life, a positive; and what was nice became fake, the cultural tag-ons that went with houses like Bushland Rd' [his parents' semi-detached].[9] Salvation from respectability and the culture of control lay, he believed, in the real working class. 'You see, what were at eleven for me the scruffy secondary moderns had become what they are – The Goods, and the They changed to We, and their way of life to Our Way of Life'.[10]

The irony, of course, was that he failed to recognize that the working classes were just another version of the culture of control. He, like many other Romantics, mistook their ritualized liminality for a whole culture. He sought out seediness and violence as a guarantee of gut emotion and real freedom. A good night for him at the Leicester youth club was one which ended with smashed furniture and a bit of blood: it witnessed to the authenticity he sought. And for all Gosling's romanticism about the working class he also tried to change the lads. He wanted them to take their lives into their own hands, to stop taking things for granted, to reject paternalism, financial strings and respectable 'activities'. In the end, inevitably, he disappointed them and they him. They were part of an integrated, tribal culture which essentially operated with clear categories of Us and Them. He was a determined individualist trying to induce them to let their liminality spill over into 'real life' – their noise and colour and apparent lack of inhibition. But they remained obstinately deferential to authority and uneasy with his refusal to *be* clear-cut authority for them. In the end they beat him up when he was technically responsible for calling the police to the club after a violent scene. He was trapped in an inescapable and unpalatable authority role and they punished him for having played at being just one of them.

Gosling's Romantic idealism has never left his writing and it is no doubt part of the recipe for his success with the progressive middle class readership which now constitutes his main audience. His flavour is essentially that of fifties' radicalism, yet his writing wears well with the progressive middle-class audience of the 1970s and 1980s because it hits the precise mid-point to which the Expressive Revolution has brought them – the *style* of spontaneous immediacy wrapping up a *political message* which is a very moderate liberal individualism. What was shockingly radical in 1961–2 is now mainstream left-liberal.

My other messengers of anti-structure were part of the swing to extremist exaggeration which ultimately stranded the Gosling position in a place not far left of the mid-point of the spectrum. My second key figure, Jeff Nuttall, is more complex and intense, less bouncily optimistic. He takes on a real prophet's mantle for the radical generation of the mid-1960s. His private Odyssey goes through the de Sade tradition of negative Romanticism and back to something more positive and communitarian, closer to Rousseau. He takes the rhetoric and praxis of anti-structure much further than Ray Gosling and in so doing runs head on into the problems of reconciling it with the aspiration to communitas. He is far more reticent about his background but the bones of his biography seem not dissimilar to Gosling's. He too was a provincial grammar-school boy, who then went to art college and on into teaching in secondary modern schools, with National Service intervening somewhere around the turn of the sixties. Nuttall is a poet of some talent, a writer and an (ex-) jazz trumpeter as well as an artist. Most of his very considerable energy and intelligence went into the Peace Movement and the Underground which grew out of it in the early to mid-1960s. He shows no sign at all of suffering from romantic idealization of the lower working class: Nuttall's romantic myth is that of the bohemian artist as the only possible agent of salvation, called to use every available anarchic technique to shock the unenlightened, out of their complacent and self-destructive 'civilized' assumptions. The Bomb in *Bomb Culture* symbolizes all that is rotten in human society: it stands for the whole of the inhumanity and violence on which he believes existing society is built.

Nuttall's vision of unfettered humanity is Rousseau flavoured with Freud, although initially at least without Freud's sense of the tragic necessity of renunciation.

I can remember realizing . . . that a religion must be instituted which each individual may enfuel and conduct from his own utterly unique sensibility, that the corny authoritarian God of the churches must be dissolved to allow a man's life to gain meaning as an ecstatic sacrifice to Being, a sacrifice richly prolonged through four score years. . . . I remember seeing clearly that if the doors could be torn off the lavatories, off the birth chambers, off the bridal chambers, off the death chambers, if those lost and desperate railway station embraces I'd seen so often during the war could be carried through to a healthy public consummation, if we could once again dance round the phallus and grow golden corn from our dung, then that would be a start.[11]

Like Gosling, there is romantic immediacy, but there is no front room any more here. One more boundary falls.

Removing the doors and taboos which hedge in privacy was to have two functions. First, negatively, it would be psychic subversion: a shock tactic to wake up the 'squares' to the recognition of the horror of the society they created and supported. Positively, it was intended as a technique for reviving the faculty of wonderment which inhibition and modern technology had jointly numbed out of existence. The two functions of boundary violation proved not so easy to run in harness and the negative seemed to lead to an aggressive nihilism. 'The future is a void . . . the only human activities which can be of any use in one's progress into infinite void are absurd practices.'[12]

Nuttall charts the 'absurd practices' which evolved out of the 'square' middle class and Labour Party protests in the early CND marches through to the wider varieties of anarchic and violent demonstrations against the Vietnam War. The only glimmer of hope that he sees is the Surrealist anarchists whose violence takes place in a carnival atmosphere: the rest have smothered themselves 'in the slimy masochism of mutual congratulation'. Nuttall pins his own hope on the Symbolist/Dada/Surrealist tradition, in de Sade, Nietzsche, Alfred Jarry, Erik Satie, Tristan Tzara, James Joyce (he calls *Finnegan's Wake* the 'bible of the sub-conscious'), Norman Mailer, William Burroughs, Allen Ginsberg, Ronnie Laing, negro jazz and the pop explosion. Art is a powerful subversive force, not just a decoration at the edge of life. 'Art is knit to society by religion. If religion becomes non-religion, corrupt, then art, in order to remain art, must divide itself off from society.'[13] Thus art becomes a religion itself, but a dangerous double-faced religion in which Nature replaces God. The early Romantics, says Nuttall, were masochists: they embraced the organic only in order to be engulfed by it (the One in the All). But de Sade (*the* key figure for Nuttall) found that power over Nature, transcendence of the organic, lay in the unnatural. 'De Sade and later Nietzsche, Jarry, Jacob, Apollinaire, Picasso hurled themselves into the Sublime Force and took over.'[14]

To face the absurd void with absurdity, to conquer Nature by the unnatural and to reveal putrefaction at the base of society, these are the prime functions of the artist, and the pursuit of them is a crusade. So paintings and constructions, poetry, jazz, a comic strip in *International Times*, happenings at the Edinburgh Festival and elsewhere, a personal Underground publication, *My Own Mag*, and the work for CND and the inner militant group, the Committee of 100, were all part of the *same* artistic activity. Art, politics, religion and life are one seamless web. Art and life are not separate, even though art and society are at war. Mix the artistic media, use art to reveal violence and ugliness not to pretty up the environment, glory in the unmentionable, do the forbidden, mangle and literally cut up language! Nuttall's technique of cut-up, following Burroughs, was frequently used in *My Own Mag* and provides an illuminating contrast with Gosling's milder variant of the same literary tactic. When Gosling wanted to convey his experience of Liverpool he ran together fragments of a novel, a short story and his notebooks. He arrived at the technique after much sifting and careful selection, in an attempt to produce a truthful overall pattern out of the mass of material in his Liverpool file. Nuttall's is an altogether more aggressive tactic. Where Gosling attempts to distil an essence, Nuttall is reaching after shock and absurdity.

The aggressive and nihilistic attack on structure produced two serious problems for Nuttall and his associates in the Underground. First, it fatally confused negative with positive anti-structure (de Sade with Rousseau) and, second, it made it ever more difficult to achieve effective and lasting cooperation. Both problems seem to have come to a head for Nuttall at the same time – around 1965–6 – and led him to modify his ideas about human nature and about what viable revolutionary tactics would be.

The use of symbolic violence in the campaign against war and societal corruption is at the heart of the first problem. The employment of motifs of lunatic violence in art as a weapon against the lunatic violence of the world creates a major ambiguity in the artist's psyche. Nuttall describes his own revulsion at the sadistic graffiti which were simulated by a construction, 'sTigma', in which he took part. The construction itself epitomizes the problem – narrow corridors, bloody heads, pornography, war atrocity photographs, religious and political propaganda, a plastic abortion, Surrealist-style human figures as furniture, a festering meal in a replica of a sleazy café, a model vagina made of a bedpan lined with cod's roe, a living-room with a drawer full of toes and much more. Absurd and violent images were juxtaposed without pre-ordained 'meaning' or sequence. Nuttall was unhappy about 'sTigma'. 'Its unrelieved obscenity was neither dynamic nor bawdy. ... You came out and the world was dimmer, the reverse of my intention.'[15] This is the recurrent double-bind of anti-structure: how can you use the *same* images simultaneously to reveal the obscenity and rot below the surface of civilization *and* to restore a sense of innocent wonderment at Natural Man and his faculties and potential?

There is one boundary problem crucial to all this too: the boundary separating image and act, art and life. De Sade simulated on stage is different from de Sade for real in the living-room. Nuttall cites several examples of this problem in which he was involved, when 'a savagery that began as satire, depicting, say, a politician engaged in some fantastic foulness, changed mid-way to a sadistic participation on the part of the artist, as he expressed himself in the mood of the piece. This was always happening to Lenny Bruce.'[16] The climax for Nuttall and many others came with the Moors Murders. 'Romantics, Symbolists, Dada, Surrealists, Existentialists, Action Painters, Beat Poets and the Royal Shakespeare Company had all applauded de Sade from some aspect or other. To Ian Brady, de Sade was a licence to kill children. We had all at some time cried, "Yes, yes" to Blake's "Sooner murder an infant in its cradle than nurse an unacted desire." Brady did it.'[17] For Nuttall a stubborn moral boundary persists between image and act. He sees Brady, Hindley and their victims as in some sense the collective scapegoats for the whole nihilist trend of the sixties Underground.

On balance, Nuttall welcomes every manifestation of protest against the corrupt *status quo*. He prefers the anarchic but feels he must approve even violent and apparently mindless movements if they are symptoms of the

Madness as authenticity: a scene from Peter Brook's Royal Shakespeare production of Marat/Sade.

incipient break-up of the old repressive social system – everything from the carnival violence of the anarchist urban guerrillas to the tribal violence of Hell's Angels, Mods, Rockers or Black Power. Social systems of a 'tribal' variety (he uses the term himself) are anathema to Nuttall, and he recognizes that they characterize the lower-working-class response. His distaste is undisguised: there is no false Romanticism about working-class freedom and vitality here; they are just surface signs of the inner cancer of society, signals that the end is near; their inability to feel and their mindless violence are created by a world which renders sensitivity merely suicidal.

Nuttall is almost as bitter and scathing about the fragmentation and disintegration of the Underground. He describes in painful detail the break-up of many enterprises, the cross-purposes, the narcissistic self-involvement, in short, the social logic of anti-structure once the first flush of liminal communitas wears off. He writes, for example, about a chaotic and fruitless week-end in which he was involved with Alexander Trocchi, Ronald Laing, David Cooper, Aaron Esterson, John Latham, Beba Lavrin and others. They were meant to be devising a forward programme for the Underground.

The group I represented was turned into the examination of their own minds, partly driven there by their fear and hatred of anything outside their own minds, with an angry contempt for most ordinary conventions and all regulations.[18]

These people *dreaded* meeting one another. Deeply they *dreaded* it. . . . The picnic table became an image of the whole meeting. Discordant, messy, runny, sticky and finally abandoned.[19]

Here we see the devoted pursuit of anti-structure leading to an angry and defensive narcissism: too many prima donnas, too many charismatic presences, too much rule breaking to make co-operation possible. Perhaps most important of all is the final example of 'nausea and humiliation' which Nuttall experienced, again a case of the anti-structural crusade turning in on the group itself. An old associate, Citron Tomazos, sent Nuttall a parody of *My Own Mag* from the mental hospital in which he was receiving treatment ('every madhouse is already a university of inner space').[20] Nuttall was angry and humiliated by Tomazos's distorted personalization of everything they had attempted together in the Underground:

Hideously accurate quotes from my conversation. . . . Finally a cut-up attributed to William Burroughs composed of every personal secret, our cowardices, pretensions and inadequacies stirred into a pungent curdle and thrown back into our faces.[21]

So in the end even the rebel individualist of inner space wants to keep a personal corner with its hiding place for secrets and inadequacies: the lavatory doors may be ripped off, but some kind of symbolic 'front room' should be kept sacred.

It is significant too that, as with Gosling, this retention of the boundary between public and private relates to a strong sense of individual selfhood which finds drugs and oriental religion repellent: the submersion of the One in the All appeals to Nuttall no more than it does to Auden or Michael Tippett. Drugs, and especially the hallucinogens like LSD, take much farther the process of 'dislocation and destruction' begun in the arts. And he despises the American West Coast hippies for copying the forms of expression of the Plains Indians without also adopting the hard, 'portable skills like hunting, riding and fortitude',[22] which underpinned their culture. The result is simply a parasitism, which encourages 'the animated arts – improvised music, aural poetry, improvised dance, informal ritual, sex, clothes, jewellery and cosmetics' but renders the 'inanimate arts of sculpture, architecture and civic design . . . well nigh impossible'.[23]

So in the end, for Nuttall, pure anti-structure is seen as a fine destructive tactic but a poor base for positive creativity. In fact, Nuttall is very close, by the end of *Bomb Culture*, to recognizing as universal dilemmas some of the things which he began by attributing to the rottenness of existing society. Alienation is not a simple creation of the squares but dates back 'to the point in evolution when the lumbering animal ape became aware of himself, became responsible for himself, became *alienated* from the cosmic energies which propelled his animal existence'.[24] The wish to sink back into that cosmic All is a death wish. So he rejects both variants of pure, unrestricted communitas, the proletarian tribal movements which are only symptoms of societal sickness and equally the cosmic pantheism and drug-induced mysticism which is a 'death wish', a sinking back to a stage of evolution long past. He remains an obstinate and clearly defined individualist. It is a difficult tightrope for anyone like Nuttall who refuses to take refuge in the solidarity of the alternative culture. In 1976–7 he was still battling for non-conformity and concrete poetry when he was ousted from the presidency of the Poetry Society: clearly, he had not given up. He is a regular contributor to *The Guardian* and to fringe theatre. His book is a classic of the British Underground, complex and powerful, not least for its honest encounter with the tensions built into the counter-cultural enterprise. It was published in hardback in 1968 but did not achieve mass circulation until the early 1970s, when it was reissued as a paperback. It was influential not with the first wave of student counter-culture but rather with the following generation, for whom it provided a guide and history. More important, it was one of the earliest Underground volumes to reach a wide Overground audience. This was very much the same audience as Gosling's, the progressive and expressive middle class.

My next Underground figure takes the story one stage further. Richard Neville is the main popularizer of the symbolism of anti-structure as 'fun culture'. Deliberately frivolous, he despises all the old ideologues of revolution as *passé*. High seriousness, consistent theory, a sense of tragedy or dilemma are 'by present standards as *out of style* as any army of drum majorettes and mastodons'[25] (my italics). Groucho not Karl, Che because his image is as powerful as that of a pop star, style not content, randomness rather than consistency, pretext before purpose; these are the new imperatives. Neville's bestseller was published in 1970. Its title is *Play Power*, and its audience was massive: the outraged bought it almost as much as the willing converts. If Jeff Nuttall recalls the Hebrew prophets, Richard Neville is the scourge of the Protestant ethic. Nothing is so *passé* as work, duty and gravity: if something gets to feel like a chore stop doing it! Neville is the colonial brand of grammar-school rebel, only marginally younger than Gosling and another journalist. He began to publish the Underground magazine *Oz* when he came to London from Australia in the 1960s.

For Neville, anti-structure is the ideal way of life as well as being a good revolutionary tactic. All roles, boundaries, continuities, expectations, structures, forms and certainties must go. Childhood is the goal of all life – no responsibilities, all play. Existing cultures must be broken up and cultural items ransacked from any source to feed the new fun culture: 'The whole world is plundered for personal decoration.'[26] The world must learn to run on principles of indeterminancy ('The world of the future may have no clocks'), immediacy, emotional (gut) reaction rather than cerebral response, flux, movement, noise and uncontaminated sexuality. The avant-garde arts and pop are central to this culture of the ephemeral. Much of Neville's book, like Nuttall's, reads like a *Who's Who* of the avant-garde arts, that small international counter-*cognoscenti*, with John Cage always prominent, with the Living Theatre, William Burroughs, Norman Mailer and above all the new leaders of pop. A heady, multi-media mixture of all these with sex and drugs liberally added will bring 'Paradise Now'.

The products of the new culture are symbiotic; they work better all together. The most memorable experiences underground are when you connect to the music, the light show, happening and movie simultaneously, while being stoned and fucking all at the same time – swathed in stereo headphones of course.[27]

This is an updated version of Gosling's love for Shakespeare and the *News of the World* – everything in, now and at once. The sex and drugs are there not just for the intrinsic pleasure they afford but because they challenge and offend the square world and provide a badge of identity for the members of the alternative culture at the same time. 'Along with mass demonstrations of cannabis smoking, "obscenity" provides a popular pretext for confrontations between Authority and the Movement.'[28] That was what *Oz* was all about. Drugs, especially pot and LSD, liberate the mind, intensify images and blur contours. Nevertheless, the legalization of pot would be disastrous for the movement, says Neville. Illegal pot smoking is the badge of identity, and its illegality is half the kick. Some other ritual of alternative belonging would have to be found if pot became licit and, worst of all, commercial. It is much the same with sex. Sex is so important to the Underground because the squares – working- and middle-class alike – are as they are because the system keeps them sexually repressed. This is what makes them such perfect material for indoctrination and political repression. Extravagant, unconventional sexuality, therefore, has the double function of liberating and satisfying the initiate and shocking the culture of control at the same time.

Casual sex, group sex, exhaustive exploration of all orifices and partnership combinations, sex as a game (and, importantly, a game without rules), these are crucial symbols of rejection of the culture of control, of ego, of body contours. 'As a girl progresses from *soixante-neuf* to human sandwiches she mentally ticks off another lost hymen':[29] all barriers and rules are there to be broken. Alternative sex symbolizes both the unbounded, individual ego *and* the boundaries of the Underground itself.

Obscenity is traditionally among the armoury of weapons employed by the alienated and frustrated ... today's militants ... use it *en masse* intersexually, instinctively, not only to entertain their listeners but as a matter of policy to communicate animosity to their enemies *and* love for each other. ... If anarchy is an essential precursor to the creation of an alternative society, so the deflowering of language, rendering it obscene and useless, is part of the process of structuring a new one.[30]

Oddly enough, it is exactly the same technique as rules the pattern of swearing among the 'Ashton' miners: obscenity as a boundary marker of the group is a very old technique, well worn in the despised culture of control.

Neville is as unconcerned by violence as he is by indiscriminate anti-structure as a way of life. He seems to imply a rather naive theology of natural human innocence which is thwarted only by sick society – the urban pastoral variant of the millennial dream. The moral complexities about which Nuttall rightly agonizes have no place in this optimistic and one-dimensional dream-world. What happens to 'squares' is their own fault; what happens (unpleasantly) to freaks is also mostly the squares' fault. No problem; no individual responsibility; only the saved and the damned, the sheep and the goats.

The religious metaphor is not imposed but constantly employed by Neville himself. For example, he writes of *International Times* as having described itself as providing an 'alternative theology', and the millennial elitism is unashamedly explicit. For the Underground, 'politics in the broadest sense has *become a religion*.'[31] The chosen vehicle of salvation, says Neville, is primarily youth, which has recently become a 'class in itself'. The corrupt old world will be broken up by the freaks among youth who must evolve a free, commune-style society before the final crack-up of so-called civilization.

The things which damn twentieth-century society for Neville are mainly work, structure, inhibitions and organization. Yet he has the characteristic ambivalence about urbanism and technology. He wants macrobiotic food but not the life of the peasant farmer, twentieth-century media and technology (you can't have light shows and stereo headphones with a medieval technology), but not the centralization and bureaucratic institutions which historically accompany the growth of technology. Neville's ideal is a cross between a media operator and an urban gipsy. In the end it remains unclear whether his alternative culture is a genuine alternative or just a parasitic enclave dependent on 'square' society; Jeff Nuttall made the same criticism of Dr Leary and his West Coast hippies. In short, Neville's anti-structure is *all* expressive, both in its negative and in its positive guise, and there is no utility base there at all: it is all culture and no society. This, indeed, was the basis of his appeal to the new culture classes, the students and the expressive professionals. Fun culture is a recipe for bohemian style for the leisured classes. It is the purest coinage of the Expressive Revolution, and by 1971 it had a ready audience.

Neville leaves most of the real questions unexamined in his easy optimism about the natural harmony of free man outside repressive systems. He pays lip-service to communalism but hates and despises the working-class tribalism of the Rockers and Hell's Angels for whom he has only superior sneers. But if Neville's book is riddled with unanswered (indeed, unasked) questions, my final exemplars of the British Underground have simple answers to everything. Mick Farren and Edward Barker offer us the purifying Terror in their glossy version of millennialism. Like Jeff Nuttall, both are products of art college and the jazz/rock scene. In 1972 they offered the Overground *Watch Out Kids*.[32] Although it did not achieve the circulation of *Bomb Culture* and *Playpower*, it is a very clear example of the harder face of Underground millenarianism, which by 1972 could travel overground and make easy contact, especially through its style of camp exaggeration, with student and rock culture. It claims to show 'how Elvis gave birth to the Angry Brigade'.

The argument is simple. Human society is divided into rulers and ruled; the rulers exploit the ruled by keeping them frustrated and indoctrinated, especially through censorship and anti-drug laws. None of this is any longer necessary because twentieth-century technology is perfectly capable of eliminating work and, with it, all necessity for inhibition and repression. 'The robots are coming – make way for the robots.'

The ideal of the alternative social system is a rock festival: 'tribes of super-nomads, artists, craftsmen (creating) new cities that stand in harmony with the earth on which they are built, where new technology can be developed that does not destroy the environment'. (And where, meanwhile, one asks, are those robots and what and who keeps them going?) Farren and Barker believed that in the 1960s such an ideal was about to come to fruition until the Rulers ruined the vision and persecuted the peaceful, unproblematic, free-fun-culture. Now the Underground has no choice but to adopt random destructive violence against repressive society:

> it will require guns and bombs to defend it against a civilization that, as it falls, would rather destroy everything with it than admit it was wrong. . . . When we have to fight we will fight like crazies. Killer acid freaks turning up where they are least expected, destroying property and structure but *doing their best to save minds.*

So the millennium will be inaugurated by the same old violent warfare but this time urban guerrilla style. And, as Auden noted, while Circe has simplified most of her disciples to flowers, she chooses an elite few and bids them DO HARM AS THOU WILT. Only thus can the revolutionary elite operate.

If the rejection of the dilemmas and complexities recognized by Nuttall is implicit in Neville, it is quite explicit in Farren and Barker. Farren is bitter about the erstwhile leaders of Nuttall's generation who betrayed the movement by arguing against drugs: Nuttall is specifically singled out for reproach. Bad drugs (heroin and amphetamines) and the self-immolation of freaks, their deaths and despair, have all been the result of persecution by vicious, 'square' society. The good, mind-expanding drugs (dope and acid) should be part of a free man's heritage – chemical ecstasy as one of the new Rights of Man, along with free shelter, food, land, clothing, music, culture, media and technology. 'Free bodies, free people; free time and space . . . everything free for everybody!!' What went wrong with the acid freaks in Britain, argues Farren, was that, unlike their Californian counterparts, they showed an antisocial tendency to hug the experience to themselves, to take trips in twos and threes instead of 'reacting to the acid experience in terms of community'. It is the nearest Farren and Barker come to recognizing the tension between anti-structure and communitas.

The content of *Watch Out Kids* is neither subtle nor profound, and for all its stereotyped condemnation of the 'fuzz,' the 'pigs' and all the 'squares' on whose behalf they conduct their repressive regime, it is, in fact, addressed to the mainstream young in ordinary schools and colleges. It was published in the justified hope that 'square' society would not repress, censor or even ignore it, but would *buy* it. 'They promised us money,' says the back cover. By 1972 the Underground message of revolution through anti-structure was pretty familiar stuff, and any self-respecting rock-music fan between the ages of fifteen and twenty would expect to possess at least one 'shocking' publication like *Watch Out Kids* – it was itself part of the *market* in anti-structural symbolism. The most magnificant thing about the book is its lay out. It is a glossier version of the multi-media Underground magazine full of photographs, cartoons, coloured images superimposed on the text, the text printed on photographs, all surface and style rather than content: punchy immediacy and the comic strip with a minimal verbal text and no page numbers. Pure pop art. Ultimately, for much of the Underground, it was hoped that the written word other than the wall slogan would become redundant, along with the bourgeois world it had served. Jeff Nuttall's associate John Latham spent the 1960s constructing sculptures ('Scoob towers') made from burnt, torn and fragmentary books to symbolize the death of the Word. *Watch Out Kids* is part of the same development. By contrast, even Neville's book is 'square', in spite of all its irreverent prose: the high priest of Fun Culture may write of 'deflowering language', but the end-product remains an old fashioned *book*, which hasn't even any distracting visual aids. Its pages are numbered and it comes complete with the proper apparatus of research, quotations, references and index. Nuttall's and Gosling's books are both far too complex and essentially *literate* to count in this particular de-structuring tactic. It is perhaps not very surprising that Mick Farren made a career for himself in the later 1970s not in permanent revolution but in a lucrative branch of commercial art, marketing posters of *Star Wars*, rock stars and the like to teenage consumers.

In most important respects, Farren and Barker are light years away from Ray Gosling's style of radicalism. In particular, there is not even a residual trace of the fifties generation's passionate identification with the working class: blacks, yes, but workers (*sic*), no; they are sunk too deep in repression and the Protestant ethic to be redeemable. It is not the proletariat then, but what Nuttall calls the 'provotariat' – students, artists, *middle*-class rebels, which constitutes the only possible Righteous Remnant in a naughty world. Teds, Rockers, Mods, Hell's Angels, all those structured tribal movements of the real working class are despised or at best patted gently on the head for being inadvertent instruments of destruction. But they are to have no place in the millennial kingdom.

The progression from Gosling to Farren illustrates a shift in the way in which the revolutionary symbolism of anti-structure was presented to conventional society. It shows an important part of the process by which the educated middle classes were exposed, if not always converted, to the motifs of the counter-culture and, in particular, to the libertarian variants of the message. These popular versions of Underground theology display the antinomian more clearly than the totalitarian variety of millennialism. For the latter, one would need to look at the tight political sects of the Underground and of the extreme wing of the student movement. The point, however, is that it was the antinomian version which caught the public imagination in Britain and America; in some parts of continental Europe, especially West Germany, something closer to a radical politicization of culture occurred and produced a much more pronounced development of the totalitarian political sect. In the Anglo-Saxon world, however, it was fundamentally a message of *expressive* anti-structure, a loosening of frames and control, and a broadening of boundaries and limits which came across as the main cultural drift of the Underground. The urban guerrilla sects like the Weathermen and even the Symbionese revolutionaries were small and their impact very fleeting: the only directly *political* movements which learned from the Underground recipes for millennial warfare were the Irish sectarians on both sides of the Ulster conflict. For the rest, what people heard and responded to was a call to make life 'sacred to the god of vertigo and his cult of disarray', as Auden puts it in his satirical poem 'The Fairground'.

Curiously enough, it was not so much the political revolutionaries of the Underground but some of its secondary offshoots which went on to exemplify to the 'square' world what I earlier called the 'brotherhood option', with its sect-like processes of total social control and group identity. The liberation movements of blacks, women and gays all took off from Underground launchings. In each case the same tensions have cropped up between the logic of anti-structure and that of in-group communitas after the first flush of euphoric liminality. Again, the symbols of anti-structure are used to attack the roles, boundaries and categories of conventional society; the same Dadaesque ploys, the carnival anarchy of bra burning, communal poetry and happenings, the taboo-breaking demonstrations – saying the unspeakable and doing the forbidden; the same category inversion which glories in all that had been despised or tabooed – 'Black is beautiful!'!'Lady, love your cunt!' 'We are the people you warned us against, mother!' But in all these cases a heavy brake is soon applied to the pure antinomian option in favour of the solidarity of the movement: the imperatives of brotherhood and sisterhood prevail over indiscriminate anarchy. Thus, movements which began by attacking their own imprisonment inside a conventional ascriptive category ('We are *human beings*, not blacks/women/gays') have ended by emphasizing that very category, sharpening its definition, defending its social boundaries and claiming ascriptive privileges, virtues and rights. Such rigid category inversion can produce a coercive tribalism far more restrictive than the old role categories of conventional culture. However, that is a separate problem. For the moment the point I want to emphasize is that all these movements were big NEWS throughout the sixties and seventies, and it was their more extreme claims to the status of a millennial elite which drew the attention of the mass media. In consequence, they too were part of the process of popularizing the symbolism of anti-structure.

The Underground and the liberation movements constituted a massive onslaught on all the old landmarks in the culture of boundary and control. Initially, it was the middle classes that felt the heaviest impact. It was their children who filled the universities and colleges. It was the expressive bourgeoisie too who lived on the culture industry which had provided the main motifs of anti-structure. It did not take them long to begin to recycle the new versions back into middle-class culture through the media of communication and through their own hip life-styles. Inevitably, the messages of expressive anti-structure eventually filtered down beyond middle-class Bohemia and into the mainstream culture. The two mass movements which were most responsible for this infiltration were the youth revolution and rock music. They form the subject-matter of the next two chapters.

CHAPTER 7

Youth Culture

'INSANITY IS HEREDITARY – YOU GET IT FROM YOUR KIDS'

Youth . . . makes the only proper bridge between the bourgeois and the state of nature; it is a pre-bourgeois state from which all student romance derives, that truly romantic period of life . . . But the recognition has come more from pedagogy, that is from the old . . . rather than from youth itself. It found itself one day presented by an era that also talks about the century of the child and has invented the emancipation of women, all in all a very compliant era, with the attribute of an independent form of life; of course it eagerly agreed.

Thomas Mann: from *Doctor Faustus*

Let me die a youngman's death
not a clean and inbetween
the sheets and holywater death
not a famous-last-words
peaceful out of breath death

When I'm 73
and in constant good tumour
may I be mown down at dawn
by a bright red sports car
on my way home
from an allnight party

Or when I'm 91
with silver hair
and sitting in a barber's chair
may rival gangsters
with hamfisted tommyguns burst in
and give me a short back and insides

Or when I'm 104
and banned from the Cavern
may my mistress
catching me in bed with her daughter
and fearing her son
cut me up into little pieces
and throw away every piece but one

Let me die a youngman's death
not a free from sin tiptoe in
candle wax and waning death
not a curtains drawn by angels borne
'what a nice way to go' death.

Roger McGough: 'Let me die a youngman's death', in A. Henri, R. McGough and B. Patten, *Penguin Modern Poets, Vol. 10: The Mersey Sound*

The arts and the Underground were the primary milieux in which the cultural vocabulary of liminality was developed during the 1950s and 1960s – ambiguity, taboo breaking, anti-structure – in short, the symbolism of ecstatic disorder. Its audience, however, was very small and specialist: the coiners, distributors and consumers of this primary culture of expressive disorder were found almost exclusively among the intelligentsia. The old intelligentsia in the traditional humanistic professions was supplemented in each generation by a trickle of the educationally mobile – scholarship boys like Ray Gosling or John Braine – but these too mostly operated within the contours of the culture of letters. Until the late 1960s the mass of the population at both working- and middle-class levels remained untouched by those cultural norms which, within the restricted spaces of elite culture and minority radical politics, were conducting so fierce an onslaught on boundaries, categories and structure of all kinds. Right up to the point at which the mass media identified these developments as part of a 'revolutionary counter-culture' most people dismissed the whole phenomenon – in so far as it came to their attention at all – as the eccentricity of an irrelevant world existing at an immense social distance from their own copper-bottomed reality.

Until the 1968 campus explosions the only point at which the riotous new symbolism of liminality seriously touched the general population was where it surfaced in what came to be known as youth culture. This chapter and the one which follows are therefore concerned with the role of youth culture and its distinctive cultural medium, rock music, in the spread of the Expressive Revolution. My thesis is that until the mid-1970s youth and rock acted as an irritant to mainstream society, but an irritant which nonetheless slowly inured adults as well as the young to new varieties of the liminal symbolism of expressive disorder. Pop, or what is now more often called rock music, along with television, performed the function of spreading the message of expressiveness outward from the intelligentsia into the traditional culture of boundary and control among the respectable working class and the non-bohemian middle class. The process was full of fascinating paradoxes and double-binds, but the end result, nevertheless, was a certain erosion of the rigidities of boundary and category, framing and classification in culture generally. By the mid-1970s rock music had taken a central place in popular culture and had secured an honourable niche among the elite arts.

The story begins with youth culture. In chapter 4, I argued that up to the late 1960s, mainstream culture in both the working and the middle classes was characterized by rituals of boundary and control interspersed with pockets of *framed* and licensed liminal excess. The period of adolescence is a major instance of this framed liminality. This is surely the point which underlies Thomas Mann's little sketch of the hayloft debates among Adrian Leverkühn's student fraternity in their *Wandervögel* phase: youth is a 'pre-bourgeois' stage, in that nature has not yet been wholly subordinated to culture. The inter-war years had cults of youth too, so we must beware of claiming anything too brand new for our own era, but these cults were probably more exclusively bourgeois than those of the sixties. Indeed, Robert Roberts's accounts of Salford[1] and Ronald Blythe's portrait of rural 'Akenfield'[2] contain pictures of an embryo youth culture which developed among the working classes after the First World War. The cinema and public transport began to open out leisure for everyone and the dance halls became the special province of the young and unmarried. Thus popular dance music and the gramophone were claimed by youth from the beginning as their own peculiar property. Here and in the street-corner cliques we can identify the precursor of modern youth culture, though it took the full employment and relative affluence after 1945 to bring it to full development.

The post-war boom of the 1950s lifted the financial pressures on parents and young alike so that for the first time in British history, there were working-class adolescents with considerable sums of money which they could legitimately spend on their own pleasures. The result was what we now accept as a distinctive culture and a specialized commodity and service market devoted to the leisure activities of youth – music, fashion, cosmetics, drink, bowling alleys, amusement parks and a segment of the car and motor-cycle trade. In particular, the rock 'n' roll of the early 1950s belonged to the young. It was a new music for the same old ritually framed liminality.

The period of adolescence and early adulthood is strictly a 'liminoid' rather than a fully liminal experience. In modern society maturity is staggered: it comes in disconnected instalments. The time between the onset of puberty (usually in the early teens today) and the point at which full financial responsibility for oneself and any dependents is shouldered (early twenties for the working class and often late twenties for the middle class) is scattered with contradictory and ambiguous social indicators of maturity. Sexual maturation, finishing school, leaving full-time education, entering paid employment, taking on a rent book or a mortgage, entering marriage or parenthood – all these important passages and margins are strung out over an extended time-scale. Even the accession of legal rights and duties has little rational order. There is thus a substantial stretch of the life-cycle in which one experiences partial independence but few responsibilities except for the self.

This period of adolescence in British society – indeed, in Western society generally – is thus an interlude of socially sanctioned immediacy and of relative freedom from the all-defining roles and structures of dependent childhood behind and full social maturity ahead. In all classes the adolescent is expected to rebel a little, especially the boy, and to be a bit wild and irresponsible before settling down. The folk sayings legitimate youthful hedonism: 'You're only young once'; 'Enjoy yourself while you're young'. Viola Klein comments on this phenomenon in her review of child-rearing practices among the working and middle classes respectively for the post-war period up to the mid-1960s.[3] Among middle-class families, in which the adolescent is more likely still to be in full-time education, the transition to 'autonomy' is less abrupt, and more a conscious development of self-reliance within the context of the educational aims is endorsed (and financed) by the parents. Certainly, those 'market' aspects of youth culture which depended on free money and free time developed for a decade or more among employed working-class youth before filtering through to the middle-class adolescent who was still in school or college and financially dependent on parental generosity. Indeed, this was habitually adduced as one of the contributory causes of early leaving among the working-class scholarship children in the studies of educational opportunity in the 1950s. Without money, full access to the new youth culture was impossible, and the pull of the affluent and glamorous peer-group style was sufficient to encourage many working-class, grammar-school children, boys especially, to prefer work to school. (Ray Gosling is a good example.) It was only in the mid- to late sixties that the universities and schools became sites for the efflorescence of middle-class youth culture, able to rival the street corner and coffee bar as meccas of liminality.

Because of the 'liminoid' character of this transitional stage in the life-cycle, the culture of youth is marked by spontaneity, hedonism, immediacy and a kind of self-centred emotional intensity which, from some angles, can resemble individualism, nonconformity or even rebellion. The immediacy and intensity stem very largely from the fact that the major preoccupation of expressive life at this stage is the existential discovery of one's own sexuality – always a dangerous, exciting, potentially ecstatic business. These 'liminoid' features are bound to give rise to motifs and symbols of structurelessness or anti-structure in the adolescent life-style. At the same time there are strong elements in youth culture of Mary Douglas's group pattern and Victor Turner's communitas, which go along with the liminal symbols of anti-structure. The most obvious is the importance of belonging to the peer group itself.

Youth is a very precarious status. It is certainly an ascriptive category, but an interstitial one − interstitial both in the life-cycle and in the social system; we inevitably grow out of it and we hold its rights to licence on licence from the wider society. Much of the time of young people is still spent relatively role-bound inside the family, which looks back to childhood, or in the institutional setting which prepares them for adult roles − school, college or work. Only identity in the interstitial status − youth − guarantees release from the duties, responsibilities, certainties and constrictions of past and future role structures. Rock music and adolescent fashions in clothes and personal decoration most of all symbolize this moment of irresponsible, hedonistic release *for the whole category*.

The paradoxical interdependence of liberation and ascriptive group membership − anti-structure and communitas − is at the very heart of youth culture and thus of rock music too. Liberation depends on membership of the category; subjective acceptance by the other members of the category depends on choosing the same form of liberation as the rest of the peer group. This is part of the explanation of the frenetic changes in teenage fashions: anyone who is slow to scent what is blowing in the wind may inadvertently count themselves out.

Some potent combination of group ritual with the liminal symbolism of anti-structure may then be expected in all variants of youth culture, but the balance between the two elements is not always the same. This brings us to a further important complexity. David Matza,[4] among others, has suggested that young people mirror, while partly transforming, the social system of their parents' milieu. I want to suggest that just such a translation does indeed occur in British youth culture. At the working-class end the youth culture which evolved after 1945 was entirely of a piece with traditional working-class cultural forms, even though its stylistic content looked superficially and startlingly new in the hands of the teddy boys, the greasers and the rockers of the first decade. As I argued in chapter 4, traditional working-class life is highly structured by group and grid: it is a culture of boundary and control regularly punctuated by socially programmed occasions in which excess, immediacy and the breaking of normal taboos is not merely tolerated but expected. By extension, working-class youth culture is the expensive and mandatory self-indulgence of the Wakes Week spiced with a touch of symbolic revolt against the adult world of work and responsibility.

The cultural artefacts of working-class youth are unmistakably tribal; that is, they take the classic form of the body symbolism of the group pattern. The point is easily illustrated if one considers the contrast between, on the one hand, the symmetrical studding on a rocker's leather jacket or the Puritan austerity of the skinhead's stylization of proletarian working clothes and, on the other hand the eclectic jumble of hippie garb or the contrived colour clashes and multiple layers of a late 1960s Carnaby Street model outfit. Fashions in hair display the same contrast – skinheads were shaved or cropped, teds and greasers *plastered* down their hair with grease, whereas the middle-class bohemian styles aimed at uncontrolled abundance. These different fashions witness to the essential tribalism of working-class body symbolism and the easy adoption of symbols of structurelessness and fluidity among the progressive middle classes on the youth scene.

The teds of the earliest rock 'n' roll period of the fifties,[5] the motor-bike boys,[6] the skinheads of the late sixties and early seventies,[7] the black Rastas and Rude Boys of West Indian sub-culture,[8] the 'lads' who leave school at the earliest opportunity to go into unskilled casual labour,[9] and the 'football hooligans'[10] are all in the tradition of lower-working-class tribalism. Their sub-cultural styles are all marked by the *machismo*, mechanical solidarity of the male horde. I argued in chapter 4 that the undermass, the lumpenproletariat was the only milieu outside the bohemian upper middle class in which anything approaching zero structure might be found. At one level this characterization is misleading. The internal arrangement of the household may be organizational and emotional chaos, without pattern or predictability, but on two points at least boundaries are very rigidly drawn among the Branch St., Ship St. and Radley undermass. Sex roles are inflexibly differentiated and the streets or blocks of flats have clear tribal boundaries.

Tony Jefferson makes a strong case for regarding the 'sense of group' as the most distinctive trait of the teddy boys, which, along with their near-lumpen status, made them peculiarly sensitive to insults, whether real or imagined. This is very like Branch St. The teddy boys' apparently random fights and aggression, and their uniform – a highly developed body symbolism adapted from an upper-class style of dress – were primarily symbolic techniques for defending their own space, both ecological and cultural. Similarly, John Clarke's analysis of the skinheads[11] centres on the notions of 'community' and 'territory'. Again, the definition and defence of the gang's space, the aggressively proletarian uniform and the football cults are all unmistakable marks of group symbolism and of preoccupation with defining the boundary, the symbolic body contour.

A particularly valuable documentary source on skinhead sub-culture is *The Paint House*,[12] a book edited from tape-recorded discussions among the members of a gang based on Bethnal Green and Stepney. These boys are the next generation on from Peter Wilmott's *Adolescent Boys of East London*[13] and in a recognizable line of cultural descent. *The Paint House* is a mine of first-hand comment which bears out the main arguments which I outlined in chapter 4 and, for that reason, is worth sketching in some detail here. The Collinwood gang was one of the first skinhead gangs formed in 1968, 'before the publicity'. The Paint House was a cellar club run on progressive, open lines. One night the Collingwood boys came and broke it up elaborately and for a laugh – the easily recognized liminal violence of the male horde. They came back to gloat, 'sitting late into the night singing football songs and chants' – a real litany of destruction. Having reduced the club to chaos – eliminated their neighbour's landmarks, totally obliterated the previous identity of the building – they began to claim it for themselves. 'Slowly the mob saw the building as theirs and felt more secure and they began doing things to make it more comfortable.' The professional youth leaders at the Paint House (the editors of the book) tried to convince the boys that they were free to do as they liked in the club but they were hard to persuade precisely because they were used to rules, authority and clear role structures. After all, how can you get that liminal thrill from breaking bounds and rules if there are none or, even worse, if they are your own creation? No rules = no danger = no *excitement*.

'When we first come 'ere you told us this was our place, to do what we liked but we didn't believe you. We tried to force you to tell us what to do . . . we didn't realise this was the type of place we were looking for.'

Even though the club slowly began to organize their own activities, not all of the members were ever able to resolve the problem of needing authority of some sort.

'A place what you can do what you like, to an extent what you like. Yeah, that's the type of place I like. I used to look at it as some place to go, weren't it? There weren't nowhere else to go, never even thought of going to the Daneford Youth Centre, it's too sad, there were no-one up there that you knew. You knew everyone up at the Paint House. There weren't no rules or nothing, you do things up there, play football and that.'

'No, you got to 'ave rules. Pubs, everywhere you go 'as rules, even public parks. You've got to keep 'em.'[14]

Even the boy who tentatively approves 'a place what you can do what you like, to an extent what you like' is obviously more at home at the Paint House because he *knows* everyone there – it's his home territory – rather than because of the free structure of the place.

The gang's many fights, their drunkenness and violence in streets and pubs and especially at football matches, were all concerned with defining their own territory and violating the territory of others. Risk-taking was essentially a group activity not an individual feat of arms or courage – several of the boys describe their shrinking terror when they were accidentally separated from the group and in danger of being caught by an opposing mob. It is significant that they relied very heavily on external controls rather than internal discipline to limit the consequences of their liminal violence. In the pitched battles at football matches they depended on the police to stop them killing each other and were quite articulate about the fact in the tape recorded discussion. They expressed their corporate identity by their uniform, their football fanship and their *machismo* swagger: 'We was the 'ardest of our time, people with long 'air was cowards, you 'ad to be a bit of a Rick & dick (thick)'; 'You 'ad to support the teams, Tottenham and Millwall.'[15]

There were no girls in the gang, and the boys seem to have regarded sexual experimentation very much as they regarded the fights and drunkenness: the code was to violate as much territory as you could get away with.

'I think all the birds were second-rate.'

'The birds used to play a smaller part than they do now. If you could get one round the corner you would. If she was Miss Universe you wouldn't really want to be walking along the street wiv 'er would yer. You just wouldn't want to be seen with 'er.'[16]

Categories just can't be mixed in this culture. Females and other gangs are treated as a separate species enclosed in their own strict borders. The game is precisely the guerrilla raids across these borders.

The same is true of the boys' view of other ethnic sub-cultures, only more so. They ritually baited the blacks, despite their brief flirtation with reggae for a few months in 1969. In particular they persecuted the Pakistanis, even to the extent of being involved in a murder. Their racial attitudes seem to have been more resistant to the influence of their liberal youth leaders and the process of growing older than any of their other views. In one of the letters written by a member of the gang commenting on the editors' draft of the book, the writer argues that the gang's thoughts and beliefs about the football and club fights now embarrass him as childish: 'I don't want to sound like an old wizard but if we could meet us as of then, we would think what childish things to do.' But Jamie's racial attitudes are unchanged – he will carry those with him into adulthood. He concludes his letter as follows:

I am sorry about the racialism but you make our views sound like a passing phase, an inheritance on this subject. I do not agree. And when you say we fear the character of the East End changing, surely if people of another borough moving in make a difference, people from miles away of another world so to speak, turn it upside down.

This is why the upper classes won't let the workers into high places, because they are afraid we will pull down the houses of Parliament, sack the Queen and destroy all the old English traditions which is probably at least half true, what with all these communists leading the unions. I think a geography book when showing people of all nations, Chinese should be yellow, Nigerians black and Europeans white. Your friends in the Bethnal Green bookshop think we should all be black. Black is beautiful, shit.[17]

It would be hard to find a clearer account of the group pattern, the culture of boundary and category in which mixed categories spell pollution. It is also a perfect case of the traditional proletarian image and value system. Classes are seen as essentially antagonistic categories *but so are races, sexes, and every kind of territorial unit.* Again, this suggests, as I speculated in chapter 4, that one of the distinguishing marks of Lockwood's 'traditional proletarian' type is that *all* its categories are seen as antagonistic, where the 'deferential traditional' is more likely to conceptualize them as interdependent and, further, that the liminality of the former is more violent and uncontrolled than that of the latter. Both, however, remain cultures based on boundary and category.

The gang's discussion of social class reveals the importance of getting the categories right and also the confusion and resentment that results when social change alters some of the contours.

'Well, when I was thirteen at school, I thought because I wasn't a tramp or living in a slum, I thought that I was middle class, ya know. So I said to me mum "we're middle class" and she said "You fucking ain't ya know; middle class is snobs." And I didn't know. I thought because you wasn't a tramp you was middle class. Thought this because there was always people at school poorer than you. Yeah, there's always people poorer than you so you might be "igher".'

They believe that there is a middle-class element developing in their area and see this as an intrusion on their basically one-class neighbourhood. These changes are not seen to be as something coming in from the outside but as a change amongst the working-class people themselves, the 'traitors'. This in turn is blamed on various environmental changes in the East End. ... Attitudes that they consider to be middle-class they see as being in direct conflict with their working-class values.

'Like middle class 'ate high class because they 'ave got more and they don't wanna mix with the lower class and despise them because they 'ave got less and they think they are not fit to be with. So the middle class, whereas the rich don't care about the rich, the middle class 'ates anybody, even theirselves. See, they're trying to keep up with the Joneses, 'cause the people next door got a colour television.'[18]

It seems to be the privatized and consumer-oriented 'new' working class who cause the worse resentment because they deny by their life-style the old group-based identities and antagonisms and thereby erode the 'proper' classifications. It is the conceptual 'dirt' thereby created at least as much as a consciousness of material or even status deprivation that fuels the gang's hostility.

Paul Willis's motor-bike boys[19] are a very similar group. For them identity is mediated through a clearly defined culture with a territorial focus, a uniform and a set of norms which reflect *machismo* and centre on taking risks on the bike. Like the Paint House skins, they tend to regard women and other status and territorial groups as separate species of beings, and they too are ethnocentric to the point of relegating coloured immigrants to a sub-human category. 'Hippies' are cowardly effeminates, as much to the bike boys as to the skinheads. Only aggressive masculinity, the ability to 'take it', to 'handle yourself' on and off the bike, to hold your own in a fight, to accept the (very high) risk of killing yourself on the bike, give you the right to belong to the group. Motor-bike culture is a particularly good example of the potent liminal communitas of shared physical danger, the death–ecstasy syndrome which I discussed in chapter 3. The other important point about this culture which all the other lower-working-class sub-cultures share is its certainty and unself-consciousness.

Values, attitudes and feelings were so deeply entrenched as to form part of an obvious commonsense reality. There was no abstract dimension to the world, no guilty reading, no burdened 'I' – just a straightforward physicality and confidence in things. The touchstones of this world were manliness, toughness and directness of interpersonal contact.[20]

In short, as Douglas argues, the life-style characterized by a group pattern and a 'restricted' code has no difficulty assimilating the image of society, reality and the self together in one process. The skinhead case, however, should warn us that this process is only smooth so long as social change does not disturb the relationship between inherited, *sacred* categories and the reality out there. Once social developments or self-conscious ideological pressures – such as the privatization process and the bohemian experiments in anti-structure – conspire to remove one's landmarks then the equation ceases to be smooth and the conceptual 'dirt' which accumulates is liable to trigger deep and wide resentment which may easily seek scapegoats.

Willis's other study of the lower-working-class lads in a Midlands conurbation, *Learning to Labour*, reveals many similar features. The lads take on the culture of adult casual labour long before they leave school. The style they adopt is part of the oppositional stance through which they reject the culture of the school – privatization, individual striving for status and, above all, the culture of respectability. They despise their conformist peers in the school, the 'respectables', who are destined for apprenticeships and even routine non-manual occupations, – they are the 'lobes' and 'ear 'oles'. The culture of the lads is, again, unmistakably a group pattern organized around territory, masculine *machismo* and a rigid dichotomization of sex and status categories. Most of their time in and out of school is taken up by deliberate and ingenious rule breaking. 'Having a laff', or 'doing nothing' becomes an elaborate art form, as it does also for Paul Corrigan's 'Smash Street Kids' of the Sunderland street corners.[21] 'Doing nothing' is the liminal state *par excellence.* It means being totally distanced from task oriented or authority-defined activities. It focuses on evading work, defying and baiting authority, if possible without provoking retaliation, and creating flurries of excitement through scuffling, taking risks and setting up 'senseless' incidents.

Liturgical swearing is a universal feature of these *machismo* sub-cultures, simultaneously manifesting internal solidarity and hostility to outsiders. It is a nice touch that one of the Paint House skinheads who wrote to the editors commenting on the first draft of the book should make a point of saying that he felt the bad language and the swearing should not go in: in cold print its meaning is disturbingly transmuted and renders it inappropriate and strictly not accessible to outsiders.

The mods of the early to mid-1960s form an interesting bridge between the unmistakably tribal communitas of the lower working class and the detailed elaboration of anti-structure which the bohemian middle-class sub-cultures developed. Their life-style is a parody of the competitive individualism of the grid pattern. There is no reliable information about the typical class background of the mod except through the journalistic impressions of the time, of which Tom Wolfe's description of the Oxford St mod scene is the best known: 'office boys, office girls, department store clerks, messengers, members of London's vast child workforce of teenagers who leave school at fifteen'.[22] They seem to have been mostly working-class adolescents who were more likely to be in the routine occupations of the consumer and service sector rather than factory hands and labourers. Certainly, the rock stars who acted as the public totems of the mod style, the Who and early Beatles, were working class, on the move through 'O' levels and even 'A' levels, college and art school. This is the 'privatized', consumer-oriented, new working class, the 'middle class from the flats not the 'ouses' so resented by the skinheads a few years later. The mods were unceasingly competitive over items of consumption, especially clothes: they invented boutique culture. Their drugs, the purple hearts and amphetamines, were not part of a mystical search for expanded consciousness, as they were for the hippies, but instead aids to keep them in the race by eliminating the uncool need for sleep and recuperation. They idealized action as perpetual self-display; they were perfect narcissists, dancing all night, moving around the cities on their motor-scooters from one dive to the next, keeping the party going non-stop through the week-end. Their *raison d'être*, their version of liminality, was a competitive hedonism based on what Dick Hebdidge calls 'fetishized' commodities.[23] The mods were not organized into gangs like some of the lower-working-class sub-cultures: they were loose and shifting agglomerations of individuals 'with a bit of style', drifting around to find the place where the action might be. They were the first real instalment of individualistic, grid-patterned competitiveness in the vocabulary of liminal anti-structure.

The bohemian end of the spectrum shifts from grid nearer to zero structure in its social pattern and cultural symbolism. Hippies, yippies, freaks, and members of the late 1960s drug scene converted the achievement-oriented individualism of middle-class culture into a liminality of self-expression. Given the humanistic ethos of the professional middle classes from which they were disproportionately drawn, this was not a sharp conversion but more a mild mutation of the parental value system. The youthful version of middle-class individualism simply devotes itself to the achievement of new levels of consciousness rather than to material success. The hippie group which Paul Willis studied emphasized fluidity and universalism in its definition of itself. In sharp contrast to the lower working-class subcultures, they had little consciousness of special territory even when they in fact monopolized particular places, houses, squats, pubs and so on. Anyone was theoretically welcome to come and go if they fitted in with the norms of the culture and sometimes even if they didn't. People, even members of the drug squad, were conceived of as individuals rather than as representatives of types, groups or roles. Boundaries and categories were fluid from choice; status and sex differences were minimized or denied, although in practice the effect in the latter case was to legitimate certain conventionally 'feminine' characteristics in males. The ultimate fluidity, assisted by hallucinogenic drugs and rock music, was that of the individual identity itself.

The hippies did not live in a world of personal certainty and had a far from certain grip on their own identities. Where in the 'straight' world this is a cause for concern, for the hippies it was a source of richness and the base for expanded awareness.[24]

One of the significant symbols of the boundarylessness they sought was the rejection of time in their music and in their lives. They too follow Hans Castorp into infinity and ecstasy.

It was not for nothing that they threw away their watches during a trip, and generally refused to be accountable to 'normal' time. They were preoccupied with the 'now' and with the attempt to change or halt that flow of time which the bourgeois order had directed through a massive critical path of careful time calculations.[25]

This, of course, is the infinity of time on the Magic Mountain, translated as 'Cloud Nine' in hippie/rock vocabulary. The hippies tried to flood the 'normal' by universalizing the liminal, and time was one of the most powerful metaphoric tools by which they made the attempt.

They wanted to experience life not as a logic and rationality unfolding itself over time, but as an immediate richness occurring outside the dimension of time, or in another statement of the same thing, in the immediately apprehended 'now'. The ultimate in the experience of this complex, varied richness was a glimpse of the mystic, divine state.[26]

Yet even here we can see the aspiration to zero structure as a technique of mystical ecstasy swinging between a real social pattern and a rhetorical ploy. Even such a structureless culture displays contradictory elements of group ritual – communitas. Hippie dress styles were as much a uniform as the bovver boots, denim overalls and crombies of the skinheads, although, as I argued above, they manifested a body symbolism of fluidity and indeterminancy rather than of rigidly demarcated body contours. Drug taking and listening to music were frequently communal activities; the living arrangements in houses, flats and squats were often communal too; and, most of all, the style of communication acted as a badge of identity. The hippies evolved a specialist language, a new 'restricted' code, which avoided cerebration, bourgeois rationality and analytic categories in favour of an oblique, intuitive (that is, context-based and implicit) mode of speech which outsiders to the culture found quite impenetrable.

The bohemian sub-cultures of youth are more varied than Willis's one study can indicate. The commune experiments quickly ran up against the awkward contradictions which occur when one tries to universalize the liminal state. The perfect fusion of opposing principles (anti-structure and communitas) can only hold for a fleeting moment in the *briefly* liminal stage in a real ritual in Victor Turner's strict sense, in the first flush of existential communitas at the start of a mass movement or at the peak of mystical ecstasy. The attempt to convert liminality into a way of life constantly forces a choice between the logic of anti-structure and the logic of communitas, and, as we saw in chapter 6 the pull of communitas frequently prevails, especially on the politically adventist wing of bohemian millennialism, while the logic of anti-structure is at its strongest among the apolitical quietist segment such as Willis studied. But the contradiction poses problems for both extremes.

Most of the lower-working-class sub-cultures displayed a sharp antagonism towards hippie culture. The bohemian life-style was despised as effeminate and weak by both skins and bike boys. There is one beautifully illuminating passage in Willis's study of the lads, in which one of the boys expresses his dismay and embarrassment when he accidentally strayed into a hippy pub outside his 'safe' territory. The elaborately casual and tattered dress of the freaks made him acutely self-conscious about his own uniform – the lads were very 'sharp' in their dress styles, specializing in Italian flared trousers at the time and spending a great deal of money on their appearance. But outside his own territory, the lad in question was made to feel he was 'done up for a wedding or something'. The bohemians didn't only arouse the hostility of the 'square' adult world – much of working-class youth also felt that someone was out to remove their landmarks.

The antagonism of the lower-working-class sub-cultures was at its greatest towards the extreme ends of the spectrum, the bohemian hippies and the puritanical Pakis, but it found targets nearer home too. The lads hated and despised the 'ear'oles', the respectables; the skins hated the privatized new working class; and the conflicts between mods and rockers (of which more below) are legendary. All these hostilities are, of course, part of a pattern of boundary and identity maintenance. But as we saw in the study of the Paint House skinheads, this process of boundary maintenance becomes more fraught and difficult when social developments conspire to introduce ambiguity where self-evident categories used to exist. John Clarke tackles this point in his study of skinhead culture.[27] The traditional working-class communities are being broken up, he argues, first by internal developments in the working class itself (the growth of a privatized and status striving element) and secondly, by the intrusion into the inner cities of, on the one hand, immigrant communities who form their own ghettoes and, on the other hand, the middle class who are buying up houses in what were once solidly working-class districts. The group phenomenon in lower-working-class youth culture is therefore not, as Matza would argue, a straight translation of the pattern of the parental milieu. Clarke sees it rather as a 'magical re-creation of community', and it is this 'magical' (symbolic) defensive function that gives it some of its violent and aggressive edge.

All the recent sub-cultural studies on which I have drawn have singled out 'deviant' or exaggerated youth styles, mostly located at the extreme points of the social-class spectrum. The mainstream, conventional adolescent has received little attention in sociological monographs, although surveys of cultural values and rock music tastes among different classes support my assumption that, at the margin, respectable working-class adolescents display stronger group elements in the social pattern and symbol system than do their middle-class counterparts. The mainstream, that is, non-bohemian, middle-class adolescent, carries stronger elements of the grid pattern into his variant of youth culture and is more ready than his working-class peer to make the shift from motifs of liminal consumer hedonism to a thorough-going elaboration of the symbols of zero structure. Working-class youth culture likes to take its liminal excesses in the form of heavy spending, the pursuit of physical excitement, especially through taking risks, and above all in the violation of rigid boundaries, boundaries which nevertheless code identity for individual and group together. Middle-class youth culture, by contrast, explores the possibility of abandoning boundaries and categories in favour of flux and fluidity, in order to achieve constantly shifting identity and expanded inner consciousness. Both class styles of youth culture share the characteristic of having enlarged the site (time, place and resources) in which liminality prevails.

Above all else, youth culture drew the attention of the adult world to the expansion of expressive possibilities. From the beginning it was devoted *only* to self-expression. Youth culture became a vastly expanded *frame* within which all the contractual, instrumental and constricting disciplines of societas held no sway – it was one long 'evening of masks and freedom'. In particular it concentrated on developing the direct symbolism of sexual expression and in spreading a scepticism of, or hostility to, authority.

Youth culture as the special province of hedonism was thus uniquely well placed to carry the message of the Expressive Revolution, the possibility of widening the frames and expanding the options for self-expression in society at large. Yet because of the nature of the liminal state, youth culture also involved the aggressive smashing of taboos and the creation of youth as a tightly defined in-group, an elect pitted against the older generation and protected by a sharp boundary which held at bay the rules, roles and instrumentality of the state of societas outside. In short, youth culture had to be, to some degree at least, an *oppositional* style. At the bohemian end it looked like radical cultural politics: at the working-class end it conjured up visions of violent and criminal gang warfare for much of middle England. At first then it seemed like a threat rather than an invitation to relax the old disciplines of culture and control.

The most influential of the studies of 'deviant' youth culture is Stanley Cohen's analysis of the confrontations between mods and rockers in the early 1960s. Cohen identified for the first time a process which is crucial to the development of both youth culture and, I would argue, the Expressive Revolution. The mass media seized upon inchoate trends in the style and behaviour of youth and by making them into news – playing up outrage, violence, disgust – defined and amplified the extreme and deviant features in youth culture and created, as it were, a set of mirrors through which cliché was refracted on to reality which in turn acted to make reality conform to cliché. Cohen shows how the boys whom the media labelled mods and rockers were initially very loose and ambiguous groupings, especially the mods, and were certainly not organized as formal gangs with leadership and role structures. The antagonism between the two types was sporadic and ill-defined until the media began to treat insignificant incidents as cases of dramatic and antisocial gang warfare. From that point the self-fulfilling prophesy began to spiral through the whole cultural system. Mods and rockers began to accept the labels and to live up to the media stereotypes of themselves. The straight world, that is the adult culture of boundary and control in middle England, was quick to focus on the young 'deviants' as folk devils who could act as scapegoats for their sense of impending loss of status, identity and certainty in a period of rapid social, cultural and economic change. It is the removal of landmarks again, of course, and as Cohen's material amply demonstrates, the vocabulary in which the folk devils were condemned is the language of purity and pollution. Cohen shows how the boys themselves were mostly in it for a lark, reading off the expected scenario of liminal disorder for fun. Having been handed an expanded script by the mass media, they played it through.

I want to suggest, with Cohen, that the very same process had occurred earlier with the teddy boys. George Melly, for instance, shows just how much of a bogey they were even to the art-school jazz scene; that traditional middle-class oppositional/liminal culture had no fellow feeling for its lower-working-class counterpart. The same sequence of media identification and subsequent amplification of the extremist characteristics took place with each new style of youthful liminality. Thus the list of folk devils runs from teds to mods and rockers, to skins, Rastas and Rudies, hippies, junkies and peace freaks, punks and new mods. I want to postpone discussion of punk until the end of the next chapter because the phenomenon is hard to comprehend without a history of rock. For the moment I will merely state in brief that punk is a superb embodiment of the ambiguities to which the Expressive Revolution has inured us all. Punk is able to be all things to all classes, fascist and anti-fascist, crude and sophisticated, vaudeville and surrealism, political and apolitical, lumpenproletarian and bohemian, all at once. The double-takes have accumulated through so many layers (just as we saw in the camp tradition of pop art), that ambiguity is of the essence of the culture. So punk is heir to *both* the group liminality of the lower-working-class sub-cultures and the middle-class tradition of anarchistic anti-structure.

The inevitable elements of oppositional stance which liminal culture always displays towards structured societas go some way to explaining the much misunderstood clichés about a generation gap. The generation gap consisted mostly of the fact that young people could institute liminality in a much greater proportion of their life-style than their parents had either been able to do at the same stage in the life-cycle or felt themselves currently able to do. Because of this a contingent and ultimately false conclusion was drawn during the sixties as folk devil followed folk devil in a quick succession of moral panics. Expressive possibility came to be erroneously equated with youth, and Richard Neville is an archetypical case of the misprision. Creative artists, as romantically liminal, of course, are given honorary status among the chosen – youth emeritus, as it were. The whole of Roger McGough's poem 'Let me die a youngman's death' is an elaborate joke using the clichés of the 'B' film to play on the self-evident absurdity of liminality in hoary old age. But if artists and poets can achieve symbolic exemption from ageing, so can everyone else in due course.

My argument is that each moral panic slowly shifted the boundaries in mainstream culture itself to accommodate increments of expanded 'liminoid' expressiveness for adults as well as the young, while at the same time affirming the continued existence of frame and boundary *in principle*. The very process of focusing on extremes, and especially on the bohemian extremes of de-structuring, moved the locus of the mid-point, changed the definition of moderation. If bohemian counter-culture tries to eliminate the frames altogether, mainstream culture can still win its battle over the landmarks by retaining boundary and frame, even though the expressive possibilities *inside* the frame encompass a wider range of liminal symbols. So it is, for example, more important to retain a system of *categorizing* films than to eliminate 'offensive', 'obscene' or 'pornographic' films altogether.

This, then, is the process by which adult mass and elite culture has re-appropriated the symbolism of anti-structure which was initially coined by the avant-garde arts and the Underground and fed out into the wider world by the mass media via the hedonistic culture of youth and the elaborate liminal symbolism of rock music, the subject to which the next chapter is devoted.

CHAPTER 8

Rock Music

NARCISSUS AMONG THE PLEBS

Two minutes long it pitches through some bar
Unreeling from a corner box, the sigh
Of this one, in his gangling finery
And crawling sideburns, wielding a guitar.

The limitations where he found success
Are ground on which he, panting stretches out
In turn, promiscuously, by every note.
Our idiosyncrasy and our likeness.

We keep ourselves in touch with a mere dime:
Distorting hackneyed words in hackneyed songs
He turns revolt into a style, prolongs
The impulse to a habit of the time.

Whether he poses or is real, no cat
Bothers to say: the pose held is a stance,
Which, generation of the very chance
It wars on, may be posture for combat.

Thom Gunn: 'Elvis Presley', in *A Sense of Movement*

Yes, people felt happier for the sight of her ... and the people's hearts beat
faster. Flowers and cheers met her, and it was clear that in cheering her the
people cheered themselves, and at the moment felt elevated and believed in
great things. But Klaus Heinrich knew that mamma had spent long,
painstaking hours on her beauty, that her smiles and greetings were the
result of practice and calculation, and that her heart never missed a beat for
anyone.

Thomas Mann: from *Royal Highness*

To himself the Brute Fact
To others (sometimes)
A useful metaphor

*　*　*

Finding Echo repellent
Narcissus ate his snot
Pee'd in his bath

W. H. Auden: from 'Symmetries and Asymmetries', in *Collected Poems*

Rock music from its beginnings in the early 1950s was *par excellence* the cultural medium through which young people explored and expressed the symbolism of liminality. First and foremost rock music is *play*. It is fun – dancing, music, sensory stimulation – it is the most purely expressive and non-instrumental feature of the life of the young and as such it is ranged against the instrumental, functional, contractual world of societas, and especially the adult world of work, and the disciplines of school. It is about feeling and experiencing rather than thinking and planning.

But liminality involves more than play: it is that same contradictory pursuit of communitas through the symbolism of anti-structure which we have already noted as characteristic of youth culture, the Underground and the avant-garde arts. Even as play, rock music must employ the oppositional and taboo breaking symbolism of liminal disorder. Its origins themselves show this. The rock 'n' roll of the early 1950s was the music of poor white youth imitating and transmuting the styles of America's poor blacks and hillbilly hicks. As the medium developed, however, we see it move along the same road as the avant-garde arts, supplementing the crudities of mere taboo violation by the elaboration of expressive ambiguities. As we had cause to note when this happens in the arts, liminality becomes an unstable and precarious condition. *Anomie* is embraced for the sake of the creative possibilities it can offer. Multiple instead of single systems of symbolic classification are brought into play so that items can express richer amalgams of meaning. And, as we have seen, ambiguity pushed to extremes can destroy communication altogether. When anti-structure is taken too far it cancels out eloquence and leaves Narcissus jabbering to an audience of one – himself alone. Then indeed he finds himself abandoned entirely to his own waste products just as Auden pictures him.

But liminality, whether creative or destructive, is also potentially charismatic. We have already seen something of the way in which youth became collectively charismatic and acted as carrier for the messages of the Expressive Revolution. Within youth and rock culture the star performers become the individual objects in which that impersonal, collective charisma is focused. In this way very ordinary boys become mythic figures of giant stature. In a quite literal, Durkheimian sense they are the totems of youth culture, incarnating the aspiration to liminality on the part of youth in general. Ray Gosling understood this very well, and, as we have seen, he too views the rock star as essentially narcissistic, putting his own most intimate feelings and attributes on public display ('your public image made up from your private parts).[1] The stars must live out in their total lives (or at least in their very public display of their lives and persons) the liminality which for most young people is merely a framed and bounded leisure-time style. The star may be 'Brute Fact' to himself but to others he is (sometimes) a 'useful metaphor', in Auden's phrases.

The role of totem or living metaphor is a phenomenally difficult one to play, full of dangers and conflicts. Simon Frith notes one of the many ironic contradictions in the position of the successful performer.[2] He behaves economically, like a petit-bourgeois individualist on the make, while at the same time trying to believe that he is really the chosen mouthpiece of the 'kids' or the 'movement'. As the Marxists like to say, this is no accident. The petit-bourgeois element is not only weak self-seeking; it is also related to an ethic of individualism, of doing your thing, of claiming full rights of self-expression, all of which are endorsed by the youth revolution. And the pious aspiration to brotherhood is more than empty rhetoric, too, even if the famous are finally protected, just as royalty is protected, from ever having to meet individuals out of the adoring crowd: it is simply an ideologically acceptable way of expressing the Durkheimian point about the star acting as totem, the momentary and ecstatic focus of the 'social *sui generis*'. As Mann says of the Grand Duchess Dorothea, in the extract from *Royal Highness* which opens this chapter, 'it was clear that in cheering her the people cheered themselves.'

In the rock world the pace can be very punishing and it is rare for a charismatic star not to find his own experience becoming anomic and meaningless at some point. Frith describes the way in which success inevitably cuts the star off from normal life.[3] His timetable is as upside-down as that of any shift worker: he must work while other people play; the more famous he is the less he is able to escape from the midnight world of groupies, booze and dope; his only alternatives are imprisonment in the luxury hotel bedroom or further impromptu displays of his image at the nightspots currently in fashion. His private world thus contracts into artificial and marginal contexts (liminal times, places and activities), and his every public appearance must keep up the required dosage of liminal anti-structure to preserve his charismatic appeal. Just as much as the politico-religious cases discussed by Victor Turner – Hidalgo or Becket – the rock star is the mouthpiece of a ready-made mythic script.

To be more precise, he has the choice of two alternative scripts: he can be prophet or priest. In the first case his followers (and maybe himself also) demand further and further increments of liminal expressiveness from him as they become inured to level after level of the symbols of anti-structure, each level quickly becoming a new bounded 'normal' which must be violated and transcended. The history of rock music is littered with the human casualties which such overdoses of liminality have produced: Dylan who needed that near-fatal motor-cycle accident as a pretext for withdrawal into a highly private domesticity; all the suicides and 'accidental' deaths brought about by the lethal life-style, of Brian Jones, Keith Moon, Janis Joplin, Jim Morrison, Mama Cass, Jimi Hendrix. The pathetic case of Sid Vicious is perhaps the clearest of all. By his time, talentless crudity was the most marketable piece of anti-structural symbolism. He played out a now over-familiar script of escalating liminal gestures and took the game all too literally. What began as a competition with Johnny Rotten for the punk limelight (if Rotten stubbed out cigarettes on his arm, then Vicious would go one better and slash himself with a knife), ultimately and fatally confused publicity gimmick with personal reality, fantasy violence with the real thing. Vicious simply made the 'Brute Fact' of self conform more and more to the marketing image, the 'useful metaphor'. Competitive liminality as a total life-style normally brings with it the nightmare abyss at least as often as the ecstasy of Cloud Nine. I strongly suspect that one major attraction of Eastern mysticism for the traumatically successful rock stars such as Townshend and the Beatles lay in the ability of the oriental monistic tradition to place positive value on their existential condition of *anomie*: it could make some kind of sense of their senseless experience of a world from which all limits had magically been removed.

The second script is that in which the charismatic totem is frozen in certain postures which convey the possibilities of liminality to his audience while confining him in a stylized idiom. Routinized liminality stands in for its experiential variant: the star becomes priest rather than prophet. Presley is the classic case. The infamous hip swivel and the sultry tone simply became a trademark. Thom Gunn's poem makes the point perfectly: he is 'our idiosyncracy and our likeness'; 'he turns revolt into a style'; and 'the pose held is a stance'. The very familiarity of the show-biz gesture of liminality simultaneously arouses the required *frisson* of danger *and* the assurance of security in the audience. 'Whether he poses or is real, no cat bothers to say.' Just that margin of uncertainty, whether the stance is or is not 'posture for combat', forms the essence of its appeal. Being a priest is marginally more likely to stave off the worst agonies of *anomie* for the star than if he is being a prophet, particularly if he is able or willing to make a ritual differentiation between real self and normal life on the one hand and liminal image on the other. Even cynical self-seeking can operate as an effective defence of the person in these circumstances, whereas a high seriousness of purpose – a fundamentalist reading, as it were, of the symbolism of anti-structure – is far more likely to bring about a painful dissolution of identity. The rock star who, like Mann's Grand Duchess, can coolly cosset his beauty, practice and calculate his effects and never miss a heartbeat for anyone may be the perfect phoney but he will not lose hold on his identity: he is simply making a craft instead of a crusade out of his charisma.

A problem common to being prophet or priest is that the heady experience of finding oneself the sacred totem of the masses is likely to be the high point of life. Is it any wonder that Narcissus often comes to see himself only in the mirror which performance and publicity hold up to him: he mistakes doctored image for intrinsic substance. Any star who defines himself by his own myth is in serious trouble. Life can then turn into a long uphill struggle to repeat the peak of ecstasy and charisma. Elvis's after life in Las Vegas was just such a sad and desperate attempt to re-live the lost Moment. And frantic repetition of old winning formulae in new contexts is a far from reliable recipe for success in such cases. So Narcissus can be trapped in and by his own image and become another worshipper at his own ikon.

Liminality can be dangerous and addictive as well as liberating and creative; the dangers are worst for the specialists who embody liminality on behalf of the mass. Totems after all are often destined to be consumed as ritual sacrifices, a point which has not escaped some of the articulate rock stars. Dylan makes extended play on his own Christ-role in some of his 1960s' lyrics; Tommy is crucified on stage at the end of Pete Townshend's rock opera; Gosling was drawn to the same image in 1962 when he described the pop star as 'paid to be crucified twice nightly'. The murder of John Lennon makes the point with tragic eloquence.

The problems of liminality as a life-style, whether of the existential or the routinized variety, are thus all too real and urgent for the performers whose public lives are displayed in what doubles as market-place and sacred temple. But the matter is rather different for the other personnel of the rock world. Management, the publicity machine and the ancillary industries can all afford a certain distancing, a more limited and instrumental (not to say cynically exploitative) view of the medium and its symbol system. To them it is primarily a commodity market. Moreover, as I have already argued, the vast majority of the consumers of rock/youth culture want their liminality framed and therefore harmlessly packaged. As Frith points out, most young people grow up to an unquestioned and barely noticed background of rock music: very few make it the prime focus of their leisure and fewer still treat it as a mission field. They are just buying ephemeral images even though such images are carved from the living substance of the performers. I have also argued above in chapter 7 that the style of liminal excess appropriate to working-class 'tribal' structures is very different from that which characterizes middle class individualism or free-floating bohemianism.

Rock music, as the major cultural vehicle of Youth is stretched over the frame of a double contradiction which at times works as a symbiosis and at times threatens to tear the fabric apart. First, for adolescents of all social classes, there is the continuing tension between the need for symbols of anti-structure expressing liberation from role and convention and the counter requirement of rituals of peer-group affirmation. But, further, there is a cross-class tension inside rock. What began as a symbiotic exchange between the tribal and the liberating elements in working-class youth culture was stretched to an ultimately unresolvable tension when the middle classes, especially the anarchic radicals, moved in to elaborate the symbols of freedom, immediacy and hostility to structures, and even to add an element of conscious political protest. Nevertheless, for a brief period in the 1960s the contradictions did work as a symbiosis and united working- and middle-class wings of youth culture, the Underground and rock, into a powerful cultural force. Yet ultimately (the Beatles' *Sergeant Pepper* album was probably the symbolic turning-point) both pop and youth culture began to disintegrate, to return to their constituent elements, to largely class-homogeneous 'markets' or groupings, though not before they had produced a significant shift in accepted attitudes on a range of issues, especially those concerning sex and authority. The progressive middle classes took rock through the logic of anti-structure until for many it ceased to be recognizable as rock and became indistinguishable from 'serious' avant-garde music. Without entirely killing the function of rock as group ritual, they shrank the relevant group of adepts for whom such rituals of belonging had meaning until the working class and the conventional bulk of middle-class youth was left behind to evolve or resurrect their own rock styles. The result has been a fragmentation of the rock scene with, on the one hand, a revival of the basic rock 'n' roll of the 1950s and, on the other, an almost infinite variety of progressive rock developments from hard, sadistic stuff to dreamy pastiches of Romantic and even baroque music.

But this is to anticipate. Before examining the chronology it is useful to locate the recurring dualism of motifs within rock, anti-structure versus group ritualism. Adorno had already noted – and deplored – this primary dualism in inter-war American jazz (by which he seems to mean everything from Delta Blues to Tin Pan Alley). It was a product of modern technology and the capitalist market masquerading as uninhibited primitivism, 'jungle music' – in fact, the old atavistic confidence trick. It consisted of simple monotonous beat apparently negated but actually reinforced by the simple trick of syncopation. 'The syncopation principle, which at first had to call attention to itself by exaggeration, has become so self-evident that it no longer needs to accentuate the weak beats as was formerly required.'[4] Moreover, it was all phoney, expropriated from the start by the structured society it seemed to be escaping.

Any precocious American teenager knows that the routine today scarcely leaves any room for improvisation, and that what appears as spontaneity is in fact carefully planned out in advance with machine-like precision. But even where there is real improvisation, in oppositional groups which perhaps even today still indulge in such things out of sheer pleasure, the sole material remains popular songs. Thus the so-called improvisations are actually reduced to the more or less feeble rehashing of basic formulas in which the schema shines through at every moment.[5]

All of this applies equally to post-Second World War pop music. And Adorno's contempt for what one might call *ersatz* liminality is echoed many times by the more 'serious' and 'committed' pop journalists. They see pop as a mission field and want its star performers to be prophets of existential liminality and not priests of a routinized variant. Yet the symbolic nature of the medium and the deep ambiguity of its consumers' pursuit of the liminal makes stylization and routinization inevitable. Moreover, it is necessary to remember that any musical form is a code: without some structure it is unintelligible; syncopation literally cannot exist without beat.

Mick Jagger, among others, was well aware of this general point. In a radio interview in 1973 he expressed deep contempt for those groups who used to appear on the British television programme *Ready, Steady, Go!* unrehearsed and relying on instant inspiration and 'spontaneity'. They only rose to 'hackneyed rubbish'. The Stones would rehearse for three days for a ten-minute spot, getting lighting, sound, camera, placing and the group's movements exactly planned. That was 'real spontaneity', Jagger claimed, when you were so well rehearsed that you knew exactly what was going to happen, and then you could dare to improvise and move slightly out of line without ruining the basic pattern.[6] In short, no spontaneity without craftsmanship; no expressiveness except through a clear code.

The same dualism which roused Adorno's despair also impressed itself on John Cage, musician and doyen of the avant-garde, who has a uniquely well-developed instinct for real liminality – and, like Jagger, for the most effective craft techniques for achieving it in art. In a famous interview for *The Village Voice* in 1966[7] Cage was asked his opinion about jazz, the old symbolic protest music of negroes and white radicals. He replied that he didn't much like jazz, principally because he found the beat oppressive: it reminded him of all the boring and only marginally useful things in life, like the ticking of a clock. 'We mustn't do anything without this lethal measurement going along with it. I myself revolt against the notion of measurement'. He did not even think much of the freedom to improvise in jazz since the so-called freedom of the soloist was dependent on the constriction of the rhythm section which had to keep the beat. (The development of free jazz by the avant-garde of that movement was precisely a response to this contradiction in a 'free' medium.) Cage found rock 'n' roll more interesting. At least everyone was in agreement there, he noted:

This business of one thing being free while something else is not being free bothers me. Everyone seems to be together in rock and roll music. With it! Another thing which is quite fascinating is its use of electronics. This makes it extremely pertinent to our daily experience ... It's a curious thing but the reason the beat doesn't oppress me as much in rock and roll as it does in jazz, I think, is because the volume is so high. In other words, one's attention is taken away from the beat by the amplitude. The volume of sound is so great that it blurs, as it were, the fact of the beat.

Cage experienced huge noise as the equivalent of silence, just as his friend Rauschenberg had all-black as well as all-white pictures to dissolve all boundaries and say everything. He believed that the results would be even better if, say, three or more rock groups played at once in different tempi and with different starting and stopping times. This would complete the logic of electronics because 'nowadays everything happens at once and our souls are conveniently electronic (omniattentive).' Something of this kind ultimately did happen at the avant-garde end of pop, and short of the electronic limit that Soft Machine or Pink Floyd approached, groups like the Who and the Rolling Stones used phenomenal noise levels to blur not only beat but lyric, melody and rhythm alike and achieve anarchic, contour-less but all-engulfing noise: freedom and instant belonging at the same time. Nik Cohn, one of the shrewdest in-group rock journalists, writes of the Stones:

All that counted was sound and the murderous mood it made. All din and mad atmosphere. Really it was nothing but beat, smashed and crunched and hammered home like some amazing stampede. The words were lost and the song was lost. You were only left with chaos, beautiful anarchy. You drowned in noise.[8]

This is what Paul Goodman calls the 'sacramental use of noise' in youth culture. It constitutes the perfect symbiosis. On the one hand there is what Cohn elsewhere calls the 'noise, the endless and perfect and changeless beat'[9] (that is, the ritual signal of recognition and togetherness), and on the other hand, an overlay of musical or lyrical anarchy, often accented by antics, appearance and body movements to emphasize the convention-smashing elements.

As these quotations indicate, it is very difficult to speak and write about rock music (especially if you are an insider to rock culture) in precise, cognitive terms: rock journalism is based on metaphor, evocation and special in-group language. Indeed, all the points made in chapter 3 might be extensively illustrated from the world of rock music and in particular, from the implicit and unarticulated meanings that its ambiguous symbols carry. While one can, of course, find the technical fanatics who will discuss chord progressions, lyrics or rock technology in minute detail (these incidentally are typically males and amateur performers rather than females or passive listeners), the more usual response of rock adepts of all classes and educational backgrounds is an insistence that rock should be directly experienced as sound, sight, feelings, atmosphere, people (definitely multi-media) rather than *analysed*. Paul Willis and Simon Frith both emphasize this. The vocabulary invokes rather than dissects and can be curiously unenlightening to the outsider.

Richard Meltzer in a valuable and extraordinary book on rock, *The Aesthetics of Rock*, does attempt the impossible, that is, the verbal equivalent of an articulate rock adept's experience of and response to the medium. The book is written in a style which is a cross between Dada and phenomenology and is very much a product of the progressive sensibility of the late 1960s. Meltzer insists that rock reaches its supreme aesthetic achievement when it 'speaks in the unknown tongue', when it obliquely and fugitively expresses the inexpressible.

Some place between the incapturably transitory and the imperceptibly infinite is the stage upon which something is acted out between the ungraspably holy and the forgettably profane:... this is the realm of the unknown tongue.[10]

Or consider this passage in the light of my earlier discussion of the power of the symbolic escape mechanisms of sex, violence and the mystical.

The greatest and most familiar analogue to the unknown tongue (anyway) in mere human experience is the (mere) orgasm. An orgasm as we all know, arises slowly as it builds up and suddenly strikes, leaving one back on earth but perceptibly richer.

Mysticism and death are his other most persistent metaphors. He argues quite explicitly that rock as a symbol system is ultimately resistant to cognitive analysis:

Rock is the best — worst suited for being verbally dissected because it doesn't matter, and at the same time rock analysis can be validly insipid and harmless — harmful enough to be irrelevant to rock as music.[11]

Perhaps it takes an ex-philosopher, ex-rock lyricist to devise such vocabulary and syntax, but it expresses the points in a vividly appropriate style. It is interesting that Meltzer often locates the 'unknown tongue' in the transitions and lesions in some of the simplest rock ditties: *too* much complexity, 'a song saturated in tongues', may defeat the object. As 1970s' rock recaptures the simplicities of the earliest rock 'n' roll, those echoes and simplicities mean something richer and more ambiguous than did their often merely crude prototypes because of all that lies between: the 'unknown tongue' depends on implicit and historically rooted sensibilities for its effectiveness. And an insider like Meltzer is better able to hear them than an outsider. Adorno may have been just culturally 'deaf' to the meanings clinging to the 'crudities' of jazz.

The (cognitively) ambiguous meanings of rock symbolism are legion.

Many of them stem from the lyrics, of course. The use of *double entendre*, of nonsense verse and of deceptive simplicity are standard form, supplemented in the late sixties by all the techniques of poetic ambiguity which we have already noted in the arts. Heavy amplification and the tricks of the recording studio can add the finishing touch by distorting or drowning the lyrics in the interests of the kind of richness of potential interpretation which cannot be checked against a fixed text: many groups in the late 1960s even refused to issue definitive accounts of their lyrics inside the record sleeve.

The most important sources of expressive ambiguity, however, are strictly products of musical forms. Rock, like any other kind of music, is made up of standard items of musical structure. It is a code, a set of techniques and standard practices however much its initiates may try to persuade themselves that it is inherently 'free' in a qualitatively different sense from other music. Indeed, this ideology of freedom from form may help to account for the virtual absence of a serious musicology of rock.[12] The alternative attitude, the dismissive sneer that rock 'n' roll (or reggae, or punk) is crude three-chord (or one-chord) stuff and not worth a musicology, is equally far from the mark: it is not entirely true and, where true, is not the whole story. The musical forms on which rock draws are very diverse. Early rock 'n' roll took its basic musical structure straight from the twelve-bar blues which in its classic form has firmly predictable shape even down to the exact chord sequence. The normal sequence is tonic, dominant, tonic, subdominant, tonic, hence the 'three-chord' sneer. The structure may look simple but the blues tradition has woven all kinds of subtleties on top of it, and, of course (*pace* Adorno), improvisation and variation is possible precisely *because* the sequence can be predicted. Rock 'n' roll also took over elements of the blues' scale modalities and intonation while nevertheless rooting itself firmly in European tonal and melodic conventions. Indeed, the white 'hillbilly' music which, along with the black blues, provided the model for early rock, was itself part of this European tradition. On to this base was grafted a jumble of items ranging from the big-band crooning styles of the thirties and forties through to jazz techniques of improvisation and gospel call and response. All this was combined with a raw adolescent energy which the poor white working-class boys brought along as their distinctive contribution.

As John Cage was quick to note, the hallmark of rock has always been that regular, emphatic, hypnotic beat. In fact, of course, there are several characteristic rock 'beats' or rhythmic structures. For example the different types of bass (usually piano or guitar: drone, pedal, ostinato, walking, rhythm and blues, syncopated or folk bass, and so on) each signal the musical tradition in which the particular piece is rooted. Over these recognized forms rock has always employed a battery of techniques to introduce an overlay of ambiguity, and not only the syncopation and decibel overkill which impressed themselves on Adorno and Cage. There are very many ways of simultaneously emphasizing and violating the beat: for instance, anticipated time, delayed beat, bent time, as well as syncopation. Indeed, whether the basic item of form is rhythm, melody, harmony or instrumentation, the standard techniques of rock (as of jazz or 'serious' music) are basically methods of stretching form just to the point of ambiguity at which it may finally be lost and then reinstating it: building tension, resolving, piling on more tension, and so on. Shifted chords and quasi-suspensions (making harmony uncertain), inflections (making intonation indeterminate), decoration and ornament and blue notes (making melody obscure), the use of the human voice as quasi-instrument and the use of instruments and synthesizers to imitate the human voice are all techniques which employ structure and anti-structure *together* as a way of wresting maximum expressive power from fundamentally simple musical items.

Additional elements of ambiguity arise from the fact that rock came to be predominantly *recorded* music. Thus repetition (a Dadaesque trick to suggest that the needle is stuck perhaps), or the 'fade' ending instead of the final resolving cadence, are both examples of amplified ambiguity. All these techniques introduce liminal effects into the clear and predictable structure of blues, ballad or folk melody.

As rock developed during the sixties, especially at the avant-garde end, principles of indeterminacy (of rhythm, melody, harmony, instrumentation and lyrics), and the practice of quasi-improvisation and the programming of (usually electronic) randomness into the music, all gained ground. By exactly the same irony as we encountered in avant-garde, many of the more ambitious groups took to minutely 'composing' the required ambiguities into the score rather than leaving them to the chance of improvisation. Everything got longer and more complicated. All the numbers recorded in the early fifties went on to 78 rpm discs: they were identical in musical form and in length. Willis's motor-bike boys knew exactly how long a fifties single lasted. Gunn got it right too: 'two minutes long it pitches through some bar.' So the bike boys timed their races round the block by Elvis or Jerry Lee Lewis on the juke box. By the 1970s though singles, which were then 45s, formed the staple diet of the Top Thirty, their musical structure was more varied and they were longer, lasting more like four minutes, while in the LP market a 'song' may last anything up to twenty-five minutes; ELP's 'Pirates', for example, is a mini-cantata, taking up one side of an LP disc.

The sophistication of rock's fast-developing technology itself stimulated much of the musical complexity of the sixties. Very little rock music begins life as marks on manuscript paper. Much of it evolves as groups mess about together with their instruments and equipment. And when a successful group is offered a whole recording studio as a playground/laboratory the urge to experiment must be practically irresistible even for someone who cannot read a note of music in the formal sense. Thus it is ironic but appropriate that groups like the Who and the Beatles who grew rich and famous on simple 'formula' songs should find themselves in a position to play musical games with space-age electronic toys. Not unnaturally, it helped to transform their product.

The visual self-presentation of rock performers illustrates the contradictory pull of structure and ambiguity even more clearly than the music itself. The earliest super group, Bill Haley and the Comets, was only one step away from the big bands of wartime popular culture. The big bands were middle-aged and wore a uniform (evening suits) that emphasized togetherness, respectability and 'sophistication'. Haley's band wore uniform too, only it was loud brash tartans in shiny materials. Moreover, they fooled around with their instruments, as some of the black jazz men had done. There is a beautiful photograph of the Comets with the bassist lying on his back with his feet in the air balancing his instrument, wearing ostentatiously odd socks. This is the first instalment of the body symbolism of anti-structure. The early rock 'n' roll singers took body symbolism very seriously, and the blue jeans, suede sneakers and cowboy shirts became a kind of convention. 'Don't you step on ma blue suede shoes' is a fifties lyric which perfectly illustrates the sanctity of the group uniform.

The early sixties saw the rise of the four-man group (togetherness) whose unity was expressed by their identical haircuts and suits. The symbols of anti-structure resided in the antics and body movements which culminated in such extravaganzas as physical fights on stage or aggressive competition between members to 'play each other off the stage' (Cream) or in smashing expensive instruments (the Who). Jim Morrison of the Doors was notorious for masturbating on stage. Some recent groups have even invited the audience to boo instead of applauding just to break the convention, or have drenched the fans with foam, spittle or obscene abuse (Black Sabbath, the Stranglers).

In the mid-sixties group uniform gave way to a more complete body imagery of anti-structure, with each member of a group not only dressed differently from the others but often dressed in crazy fancy-dress costumes. A 1976 concert given by Bob Dylan and Joan Baez ('Hard Rain', televised by the BBC in December 1976) displayed a riotous amalgam of religious, ethnic and political body imagery – crosses, Stars of David, Arab (or Vietnamese?) guerrilla headbands, gypsy bandanas, ethnic shirts and belts (South American, Balkan, American Indian?). In the course of time, then, the body symbolism of anti-structure has become ever more extravagant, leaving the occasion itself to carry the gestures of togetherness. Punk gigs in the late 1970s were riots of surreal fancy dress for audience and performers alike.

The same dualism runs through the other most characteristic features of rock. For example, it is both a solitary pursuit and a public ceremony – private fantasy alone in the bedroom with the record player, the photographs and the fan magazines or group euphoria at the disco, the pop concert or the rock festival. The invention of the rock festival is a very clear indication of the desire to create temporary social systems exclusive to members of the rock/youth culture. The rock festival offers a brief and therefore relatively unproblematic taste of structureless Utopia, week-end commune life for secretaries, students and stockbrokers' clerks.[13] Again, one has the ritualism of instant, painless and costless belonging signalled by common pursuit of the same symbols of structurelessness.

The fan clubs and fan magazines are some of the most obviously ritual elements in rock. They look very like the temples and sacred scriptures of an esoteric cult. The obsessiveness with which the most trivial items of fact are chronicled in the 'fanzines' is redolent of a certain kind of text-swapping normally found only on the most fundamentalist fringes of Islam and Christianity. As I have already argued, the role of the pop stars too has strong ritual and religious overtones: 'Clapton is God' is one of the (only half-jocular) slogans Cream fans used to use. Even the commentators most anxious to play up a prosaic view of pop are seldom able to avoid terms such as 'idol' or 'shaman' for long and 'charisma' has become an indispensable part of the pop journalist's vocabulary (also affecting the names of pop record companies). Gosling, as we have seen, was inside the pop phenomenon from its beginnings in the 1950s. He writes brilliantly of the way in which public pop produces an intense identification between singer and audience giving the latter an experience of common belonging and at the same time a heightened version of their own most personal experiences, disappointments, dreams and desires. The star he sees as a boy-god, the Ishmael figure, the lonely, uncommunicable but desired outsider, selling his youth and beauty in a public ritual created from all the most private and tabooed items of experience. Wilfred Mellers, the musicologist, makes a related point.[14] He likens the vocal technique of certain pop stars, Mick Jagger and Jimi Hendrix in particular, to the chanting of different kinds of medicine men and notes the increasing concentration in pop on symbols and images alien to Western Christendom as more convenient carriers of a rebellious gesture. So, again, one has the ritualization of an anti-conventional, anti-structural symbolism.

The importance of the defiant gesture and outsider status cannot be over-emphasized. It operates both as a slap in the eye of the square adult world and as a banner around which youth can rally. The selection of an illegal (pot, acid) rather than a legal (alcohol) stimulant had as much to do with peer-group identity as with a search for neo-mystical or truly liminal experience. To have rock idols like Jagger in a martyr role *vis-à-vis* police and convention is splendid for in-group cohesion. The preference for the pirate radio stations and their anarcho/vaudeville disc jockeys rather than the BBC serves the same kind of function.

The extravagant flouting of adult conventions, the aggressive emphasis on raw sexuality and especially on narcissistic male sexuality and potential violence, has been a continuing thread in rock. From the earliest years of the fifties' rock 'n' roll the quality of the threat and menace has been a basic ingredient of rock. There is an often repeated theory that this threat is in some sense 'genuine' but is cunningly deflected by commercial capitalism which in George Melly's view tempts the wild roaring bull with a 'golden mash' and then slips round the back to castrate him while he is distracted: thus 'the masculine rebel is transformed into a masturbation fantasy-object for adolescent girls.'[15]

Adorno employs the castration imagery in a similar way. What this interpretation misses is as important as what it gets right. The first point is that from Elvis Presley onwards the *most* crudely aggressive performers have *not* been the largest commercial successes: the progressive *cognoscenti* nowadays revere, say, young Chuck Berry or Howlin' Wolf far more than Elvis, who was white and, by comparison, tame: they prefer the Stones and the Animals to the Beatles and so on. But the fact remains that it was Elvis and the Beatles who became international idols: their records sold not merely through the machinations of company entrepreneurs but because the market wanted that product and not the 'rawer' and 'more authentic' variant. A close perusal of the Top Twenty charts and the record sales figures underlines this point over and over again. Just one example may be sufficient here. In a compilation of Top Twenty records in Britain between 1956 and 1969, that smooth and ageless PR man for fundamentalist Christianity and clean-limbed youth, Cliff Richard, comes second to Elvis in total hit records and third after the Beatles and Elvis in Number 1 hits.[16] All these charts demonstrate that the real 'hard stuff' is a minority taste and has largely an LP, not a singles, market. Cliff Richard versus, say, Jagger, or the Osmonds versus Alice Cooper is another undertow in rock. The polarization between delinquent rebel and boy-next-door operates not merely between stars but within the dual image projected by individuals. Elvis was not only the embodiment of animal sexuality and male arrogance but a gospel hymn singer and mother worshipper. Tommy Steele, his best-known English copy, was more energy than aggression and made a career out of legitimate show-biz by exploiting proverbial cockney cheek and charm, an old formula in a new mould. One could multiply examples.

The point after all is that the medium – pop, show-biz – is a symbolic medium and so is all gesture and style. Real, hard rebellion must take on tougher channels – politics, crime or whatever. So the result is that the rebelliousness of rock is *stylized*. Few of its stars want it otherwise, however much they may get carried away by their own rhetoric of liminality. Even the Rolling Stones ultimately failed to move rebellion off the stage and merely accepted it as a ticket-of-entry to the free-floating life-style of the international jet set, and many of the angriest rock personalities merely succeed in destroying themselves with overdoses of *anomie*. Moreover, most of the teenage consumers are only playing at liminality. The point is not that capitalism wants order and youth wants revolt but that most young people want the semblance and symbol of revolt without its reality, they want to threaten without cracking known social moulds, while the world around remains familiar and therefore safe. Thus rock is the ritual gesture of liminality not a first instalment of revolt: the image and not the substance.

And what youth wants at least as much as these things is the symbol of generational belonging and the sense of exclusiveness that this gives *vis-à-vis* other generations. Thus the kiss of death to a rock style is either adult approbation or the intrusion of teeny and weeny boppers, lollipop, kiddypop – in other words, the generation of little brothers and sisters. Hence the increasingly frenetic changes of style and the accelerating shortness of a pop generation as each style is passed by the mass media up into adult popular culture and down to the child market. Generational exclusiveness is far more elusive and fleeting than the institutionalized symbols of revolt which form the common element of threat which links style to succeeding style.

The other dialectic in rock is best seen through a brief résumé of its chronology. The problem is that though all social classes in the youth/pop culture are juggling with symbols of de-structuring against peer-group rituals, at the margin the progressive middle classes want the symbols of de-structuring and the working classes want peer-group rituals. In a nutshell, what happened was that after an initial stage when pop was exclusively proletarian (simple, repetitive and very ritualistic), the progressive middle classes and the Underground moved in to use the new popular medium as a vehicle for their message. After a brief success in the 1960s the extremes of progressive rock provoked a reaction particularly among the working classes, who reverted to the basic rock of the 1950s and took up reggae, the West Indian variant, in considerable numbers, then soul, and then briefly punk rock, followed by the New Mod style. I suggest that this history falls into four clear periods. The first is rock 'n' roll; the second is the era of the Beatles and Stones, when English provincialism became briefly cosmopolitan; the third begins as the Greenwich Village and Los Angeles folk and protest invasion and develops into a full-blooded millennial movement which is at its height in student revolution year, 1968; and the fourth is the multi-dimensional seventies, with a multiplicity of styles coexisting each with separate and largely class-homogeneous publics.

In its first stage pop was exclusively 'prole' – 'rank if vigorous', as George Melly describes it with the superiority of a middle-class jazzman. Jazz, in fact, insulated middle-class British radicals from pop for over a decade.

Rock 'n' roll was a graft of American negro rhythm and noise on to white crooning styles and it was the first specifically teenage music. The beat was simple and heavy, the images were all teenage possessions, activities and feelings. There was much more open sexual innuendo than popular music had recently carried, and a good deal of aggression and energy. The lyrics were simple, either conjuring the concrete items in the teen life-style, blue jeans, suede shoes, American cars and Saturday nights, or it was nonsense rhymes such as Little Richard excelled in. Nik Cohn, almost alone among rock journalists, captures the essence of the phenomenon:

Rock 'n' roll was very simple music. All that mattered was the noise it made, its drive, its aggression, its newness. All that was taboo was boredom. The lyrics were mostly non-existent, simple slogans one step away from gibberish. This wasn't just stupidity, simple inability to write anything better, it was a kind of teen code, almost a sign language, that would make rock entirely incomprehensible to adults.[17]

In so far as this teen ritual carried de-structuring motifs they were not in the form of social protest or global hostility to structure but were the working-class adolescent's irritation with the waste of time in school, delight in baiting authority but most of all the imagery of an endless Saturday night rave-up. It was music to dance to and it was the music of first teds and then rockers. Its stars in England were given appropriately aggressive male names – Steele, Fury, Wilde.

The next phase, the era of the Beatles and Stones, is the age of the mods. If the Who stayed the archetypal mod group for longer and wrote the most concise anthem of youth ever in 'My Generation', one should not forget that before their Progressive Enlightenment the Beatles too were just 'sharp little mods', as Jeff Nuttall observed. The shift of style in this phase was from solo singer to group and the names of the groups were often acid little jokes, Beatles, Animals, Kinks. The emphasis moved from London to the provinces, partly because the rawer provincial cities such as Liverpool and Glasgow had become the centre of flourishing teen clubs where jazz-influenced youngsters, often with 'O' and 'A' levels, were experimenting with new grafts of the negro blues idiom on the fifties' rock styles and attracting personal local following.

I do not propose to explain the phenomenal success of the Beatles but merely to point to some of its social ingredients. First, they represented a social step on from early English rock despite their deliberate playing-up of their working-class identity. They were the essential mods, upper-working to lower-middle class, and on the education conveyor belt. They kept some of the anger and channelled a good deal of it into the backlash of the periphery against the centre, delighting in making London look phoney. They displayed cool, adolescent cheek and smooth, fashionable dress. They were, in fact, the perfect mixture for everyone: a bit of jack-boot harshness

(Lennon), the pretty boy-next-door (McCartney), the soulful loner (Harrison) and the genuine working-class comic drummer (Starr). This, in fact, constitutes the tension and symbiosis of rock itself and their subsequent careers since the group broke up illustrate the point clearly. Lennon, the art school drop-out, for a while found his promised land in the anarchic wing of the avant-garde arts-cum-social protest and ran the whole gamut of progressive gestures from Warhol-like films of his own genitals to anti-war happenings. McCartney stayed pretty and melodious and apparently integrated fairly painlessly into fashionable and wealthy east coast America. He still looks pretty and plays tuneful pop with his group Wings. Harrison predictably got stuck at the Eastern mysticism stage they all toyed with, but in a gentle variant. Only Ringo Starr stayed anywhere near his origins and carved a successful career in show biz strikingly similar to Tommy Steele's.

The Beatles encapsulated the whole strength and problem of rock: avant-garde to basic working class; ideas versus beat; aggression versus romantic sweetness. Their greatest successes were the simple, ritual, teen formulas or affectionate nostalgia for the life of the terraced house.[18] Of course, the symbiosis cracked in the Beatles themselves. The avant-garde end began to swallow up the rest. Their conversion to drugs and Eastern mysticism as the latest prerequisite of selfhood (liminality again, of course) was the turning-point for the group and for the medium.

Sergeant Pepper, acid rock, psychedelic lyrics and oriental instruments all endeared the Beatles to the colour supplement progressives, who loved and hailed as significant the ambiguous meanings in the lyrics, the eclecticism of the music and the avant-garde sadism of the humour, such as references to the Moors Murders. They began to say and do what the Underground had preached for a decade or more. Not only the week-end progressives but even some full-time radicals hailed them as the authentic voice of youth and truth. Jeff Nuttall, wrote:

The Beatles were, and are, the biggest single catalyst in this whole acceleration in the development of the sub-culture. They robbed the pop world of its violence, its ignorant self-consciousness, its inferiority complex. They robbed the protest world of its terrible self-righteous drabness, they robbed the art world of its cod-seriousness.[19]

An equally shrewd commentator, Pete Fowler, who has the merit of being in touch with working-class youth, had a very different verdict: 'For all those who thought the Beatles were the Saviours of Rock, there were at least twice as many who thought John Lennon was going round the twist.' Fowler has a graphic quotation from one of his skinhead informants, a Birmingham apprentice who was fifteen in 1967: 'I hated fucking *Sergeant Pepper* and that thing the Stones did with "She's a rainbow" on it. Me and my mates spent most of the time in the pub after that.'[20]

This was the writing on the wall but no-one read it in 1967–8. The Beatles' conversion and similar flirtations with drugs and mysticism by all the leading groups – the Stones, the Who and so on – inaugurated the third historical period, the age of the hippie. This, the Greenwich Village/Los Angeles millennial stage, is a muddle of avant-garde motifs which exactly reflect and repeat the anarchic themes of the arts and the Underground. It was Rousseauesque, anti-urban Utopianism shot through with the blacker, more violent Romantic heritage of de Sade and Nietzsche. This was the exact musical equivalent of hippie millennialism, even down to the normal sectarian bifurcation into a passive and a violent wing which perfectly mirrors the double thread in Romanticism: peaceful English hippies at Glastonbury or Charles Manson in California. The gentle variant was all acoustic guitars, 'folk' intonation, oriental instruments and hymns by urban youth to a pastoral idyll. The message was 'Love not War', an end to greed and pollution, politics and bureaucracy. Drugs were benevolent aids to consciousness. The attempt in the music, the dress (pre-Raphaelite, or jeans and beads) and the life-style was to combine anarchic eclecticism with commune-style togetherness, zero structure and group ritual. This was the point at which the pop festival appeared as the major ceremonial focus. Drugs were doubly useful: they could act as the identity symbol of enlightenment and also blur contours, produce fantastic, nonsensical, surrealist juxtapositions of images, and transform twentieth-century technology from science (bad, 'square') into magic (good, liberating). Acid rock kept the ritual beat underpinning dislocated melody and surrealist lyrics.

The paradoxical combination of violence and gentleness is well illustrated by the leading minstrel of the period, Bob Dylan. It is the classic combination of violent condemnation of the adult world and urban society inside a form which idealizes gentleness. His tone is harsh and his love songs are just as bitter as his social-comment songs. Dylan's career illustrates many of the fundamental tensions of the rock world which come to a head in the late 1960s, the time of his greatest triumphs. He seems always to have been a chameleon figure, uncertain of his own identity, ashamed of his small-town, lower-middle-class Jewish background and trying on all kinds of alternative fantasy identities from early adolescence onwards. In this sense he was the perfect case for totemization – a boy who could only find an identity via public adulation, someone who would settle for nothing less than myth status.

His adolescent years in school saw him imitating and idolizing the rock 'n' roll stars of the fifties, particularly Little Richard, but in his late teens he abandoned this for an alternative dream and followed the Woody Guthrie myth into the folk protest tradition, where he finally made a name for himself, largely, it seems, through taking his own white – 'hobo-of-the-road' legend with total and dedicated seriousness. In 1963–64 Dylan rediscovered

Dada and surrealism woo the masses again: rock and youth culture domesticate the avant-garde gesture, as here on a record sleeve.

rock and virtually invented the genre of folk-rock. He abandoned protest and the movement without a qualm and took on another identity, shifting music, subject-matter and self-image at the same time. As Dylan put it in a conversation with a friend:

There's no yesterday, so what's left is today.... I was me back then and now I'm *me*. You dig? I can't ever be the me from back then, I can only be *me* from today. And the me from today is involved in a bigger circle of people.[21]

The image now was not old, neglected Woody Guthrie but the Beatles crossed with Rimbaud and T. S. Eliot. Moreover, the coming ideology of self-expression was already speaking through Dylan who always acted like litmus paper in registering what was 'blowing in the wind'. In 1964 Dylan said of his album, *Another Side of Bob Dylan*:

There aren't any finger-pointing songs in here. Me, I don't want to write *for* people any more. You know – be a spokesman. From now on I want to write from inside me. . . . The way I like to write is for it to come out the way I walk or talk.[22]

That was the new ideology, but there is a lot of the Grand Duchess Dorothea in Dylan too. The effects, even the effect of total spontaneity and sincerity, are carefully crafted. 'He never made a mistake in terms of theater,' said an associate. 'That comes out in his songs – theater, and the theater never went wrong.'[23] Another illuminating comment from one of Dylan's early friends and musical rivals reveals him as master of the key technique for achieving expressive ambiguity, that simultaneous affirmation and violation of musical form which I discussed earlier in this chapter.

He was something of a natural – a cat who seems to know all the rules and systematically breaks them. He gave the appearance of not knowing anything, but you could just feel he knew what it was all about and he was deliberately breaking the rules and making it work.[24]

It was entirely appropriate that Dylan should find himself in his first film role in 1973 hymning Billy the Kid as Sam Peckinpah's ideal of the free man: violence as the prerequisite of freedom always lay inside even the passive variant of hippie ideology and is a powerful, implicit strand in Dylan's music. His latest film, *Reynaldo and Clara*, written, directed and acted by Bob Dylan and featuring both Mrs Sara Dylan and Joan Baez, is an even better illustration of the essence of Dylan and in a sense of sixties rock itself. Dylan is both subject and object: the film is Narcissus's apotheosis. It is a surrealist play on the multiple myths of Dylan, on all the public speculation about his life and loves and his slippery uncertain identity. It is a new meta-myth of and by the old shape-shifter, an incestuous, Dadaesque and grossly self-indulgent (it lasts four and a half hours) account of Dylan's fame.

Dylan's career also illustrates an interesting competition between two important variant motifs of anti-structure. The problem is whether the imagery and techniques of twentieth-century machine technology stand for the devil of the 'square', adult bourgeois world or whether they can act as symbols and agents of youthful liminality. The folk/student protest tradition has tended to fear and despise all this urban technology and to cling to what Adorno would dismiss as a phoney and atavistic primitivism. Dylan's adoption of electric amplification and rock backing groups in 1964 caused an enormous furore – it was a kind of heresy at the time, though ultimately many members of the folk protest school followed and rejoiced in the further instalments of ambiguity (and public notice) which it made available to them. The counter-tradition, from Chuck Berry in the fifties to Bruce Springsteen in the seventies, has used modern technology, and especially the car and the motor-bike as a metaphor for sexual and personal power and freedom. It is the same use of machine imagery which is found in the Futurist art movement. In the sixties, however, the pastoral tradition mostly took the form of a naive, anti-technological and anti-urban Utopianism, assuming that release from sexual inhibitions and a penchant for watching flowers grow ('feeling groovy') would produce natural social harmony. This side of the movement released a stream of gentle melody, and a rediscovery by middle-class adolescents of serious Romantic music from Mussorgsky to Vaughan Williams (King Crimson; Focus; Emerson, Lake and Palmer).

The adventist side of pop is harder to pin down in Britain than in America. The Beatles flirted with it in songs like 'A Day in the Life'; the Stones found new springs of anger and aggression; and the university campuses produced zanies like Arthur Brown, whose act was a mixture of voodoo, science fiction, Aztec ritual and the comic horror film. In Britain Jimi Hendrix was probably the major figure, with Afro hairdo, drugs, violent guitar sound and vocal overkill, and heavy hints of Voodoo, black magic and the like. In America it was all more explicit. Groups like Tuli Kupferberg's Fugs and Frank Zappa's Mothers of Invention used every trick in the violent avant-garde book; they were the darlings of the student revolutionaries. They preached dadaesque doctrines and used all the usual taboo-breaking techniques. Zappa, for instance, produced a publicity picture showing himself sitting maked and scrawny on a lavatory. Tuli Kupferberg proclaimed, 'Everyone who will not dance in the streets will have to be shot.' Jim Morrison and the Doors probably get as near to the Charles Manson style of millennialism as commercial pop ever could with their message 'Divine is Free', 'Break Loose', do anything so long as it is unrestrained, the road to salvation is down the dark path of daemonic excess.

In the big cities in Britain the progressive segment of youth took up multi-media experiences, organized 'Legalize pot' rallies, ate macrobiotic foods, dabbled in oriental mysticism, black and white magic, rediscovered the attractions of myth, allegory and simple fairy stories. Tolkein was the inspiration of the gentle variant (even the Who use Tolkein references; the main London venue of the avant-garde was Gandalf's Garden), and Hermann Hesse of the darker wing (one popular American group was called 'Steppenwolf', for instance). Magicians, moon goddesses, untouchable distant ladies, demon lovers and devil children cropped up as part of the new vocabulary of rock. The groups took surrealist or science fiction names, like Pink Floyd, the Soft Machine (echoes of Oldenberg's canvas medicine chest?), Led Zeppelin, Moby Grape, Jefferson Airplane, the Grateful Dead. Record sleeves and concert posters became major works of pop art, surrealist pastiche, art deco. No one was really laying the foundations for revolution but everyone was employing some variant of the motifs of zero structuring against conventional society, and everyone was busily coining new rituals of enlightened togetherness with a rock beat. Some groups like Pink Floyd and Soft Machine moved into the realm of avant-garde electronic music and were even invited to perform at the Albert Hall and the Round House. But as Fowler's Birmingham skinhead bitterly noted, you couldn't dance to the music any more.

All this was splendid for radical students, young dons, the art schools and the real Underground, but how many Birmingham skinheads really appreciated free verse, or abstruse mysticism, or references to T. S. Eliot and Ezra Pound, such as Dylan indulged in? The consequence in the early seventies was a revival of fifties rock 'n' roll and the skinheads' acceptance of reggae, the West Indian heavy beat style, as the only way back to simplicity and music you could dance to. The old men of the fifties got a new lease of life, particularly Elvis and Chuck Berry, while new groups tried out a fifties sound. Films and musicals of fifties rock 'n' roll began to appear and even some of the avant-garde began to dig back to the 'classics', partly as 'camp' and partly because the de-structuring tactics had gone so far as to become self-defeating. It is interesting to note that just as hippiedom produced a counter-trend in the Jesus people, so the appearance of Jesus rock in the late sixties is a minor but parallel reaction in pop. In part it is the backlash of the lower middle classes, in part the pursuit of 'camp' by the progressives and in part the reinstatement of the familiar religious tradition into the pot-pourri of items in the eclectic jumble of motifs: if Jesus can figure as the James Dean of the first century, even he may be admitted to the pantheon of outsider heroes. Dylan's much publicized conversion to Christianity in 1979 was perhaps the most spectacular validation of that old tradition.

The 1970s have seen all the same ingredients in the mixture as before. In the quarter-century of rock's history the medium had already discovered all the available techniques for expressing symbolic liminality through motifs of anti-structure which could then be deployed in rituals of age-specific communitas. The seventies added nothing new to the vocabulary but it has been re-used in some interesting ways. Here we need to consider three particularly characteristic processes. The first is the break-up of the market into different publics organized on all the usual principles of social differentiation of age, sex, class, education and region. Of these, social class and age are the most important. The second process is that of institutionalization and expropriation by the wider structures of society. The third process derives from the self-defeating nature of anti-structural symbols. All three processes are interdependent but for the sake of descriptive clarity it will be best to discuss them separately.

First, let us consider the splitting up of the rock world after the brief period of near-classless communitas which characterized the Beatles' middle period. A number of recent studies have shown distinctive patterns of class and regional variations in musical preferences: class of destination as indicated by educational level is more important than class of origin in this respect. Indeed, pop journalism in the seventies has worked on the unquestioned assumption that, crudely, proles and students like different kinds of rock. I will quote only one study here to give a general indication of the broad class differences in taste. Graham Murdock and Robin McCron studied a cross-section of teenagers in Midlands schools in the early seventies. They found a very clear distinction between the preferences of sixth-formers destined for (and normally from) the middle classes, and those of early leavers, the working-class segment. Each group despised the other and its music. The sixth-formers described the early leavers as 'CSE cretins' or 'stupid skins', and identified themselves and those who liked the same progressive rock as 'people who listen deeply to records and think about them' or 'people who are really into music and not just liking it because their friends do' − a personalistic and individualistic ideal. The early leavers described the progressive fans as 'weirdos', 'freaks' and 'scoobies', and saw themselves as 'people with a bit of taste', 'people who like to dance', 'people who are in with the crowd'.[25]

The terminology of Us and Them varies with place and time, but the general pattern repeats itself: Willis, Frith, and Sugarman[26] have all documented the phenomenon. It is the reason for the sectarian-style quarrels among pop *afficionados* as to which groups deserve precisely which label − rock, soul, heavy metal, rhythm and blues, progressive, new wave, and so on. The particular performers who find favour with different class publics also change over time. The working class of the late sixties took up re-issued versions of early fifties' rock 'n' roll, updated fifties rock with more powerful amplification (Status Quo, Sweet) or a harsh amateurism which reasserted the old dream that any working-class kid could do it if he had the chance (Deep Purple, Eddie and the Hotrods, Black Sabbath). They flirted later with the aggressiveness of David Bowie, perhaps as much for his chauvinistic, 'fascist' pronouncements as for his music. While it was still in its earliest phase many of them moved on to the latest stylization of the lumpenproletarian style, punk rock or new wave (journalistically labelled 'dole queue rock')[27] with its Nazi insignia, the paper clips and safety pins through the ears, hennaed hair and brothel make-up for the girls, and carefully tattered clothing for the boys. It looked extravagant, its names sounded menacing (Stranglers, Sex Pistols, The Damned), and musically it sounded exactly like 1953 with a bit of extra obscenity and a synthesizer to add to the guitars. Above all, however, British working-class adolescents adopted 'black' beat music, first reggae and then soul, perhaps because it was 'outsider' music but particularly because they could dance to it. One 'soul chord' and a heavy repetitive beat is virtually all you need. The northern working-class disco-club circuit in particular has become the heartland of soul music.[28]

The middle-class and student populations have their own favoured styles and continue to patronize the progressive political and avant-garde music of the late sixties. They prefer to listen to serious rock, not to dance to it. Bob Dylan, for example, has an apparently permanent market here and was a runaway success in his 1978 London concerts. But the middle-class end of the rock world is a very slippery customer. Middle-class rock fans tend to maraud across the ethnic and class boundaries to seek out the 'authentic' reggae, soul, punk and gay performers while despising the plastic imitations which seem to satisfy the mass market. The 'committed' rock adept will accept only genuine, not managed, charisma, though it is often hard to tell the difference.

The difficulty in generalizing about which groups and styles are favoured by different publics is partly a consequence of the speed of change. Styles are born, matured and passed on up and down the age and class hierarchy all the time. Moreover, the wheel turns ever faster as pop entrenches itself in the media of instant communication. After all in the fifties few young people had their own private record players or radios or even a family television set. Today most adolescents have access not only to family radio, TV and hi-fi, but will own private transistors, car radios, tape recorders and stereo or quadrophonic record players. So styles are able to travel very fast. A performer initially adopted by one public may be dropped by his original fans when they find some despised out-group sharing their taste (Slade; T. Rex; Rod Stewart; 10CC – the process is virtually universal). And too much commercial success is almost certain to alienate the intellectual fans.

The problem is not only one of class and educational differences; it is just as much a generational one. Indeed, Simon Frith shows that age differences are much easier to document, because more generalized, than the class differences. Styles filter very fast down into the child pop market. By 1970 *Top of the Pops*, the BBC programme, was virtually children's television.

Nothing illustrates these processes more clearly than the brief history of punk, which as I have already hinted is a vastly accelerated chronology of rock itself. The term punk really only surfaced in 1975–6 but within a year all the rock magazines were featuring regular obituary articles arguing that punk was dead. It seems to have begun life in a few obscure London clubs with a largely working-class clientele, and in its beginnings it may have been an authentic backlash of the lumpenproletariat re-creating simple beat, music that needed no special skills, and spitting out both the general alienation of the unemployed and the *machismo* and chauvinistic attitudes native to many lower-working-class milieux (after all, we are only one brief generation on from the skinheads). The middle classes invaded it very early, scenting a new, raw, non-commercial, underdog authenticity here. The typical pedigree of the punk managers and promoters now seems to be the old art school and/or public school pattern and many of them are the not-so-young rock entrepreneurs of the late sixties wearing new hats: Malcolm McLaren, manager of the now defunct Sex Pistols, is a typical rather than a maverick case.[29]

Just as it did in the sixties, the take-over of the bohemian middle class turns lumpen crudities into sophisticated subtlety. Simple if violent taboo breaking gives way to camp double-takers and all the usual apparatus of anarchic anti-structure derived from the avant-garde arts, vaudeville and the rest. Surrealism, Dada and pop art are easily detected as direct influences on dress, self-presentation, lyrics and music. For instance, Poly Styrene of X-Ray Spex is a kind of rock Andy Warhol ambiguously celebrating a world of plastic day-glo; the members of the Clash are ex-art students explicitly playing with the old apparatus of Surrealism; and so on.

If 1967 was the year of peace and love (*passé* now because it has been done before), then 1977 has to be the year of hate (symbolic inversion and simple binary oppositions again). Both will stand for the liminal freedom of the young against all odds, of course. The fascist insignia which in 1976 had the student far left screaming that punk was just the musical face of the National Front have to be re-interpreted. They are now seen as a clever double-take, just breaking the taboos of the 'square' old guilty adult world. So in 1978 we had festivals of Punk Against Racism in the London parks. Nobody knows any more whether punk was or is 'really' sexist or racist, and the power of its over-exposed symbols rests precisely on that ambiguity. It can be all things to all classes – the embodiment of everything that rockers and skins stood for in their time, for the tribal working class, and simultaneously the latest version of protest, authenticity and anarchic self-hood for the bohemian radicals. Yet that very ambiguity also lends it a certain irony and provisionality.

In the course of this development it becomes ever more difficult to differentiate punk or new wave from any other kind of rock. It loses its early crudity as performers re-invent (or dare to remember) more complex musical techniques which have already been tried in the past. A group like Ian Dury and the Blockheads is a superb example of all this. The music is complex, powerful, clever and deceptively simple to listen to. The lyrics are witty, and the performance is professional in every sense. Dury (another art school graduate) is the antithesis of the glamour image (useful anti-structure there): he is pushing forty and crippled. He is a master of double-take and of carefully calculated taboo breaking. He creates a most effective image of the lumpen 'blockhead' through an intelligent and subtle musicianship and skilful theatre craft. It is the old story: genuine talentless crudity is less effective than clever artifice.

A similar twist has occurred in punk journalism. A whole new cult has
grown up devoted to castigating punk for having sold its pure crude soul for
mere fame and fortune. The high priest and priestess of the cult, Tony
Parsons and Julie Burchill, may well be totally sincere but they make a good
living out of it. In fact they have even become quasi-stars themselves on the
basis of their weekly jerimaiads. If punk has revealed nothing new it has
effectively demonstrated the permanent marketability of colourful disillusion.

Now, all this makes boundary maintenance increasingly difficult for each
rock generation. Nothing remains exclusive for long, not even the cultural
coinage of teenage liminality. And it is not only the generational boundaries
within youth culture which are hard to defend but the broader boundary
between youth and adult worlds. Within six months of punk taking on the
role of current folk devil, haute couture was copying punk hair styles, make
up and clothes for the international jet set. Rock styles move up the age
ladder too and into the world of adult popular entertainment. Smoothed and
sweetened variants of rock crop up in TV and theatre variety shows, the
Eurovision Song Contest and the like. Like denim, pop has become ubiquitous: music for housewives and air travellers.

The adult intelligentsia takes its toll too. While show biz incorporates pop
at one end, the avant-garde opens its arms at the other to expropriate the
vitality of youth's special medium. Jagger appears in films.[30] Ken Russell
takes Pete Townshend's 'rock opera', *Tommy*, and makes it into a film, thus
putting the Who at the end of a line which includes Elgar, Richard Strauss,
Mahler and Tchaikowsky. He then caps it with an even wilder pop art
extravaganza in *Lisztomania*, the life of Liszt, Wagner, and the Hitler
regime couched in a rock idiom and again featuring the Who, this time with
Ringo Starr. The Göthenburg Ballet dances to music by Emerson, Lake and
Palmer. Rick Wakeman boasts that his music will figure in public exams
within a decade. Leonard Bernstein plays the Beatles with a full symphony
orchestra.

Nor is this expropriation a one-way process. Rock sends out its tentacles
and draws in material from wherever it can: its devotion to the cause of
boundary violation results in an indiscriminate eclecticism. So all the
resources of both popular and elite culture can be ransacked. Allusions to
media idols from Chaplin to Monroe; internal quotations from earlier rock
styles, from despised ragtime, Tin Pan Alley and the music hall as well as
the normatively preferred jazz and blues. The music quotes too from Bach,
grand opera and even the odd hymn tune. Van Gogh joins Christ and every
jilted adolescent among the hero figures of the pop lyric. Record sleeves
recall cubism, Dada, Picasso, French Impressionism, just about everything.
At least three current record sleeves use Magritte's surrealist *Portrait of Mr
James* as their model. Emerson, Lake and Palmer present themselves as

three Renaissance angels on one of their record sleeves (*Trilogy*). Queen, among others, use falsetto and counter-tenor effects to invoke early ecclesiastical music and the operatic *castrato* sound. Poets ancient and modern are cited, plagiarized and copied.

The medium is so voracious for new material, then, that it constantly compromises its own exclusiveness and leaves only a very weakened boundary between its sacred self and the profane outside world. If a boundary is violated often enough, it ceases to be a boundary, and then its violation can no longer act as a symbol of anti-structure. One interesting symptom of this can be found in recent rock journalism. Rock has become obsessed with its own history. In the last three years or so radio, TV and magazines in Britain have built up the genealogical table of rock: Radio 1 in England spent six months on the history of the blues as one of the roots of rock, and in Spring 1977 ITV ran a six-part serial history of popular music which also appears in book form.[31] The main rock magazines and some of the Sunday newspaper colour supplements have issued photographic summaries of the development of rock. There are rock encyclopaedias and archives of rock records. All this attests to the institutionalization of the phenomenon: it has been enshrined and routinized in official documents. Yet it began as the medium of instant expressiveness. George Melly, when he tried to define pop as late as 1970, looked to its fleeting and impermanent nature for its essence: the moment is always more liminal than the monument. He wrote:

|pop| is sensitive to change, indeed it could be said that it is sensitive to nothing else. ... It draws no conclusions. It makes no comments. It proposes no solutions. It admits to neither past nor future, not even its own.[32]

Nevertheless, the most recent books on the subject are specifically concerned to trace the roots of rock; to deny the newness of what happened in the early fifties and to stress the continuous nature of the tradition that produced contemporary rock.

This discovery of the ancestry and inheritance of rock is related to a number of phenomena. We have already seen it as in part the consequence of the eclecticism of pop which breaks down its own exclusiveness. But it is also partly attributable to the limited and self-defeating nature of the symbols of anti-structure, especially when they have to use institutions as vehicles of expression. It is important at this point to recall the dependence of anti-structure upon structure for its own meaning and intelligibility. Yet we have seen that structured *societas* (adult mass culture, elite culture, child culture) constantly shifts to adopt the precious symbols of pop liminality. This forces rock into ever more extreme gestures of taboo and boundary violation in order to insist on its special identity. But its identity rests on institutional as well as symbolic foundations, and the institutional base of pop is big business. The entrepreneurs of the pop world are for the most part a quite distinct group from the performers and the youthful consumers. Many of the early ones in Britain were astute public school boys who took to managing the inexperienced working-class stars of the first fifties boom. The entrepreneurs as we have said are in the business to make money and are not in it as missionaries of existential liminality. They co-operate easily with the managers and promoters of popular culture in films, television, radio and the clothing and cosmetics trades, and indeed often use a successful toe-hold in rock to diversify their own business interests in just these directions. The Sex Pistols may have been the latest word in angry, oppositional rock in Jubilee year, but their manager, Malcolm McLaren, an ex-art student, ran a profitable line in selling the mandatory punk uniform in his special boutique. He was quick to turn the murder of Nancy Spungeon and the arrest and subsequent suicide of Sid Vicious to good commercial advantage, breaking all previous British records in tastelessness with his special shirts mourning Nancy and his coffin posters of Sid. The example is extreme but not untypical: all publicity is good publicity, provided it sells products.

Institutional processes also accelerate a development which is inherent in the nature of symbols of anti-structure themselves. I have referred to it in an earlier chapter in Kenneth Burke's term the 'principle of entelechy' and in Arthur Koestler's concept of the 'principle of infolding': once all the main features of a style have been developed it naturally moves into more extreme and emphatic versions of itself until it exhausts its own logic and provokes the introduction of a counter-style. Some such process has surely happened time and again in rock music. We have already seen the way in which excesses of anti-structure in the late sixties provoked a return to simpler rock styles, a kind of re-primitivization exactly parallel to the movements in the visual arts discussed in chapter 5. A more recent example is the return of complex choreography complete with instruction manuals and disco dance studios after a decade or more which has exhausted the style of extreme informality and improvisation in rock dancing. The new style has the added advantage of providing a counter-pole to punk unmannerliness. The Stigwood/Travolta films *Saturday Night Fever* and *Grease* have been crucial in popularizing these new fashions of neo-formality and standardized forms which disco dancing now entails.

We noted above that the most powerful symbols in any cultural vocabulary tend to cluster around sex, violence and mysticism. In the case of youth culture one must add authority and control as the other obvious boundary markers between the young and the adult worlds. So gestures flouting authority and celebrating hedonism are also bound to figure centrally in the symbols of anti-structure. But there is a limit to what can be done with these symbols without being self-defeating. Take the theme of male sexuality which symbolically focuses sex, violence and authority in one economical set of gestures. The early white stars, with a few notable exceptions like Jerry Lee Lewis, tended to combine these gestures with their own opposite – the boy-next-door image. Rock history has prised apart the two halves of this polarity, at least as far as public image goes. The demon-lover image has been pushed to ever more extreme expressions. The sexual aggressiveness of Presley in the fifties looks strangely 'classical' and indirect if one compares it with say Jim Morrison in the sixties or Alice Cooper or David Bowie in the seventies. Cooper and Bowie represent different but equally important evolutions of the principle of breaking the sex/violence/authority taboos. Alice Cooper features songs celebrating mass riots, child murder and necrophilia (though his greatest hit was a fifties' formula song beginning 'School's out, forever!'). He has burst bladders of

The body-symbolism of anti-structure pushed to its show-biz extreme: threat and menace evaporate in the camp giggle. Alice Cooper was an early seventies perpetrator of theatrical outrage with songs and a stage act based on carnage, riots and necrophilia.

blood in a montage of baby slaughter, and has thrown the warm, twitching bodies of headless chickens at his audience. Bowie takes a different route to liminality. He is ostentatiously androgynous (unisex or multi-sex) and at different times has played with imagery of fascist violence and science fiction mutation.

In a minor way the representation of female sexuality has undergone a similar development, with aggressiveness and role ambiguity becoming marginally more noticeable. Yet pop performers remain predominantly male and images of sexuality are overwhelmingly masculine and narcissistic as McRobbie and Garber show.[33] Now the process of exaggeration can become self-defeating in two senses. If it is pushed far enough the sense of menace evaporates in a giggle and becomes the *Grand Guignol* of the camp horror film. Alice Cooper and his various imitators (like Wizard or Kiss) often tip over into the comic, and therefore become unthreatening. It is also self-defeating because the moment some new symbol of, say, sexual sadism is coined it is instantly 'hyped' as the rock trade puts it, that is, oversold by promotion and advertising, disc jockeys and reporters. Then it is copied by a host of imitators – as Bowie is followed by Roxy Music, Iggy Pop and others – and passed on down the market. And finally it is laundered for child and adult consumers and the rock innovators are left to think up some new gimmick to carry the message of anti-structure.

A particularly nice example of what happens when the symbolism of anti-structure is exaggerated to the ultimate degree has been furnished by a late seventies cult in some American university cities. The film of *The Rocky Horror Show* – itself an example of the comic/'camp' *Grand Guignol* which lies just beyond the serious threat and menace – has become an object of regular pilgrimage. Audiences return again and again to take part in a collective comedy which combines slapstick and Surrealism in a new and *wholly predictable* ceremony of group togetherness. When a girl in the film gets out of her car in the rain and covers her head with newspaper one half of the audience copies her while the other half squirts water pistols.

Rising shakily from the dinner table (which balances on a glass-topped casket containing Meatloaf's deep-frozen *membra disjecta*), Tim Curry as the predictably evil Transylvanian transvestite, Dr Frank N. Furter proposes a toast, whereupon the air is filled with slices of toasted bread frisbee-ing in rococo trajectories across the screen.[34]

Rayner Banham comments that the audience is

out-smarting even smarty-pants Richard O'Brien who must have set out to do just this sort of thing himself when he devised the original stage show, but couldn't have seen just how very much further the children of Leslie Fiedler, Tom Wolfe, Bevis Hillier and Anthony Haden-Guest could carry the joke.[35]

So the last word in crude/sophisticated anarchy simply turns into the purest form of group ritual, strongly reminiscent of the American fraternities or English rag days of the 'square' old 1950s.

Even the drive to explicitness of expression in rock music can be inherently self-defeating. Obscenity probably has less impact in the mid-1970s than did the innuendo or the ambiguous body movements of earlier periods. Townshend's 'Why don't you f-f-f-fade away' at the end of 'My Generation' was far more powerful than any number of completed four letter words. The stuttered 'f-f-' is a perfect case of Richard Meltzer's 'unknown tongue'. And when the Sex Pistols proclaimed in 1977 that they believed in sex without love the public could only sigh wearily and feel they had heard it all before. Or they could well decide, as many clearly did, that if that was what it is all about, they might as well go back to the classics: Elvis and Chuck Berry had said it all, and more economically.

Paradoxically then, the very speed of change is beginning to have the same immortalizing effect on rock as it has had on the products of the Walt Disney studios: *Bambi* can be reissued every few years to a new generation of children. And those same children a few years on can rediscover the Beatles. The fact that a film based on their *Sergeant Pepper* album could be a commercial proposition in 1978 bears witness to this.[36] The continuing success of a few super-groups who started in the early sixties (the Stones and the remnants of the Who) is part of the same phenomenon. So, although the medium may have left itself nowhere new to go, it can re-tread the same ground innumerable times.

This brings me to the final point, which in a sense is the very first point of the argument. Symbols have the primary function of orienting us to our world. It is true that rock elaborates the liminal moment – the rave-up, the emotional heights and depths of love and despair, egoism and isolation – but it also rests on images of the taken-for-granted world. It holds up a mirror to the urban street – to cars and clothes, to friendship and sexuality, to play (and occasionally work), to landscape and townscape and to the shared values and assumptions of classes, genders races and regions. It is one of the major modern repositories of myth – of heroes, legends, ballads, stories and minstrelsy – which have always served to heighten and express the nature of social arrangements, to embody models, to exhort and to warn us. Greil Marcus offers a brilliant analysis of just this aspect of the way in which American rock communicates and helps to perpetuate certain key images of American society.[37] Though it has not been my primary concern in this chapter, it would leave an unbalanced account if I failed to emphasize now those important aspects of rock which reinforce cultural continuity and which by giving meaning and significance to the ordinary contours of life come down on the side of order in the order/disorder dichotomy.

Of all the features of social order which rock organizes, mediates and reflects, sexuality is probably the most important single element. I have said a great deal about sexuality, as a powerful metaphor of liminality, but sexuality is also related to gender roles and rock plays a major part in this role socialization. Most young people today discover their own sexuality in and through rock music. The symbolism of rock parallels the praxis of puberty as the young translate theoretical knowledge into experiential understanding, as they try on emotions and roles both vicariously and for real. On the whole rock music has always tended to reinforce gender differences: to paraphrase Simon Frith and Angela McRobbie from a conference presentation,[38] 'cock rock' is for (and by) males (for example, Thin Lizzie); romantic love for females and teenyboppers (say, David Cassidy). Even the counter-cultural rock of the late sixties was more about mother goddesses than about sexual equality. The dichotomy may be getting less sharp at present but the process is very slow. If there *is* a change, it is coming by two routes. On the one hand, a few female rock performers are taking on the sexual aggression of the 'cock rock' tradition (examples are Millie Jackson, Patti Smith, the Slits) and using punk or women's liberation shock tactics which are often strongly reminiscent of the toughest early blues queens like Ma Rainey. On the other hand, the male performer seems very reluctant to renounce raw, male aggressive sexuality since it is such a central weapon in the taboo-breaking armoury of rock symbolism. Only when the mainstream rock tradition begins to parody or invert male machismo as a taboo violation *internal* to the rock medium can any real convergence of sex roles begin to be expressed. As yet there is little sign of this, except in the 'camp' wing of rock, although gay and punk rock may well experiment more on these lines (for example, the Tom Robinson Band). Meanwhile the central paradox of rock is that it uses its most precious symbol of liminality, that is overt sexuality, to reproduce and reinforce the sexual role differentiation of the wider society, and in particular the rigid pattern of the lower working class.

Rock music then, like all cultural media, is ultimately revealed as Janus-faced: it affirms order and meaning, reinforces conventional roles and simultaneously sacralizes the liminal symbolism of disorder. Its power rests not in one rather than the other half of this paradox but in the combination of the two functions. The fact that rock is play, leisure time self-expression for the kids, does not make it trivial. Human beings persistently experience the frivolous and the profound, the ephemeral and the elemental, in the *same* activities. This is as true of rock music as of sex itself, and it is this fact which renders it such a powerful medium of cultural communication in contemporary society. It has certainly acted as the single most important vehicle for the spread of the hedonistic messages of the Expressive Revolution, passing them up and down the age and class hierarchies in ways which have become so normal that we no longer even notice the radical nature of the change which has occurred in our cultural presuppositions over these last three decades.

CHAPTER 9

The Expressive Professions I

RADICAL PEDAGOGUES, THERAPEUTIC PASTORS AND CARING POLICEMEN

Seeking for a return blow [Herr Settenbrini] left the enemy time for a further onslaught upon the classical ideal in education, the rhetorical and literary spirit which characterized the whole of the European educational system and its splenetic partisanship of the formal and grammatical, which was nothing else than an accessory to the interests of bourgeois class supremacy and had long been an object of ridicule to the people. . . .

. . . [T]he literary person, true son of humanism and bourgeoisiedom, could always, certainly, read and write – whereas the noble, the soldier and the people never could, or barely – but he could do and understand nothing else in all the wide world, being nothing but a Latinistic windbag, who had power over language, but left life to people who were fit for it.

Thomas Mann: from *The Magic Mountain*

An educational system which still conceives itself as a child of the age of enlightenment, with criticism as its chosen medium of instruction, the liberation and cult of the ego, the solvent of forms of life which are absolutely fixed – such a system may still, for a time, reap an empty rhetorical advantage, but its reactionary character is, to the initiated, clear beyond any doubt. All educational organizations worthy of the name have always recognized what must be the ultimate and significant principle in pedagogy: namely the absolute mandate, the iron bond, discipline, sacrifice, the renunciation of the ego, the curbing of the personality. And lastly it is an unloving miscomprehension of youth to believe that it finds its pleasure in freedom: its deepest pleasure lies in obedience.

Thomas Mann: from *The Magic Mountain*

I see the Church, even as she is today, secularized and reduced to the bourgeois, a citadel of order, an institution for objective disciplining, canalizing, banking-up of the religious life, which without her would fall victim to subjectivist demoralization, to a chaos of divine and daemonic powers, to a world of fantastic uncanniness, an ocean of daemony. To separate Church and religion means to give up separating religion from madness.

Thomas Mann: from *Doctor Faustus*

Believe me barbarism even has more grasp of theology than has a culture fallen away from cult, which even in the religious has seen only culture, only the humane, never excess, paradox, the mystic passion, the utterly unbourgeois ordeal. But I hope you do not marvel that 'The Great Adversary' speaks to you of religion. Gog's nails! Who else, I should like to know, is to speak of it today? Surely not the liberal theologian! After all, I am by now its sole custodian! In whom will you recognize theological existence if not in me? And who can lead a theological existence without me? The religious is certainly my line: as certainly as it is not the line of bourgeois culture. Since culture fell away from the cult and made a cult of itself, it has become nothing else than a falling away; and all the world after a mere five hundred years is as sick and tired of it as though, salva venia, *they had ladled it in with cooking-spoons.*

Thomas Mann: from *Doctor Faustus*

Most of the work in distributing the principles of expressive anti-structure was achieved by youth culture and rock music. Their effectiveness in this task is nicely summarized by the American car-sticker and tee-shirt slogan from which chapter 7 borrowed its title: 'Insanity is hereditary – you get it from your kids.' Surrealism as humour, as advertising gimmick, as sartorial style, the 'egalitarian' manners of informality and immediate intimacy, the apparent disdain for authority, and above all the careful cultivation of unashamed and guilt-free sexuality, all went to make up a culture which was passed backwards through the generational hierarchy. Folk devils had transmuted into arbiters of taste. Of course, both youth culture and rock music were operating in purely expressive areas of life and therefore were able to witness to the cult of self-expressive disarray in its most highly developed and uncompromised form. After all, they were just leisure time pursuits, and as such were protected from too much encroachment by the dismal requirements of utility and instrumentality. But there was another important sphere in which this cultural revolution made an almost equally massive, but this time more equivocal, impact. This was the area of the vastly expanded service professions, that disputed ground in which the expressive and the instrumental vie for supremacy. Above all it was in the now enormous education industry and the so-called 'caring' professions like social work that the new imperatives found most resonance.

I now want to examine the form which the Expressive Revolution took in these spheres. The general argument is that up to the mid-1970s, all the expressive professions display powerful movements of an anti-structural kind. In each case, however, the problems which lie in the self-defeating logic of pure anti-structure are thrown into even sharper relief in the service professions than in the cases we have already examined. In part this is caused by the admixture of important elements of utility and instrumentality in the activity concerned – that awkward 'But what does it *achieve?*' These problems lead to the re-discovery of the importance of structure and control even as a *prerequisite of self-expression*, let alone as the precondition of complex skills. A complicating factor in all cases is the process of professionalization, especially when applied to problems of status uncertainty. By the early 1980s the net result has been a routinization and institutionalization of strong expressive imperatives in these professional activities, but something which stops far short of the goal of universal liminality.

The long duel between Thomas Mann's two pedagogues, Settembrini and Naphta, for the mind and soul of Hans Castrop constitutes a fictional summary of the paradoxes and conflicts which infest the modern world and its educational institutions and which were brought to one of their periodic climaxes by the counter-culture of the 1960s.

In fact we need to see Settembrini and Naphta as the two halves of the polarity we have regularly encountered in this exploration. Settembrini's humanistic tradition, despite its deep reverence for rationality, was, as his rival rightly charged, the source of 'the liberation and cult of the ego, the solvent of forms that are absolutely fixed'. In short, it was the pedagogy of anti-structure. Naphta's romantic idealism was the other liminal thrust: it was collectivist, it stood for communitas, for values which transcend cold, calculating rationality, for the experiential, authentic knowledge of the 'folk' as against mere book knowledge. The first leads to the cult of self and the second to the pedagogy of collective terror.

Both strands have a long history of coexistence but had been held back from their own extreme logics by a framework of classical structure and by the overarching imperative of reason. The romantic counter-culture of the 1960s attacked these classic elements of form and found reason compromised by its bourgeois and instrumental connotations. In assaulting the restraining frame they thus freed egoistic individualism to pursue anarchic subjectivity and let loose romantic idealism to assert the superiority of collective being over disciplined ratiocination. Knowledge transmuted from the objective to the subjective mode.

What is particularly significant, however, in Mann's treatment of the conflict is his unequivocal attribution of the cult of the Self to Settembrini's tradition of classical humanism. In short, all those precious gestures of liberating anti-structure *are a natural product of the pedagogy of the bourgeoisie.* It is a point all too easily overlooked if one concentrates only on the other characteristics which Naphta attributes to bourgeois education, that is its 'formal and grammatical' nature. The student revolutionaries of 1968 saw the gestures of symbolic anti-structure with which they attacked that 'formal and grammatical' base of education as inherently revolutionary. Of course, they were nothing of the kind. Their origins, like those of the students who wielded them, lay in the tradition of privileged classical humanism. The educational axioms of the counter-culture were simply logical extensions of principles which had long been enshrined in elite education in Europe. That tradition was composed of mixed strands of Classical humanism and Romantic individualism, and although Naphta calls it 'bourgeois', in fact, it also retained a good deal of the patrician about it. Indeed, it was its elite location which allowed it to value the expressive above the instrumental – a luxury which the 'people' can seldom afford.

In the late 1960s, the educational institutions of Britain, along with the rest of the Western world, were subject to an onslaught by the champions of expressive anti-structure, starting in the universities and spreading outwards and downwards through the system. The active crusaders were a small (and largely bourgeois) minority but the reverberations of the movement spread wide. The counter-culture by no means overwhelmed the education system but it did produce shifts in policy and practice. It is an equivocal legacy, however. The self-defeating consequences of pure, Romantic anti-structure were not immediately evident, although some of the more extreme experiments still stand as cautionary examples. By the mid-1970s educational research, policy, and practice had slowly re-discovered, or perhaps one should say re-emphasized, the importance of rule and structure even though the system will perhaps never be quite so 'formal and grammatical' again. Much the same process has occurred in the therapeutic professions – which are themselves based on a species of pedagogy, of course – and for similar reasons.

Religion, by contrast, is a very different matter: one might almost consider it the reverse case. Mann puts the argument with mangificent cogency in *Doctor Faustus*. If culture embodies a society's knowledge and practices, its recipe for reducing chaos to order, then religion in its very essence bursts the bonds and bounds of order. Above all other human activities, religion is the pursuit of the transcendent possibility, of that which escapes the confines of coded meaning, of rules and order. Religion addresses itself to the lurking irrealities, the jungle of alternative possibilities and meanings, to the source of ecstatic disorder. The churches have a tricky double-function here. They haul back the transcendent possibility from the dangerous and disordering chaos beyond the bounded *nomos*, and confine it within a framed, sacred space, in beliefs and practices which reduce to order that which essentially confounds order. The transcendent then acts as the sacred legitimation of a society's particular system of order and rule. At the same time, however, it enshrines in its symbolic representations, the memory and reminder of that transcendent possibility. It is thus a permanent incitement to the pursuit of the impossible, to the heroic alternative, to the release of the 'chaos of divine and daemonic powers ... a world of fantastic uncanniness, an ocean of daemony'. Thus, as Adrian Leverkühn argued against his young theological confrères, even when 'secularized and reduced to the bourgeois', the Church is still an indispensable source of 'objective disciplining', and of an order which keeps at bay the chaotic daemony and unrestrained experimentation in the transcendent possibility which would otherwise arise.

The second quotation from *Doctor Faustus* is part of the Devil's seduction speech. Only Lucifer remains to represent the transcendent possibility because bourgeois society has reduced religion to mere culture: 'only the humane, never excess, paradox, the mystic passion, the utterly unbourgeois ordeal'. 'Secularization and the reduction to the bourgeois' have obscured the true *raison d'être* of religion, and left the empty husk of institutions which are concerned *only* with the maintenance of order. What else, then, can truly represent the theological but the Devil and barbarism? If bureaucratized religious institutions stand for order, reason, and control, then the reassertion of the transcendent possibility can *only* take a black, negative, daemonic form. In the age of the 'liberal theologian', the last place anyone will dream of looking for religion is the Church.

The counter-culture certainly listened to that persuasive half-truth which Mann puts in the mouth of the 'Great Adversary'. In general, they grasped at the transcendent possibility via oriental religions, simply ignoring the home-grown Judaeo-Christian tradition, and only rediscovering its mystical and ecstatic potential in the mid-1970s. Many inside the conventional churches listened too to the charge which represented the churches as empty husks with the religious spirit evacuated from them. What they forgot was the other half of the truth which Auden puts with force and clarity in a discussion of the Protestant mystics:

An institution which makes it its professional business to keep alive the memory of the (divine and redemptive) event – otherwise later generations will be unaware that it occurred – and to assert its redemptive importance – otherwise later generations will take it as one historical event on a par with an infinite number of other historical events and devote no special attention to it – is essential. The function of the Church as an institution is not to convert – conversion is the work not of men but of the Holy Spirit – but to make conversion possible by continuing to preach its good news in words and liturgical acts. She must go on repeating herself, no matter whether her repetition be passionate or, when faith is low, lifeless and mechanical, to preserve that possibility.[1]

The Jews have always appreciated this point, but Christians and especially Protestants often lose sight of it. Of course, it is a delicate business preserving a lively balance between the direct apprehension of the transcendent and the preservation of the possibility of such a vision through symbolic and institutional forms. The religious counter-culture inside the church took two main forms, neither of which respected that tricky balance. The first form was an attack on the institutional husk (its associated risk was that it might compromise or mislay the vision enshrined in the institution). By a sad irony, many of the techniques of symbolic anti-structure inside the church had the net effect of reducing it even closer to mere 'culture', in Mann's sense, and letting yet more of the religious essence escape. This is particularly the case with 'improvements' and updatings of the historic forms of liturgy, language, and church organization which, like the 'liberal theologian', seek to render the Church more like ordinary, mundane life. The erosion of the boundary between the *Church* and the profane world thus pushes *religion* the more surely into the arms of daemony, and, as Mann's Faustus remarked, that means to 'give up the separation of religion and madness'. Indeed, quite literally so. One of the most influential views in the counter-cultural *mélange* was that of the existentialist psychiatrists, who saw in madness the only true vision in an insane world. So the radical therapists were rediscovering the ancient religious connotation of madness at the same time as many clergy were busy demolishing the distinction between the Church and the world, and, in so doing, inadvertently abandoning the religious in favour either of secular politics or of a mildly therapeutic pastoral role: 'only the humane'; no dog collars; no mystery, just good citizenship and informal mateyness. This particular style of anti-structure emanates from that strand of Protestantism which mistrusts the collective and ritual aspect of religion as 'inauthentic' and which has, as an unintended consequence, the extrusion of mystery and the reduction of religion to the ethical. Paradoxically, as Auden understood, the very mechanical repetition of ritual is inseparable from the mystery of which its re-enactments are a reminder: destroy ritual or reduce it to the banal, and you are well on the way to destroying the mystery.

The second thrust of counter-cultural anti-structure comes again from the Protestant tradition. It is the antinomianism which lies behind both Protestantism and the political Underground. As I also argued above, the antinomian option always tends to bifurcate between the logic of unrestricted anti-structure and that of the disciplined millennial sect. This proved as true of counter-cultural religion as of Underground politics. Both inside and outside the mainstream churches there has been a marked tendency for antinomianism to transmute into a sect-like exclusiveness. This is the result of two processes with which we are now thoroughly familiar. First, the antinomian crusaders, because of their certainty that they hold the ultimate truth, behave like a spiritual elite, symbolically marking off the boundaries of the chosen group from unregenerate outsiders. Then principles of belonging may come to take precedence over personal vision.

Second, excess of anti-structure as a recipe for living tends to give rise to distressing *anomie* which is not always compensated by the mystical (and sometimes drug-induced) intensity which is its positive attraction. As in the case of narcissistic self-knowledge, so purely antinomian religion may leave the precious self stranded in lonely isolation. When this happens, cults and sects which offer absolute certainty and total belonging, or even a small, structured 'life world' may be welcomed with relief. Thus the *anomie* and existential anxiety produced in the wake of hippie and drug culture, oriental mysticism, and expanded personal consciousness, left casualties ripe for the brotherly embrace of the total sect. This was the recruiting ground, in the 1970s, for Jesus Freaks, the Children of God, the Unification Church and the other movements of total commitment, which draw their membership disproportionately from the offspring of the bourgeoisie who have already tried the recipes of liberating anti-structure and found them wanting.

In order to take the argument further, it is necessary to move on to a brief institutional analysis of the service professions in the 1960s. It may then be possible to assess the impact of the Expressive Revolution on them and on the culture of control into which they all reach as part of their professional activity.

As the economy of advanced industrial society comes to rely more and more on the service sector, so it causes the manual working population to contract as a percentage of the work force and to become more homogenous while the white-collar occupations are in a state of rapid expansion. A zone of routine white-collar occupations, clerical, technical, sales and services, with low 'classness' but many objectively proletarian features, appears and merges into the lower reaches of the semi-professions and the professions which are also in a state of rapid expansion. The middle class proper can be divided on a number of axes: professional/commercial, old/new, expressive/instrumental. I have chosen to focus on education the welfare professions, and the churches because all three are part of the expanding professional and semi-professional sector which is predominantly 'expressive'. They all straddle the intermediate zone and the middle class proper, that is, they each involve a status range which extends from the quasi-proletarian lower rungs of the routine service sector up to the highest professional level of the upper bourgeoisie. The clergy are members of an old middle-class profession experiencing a sharp decline in status and relative affluence. Their recruitment increasingly depends on the lower and newer white collar stratum, and by the 1960s they can no longer be regarded as an automatically elite cadre either in terms of status or of influence, even though the Anglican Church retains an upper layer which is continuous with the old gentlemanly classes. Education is the point of major growth among the predominantly 'expressive' service segment, and the main bulk of professional educators, are the schoolteachers, roughly half of whom are the socially mobile sons and daughters of the upper working and routine white-collar classes. Most welfare professionals in terms of status and recruitment lie roughly parallel to the schoolteachers.

All three of these professional activities involve elements of the instru-mental in their activities despite having a predominantly expressive *raison d'être*, although this is less true and more complicated in the case of the churches. The covert tension between expressive and instrumental norms is part of the explanation of how each profession reacted to the counter-culture. It is very important to recognize that all three professions are, or have been, crucial elements in the processes of social and political legitima-tion and control. Historically, however, the balance has shifted between the three with the welfare agencies and education taking over many of the control and legitimation functions which were formerly invested in the church. One of the universal processes observed in all industrial societies in the twentieth century has been a tendency for the Churches to lose their monopoly control of the definition of meaning, and of legitimate knowledge; education; family law and practice; of the legitimation of power and hierarchy, and the disposition of social resources. The process of institutional differentiation has pushed the Church from the centre to the periphery of society. It is this process, as much as anything, which has eroded the status of the clergy and is inexorably reducing them to the social level of the lower service class.

At one level this process assists the Church's 'reduction to the bourgeois' because it transforms its services from a central prop of social existence to an item of voluntary individual consumption: at its lowest, this, especially in Protestant cultures, makes religion a leisure time commodity – a bit of 'culture' which has been 'ladled in with cooking-spoons' for so long that 'the world is sick and tired of it', exactly as the Devil persuaded Adrian Leverkühn. Yet the very loss of centrality and of social control functions allows the Church to re-emphasize not just its purely expressive functions but its potential for propagating the alternative vision: both its prophetic critical function and its a-social pursuit of the transcendent possibility, are released from the constraints which the power and social centrality of the Church inevitably entailed in the past. Hence the Church is a fruitful recruit-ing ground for converts to the gospel of anti-structure.[2]

Yet this is only one side of the story. Another universal process runs in quite the opposite direction: this is a tendency towards the bureaucratization of everything. With it goes not just an organizational mode but a set of criteria for judging efficiency on the analogy of a measure of 'output'. The Churches have been progressively bureaucratized, and management criteria have spread so that clergy 'efficiency' and 'productivity' become an issue. The social and the self-image of the religious professional shifts uneasily from the old models of evangelist, sacramental priest, gentleman to those culled from the contemporary economic world; ecclesiastical executive, God salesman, Church bureaucrat. The cleric and the layman look for evidences of 'success' or 'failure' and find them in measures of congregational size, busyness, participation or innovation: are we a profitable firm or not? The fundamentally disturbing religious messages of prophecy or ecstasy do not readily fit into this package and can even be a distinct embarrassment.

However, one role drawn from the modern professions, that of the pastoral therapist does have a ready appeal. If prophecy and mysticism are too strong, then ethical devotion to one's neighbours can stand as a mark of the Church's difference from the world: it can be the supreme 'caring profession'. Helping one's less fortunate brethren can represent the human (but again 'only the humane') against the anonymously bureaucratic; the (non-controversially) political against the egoist privacy and profit; self-sacrifice – and a convenient moral legitimation of the relatively declining living standards of the clergy – against a prevalent secular materialism. So, clergy learn less Greek, Latin, Hebrew, and classical theology but more social science. They become a species of semi-professional therapist with a roving brief, generic case workers for the parish with a mildly spiritual aura.

There is a further awkward paradox in the role of the Churches. The more religious institutions move to the periphery, the more religion becomes privatized: it becomes a matter of individual, personal concern rather than of public affirmation, ritual, ceremony, and social resonance. Again Protestant cultures like the British have moved further along the path of privatization than have Catholic cultures like the Spanish or the Italian, in which religion is regarded as intrinsically communal and organic. Yet at the same time, because of its history, religion is still deeply woven into the fabric of cultural identity. Even in an apparently secularized nation like Britain, where only a smallish minority of the population is involved in regular public worship and Church activities, regional, local, ethnic and sectional identities still find articulation through a residual denominational loyalty. The whole notion of belonging to the nation, of being English (or Scots or Welsh) seems inseparable from a need to claim the title Christian.[3] Again the only serious exceptions to this are the same social groups which we have seen as lodged outside the mainstream culture of boundary and control, that is the lumpenproletariat at the bottom and the bohemian intelligentsia at the top. So a nominal denominational loyalty is a routine part of the British identity. At one level, church-going may have become merely a matter of taste but at another equally important level, most members of the population do not merely feel that they belong to the Church (which they rarely visit) but that the Church belongs to them. They claim the rites of passage as rights of citizenship and see the Church, and especially the national Church, the Church of England, as part of their natural heritage much the same as the National Health Service. All this, of course, is a crucial aspect of religion's role as culture – the vehicle of order and the source of a sense of secure membership of a natural community. This aspect, however, is the one *least* palatable to the religious professionals. The clergy tend to resent their role as hapless providers of the rituals which go along with mere citizenship. They do not often like to see themselves as civil servants in the Durkheimian cause of social cohesion: hence the alacrity with which the neo-therapeutic function is often seized upon. Given the power of prevailing economic criteria and their own declining status, the clergy must insist on the fundamental usefulness and relevance of what they do, and religion-as-social-work fits that need.

This therapeutic model of the role of the clergy is perhaps the most popular because it has the merit of solving relatively painlessly, or rather of masking, the major problems of changing status and function. Yet there existed two other alternative models. The first is the prophetic role. The release of the Church from its functions of control and legitimation has enabled a significant and vocal minority to take up the cause of secular radical politics. 'Liberation theology' and the numerical dominance of Third World Christians in ecumenical organizations such as the World Council of Churches gave an impetus to this development. It slotted neatly into counter-cultural radicalism. Priests and pastors who followed this line tended to gravitate into specialist ministeries. Simultaneously there developed a Conservative Evangelical revival as a counter-blast to the radical option. In the sixties recruitment to theological colleges was heavily split between the radical and the Conservative Evangelical groups. The Conservative Evangelicals, often biblical fundamentalists and political conservatives, reasserted the specific and special nature of the religious calling in response to the radical attempts to merge the Church and the world: they were called to save souls and not to act as a species of cultural/political guerrilla movement. But both Conservative Evangelicals and radicals disliked and rejected the traditional Durkheimian function of the Church. In John Robinson's famous phrase, they wanted 'to melt the fat of tribal Christianity', thus further eroding the institution's natural community base.

The development of the welfare or caring professions displays a curious cross-over with the trajectory of the clergy. The growth of these professions, like that of education, is an example of the way in which certain of the Church's old functions (pastoral care, education) are hived off to specialist secular agencies in the process of modernization. In the case of the welfare professions there is a reverse movement from that of the Churches. They began in instrumentality and in time came to lay claim to expressive functions. Social work and associated activities began as the unequivocal agents of control. The lady bountiful and all the pioneer educators of the poor in Victorian England were representatives of religious bodies anxious to reduce to order (and, if possible, lift to salvation, though often the two were conceived of as synonymous) the unruly enclaves of the 'dangerous and perishing classes'. Certainly, there were humanitarian and religious values there too, but fundamentally and quite explicitly the social objective of the voluntary and public provision of what became social welfare services was to control deviance and bring the poor under the culture of control, preferably by getting them to internalize its rules or failing that, by imposing on them coercive and custodial policies. Thus Christian love for the poor and unfortunate consisted in introducing them to the benefits of discipline and order. It was not entirely unsuccessful, although the lumpenproletariat has always 'played the system' while rejecting its values. As time went on, this control function was overlaid by an increasing stress on the provision of resources to the needy, and the state took an ever greater hand in the matter. By the twentieth century this had produced a whole crop of new professions and semi-professions, the bulk of them financed by public funds.

In Britain the pure custodial/control function has never carried much kudos: to be a sort of social policeman is not a status-enhancing image. The mere distribution of material resources – storekeeper for the poor – is no better. Therefore as these professions developed, a tension was set up, compounded of a number of elements but manifesting itself in the playing down of the control function and the insistence on an expressive *raison d'être*. Let us examine the ingredients in this mix. The first is the tendency to routinization and bureaucratization which we noted in the Churches. The standardization of procedures, the growth of purely administrative machinery, record-keeping and so forth affects the structure of the social welfare agencies. The workers at the therapeutic coal-face are supplemented by the usual Parkinsonian swelling of the bureaucracy. A complex and initially messy, discontinuous and inconsistent set of functional and status differences in the diverse voluntary and public agencies is slowly squeezed into something more like uniformity, culminating in the professional reconstruction of the 1950s and 1960s.

At the same time, and continuous with these developments, a process of professionalization is occurring. This too is common to the whole of the new white-collar segment and is sufficiently familiar to need little rehearsal here. The new claimants to professional status have to juggle with apparently incompatible needs. A profession on the model of the old high-status occupations like law and medicine first requires a definable skill, which is usually tested by formal qualifications and monitored by a professional council of some sort. This requirement confers both status and an economically valuable capacity to control entry through the power of deciding who is and who is not a qualified member of the profession. Over an extended period low pay will become incompatible with high professional status, yet the aggressive use of industrial action to raise pay involves the risk of looking more like a trade union than a profession: this status risk is exacerbated if, as in the case of the welfare professions, a substantial segment of your recruitment is from a relatively lowly zone and is predominantly female in addition. If pay is low in part because in its early stages the profession received a hidden subsidy in the form of high status, unpaid voluntary labour, then you are tightly double-bound. Industrial militancy may finally rub away your one feeble claim to ascriptive high status, the lady bountiful ancestry.

The welfare professions had all these problems and more. An aggravating element in the status uncertainty was the fact that in the most privileged segment of the profession, that is, in psychiatric and medical social work, the social worker was an inferior ancillary to a 'real' profession – medicine, both psychiatric and physical. This in itself was one of the factors which helped to popularize the 'therapeutic' label: if you are claiming professional status, it is very helpful to have a model in an established (and heavily male) area like this on which to model yourself. The other important factor was an increasing emphasis in society itself, especially after the post-war reconstruction, on the enhancement of the quality of life as a desirable social goal and indeed one which the state could promote as a basic human right. This enabled the social welfare occupations to develop a professional rhetoric which presented them as servants in the cause of expressive enrichment and minimized, at least in public, their custodial and control functions. It provides a comfortable and uplifting self-image while also carrying the positive moral overtone which any convincing profession must have – the equivalent of the Hippocratic oath.

Despite all this, however, one difficulty remains, that of providing a precise and credible definition of the skills involved which will distinguish the 'caring professions' from voluntary meddlers, pastors, or just good neighbours. Any casual perusal of the main professional journals from the sixties onwards will confirm the point: every issue produces a crop of letters and articles which are in effect public breast-beating about the elusive 'specialness' of the profession and the difficulty of convincing the public of the fact. One characteristic attempt which is perhaps more soft rhetoric than hard definition is that of the British Association of Social Workers (BASW). The official working definition of BASW appeared on the front cover of the journal *World Medicine* in January 1978. It is printed in gothic lettering with an elaborate medieval-style arabesque around the first letter:

Social work is the purposeful and ethical application of personal skills in interpersonal relationships directed towards enhancing the personal and social functioning of an individual, family, group or neighbourhood, which necessarily involves using evidence obtained from practice to help create a social environment conducive to the well-being of all.

The expressive imperative could not be more clearly put. Nevertheless, the fact remained that most of the 'clients' of the public welfare services were involuntary: they came disproportionately from among the poor and deprived, and the status of the client has an unfortunate tendency to contaminate that of the professional. Yet serving the unfortunate can offer compensatory moral or ethical status which helps a profession to legitimate itself. Thus while one segment of the profession proclaimed that its mission was to convince the ordinary citizen of his need for professional assistance in life-enhancement, another segment developed a heavy identification with the underdog/client as a category. This latter led to movements for community action, citizens' rights, and consciousness-raising which meshed easily with certain forms of counter-cultural radicalism.

The point in a nutshell is that when the counter-culture made its first dramatic impact, the welfare professions were in a difficult and internally contradictory state. Their status, pay, recruitment and work placed them relatively low and insecurely among the established professions; their special skills were not easily defined and, for a series of reasons, their professional rhetoric was shifting away from an instrumental towards a heavily expressive justification. As in the Churches, a significant and vocal minority took up the option of political radicalism in part at least as a way out of the impasse over professional identity and as a gesture which publicly renounced the conservative, custodial/control functions.

The situation among professional educators contains many similar elements and one highly significant difference. Where social work and its sisters are raw new professions, education is a very old one. Again it is the offspring of the Church and derives from a time when clerics were the only literate profession. The point of this is that the highest stratum in education has an ascribed status with a pedigree that stretches back to Abelard and links the universities and the intellectuals with the Greeks, the Renaissance, the monastic scholars of the Middle Ages and the gentlemen scholars of the eighteenth century. In the twentieth-century era of mass education that elite segment may be popularly seen as 'bourgeois', but the tradition in which it stands has patrician and monastic elements too. In other respects, however, education shares most of the characteristics and inner contradictions of the welfare professions. Most teachers come from the same social level as the welfare professionals and their education and training run together most of the way. The problems of status and of the definition of skill are less acute, yet the same difficulty exists of an internal contradiction between diverse goals and functions, some of which are more acceptable than others, and of a permanent tension between expressive and instrumental imperatives. Educational institutions cannot escape their instrumental functions. They too are involved in custody and control and this role becomes vastly extended as societies move into the age of compulsory mass education.

They become major agents of socialization and distributors of the values and culture of order in whatever form is current in that particular society and time. They take a prominent role in social placement, both in the sense of feeding the various levels of the labour market with an appropriate input, and in the sense of distributing persons in the social and status hierarchy of the wider society. It cannot be too strongly emphasized that educational institutions are not the *source* of that hierarchy, but that they cannot help but relate to it: they may marginally redistribute persons but they can neither make nor break the stratification patterns of the society in which they operate. And finally, in directly instrumental terms, they inculcate and extend skills and knowledge some of which have direct economic and political uses.

In the course of the twentieth century educational institutions in this and other Western states have been prominently featured as the focus of political policies of social redistribution. For various complex reasons, both the social democracies and the communist states of Europe have attempted to increase first of all the formal availability of education and second the capacity of the less privileged sections of society to make use of that provision. Part at least of the rhetoric of the development was ideological and part was instrumental – the idea that education should be seen primarily as an *economic* investment and that industrial efficiency demanded the replacement of ascriptive by achievement criteria: meritocracies were meant to be economically more profitable. It is important to remember that the vast expansion of university provision in the 1960s was justified predominantly in these terms.

The realities, however, were rather different. First, the ideal of redistribution, of equality of opportunity and of the prevalence of criteria of achievement, were soon shown to be at least partly illusory: the pattern of stratified privilege had shifted rather little between the mid-1930s and the late 1960s. It was not that *no* changes had been made – many more children from all social classes were enjoying the benefits of higher education – but rather that the *relative* life chances of the family of an unskilled worker were still much inferior to those of the families of the bourgeoisie. Crudely, the working-class child remained far less likely to do well in education than his middle-class contemporary, even when both had the same measured intelligence quotient. The reasons for this are too complex to discuss here and would stray too far from the argument in hand. What matters at this juncture is the fact that the teaching profession itself, particularly in view of its heavy recruitment from the educationally mobile, tended to act as an agent of the liberal or egalitarian ideology: the pronouncements of the British National Union of Teachers consistently and vividly illustrate this commitment. The teaching profession had very little incentive or inclination to stress those functions which were not merely instrumental in the sense of useful but also in the conservative sense of maintaining and reproducing the fabric of social inequality. The professional self-image therefore is pulled away from custody, control, and social reinforcement towards a stress on social 'progress', justice, and equality. Again, this has the merit of providing a high moral justification which reinforces the claim to proper professional status.

The tendency of the education profession to play down its control/legitimation functions is also, ironically, reinforced by the patrician heritage of higher education. In England in particular it has for a long time been more gentlemanly to be useless than to be useful: the expressive carries more kudos than the instrumental. The difficulty however is that the lower one lies in the stratification system, the more difficult it is to justify one's existence in purely expressive terms, and that is precisely the double-bind in which the teaching profession is caught. In Britain, more markedly than anywhere else in the modern world, high status education tends to be associated with pursuits which claim no direct utility: classical humanism has for centuries been the province of the gentleman, while knowledge useful to trade and industry has carried a lower status connotation. The nineteenth-century, self-made captains of industry created the public school system in order to convert their sons into gentlemen via Greek, Latin, manly sports, and patrician contacts. To the ambitious among the poor they offered useful knowledge in science and political economy in the Mechanics' Institutes. The dichotomy has maintained itself into the 1980s in British education; it is embedded in the binary system which keeps universities organizationally and financially separate from the polytechnics and maintains a notably different pattern of class recruitment in the two sectors. The children of the elite filter naturally into the universities, and the humanities and pure science, while the educationally mobile children of the less privileged go into the polytechnics, applied science and social science (or, if they are girls, into teacher-training).

What all this reflects is the differential status of contrasting types of knowledge. Humanistic knowledge is useless but bears status and can open the door to elite occupations, not just in the professions but in business and politics too. The cult of the gentleman-amateur is far from obsolete; it is still the natural educational route of the most powerful in the land. On the other hand, 'useful' knowledge in the applied sciences and social sciences has less status but more immediate economic and vocational relevance. The contrast is less sharp in America, France, Germany and Japan.

Within the educational system itself then, the privileged model is that of classical humanism. Certainly education is seen as offering usable skills and applicable knowledge, but its highest achievements are seen as the classical scholarship of an idealized university tradition. The academic model of disinterested humanistic learning became the benchmark against which educational 'success' or 'failure' was measured. Approximation to this apex ideal was the main coinage of what Bourdieu has called 'cultural capital'[4] and as he points out, the market value of this 'capital' is less the direct instrumental utility of its content than the status label which it carries. This elite tradition of pedagogy contains both a classical and a romantic strand of individualism. The classic strand values abstract truth above social usefulness: it enjoins the scholar to sacrifice self-interest, humanitarian considerations, social expediency and charity alike if they conflict with academic integrity. The romantic prizes knowledge for the sake of self-development and self-expression. Neither has much time for the utilitarian or instrumental *per se*. Thus the romantic, the classic and the gentlemanly elements in this elite tradition all lean away from the instrumental pole; the romantic because its goal is subjective experience and self-expression, the classic because truth comes before utility and the gentlemanly because knowledge is a form of amusement and self-satisfaction. So inside what Naphta misleadingly calls 'bourgeois' pedagogy, the true end of knowledge is more expressive than instrumental. For the elite, knowledge is a form of self-cultivation unimpaired by alien and alienating instrumentalities: it is also, paradoxically, the most marketable form of knowledge.

The privileged status of this elite pedagogy encouraged the further accentuation of the expressive imperative in education at lower levels of professional activity, first by what I have elsewhere called 'status drip',[5] which is the old trick of modelling oneself on the top layer in order to appropriate something of its status to one's own level, and second because it fitted nicely with a popular version of liberal egalitarian ideology. This was the view that education should never be alienating but ought to be based on the inner needs of the individual personality: it should be geared not to external criteria like market requirements but rather to the aim of developing as fully as possible the autonomous individual. This philosophy already shows itself in the famous phrase in the 1944 Education Act, that each child should receive the education best suited to his 'age, ability and aptitude'. It comes to full expression, however, in the Plowden Report, of which one of the most frequently quoted paragraphs (describing the ideal progressive school) includes the following: 'The school sets out deliberately to provide the right environment for children, *to allow them to be themselves* and to develop in the way and at the pace appropriate to them.'[6]

But Plowden, like my argument so far, overstates the case. The expressive imperative does not go completely unchallenged. The 'bourgeois' tradition is not confined to the kind of humanistic individualism which Naphta attributed to it, but importantly includes a school of thought which demands that education should justify itself by its economic relevance and profitability. In early modern England, the incipiently bourgeois dissenters developed scientific academies and in the nineteenth century, the intellectual spokesmen of the entrepreneurial class invented the dismal but useful sciences of political economy and social statistics. That tradition, running from Puritan dissent to bourgeois rationalism, stands powerfully alongside that of gentlemanly humanism, although it never quite stormed the commanding heights of the education system. It too can claim a certain natural affinity with a variant of the liberal/progressive ideology of popular education in that it encourages individual competition and meritocratic principles. It is an anti-romantic individualism perhaps stronger in America than it is in Britain.

Thus we see two forms of individualism in education, the meritocratic/instrumental and the romantic/expressive. The latter is strong in the arts and humanities, in the universities and the professional upper middle class (especially all the communicators). The former is the tradition by which the vast economic costs of the education industry were usually legitimated and was strong among the commercial middle class, politicians and the non-humanistic middle ranks of the teaching profession. It also found a natural home among most of the working classes who valued book learning, if they valued it at all, as the source of marketable skills and qualifications. The important, small minority of the working class which held a view of education close to that of classical humanism was Robert Roberts's self-educated and politically articulate proletarian intellectuals who valued learning for the truth, the social prophecy and the self-development which it held out to them.

This was the state of affairs on to which the counter-culture exploded. The next chapter traces its impact on these three professional areas in which the axial principles of the Expressive Revolution had already put down deep roots.

CHAPTER 10

The Expressive Professions II

CHAOS DOMESTICATED
OR
THE TAMING OF THE COUNTER-CULTURE

Dare any call Permissiveness
An educational success?
Saner those class-rooms which I sat in
Compelled to study Greek and Latin

* * *

The Book of Common Prayer *we knew*
Was that of 1662
Though with-it sermons may be well
Liturgical reforms are hell.

W. H. Auden: from 'Doggerel by a Senior Citizen' (for Robert Lederer), in
Collected Poems

It is easy to see why the universities were a natural base for the development of the counter-culture and the Expressive Revolution, and why within the universities the effect was greatest in the humanities and social sciences. The site of the elite tradition of classical humanism was, as we have seen, also the home of romantic individualism and that 'bourgeois' cult of the liberation of the ego out of which the counter-culture grew. The education system was internally torn by a (mostly implicit) struggle between expressive and instrumental imperatives. In that struggle, the gentlemanly ideal of Renaissance man and the 'bourgeois' cult of the liberated ego mostly colluded together in championing expressive imperatives while 'bourgeois' philistinism made common cause with economic and bureaucratic rationalism to fight for instrumental imperatives. The social sciences, lacking both gentlemanly validation and unequivocal usefulness, found themselves engaged in documenting and de-mystifying exactly those functions of education which were most objectionable and embarrassing to expressive norms and egalitarian principles – social and status placement, control, legitimation and the perpetuation of hierarchy. An exactly parallel situation existed in the welfare professions. There, too, the intelligentsia was busy uncovering the self-perpetuating nature of privilege and deprivation in society and unmasking the policing functions of a would-be profession whose claim to social status and ethical validation rested to a significant extent on denying or ignoring those functions in favour of a stress on therapy, social redistribution, and expressive enrichment.

In all three cases, education, social welfare and religion, the intelligentsia of the profession contained a visible and high status segment which was directly involved in the Underground exploration of expressive anti-structure in the late 1960s. Those setting the tone were the student 'revolutionaries' in education, the radical existentialist psychiatrists in the welfare services, and the liberationist radical priests in the churches. The three overlapped of course. The status-bearing connotations of expressiveness as against instrumentality helped to make the counter-cultural package attractive to parts of the lower professional and semi-professional layers, as did a sense of being ethically compromised by the conservative functions of legitimation and control. So the rhetoric and praxis of expressive anti-structure travelled down the hierarchy of all three professions through a process of 'status drip' from the top.

The familiar pattern recurs of attacks on boundary, structure, form, and limits. Institutions as such are anathematized as restrictive, bureaucratic, and dehumanizing. The distinction between professional practitioner and client is eroded: priests refuse the dog collar, nuns and monks the habit, and even the Catholic tradition of clerical celibacy is put in question; radical psychiatrists and progressive social workers abandon devices of professional distancing and become mere human beings on the same plane as the client who may even be revered as social scapegoat and sacred victim rather than being viewed as sick, deviant or inadequate; the schoolmaster wears jeans and insists on being addressed by a pet name instead of a respectful title and so on. The same bifurcation into antinomian and totalitarian variants of anti-structure is found exactly as in the Underground and youth culture: counter-cultural experiments in education, 'caring', and religion split down the middle into disintegrating anarchy or tight disciplined cells. Free schools and Free universities become cadres of ideological uniformity, radical experiments in Free therapy become rival schools of theory and praxis. The same self-defeating inner logic of pure anti-structure is found here too. Radical priests violate the boundary between Church and the world only to find that their religious vocation gets mislaid in the process. Educational radicals, seeking to avoid the condemnation of being 'Latinistic windbags' elevate experience and topicality above cerebration and abstraction, and in so doing lose their distinctive function and simultaneously undermine the claims of testable knowledge by relativizing everything and replacing the objective by the subjective mode of understanding. Social workers, determined to humanize the client as the equal of the therapist, further deny their already precarious aspiration to special knowledge and skills, thus rendering their 'professionalism' ever more suspect.

All these problems are compounded by the fact that in all three cases the appeal of expressive anti-structure is far greater among the professional practitioners than among the consumers of the service. Even in the late 1960s the mainstream culture of control was still inhabited by Church congregations and mere 'tribal' Christians, the clients of the welfare services and their neighbours, and the mass of students, pupils, and parents, who were not yet tuned in to the progressive/expressive message, even as a leisure-time style, let alone as a total way of life. Yet again, it was a question of the counter-culture removing the landmarks. The range of contradictions which this produced will perhaps be clearer if we take each of the three professional activities in turn and look briefly at the most characteristic manifestations of symbolic anti-structure and their consequences.

The so-called student revolution involved everything we have already examined in the arts, the Underground, youth and rock culture, plus some distinctive pedagogic gestures.[1] I will concentrate on the last of these. The violation of boundaries, rules, and taboos was, as ever, at the centre of the enterprise. Thus, for example, student rebels sought to eliminate the distinction between teacher and taught in all kinds of ways — by demanding an equal say in curriculum content; by either eliminating or participating in assessment; by taking control of student recruitment and staff appointments; by abolishing or invading separate staff dining and common rooms, studies and offices; by denying teachers the right of privileged access to personal information about students and colleagues. All information was to be open to all. This in common with many other demands constituted a denial of the distinction between public and private (places, information, behaviour, roles), between relevant and irrelevant (knowledge, duties). It was all of a piece with the elimination of the boundary between different subject areas (no departments, faculties, or specialisms); between cognition and feeling; between book learning and random sense impressions; between high culture and mass culture; 'taste' and 'vulgarity'; the important and the trivial; between the university and life. Thus occupying a public park 'for the people', or squatting in empty property, listening to or making music, or smoking pot, could be regarded as at least as valid as academic work in defining the student's proper activity.

Much of this involved a denial of social roles and of defensive or functional distancing techniques which traditionally protect the person from existential overload. The student radicals assiduously assaulted those particular defences with their requirements of instant and total intimacy. But my favourite illustration of the (literally) surreal lengths to which symbolic boundary denial could go took place during a student occupation at the

London School of Economics. The students not only tore down the separate 'Ladies' and 'Gentlemen' notices from the lavatories (though they did not follow Jeff Nuttall's advice and rip off the doors too), but they even painted out the distinction between the first floor and the second, between the second and the third and so on: even purely functional classifications of space had to go, just as the watches and clocks were to be discarded in order to free time. The boundaries between human beings were symbolically attacked in innumerable ways. Conventional, role-distinctive forms of address were dropped (hence, for example, the now ubiquitous 'Ms'); instant personal intimacy was claimed; the protective walls around private or vulnerable parts of the personality were indignantly destroyed. The concept of academic production as individual private property in knowledge was anathema to many radicals and gave place to the collective project.

We see the familiar seesaw which antinomian anti-structure sets in motion. While overtly individualistic, it constantly transmutes into a constrictive collectivism. Again we find the tension of coexistent anti-structure and communitas. Indeed, peer-group pressure to uniformity – of dress, speech, ideology, gesture – was one of the most striking features of the so-called student revolution. The collectivism was often deliberate, and not merely the unintended consequence of boundary destruction. As we noted earlier in the political Underground, certain selected boundaries and categories were given a new salience. A particular attack was launched on the classical academic assumption that all scholars are in a certain sense equal and alike through their common acceptance of basic humanist and rational norms which govern the pursuit of truth. This ancient egalitarian assumption met resistance on the new grounds of subjectivism, relativism and the superior moral worth of the underdog. Thus women and ethnic minorities in particular came to be treated as special ascriptive categories with their own world view, value system and self-orientated subject-matter. Women's studies, black studies and the like often explicitly deny the possibility of impartiality, objectivity, comparability and equality in scholarship. Policies of 'reverse discrimination' in favour of these disadvantaged groups have been put into practice in some parts of the educational establishment of the Western world, most notably the United States university system, and with highly controversial consequences.

In the case of the student 'revolutionaries' it is relatively easy to trace the natural logic of expressive anti-structure because there appeared a sufficient number of pure cases – Kenneth Burke's 'principle of entelechy' working itself out relatively unhampered in the rarified air at the top of the academic mountain. On the one hand there was the elaboration of the antinomian alternative, which in educational terms rejects knowledge in the objective mode (and the neo-classical pedagogy which most naturally accompanies that mode) in favour of knowledge as subjective and relative. A romantic, 'open' pedagogy based on individual feeling and a rejection of fixed sequence, of a formal hierarchy of levels of understanding and of invariant roles in the pedagogic process, is the proper partner of the experiential, subjective mode of knowledge. On the other hand, there was the pure collectivism of the millennial sect which in educational terms sees all knowledge as based in, and subordinated to, the objective interests and subjective identity of the group. Thus 'working-class knowledge', 'women's knowledge', 'West Indian knowledge', 'revolutionary knowledge', 'kids' knowledge' become absolutes for their respective groups (or rather for the pedagogic champions of such groups). They are praxis, not mere theory. They cease to be subject to 'bourgeois rationality', criticism, testability, comparability, or, importantly, to individual dissent. There is a serious strand of anti-intellectualism in both the antinomian and the collectivist version of the new knowledge. Moreover, both knowledge and pedagogy can no longer be taken for granted: we must always ask whose and which knowledge? Whose and which pedagogy? Thus a kind of *lutte des paradigms* sets in in academia. Further – and this may account for some at least of the prevalent dislike of sociology among the older disciplines – it constitutes a new intellectual imperialism which implies that sociology (or rather sociolog*ies* since the claim to 'value freedom' has been scornfully discarded) have a privileged access to the bases of all the supposedly specialist and autonomous types of knowledge.[2]

Only a small minority of students and academics were directly involved in these extreme developments of the counter-cultural logic. Most, even among the activists, were merely caught up in piecemeal expressions of peer-group effervescence and solidarity in which the exact pretext for action was relatively unimportant and frequently a product of, rather than the inspiration for, the action. The Academic Carnival was as much as anything a manifestation of tribal solidarity among affluent youth isolated together in large, anonymous, impersonal campuses. Indeed the institutions which experienced the worst disruption were not the most traditional and classical (which were anyway privileged enough to have retained small-scale personalized social relationships), but the newest, rawest, and, in ideological terms, the most progressive universities and colleges: Essex and Berkeley rather than Cambridge and Harvard. It is as well not to get the 'student revolution' out of perspective: it should be seen in functional terms as a middle-class parallel to the mods, skins, and punks. It was always primarily a vehicle of age-group solidarity and expressive excess. That is why rock music was so central an element in student praxis. As Tim Curry, star of *The Rocky Horror Show*, recently said: 'It's the Dionysiac bit in rock that really interests me. I like music you can behave badly to, and behave badly doing.'[3] Just so the 'student revolutionaries' who occupied administrative offices and held mass meetings and demonstrations to the sound of Jim

Morrison, Jimi Hendrix, the Rolling Stones, the Grateful Dead and the rest. It was anti-bureaucratic Utopianism to a rock beat.

Nonetheless, the half-inadvertent application of the logic of anti-structure has left a long-term deposit in our institutions of higher education. It is a highly equivocal legacy, not least because some 'liberal' and 'rational' academics and administrators took as literal many gestures, demands and claims which were essentially symbolic. The most serious, though by no means wholly negative, long term consequence of the counter-culture in education is a continuing debate about the nature of knowledge itself.[4] At its worst it results in a loss of intellectual nerve, especially about the validity of the objective mode of knowledge and not least about Western science (although commentators from the arts are more prone to suffer from this than practising scientists). It produces, too, a tendency comparable to that which we noted in the arts, in which the concentration on the *structure* of knowledge can evacuate the *content* of knowledge, what one might call a drift towards the meta-level in everything. At its best, however, like all fresh doses of ambiguity, the debate about the nature of knowledge can stimulate new insights and creative energies. The counter-culture also leaves behind a continuing provocation to inter-disciplinary work which can of course be trivial (because merely fashionable) but which, like all marauding across fixed boundaries, can yield a rich bag, often the more pleasurable for having been the fruits of poaching.

The major organizational consequences of the counter-culture in higher education are almost unrelievedly negative, however. The main achievement of the radical sixties has been to strengthen the thrust of the bureaucratic ethos at the expense of the traditional and the personal.

Where the student radicals were heeded, they inaugurated a mechanization of choice and an expansion of the machinery of participation, which simply multiplied the bureaucratic boxes. Where, as was usually the case, they evoked heavy, negative reactions, they succeeded in contaminating the public and the political image of higher education and in particular the reputation of the social sciences and of the ancient humanistic love of learning for its own sake. The counter-cultural pursuit of conspicuous expressive uselessness in the late sixties has immeasurably strengthened the hand of the champions of immediate utility in the late 1970s, not least because so many parents and young people have rejected the higher education option altogether in recent years of restricted job opportunities and heavy competition. So the culture of control did not simply crumble before the onslaught of the new, sophisticated hedonism in learning: on the contrary, from the mid-1970s, the conditions of economic stringency strengthened its base and, above all, gave a new lease of life to that other tradition of 'bourgeois' pedagogy, that of meritocratic and utilitarian individualism. The student radicals helped to explode the myth that unrestricted university expansion was a prerequisite of economic prosperity: they drew the attention of the political paymasters to all those purely expressive activities which, in the past, had been a luxury of the gentlemanly class, but which, in the era of mass higher education, had looked set fair to become part of the new rights of the common man. It is hardly surprising that governments of all political colours responded by tightening the financial strings, by sharpening the insistence on the instrumental functions of education and by encouraging a shift away from subjects which in the late sixties were troublesome, 'useless' and vocationally irrelevant. In short, the social and political establishment made clear its view that the expressive imperative is all very well in its proper place (and its 'proper place' seems to be leisure and entertainment), but that there must be proven value for money from the very expensive education industry.

The lower reaches of the education system constitute a much more complicated case. The symbolism of expressive anti-structure percolated down to the schools partly via youth culture and partly by the process of 'status drip' within the teaching profession, assisted by a minority tradition of progressive educational philosophy and practice which itself had an impeccable high-status pedigree. In the schools, too, this progressive movement involved a sharp attack on boundaries, categories, roles, rules and ritual and was characterized by a fundamental mistrust of institutions as such. Ivan Illich, the international prophet of deschooling, put the case most flamboyantly,[5] though many teachers who had never read Illich and who would have been astonished to be thought of as part of a counter-culture, shared that generalized mistrust of the routinized and institutionalized in education. The merging of categories and elimination of boundaries was also something which few schoolteachers held as an overt principle (unlike the student rebel leaders), but which simply happened to be taken on board with what they accepted as a liberal cargo. All-in comprehensive schools were favoured rather than specialist or selective schools, and co-education inexorably squeezed out the single-sex school. Architectural boundaries were swept away (or rendered movable) in open-plan buildings and subject boundaries were eroded by new subject groupings. Pedagogically, the stress shifted from the pupil as recipient, 'vessel', or apprentice, to an insistence on his self-determination. Learning through exploration, feeling, self-discovery was ideologically preferred to the older, more classical models which assumed a hierarchy of skills, a structure of rules, sequences and rituals and which endowed the teacher with the role of expert and authority on the basis of his superior knowledge and training. At the same time those rituals which traditionally embodied and expressed collective identity (communitas), group symbols such as uniform, speech day, school assembly, school sports and the house system, all fell out of favour as constricting individual liberty. Hierarchy, authority, and honourable, achieved leadership roles (prefect, house captain, and so on) were also frowned on as anti-egalitarian. So instead of formal rituals of overall communitas, many schools came to be dominated by the symbolic vocabulary of anti-structure and new, informal rituals of peer-group conformity.

In part, these de-structuring moves have been an explicit ideological assertion of the superiority of openness, informality and fluidity over closure, formality and structure. In part, they have simply been a reaction against anything, however contingent, which happened to have been linked with elite educational forms and practice. And here lies a major problem and contradiction. The progressive package is the natural vehicle for an assertion of the primacy of expressive norms; the value and relevance of education should rest on the inner choices of the learner and ought not to be determined by system needs or by formal, external requirements – hence the dislike of public examinations as coercive, arbitrary and alienating. Yet such a viewpoint has historically been a luxury afforded only by elite education and its gentlemen consumers. At the middle range of the education profession the progressive is placed in an awkward double-bind over criteria of usefulness, especially on egalitarian grounds. The temptation to despise 'merely useful' skills because they are vocational and instrumental both smacks of snobbery and in practice is likely to prove more damaging to working-class and immigrant children than to the offspring of the professional classes: the relatively deprived *need* specific competences and not just sensitive souls with which to confront the labour market. Furthermore, as one moves away from the university sector, professional educators become less willing to rest their claim to the validity of their calling on unashamedly expressive criteria: for most schoolteachers, some kind of claim to usefulness seems indispensable. So whereas the radical *haute bourgeoisie* can (in status terms) *afford* an extravaganza of anti-instrumental anti-structure with its subjectivist and relativizing definitions of knowledge, by contrast the schoolteacher, even when he is of progressive persuasion, can seldom go so far without putting an intolerable strain on his professional self-image. Thus the social logic of progressive anti-structure runs into some awkward contradictions in the school as distinct from the university.

The bifurcation into pure antinomian subjectivism, on the one side, and the total collective sect, on the other, is less well developed, though there are some traces of such a polarity. There is a certain amount of counter-cultural collectivism – some of the Free school experiments and certain strands of aggressive egalitarianism almost become sect-like. One tendency, for example, defends the autonomy and validity of underdog sub-culture (the working classes, the black population, the inner city undermass), with such single-minded fervour that the logic of the position becomes a form of cultural apartheid. Another sect-like type of reaction ignores the actual culture and priorities of the local community within which it operates, because the teachers' collective is believed to be possessed of a revealed truth which contains the only knowledge that can genuinely free that community from the shackles of its 'false consciousness'. The state has not encouraged extreme examples of this sect-like tendency and it is easier to find cases outside the state system (in voluntary experiments such as truancy centres or Free schools, for example), than in regular local authority provision. The purely antinomian alternative is also less well developed than in the university counter-culture. While examinations and job requirements may be mildly despised as getting in the way of ideal educational ends, the traditional aims of education and the objective definition of knowledge have nevertheless been retained in the progressive movement.

Just as external qualifications are not dismantled even though they may be despised at a superficial level, so too we find that the progressive movement in schools does not seriously abandon the objective mode of knowledge. It is simply claimed that an open pedagogy is more humane, up-to-date, and efficient as a method of imparting traditional educational skills. Thus we characteristically find an attempt to combine the pedagogy of anti-structure with only a minor, expressive modification of the objective definition of knowledge. This contradiction goes a long way towards explaining the confused state of the public debate on education in Britain. The retention of important objectivist and instrumental norms muddles a phenomenon which at the university level became quite openly a contest of paradigms – paradigms both of knowledge *and of their logically associated pedagogic styles*. Yet, in the contest between the champions of 'progressive' and 'traditional' education in schools, both sides claim superiority in imparting the three Rs, and neither side, publicly at least, argues that the sequence and pacing in the acquisition of the old skills might logically be expected to take radically different patterns according to the type of pedagogy.

The fact is that from the beginning progressive pedagogy covertly smuggled in many elements of form, structure and sequence from the traditional system while overtly institutionalizing openness, fluidity and apparent pupil autonomy. Today advocates of *purely* subjectivist pedagogy are nowhere to be found: there is no serious championing of real student self-determination in schools any more than there is championing of an unadulterated experiential definition of knowledge. In part, of course, this is due to the fact that some extreme experiments have demonstrated the self-defeating logic of the pedagogy of pure anti-structure. The problem is also akin to the one we traced in the arts, where it was found that a romantic/expressive technique was no guarantee of an effective romantic expression in the finished work of art, but that some of the forms and techniques of classicism were necessary to achieve that objective. Exactly the same applies in pedagogy. Thus the progressive movement in schools, especially at the secondary level, has brought about the spread of an *apparently* expressive 'open' pedagogy as the widely-favoured style, which nevertheless covertly rests on sequence, structure, and teacher authority. It has allied this style with assumptions about the nature of knowledge which have largely retained an objectivist base but overlaid it with an expanded rhetoric of subjectivity and expressiveness. Thus both the pedagogy and the knowledge mode of the progressive movement in schools rest on uneasy contradictions. This is one of the reasons why research into the effectiveness of different styles of teaching constantly produces unsatisfactory and ambiguous results[6] – the packages themselves are too full of contradictions to be easily disentangled at the level of empirical measurement.

Nevertheless, one of the important consequences of this partial and contradictory institutionalization of expressive anti-structure in education is both an anti-egalitarian and an anti-individualist thrust. It carries a serious danger of imprisoning children inside the philistinisms of peer-group culture or in the specificities of local sub-cultures: in schools as well as universities, the favoured mode of self-determining individualism all too often turns into peer-group conformity.[7] In these circumstances, only strong and impartial adult authority can protect and hedge about the precarious autonomy of the non-conforming child, and that is easier if adult authority is overt, not covert. The danger is almost certainly greatest for the child from a non-academic household for whom school is the major source of alternative cultural potential. Worse – and this now seems to be a widely accepted point[8] – the free-floating, unstructured social vocabulary of the progressive/expressive school is likely to be experienced as alien and disorienting by the typical working-class child whose family operates within the classic culture of control. In such a context the working-class child may well find it harder to acquire definable skills than he would in a more overtly structured system. Of course, many middle-class children outside the world of the bohemian bourgeoisie may find a radically de-structured milieu difficult to cope with too, but at least they are likely to pick up basic educational skills and motivation from home.

In fact, as Basil Bernstein has vigorously argued, the battle between open and closed pedagogies is really a struggle *within* the middle class, between the old formal segments and the new informal sector of the *haute bourgeoisie*.[9] The latter now use the state education system in significant numbers and the main casualties of the struggle are the children of the working class: 'self-determination' for the offspring of the respectable culture of control means bewilderment and for the lumpen 'lads' a perfect opportunity to practise the art of 'doing nothing' with impunity. By contrast, the middle classes, both old and new, structured and free-floating, can endow their children with cultural capital in the form of specific and transferable educational skills, whereas the working classes have never really known how to supplement the School Game, and least of all the new Open School Game. Moreover, the assumption about openness and flexibility is grossly misleading anyway. Andy Hargreaves has cogently demonstrated that 'open pedagogy' is not open at all, but only in Bernstein's sense 'invisible'.[10] It is a pedagogy of *implicit* rules and *hidden* meanings, a veritable Underground system of education, and most of the working classes are simply not cued into it. Thus, for the relatively deprived, it is more effectively closed than the old 'formal and grammatical' system in which rules, power, and authority were nakedly visible and not masked by any symbolic rhetoric of boundaryless expressiveness.

It is very difficult to assess with any accuracy just how far any of these principles of progressive pedagogy have spread in the school system because there is no research which has attempted seriously to trace the extent of the phenomenon. Certainly, many elements of the style will be found today even in supposedly more formal schools. Yet there is no doubt that the popularization of the movement began to meet with serious resistance from about 1973 onwards. A series of critiques of the progressive panacea appeared from a variety of sources. It slowly became possible to separate the politically loaded issue of 'comprehensivization' from problems of knowledge, pedagogy and school organization – for example, the dangers of depersonalization in very large schools is now the subject of lively debate. Private, governmental and professional educational research and comment are slowly raising specific questions about the harvest of the progressive revolution in the schools. In remedial education, the vital role of sequence, repetition and structure has again been given central place. Bennett[11] and Rutter[12] have both documented the importance of structure and sequence and above all of the teachers' willingness to abide consistently by the rules, commitments and duties of the authority role as a key to pedagogic success. Inspectors of mathematics and science have joined university professors of those subjects in warning against a too literal use of subjective pedagogies. The Government and the Schools Council have bowed to the weight of opinion in higher education and have (perhaps temporarily) abandoned their plans for introducing undifferentiated school-leaving examinations. Uniform tests and standardized curricula are being seriously canvassed. And, of course, there were the Black Papers[13] and the various national bodies which sprang up in their wake to 'protect educational standards'. The first Black Papers were certainly seen as the educational equivalent of the Festival of Light and Mrs Whitehouse's National Viewers' and Listeners' Association – the vicious backlash of the articulate culture of control against the progressives who were busy carrying off their neighbours' landmarks. Indeed, in part they were just that, and it is very significant that most of the prominent contributors to the Black Papers were first-generation grammar school and university products. They were acting as righteously angry spokesmen for all the lowly offspring of the respectable and underprivileged classes whose precious access to the true liminality of the book was being threatened by the expressive excesses of the *haute bourgeoisie*. If much of the Black Papers was angry rhetoric, they nevertheless constituted more than a rhetorical challenge to the progressive party: they refused to take for granted the moral superiority of the new expressive values and perhaps stimulated some cool reappraisals of what had begun to be taken for granted.

The history of the contradictions of the Expressive Revolution is very similar in the welfare professions. In the first place, there are clear similarities with some of the institutional boundary demolition which we observed in education. In this respect the counter-cultural message meshed easily with the trajectory of professionalization. The plethora of types of training, work, and recruitment was reduced to bureaucratic order in the period between the 1950s and the 1970s. Instead of vertical distinctions between, say, child care, probation, psychiatric and medical social work and so on, a new, all-in category was created, the generic social worker. This move involved anti-elitist elements like those in the comprehensive school movement and like that movement, its results were often far from egalitarian. In the case of the welfare agencies, the old vertical distinctions were replaced by a partly concealed horizontal hierarchy in which educational level and length of training rather than field of specialization became the status-bearing criteria. As in the case of the universities, the long-term consequence is one of increased bureaucratization. Indeed, this is hardly surprising, since the development was dictated more by the normal process of routinization and the need for uniformity of professional qualifications than by the ideological imperatives of boundary demolition. Nevertheless, the anti-boundary fashion of the late sixties assisted the change. It also accelerated the erosion of the distinction between deviance and other 'presenting symptoms' of client need. The move towards family courts, the decriminalization of the child delinquent, and the establishment of the generic case worker all assisted in blurring the distinctions between clients of the welfare agencies who had broken the law, who showed signs of mental disturbance or inability to cope, or who simply suffered material deprivation. A quasi-medical language of therapy and treatment replaced the language of social control.

A radical revision of the ontological status of the client is in fact the main hallmark of the counter-culture in this sphere. The relevant theory and praxis of anti-structure was largely developed, not in the welfare professions as such, but in the Underground of radical psychiatry especially associated with R. D. Laing, David Cooper, and Aaron Esterson (all of whom were for a time close associates of Jeff Nuttall). The superior sanity and exemplary suffering of madness was the particular contribution of this sector to the popular counter-cultural message. Its general outline is too well known to need repetition here. Again it led a vocal minority into either the antinomian option or to collective sectarianism in the usual polarizing fashion. The antinomian variant in the welfare professions largely consisted of the professional rejecting the control function *in toto* even under the guise of therapy and accepting the client's condition and definitions of reality in the client's own terms. By category inversion, if 'pathology' is a spiritually and morally superior state to 'normality', then the attempt to reconcile the client to 'insane' normality and to lead him to a realistic adjustment to the possible must be not merely useless, but wicked. Popularized Laigianism, which is of course much cruder than Laing's own subtle and ever changing thought, has given rise to books, plays, TV programmes and films which straddle the fiction/documentary divide and have entered into the stock of folk wisdom. The phenomenon has a good deal in common with the medieval cult of the suffering saint: the progressive bourgeoisie can receive benison from public displays and ritualized re-enactments of saintly suffering by society's scapegoats.

The collectivist alternative is one which rejects not only control but therapy. If the social system is insane then the only proper activity for the caring professionals is to organize or encourage the deprived to aggressive political action: it is the powerlessness, of the deprived which renders their culture 'pathological' in society's eyes and which generates material lack; society will only remedy that lack at the price to the recipient of accepting the 'pathological' label: 'therapy' and 'caring' are thus just a legitimating cloak for control and interference by the powerful in the lives of the powerless. Thus on the one hand, the antinomian logic is simply to proclaim 'Behold the Man!' and to treat suffering as akin to religious ecstasy and/or prophetic martyrdom. On the other hand, the collectivist logic is to form the client category into a kind of aggressive political sect.

Interestingly enough, just as happened in education, a bourgeois rational individualism re-emerged to combat the patrician romanticism of the counter-culture. The American Thomas Szasz[14] is the clearest voice making the case for rational individualism in psychiatry, and by extension for the 'caring' professions. This position also starts with an attack on the therapeutic role as concealed interference and control: the therapeutic model reduces the human being to a psycho-social cipher: the client (madman, murderer, deviant, or whoever) is treated as if he were incapable of making free choices or calculated decisions; he is also denied the right to accept punishment or make reparation for wrong-doing. The transformation of overt control and punishment into an emotion-soaked rhetoric of humanitarian care and individually tailored therapy is a confidence trick which removes individual freedom and draws a veil over the real nature of the welfare professional's role, that of combined priest and policeman. Szasz's basic premises had a long pedigree not just in rational individualist thought but in the Christian theology of sin and free-will.

In practice the pure antinomian option made rather little headway in the mainstream of the welfare professions, but remained largely confined to counter-cultural experiments in which little or no public money was involved. It never became much more than an in-group game among the radical bourgeoisie and simply provided a bit of oppositional rhetoric for social work students. The collectivist alternative had more success and put down strong roots in the voluntary and local authority welfare agencies. Community action, clients' rights, and consciousness-raising have become an established, though perhaps fairly restricted, part of social welfare organizations. It is a development which entails an awkward set of double-binds, however, which were signalled by the very need for 'consciousness raising'. The theology of client self-determination (like that of pupil autonomy) makes it difficult for the professional simply to take (and be seen to take) the active leadership role: the group must act on its own behalf. It is the problem which Ray Gosling failed to solve with his Leicester youth club, in fact. The client group is mostly unlikely to think of doing something radical on its own behalf without the stimulus of outside authoritative initiative. It is usually an aggregate of scattered and often desperate individuals rather than a real group – the homeless, single parents or the old may all share common problems but they tend to exist in highly privatized and isolated units. Moreover, one important category of regular clients is the lumpen undermass, the Learys and their kind, who lack the cultural vocabulary of organization, political mobilization and self-help which come from the culture of control.

And here again we meet an old dilemma. The working-class culture of control evolved precisely to make possible some degree of personal autonomy in conditions of scarcity and insecurity. One insidious effect of the popularization of the counter-culture's expressive values has been to invert the categories so as morally to stigmatize the culture of control and respectability while representing the culture of unstructured short-run hedonism as ideologically preferable: the latter is not only the style of the bohemian bourgeoisie but of the undermass itself. There is an inbuilt temptation in the role of the social worker today: if he makes a strong empathic identification with, say, the victims of the cycle of self-perpetuating poverty, he may lose sight of two important and often uncomfortable considerations. First, he may, perhaps unintentionally, symbolically devalue the achievements of the respectable working classes and induce in them an inchoate resentment. Second, no amount of redistribution of resources will endow the victim with real autonomy if he does not also acquire some of the skills and powers which the culture of control has traditionally carried. This internal double-bind in the practice and ideology of the progressive element in the welfare professions tends to resolve itself in exactly the same way as it does for the progressive schoolteacher. It becomes a rhetoric of openness, of 'enabling', of 'client self-determination', which conceals the reality of control and direction which is in practice exercised by the most successful professionals. As Geoffrey Parkinson recently remarked *à propos* high-risk probation clients, 'If there is one single feature that characterizes serious potential recidivists, it's that they don't want to be helped, except occasionally by cash and partial collusion.'[15] So a literal application of client self-determination would reinforce the sub-cultural inequalities just as effectively as would real student self-determination in schools. And, of course, no one is really asking for that, whatever their rhetorical style.

Nevertheless, shifts in the direction of expressive self-determination are more than merely rhetorical. The de-stigmatization of the traditional client has been part of a consistent set of egalitarian and humane developments in law and social policy: the laws of bastardy, the rules which determine entitlement to unemployment pay and social security benefits (such as the removal of financial penalties for 'cohabitation' or the entitlement of strikers), are examples of a change in the conception of the role of the welfare services away from the control function to that of enhancing the quality of life and allowing even deprived or deviant groups to choose and justify their own life-styles. But there remains the problem of how this rebounds on to the culture of control, especially at that crucial margin where the respectable working class and the undermass touch. While research convincingly demonstrates that all this has done very little to alter the self-perpetuating structural nature of most gross deprivation, this is not the message which is heard or heeded in the mainstream culture of control and importantly by the respectable working class. The rhetoric of the Expressive Revolution in the welfare professions has been too widely understood as a soft justification for not merely not evicting but for re-housing Muriel Spark's Learys or Robert Roberts's Ignatius and giving them regular cash doles: it induces a suspicion that the leaders of opinion have lost their respect for respectability. The regular (and ill-documented) campaigns in the tabloid press against 'scroungers' and 'fiddlers' are not just journalistic National Front-ism, they appeal (and help to sell newspapers) because they reflect an inchoate unease among the readership, not about 'respectable' deprived groups, like the old, but about the symbolic implications of moral tenderness on the part of high status groups for the culture which the 'low and no class' dregs has always embodied. Hence the almost mythic image of the Superman Scrounger with twelve children and no job as the archetypical trickster and popular folk-devil of the late 1970s. The latest journalistic exposés of waste and wantonness in the welfare state may look like beasts of a very different colour from the Black Papers on education, but they have this at least in common: they express the anger and puzzlement of the culture of respectability, self-control, and hard work against the way in which the cultural spokesmen of the expressive bourgeoisie have carelessly carted off the old moral landmarks and stowed them away in an inaccessible attic.

The legacy of the counter-culture in the state-financed welfare services is as internally contradictory as that in education and for the same reasons: a modified rhetoric of expressive anti-structure has become a part of the professional vocabulary and self-image while criteria of success and utility are nonetheless applied both in the unspoken ground rules of professional praxis and even more sharply in the overt requirements of public policy. The financial squeeze is at least as acute in the welfare services as in education since the late 1970s and has the same consequence of strengthening the value-for-money lobby. In one respect, however, the welfare field differs markedly from education. It has grown an ever more luxuriant fringe of private therapeutic agencies which are in effect continuations of counter-cultural experiments. This world of the therapeutic cults merges imperceptibly with that of the fringe religious cults or 'new religions', so much so, in fact, that one observer has proposed the blanket category 'self-religions'[16] to obviate the awkward necessity of deciding what is secular and what is religious in this new milieu. The therapeutic fringe cannot be put into proper perspective, therefore, without a discussion of the counter-culture's impact on religious institutions. Accordingly, it is to this that we now turn.

We have already noted in some detail the important role of cults of Eastern mysticism in the development of the symbolism of ecstatic disorder. If, as Thomas Mann so rightly noted, the Church is shrunk to a mere bureaucratized organ of culture, then religion will go elsewhere. A neutered Church will leave a vacuum which will be filled by both antinomian and totalitarian daemony. Many of the religious elements in the counter-culture were diffuse and imprecise – Colin Campbell has called it a 'cultic milieu'.[17] It consisted of such things as a generalized dabbling in the literature and history of the occult, mandalas (Jungian and other), tarot cards, astrological prediction, yoga, techniques of mystical ecstasy (with and without drugs) in meditation and expanded consciousness. Many of these were a kind of do-it-yourself kit of spiritual self-development (or prophylactic against *anomie*) passed around by word of mouth and the odd paperback book. Some influences remained diffuse even when it was possible to associate them with specific cults or movements like the Transcendental Meditation of the Maharishi Mahesh Yoga (of fleeting Beatles fame), The Divine Light Mission of the Maharaj Ji or the neo-political Ananda Marga.

Cults of mysticism, occultism and/or self-development had lain around on the bohemian fringe of the *haute bourgeoisie* since the turn of the century at least, enjoying periodic revivals in the decadent twenties and thirties. The late sixties saw a new efflorescence: most of the best-known of the modern cults and sects were either founded (the Jesus people, for instance) or began their significant spiral of growth in the West (Krishna Consciousness, for example) around 1968/69.[18] All the 'new' cults, the Children of God, Meher Baba, TM, the Divine Light Mission, The Church of Satan, the Aetherius Society, the Unification Church, The Process, Scientology, Nichiren Shoshu, The Jesus People, Krishna Consciousness and so on, drew their major body of recruits from the student/youth population which was the home base of the extravagant culture of expressive disorder. The picture which most students of the new religions give us[19] is of a fairly widespread shopping around, with young counter-cultural converts trying one spiritual panacea after another, shifting between varieties of antinomian and sect – like groups before settling into one specific movement. Thus there is a certain fluidity of personnel and of ideas in the new religious melange. There is also an imperceptible merging of the secular and the religious elements, so that it makes more sense to discuss the cults of self-therapy, like the Human Potential Movement, Primal Scream, Synanon or the Process, together with the self-defined 'religious' movements rather than in arbitrary separation. Thus, for example, while TM, when it originally came to the West, was more religious and exclusivist than it is today, Scientology, largely for reasons of taxation and legal protection, became steadily more 'religious',[20] and Janov's Primal Scream began as an overtly even militantly secular therapy and has only in the last three or four years begun to elaborate a theology of the individual's mystical recapitulation of evolution and of the transmigration of souls.[21] This kind of cross-over of emphasis is typical rather than exceptional and such volatility (not unrelated to a shifting recruitment pattern) is one of these features of the new religions which makes them difficult to categorize.

Roy Wallis has suggested that they be divided on Weberian criteria into world-affirming and world-rejecting cults.[22] The former he characterizes as individualistic and egoistic: they offer esoteric techniques and forms of knowledge (sometimes in a scientific and sometimes in a religious and usually oriental vocabulary) as aids to success and personal psychic health in a competitive world. They may despise or approve that world, but the essential point is that they accept it as the only possible context for their members' lives. The world-rejecting movements are more obviously collectivist. They set out to protect their members from a debased and corrupting secular world by offering an alternative community of total belonging in which rules and control are absolute and are based in the group and not in the conscience and will of the individual: *extra fraternitas nulla salus*. For most purposes this is an admirable categorization, but it does not point up sharply enough certain aspects which are important for my present

Two types of liturgy.
Rock to religious ritualism: an easy passage. Buddhists on Bodmin Moor (above).
New liturgies of touch: pioneered in the cults and sometimes adopted in the mainstream churches (below).

analysis. Wallis's distinction lies parallel to my delineation of the antinomian option as against the total sect: the antinomian roughly corresponds to his world-affirming category while the total sect refers to much the same range of movements as his world-rejecting category. The difficulty lies in the fact that the criterion of affirmation or rejection of the world does not entirely encapsulate the essence of the relevant distinctions. The clearly ego-based (even egoistic) cults of therapy and self-development (Scientology, The Process), as well as the cults of the mystic East (Hare Krishna, Vedanta), largely fall into the world-affirming group. Many of the mystical cults echo the traditional oriental mistrust both of the ego and of the material world and involve self- and group-discipline as part of the spiritual recipe for expanded consciousness. Indeed, as we have already seen with the hippies, the ultimate expressive ecstasy may be found in the fusion of the One with the All, the blurring of the contours of individual identity and the merger of self with cosmic essence. Thus both the attitude to the world and the concept of self are somewhat, even radically, different from what is normally implied by world-affirmation. On the other side, as Wallis himself notes, many of the world-rejecting movements in fact incorporate some positive, world-affirming principles in their own communities while nevertheless condemning the profane world outside. Thus though many of these sects enforce strict rules of sexual chastity, they may also value procreation, mutual affection, and even on occasion condone the use of sexual generosity as a part of missionary endeavour. It may therefore be more accurate to see the total sect as distinguished by a vision of salvation which is essentially social and therefore condemns the corrupt sociation of the profane world. By contrast, the mystic cults are asocial in that their vision of salvation concerns only the level of consciousness and has no social component whatever: thus both their individualism and their assessment of the relevance of the world differs from those of the manipulative therapies with which they share Wallis's 'world-affirming' category.

I make these points not to quibble with Wallis's concepts but simply to draw attention to the fact that these internal contradictions in the movements themselves make more sense if we relate them to the features of the expressive pursuit of liminality which characterize all the cultural phenomena that we have examined. The first of these is ubiquitous taboo violation. The breaking of taboos, as we have noted many times, involves a whole series of contradictory logics. Thus La Vey's Church of Satan can cock a snook at the Protestant ethic by its libidinous sexual ethics while the Unification Church can shock conventional society from the other direction by its ultra-Puritan approach to sexuality and its arranged marriages. Even more important is the search for ecstasy, for the mystic escape from structure and from the merely and mundanely social. It may be immanentist or transcendentalist in its underpinning theology, in-the-body or out-of-the-

body, transcendence or transfiguration, but whatever form it takes, its substance is the utterly asocial moment of pure being, unemcumbered by
categories, roles or even meaning (all those may precede and follow but they
are not of the existential essence of ecstasy). And what characterizes most
of these movements is precisely the pursuit of ecstasy.

Once again the phenomenon falls into two polar types, leading
respectively to what Auden calls the heaven (or hell) of the 'Pure Self' or to
that of the 'Truly General Case'. The 'self-religions' (The Process, Primal
Scream, Kerista) in which the exclusive focus is ego and his mental, spiritual
and physical perfection come under the first rubric, as also at the other
extreme do the mystical movements in which the total subjugation of the self
is the accepted route to mystic ecstasy (Zen, Vedanta). Both are variant
developments of the antinomian option. The total sect on the other hand (the
Unification Church, some Jesus groups) marches towards the heaven of the
'Truly General Case', where ecstasy, like salvation, is collective or it is
nothing. I will take these types in turn.

First let us examine the double trajectory of antinomianism. In the case of
the 'self-religions' pure, rule-free expressiveness as the key to salvation
results by an impeccable but ironic social logic in highly commercialized
and smoothly marketed therapeutic services – encounter groups, rebirthing,
e.s.t. – which are offered as scientifically tested recipes for personal integration and the maximization of the individual's expressive potential in a world
of anonymity, competition and privatization. It is quite simply a case of the
usual process by which a charismatic message, this time expressive
spontaneity and individual authenticity, becomes routinized and institutionalized. If the do-it-yourself method brings you no satisfaction (and
after all, spontaneity as a *method* is most likely to bring endless repeats of
old miseries and mistakes), then you must go to the successful firm to get
yourself de-programmed. The odyssey of Jerry Rubin is the best publicized
case – from surrealist yippie to growth counsellor in a mere decade.[23] So the
belief in the primacy of the inner-determined self and the flight from externally structured (and therefore coercive) social roles transmutes to create a
market in off-the-peg private identities. Moreover, the cure comes to be
indistinguishable from the disease. The erosion of secure, socially rooted
identities began in the social changes which brought complexity, mobility
and differentiation. It was accelerated by the counter-cultural onslaught on
roots and boundaries so that the members of the expressive bourgeoisie do
indeed often experience acute and chronic identity crises. The ideologically
preferred recipe for expressive life-enhancement, however, tends to render
identity more rather than less problematic: the characteristic modern
malaise is not too much repression but a precarious ego.

It is for these reasons that the most appealing 'self-religions' combine a
rhetoric of expressive self-discovery with a praxis which creates alternative

sources both of belonging and of self-definition. In short, they offer what Berger and Luckmann call 'plausibility structures' which prop up the subjective self. They claim to be liberating while much of their real appeal lies in the latent function of providing firm and definitive conceptions of private individual identity which can be strongly internalized and which are usually backed up by psycho-social support structures. The fact that the vocabulary is one of 'growth' and 'development' should not blind one to the formulaic (and therefore predictable, structured and security-bearing) nature of the identities on offer. The therapeutic process itself is frequently similar to religious conversion, and descriptions of, say, intensive T-groups or weekend sessions of Primal Scream or e.s.t., where participants have minimal sleep, food and privacy, are startlingly close to Victor Turner's delineation of the ritual process through which old identities are stripped away during a liminal passage characterized by symbolic anti-structure (mutual abuse, gross fatigue, despair and psychic degradation), culminating in joyous re-integration into a new identity. The latter may be an unequivocally ecstatic experience and is usually reinforced by instant collective euphoria (pure communitas), the display of expansive affection between erstwhile strangers, and so on. Because the therapeutic cults are fundamentally individualistic – indeed, almost the sanctification of subjective, private identity – their plausibility structures are less obvious than those of the total sect. Nevertheless, the movements do find ways to underpin the new, post-therapy identities of their converts/clients through their publications and a structure of individual and/or group contacts which can be re-activated at need. Some of these movements are even showing signs of spawning experimental therapeutic communes as semi-autonomous spin-offs.[24] It is in some ways an obvious and natural development precisely because of the problem of the precarious plausibility structures of the individualistic cult.

A similar internal tension exists in the religions and quasi-religions of ego-less mystical ecstasy. Again they derive from a strand in the counter-culture which set out to elevate the subjective/expressive above the objective/instrumental: inner states of subjective consciousness are the only good end in life. This version of expressive antinomianism, however, had to come to terms with the fact that mystic ecstasy is simply not there just for the asking, even, ultimately, with the assistance of drugs. As mystics at all times and in all cultures have discovered, the surest route to ecstasy is self-discipline, the objective is often a surer approach than the subjective to mystery and transcendence and the renunciation of any obsession with ecstasy itself is a necessary prelude to the experience which more often comes as a gift of grace unsought than to those who pursue it with egoistic passion. As C. S. Lewis once said, the only remedy for those who are haunted by the scent of unseen rose gardens is work. Thus once more the paradox of *coincidentia oppositorum*. So the diffuse counter-cultural pursuit of subjective ecstasy gave rise to certain highly-disciplined movements of Eastern style mysticism in which the virtues of poverty, chastity and obedience are strongly reintroduced. Self-expression leads to shaven heads, saffron robes, begging bowls and all the disciplines of classical asceticism.

There is another logic, too, lying inside this development. As I argued in the case of the charismatic rock stars, one of the attractions of Eastern-style mysticism is its capacity to reaffirm meaning and sense by representing as a spiritual achievement the otherwise distressing, existential condition of *anomie.* Cults like Krishna, Zen and Ananda Marga recruited heavily among the casualities of the drug scene. They were able to offer a permanent 'high' that needed no chemical assistance. At least as important, however, is their communal structure. Far more clearly than in the case of the therapeutic self-religions (with which, anyway, they merge at the margin, as in TM), their not-so-latent function is the provision of alternative structures of secure identity, in this case usually well-developed and internally cohesive face-to-face communities which act as quasi-families as in the Hare Krishna cult. In many ways they are the perfect solution to the problem which the counter-culture posed itself: they routinize both anti-structure *and* communitas, by making discipline equally the basis of group belonging and of the transcendent possibility. They break all the correct taboos by being outside the Judaeo-Christian tradition and thus preserve a clear symbolic rejection of the parent culture: they remain 'alternative society'. Precisely because they are trying to hold on to both halves of the logic of liminality, these collectivist cults of eastern mysticism lie half-way between the institionalization of pure anti-structure and the sectarian routinization of total communitas.

The groups which resolve the dilemma in favour of communitas at the expense of anti-structure are those I have referred to as total sects and which Wallis calls the world-rejecting cults, the Unification Church, some of the Jesus People and the Children of God are examples. Again these movements mopped up the leavings of the drug and protest culture of the late sixties. Their converts opt for a clear structure of belonging, security, firm and absolute rules and values, explicit hierarchy, overt control and a radical curtailment of both privacy and personal choice without even the promise of individualized ecstasy which the mystical cults can offer to compensate for discipline and obedience. The 'high' here is a group 'high'; certainty and belonging are the major benefits. It is interesting that many of the investigators of these movements now stress the conscious and intelligent choice which most 'conversions' entail, the recruits are not 'brainwashed' as the popular stereotype suggests but are quite lucid about the rationale of their decision;[25] clearly, the same might be said for the clientele of the therapeutic cults who also know pretty precisely what they are bargaining for. In the communitarian sects there does, however, remain a strong remnant of symbolic opposition (the quality that Wallis identifies as world

rejection), and the very choice of exotic and deliberately exclusive movements still carries over that counter-cultural utopianism about being an
'alternative society'. Indeed, we have here yet another popular folk devil in
the exclusive sect. Groups like the Unification Church are feared and
disliked by the liberal elite because they are closed, disciplined and premised
on 'irrational' religious dogma; they are equally anathematized by the
culture of control precisely because they are such effective *alternative*
control systems cutting across all the natural societal ties of family, race,
generational connection and local community.

Some of the fringe sects of communitas do however exist within the
Judaeo-Christian tradition, more particularly the Jesus groups. Here the
oppositional element is less total (except perhaps among the well-named
Jews for Jesus), and many observers have noted the capacity of these
groups to act as half-way houses between the counter-culture and mainstream society. Their re-integration into an alternative culture of control
enables some sect members to make the further move back into conventional society, back to families of origin and the ordinary Christian
denominations. Even some of the more exotic eastern movements like
Krishna Consciousness, Meher Baba and some of the tiny Islamic communes can have this 'staging-post' function.

As the research on communitarian groups proceeds, the question remains
unresolved as to just how total the control really is. With the important
exception of the People's Temple in Guyana, most of the sects in the
Anglo–American world probably leave more room for choice and
manoeuvre and certainly for personal interpretation of doctrine than the
term 'total sect' would imply.[26] My point, however, is simply to establish as
a heuristic device the contrast between those new religious movements
which lean towards the institutionalization of communitas as an antidote to
overdoses of anomic anti-structure, and those which lean towards the
institutionalization of antinomian expressiveness. The latter type itself splits
between the egoistic cults of privatized self-religion and the cults of mystical
ecstasy. Specific groups will seldom be pure cases of any of these types, not
least because all three are products of the uneasy tension between the
different logics of expressive liminality; and in any case, the emphasis in any
actual movement tends to shift over time. It is perhaps of some interest
nevertheless that the counter-cultural young favoured the mystical cults and
the re-integrating sects of communitas while their parental generation
supplied the clientele for the bourgeois commercial cults of ego therapy.[27]
Only the generation which had tasted the real if fleeting pleasures of existential communitas *and* the extremes of drug-assisted flight from identity into
cosmic consciousness was prepared to pay the price of the communitarian
option. The middle-aged cling stubbornly to a hard-edged individualism
which anyway has more affinity with the direction of economic change and

the conditions of middle-class occupations. After all the communitarian option frequently necessitates a rejection of normal middle-class job opportunities.

The religious legacy of expressive disorder is not by any means confined to exotic new sects and cults. A significant minority in the Churches and especially among the clergy responded to the counter-culture's usurpation of their religious role by the sincerest flattery — imitation. Every item of counter-cultural anti-structure finds its reflection in the mainstream religious institutions. It is perhaps most clearly illustrated at the point where mainstream and alternative religiosity are closest together on the spectrum. In the Jesus movement, we see a combination of something like Conservative Evangelical theology, an insistence on the uniqueness of the Christian message and a strict Puritan ethic, all of which can be found also in mainstream Churches. Along with this go certain strikingly visible counter-cultural ingredients — youthful communitas expressed in colourful demonstrations of public witness, diffuse but uninhibited mutual affection and even in some rare cases the Gift of The Spirit, that is, tongues, glossolalia. This latter manifestation above all has close affinities with some of the most crucial counter-cultural motifs. It is a meta-language of universal brotherhood, the speech of the transcendent reality which rises above the Babel of specific tongues, roles, races, sexes and Churches; the direct experience of individual ecstasy as divine grace, which also acts as the cement of group cohesion. In short, it is the Christian equivalent of 'Orghast' and the evangelical answer to mystical ecstasy. The Charismatic Movement in Christianity runs all the way from Jesus Freaks and the Pentecostal sects to the mainstream of Non-conformity, Anglicanism and Roman Catholicism. It is a minority movement of renewal inside the conventional Churches which re-frames the special symbols of ecstatic disorder inside the religious institution.

The Charismatic Movement grew out of the same 'cultic milieu' as the rest of the religious counter-culture.[28] Like the rest of the sixties' cultic activists, the charismatics are drawn overwhelmingly from among the professional middle classes. One wing of the movement is quasi-sectarian, tending to take over particular local Churches *in toto*, while the other wing exists fairly happily within non-charismatic congregations. Its development makes more sense if we take account of the extensive lending and borrowing of motifs across the whole spectrum of the cults. Since about 1973 some of the charismatics have developed in a distinctly communitarian direction evolving a system of house fellowships and a highly articulated small group structure in which every aspect of life is provided for and children are very carefully trained. The authority structure is absolutely clear: women and children submit and men take decisions in family, work and religious life. The system of 'shepherding' extends the group's social control into even the most 'private' corners of life: like many of the therapeutic cults, it employs techniques of confrontation as well as consultation. The moral norms are very strict (absolutely no sexual permissiveness), but though the *content* is a culture of extreme control, the style incorporates strong elements of spontaneity, not just glossolalia itself, which is very much a minority phenomenon, but the fact that there is no set order of worship, a great deal of informal folk style singing of a secular kind, and so on. In fact, the Charismatic Movement lies somewhere between Primal Scream and the Unification Church, routinizing and re-framing elements of liminal anti-structure inside a system of normative communitas which eliminates all uncertainty about norms and roles. In fact, it is the perfect case within contemporary Christianity of what Kolakowski calls the 'counter-Reformation' syndrome: it takes into its own arsenal the most successful weapons which the opposition (secular and cultic) has deployed against it.

At the extreme end of the spectrum from the puritan norms of the charismatics, the Churches had their own Underground movement which merged imperceptibly with the 'secular' counter-culture. It was based on liberation theology, peace, love and support for the revolution of the oppressed, in the usual complex and contradictory mix. It was super-ecumenical, looking towards the eastern mystical cults and paying little heed to denominational boundaries within Christianity. It mistrusted Church hierarchies, condemned institutionalization, bureaucracy, arbitrary authority and the capitalistic role of propertied religious bodies. This religious Underground produced several magazines in the late sixties and early seventies including a short-lived Christian Marxist publication, *Slant*, and the widely-distributed *Catonsville Roadrunner* published in London and Berkeley, California. The format of *Roadrunner* is exactly that of the Underground press of the time: it looks exactly like *International Times* and claimed to be a sister magazine to *Oz*. Something of its flavour may be conveyed by the following extract from the editorial of issue 20 (no date) on drugs by Karma Lodro Zangmo. (The echo of Grace Slick and Whiter Shade of Pale is unmistakable.)

At one point in time it was said 'The Kingdom of Heaven is at hand' or 'The Kingdom of Heaven is within.' By this we mean 'A New State of Being', a new state of awareness of Inner Sight. We must be ready to cultivate 'awareness' through Meditation so that we may transcend like the immortal Alice, who by becoming so small with humility was able to enter through the little door into Wonderland after falling down a rabbit-hole. She also found that when she was too high she could not enter through the little door. She was in a fix. It is only by being in the right state of mind that we can find what we are seeking.

...My attitude to drugs is neither one of approval or disapproval, you have to try and see for yourselves. For some it has been necessary to take a trip into the 'unknown' in search of Reality, a search which proves disastrous for some and enlightening for others. Those who have attained knowledge this way must come out in the open and help one another, forming a new brotherhood.

Priests who followed this line often sported posters of the variety 'God bless the grass that grows through concrete.' The double-face on drugs is paralleled by an equal equivocation about violence and revolution: should the alternative society be ushered in by violent political action or not? One page of that same issue of *Roadrunner* contains a moral condemnation of prelates who did not instantly endorse a report of the British Council of Churches which advocated financial support for guerrilla movements in southern Africa. The next page contains an article which includes the opposite approach: 'The spiritual revolution is in fact far more important than political or social revolution, for the key is the consciousness of the people in power. The attack on the *form* of the Establishment is not as effective as the attack on the consciousness of the people.' In short, *Catonsville Roadrunner* displays exactly the range of contradictory Underground convictions that we traced in Jeff Nuttall and Richard Neville. This particular issue also contains a 'Directory of the Liberated Church in Great Britain'.

This movement of avowedly 'alternative' religion was, like the fringe cults, a minority phenomenon, but it helped to set the tone and style for movements which touched the mainstream more closely. The ecumenical and social experts in the Churches' special ministries, on the committees of the *British* and the World Council of Churches and the central boards of all the denominations (who were after all, some of the major public spokesmen of official Christianity), often echoed a modified version of the radical counter-cultural message,[29] as did a minority of active innovators in the local congregations. A number of studies of the clergy give us a picture of 'progressive' clergy who emerged as a distinctive force in the Churches at the same time as the secular counter-culture appeared. In his study of Anglican ordinands, for example, A. J. Russell identified a significant minority (about one third of his sample) whom he labels 'anti-Puritan'. This group of ordinands tends towards an immanentist theology with a concept of a deity who works in secular affairs and is served by an invisible Church. They welcome the numerical decline of the Church and its loss of power and status. Russell in *The Clerical Profession* writes:

This line of thought ... undermines the distinctions between the Christian and the non-Christian, between the Church and the world, because it sees the structures of the Church as in many ways working against the will of God, and because it sees the very drawing of a line between 'us' and 'them', as contrary to the idea of a God who creates and redeems the world.

So again the response of the radicals is to destroy the boundaries. The dilemma that this produces for them is the tendency to find that they have dug the grave of their own specifically Christian vocation along with that of the institutional Church, the conventional parish and the old role of parson and minister. Furthermore, although they dislike and oppose what they see as an inturned, sectarian character in the 'gathered Church', they nevertheless find themselves engaged in activities which mark off them and their kind in a sharp sect-like fashion, leaving both the conventional and the tribal Christian outside the charmed circle of the radical elect.

In other ways, too, the progressive clergy deny their special vocation. M. W. Moore in a study of radical Anglican priests quotes one of his respondents as saying: 'One's overall aim is to release Christianity from things ecclesiastical, be they church buildings or persons, and give them back to the laity, to free it so that it becomes not an institution but a movement.'[30] In all sorts of ways, therefore, the radical clergy destroyed the symbolic boundary markers and the insignia both of the Church and of their own special office: they wore denims and threw away their clerical collars; they celebrated the Eucharist in homes with real bread, not flimsy token wafers; they lived in communities, squats, council houses and not apart in rectory and manse. They were in the business of de-formalizing and de-institutionalizing religion: the spirit should blow where it listed.

One of the main symbolic foci for this boundary destruction was the liturgy. As one of Moore's curates put it: 'I look for liturgical change in the direction of letting it express what we want to say and celebrate – for it to become a much more human occasion, you know – one wants to breathe some warmth into it.' So spontaneity and subjectivity invade the ritual core of the religious act. Improvisation, dance, rock music, noisy children, lay participation, movable altars (or none) and what Americans graphically call the 'whole touchy feely thing' – real kisses of peace paralleling the real eucharistic bread – come to characterize the progressive Church service. Moreover, this penchant for liturgical innovation spread well beyond the radical epicentre into the parish strongholds of the much despised 'suburban Christianity' and even into Conservative Evangelical congregations. Like the Charimatic Movement, the adoption of informality, tactile demonstrations of mutual affection (real or affected) and all the apparatus of religious anti-structure and congregational communitas acted as a kind of 'counter-reformation' innoculation against the counter-cultural disease. The radical style was employed to protect a conservative or traditionalist religious core. But style, as I have had many occasions to argue above, is not a mere frill but carries its own awkward logic. The logic of all the liturgical innovations of the last decade is the same as the logic of anti-structure in the arts, the Underground and everywhere else that we have traced the effects. The basic point is eloquently caught by David Birch, writing largely of the Roman Church, who draws all the relevant analogies, many of which would startle the middle-of-the-road cleric who has been inadvertantly caught up in the counter-Reformation deployment of the radical style. Birch writes:

The aim of a liturgical celebration, like that which Craig called a 'happening' in the theatre, is to allow the audience or congregation to get beyond itself, not into a land of make-belief, but into a close-knit member of a community. . . . While Artaud and his followers were trying to get rid of an inactive audience, mere spectators, so the church, after the Lambeth Conference of 1958 and the Second Vatican Council of 1962, began to break down the barriers that separated priest from people; individual from community. Both church and theatre sought a higher degree of involvement from all. One was no longer to 'hear' Mass, but to 'celebrate' the Eucharist; in the theatre, entertainment was to give way to audience participation, to 'stimulation'. As contemporary English was to replace Cranmerian English and Tridentine Latin, so Brecht, Pinter, Wesker and latterly Handke and Poliakoff were to replace the stereotypes of 'Hobson's Choice' and 'Charley's Aunt'. The 'closet drama' was to become in Brecht's terminology, 'total theatre'. . . . Likewise, private devotion at Mass was to become 'the prayer of the faithful', the once private canon of the Mass was to become 'the prayer of the Church'.

As Genet, Ionesco, Albee and Durrenmatt called for theatrical freedom, so the members of liturgical commissions began to formulate the dictates of Vatican II, bringing a greater sense of freedom to the liturgy. As the proscenium arch is being replaced by small studios, theatres 'in the round', and so on, so the rail gates enclosing the sanctuary were removed. The elimination of the alienating symbols of arch and rail enabled barriers to be broken down both physically and symbolically. The priest was not now enclosed, and therefore neither was the Eucharist. Likewise the actor ceased to be a fancy dress figure on an unapproachable stage. As Beckett was to strip the stage of all unnecessary rubrics added over the years.[31]

I have quoted this passage at length because the parallels in the practice of boundary demolition in Church theatre are accurate and relevant. As we have seen in all these spheres, boundary destruction results in unintended losses as well as some expressive enhancement: at its worst it can be totally self-defeating. Birch clearly recognizes something of this dilemma. The Church loses spiritual force to the degree that its system of symbolic communication is reduced to, equated with and becomes ultimately indistinguishable from that of the profane world, and language is the classical agent of this inadvertent loss. He writes:

Advertisements, broadcasts, newspapers and magazines are fighting a war of attrition with the meaning of words. In order to maintain the maximum semantic force of the language of words in the liturgy, we must therefore follow the lead of the theatre and aim towards a language of senses, where we gain a 'total liturgy' and not simply 'old wine in new skins'. Everyday language may bring an immediate understanding of the Mass or Communion service, but beyond the surface there is a gradual wearing away at the meaning of the words used. Once powerful symbols of 'love', 'grace', 'charity', 'wonder', 'offering', 'sacrifice', 'light', and 'fellowship' are as much part of the advertiser's lexicon, his vocabulary as they are of the liturgist; as such their meanings in relation to the message of the church degenerate.[32]

Birch reflects and fails to solve the contradictions which we first met in the arts. He echoes George Steiner's lamentations about the devaluation of the Word and in this passage he sees a hope of filling the vacuum by supplementing the neutered Word with the 'language of the senses'. Yet in the previous passage he seems to imply that liturgy, like theatre, is rediscovering a minimalism (of ecclesiastical rubrics as of theatrical props and scenery). So again we see implications for liturgy in the new fashions which lead us both to Beckett and to Richard Neville or John Cage – a liturgy of bareness and silence or a communion of sensual stimulation; minimalism or the multi-media carnival. In either case, we also see the role of the priest becoming more like that of the theatre director, the unseen head who is responsible for orchestrating all the experimentation: where there is no script (or liturgical text, or musical score), the conductor or director becomes all powerful. In practice, as Birch recognizes, the result is often neither minimalism nor carnival, but just empty banality. In fact the most frequent consequence of the radical liturgical innovations is to accelerate that process of 'secularization', that reduction of religion to mere culture and the evacuation of the religious essence. Once again the attack on boundaries results in the opposite effect from that intended by the radicals who inaugurated it.

Where Christians redeployed the symbolism of expressive disorder and radical communitas they usually succeeded in eroding the distinctiveness of the Christian (or, indeed, the religious) message itself: in trying to transcend boundaries they merged with the profane world. They were sometimes able to relocate the new symbol system in quasi-communitarian enclaves of committed priests and laity but in so doing they set themselves apart as an 'alternative' elite. They simply redefined *which* boundaries separated the saved from the damned so that the radical enclave rather than the conventional Church became the 'inside': then they needed a 'Directory of the Liberated Church' in order to recognize fellow 'insiders'.

Exactly parallel consequences follow from the adoption of the same style by traditional or conservative groups within the Churches. The shared symbolism of spontaneity, informality and in-group communitas serves to mark off the committed regulars from the periphery of tribal Christians (which includes most of the working classes, of course) who have not been initiated into the new symbol system and vocabulary of 'open' brotherhood. This cultivation of demonstrative openness simply serves to accentuate the division between the in-group, who can operate the style with skill and without an embarrassed self-consciousness, and the outsiders, who are not merely uninitiated into the style but who frequently are repelled by a mode so alien to the English culture of control. Thus the ancient Durkheimian functions of the institutional Church as the natural vehicle of national and local identity are further attenuated as congregations typically become more in-turned and exclusive, all in the name of openness and mission, of course. Again, 'invisible pedagogy' rebounds on itself to foster *de facto* elitism. This further colludes with just those social processes which are undermining the bases of natural community and making privatization ever more common. In fact, we have travelled back around the same old circle of inchoate malaise, followed by prophylactic action which intensifies rather than alleviates the ill. After all, it was these same processes of privatization and the shift of the Churches from the centre to the periphery of social life that originally triggered the clerical anxieties which in turn induced so precipitate a copying of the counter-cultural style. It seemed to offer immediacy, topical relevance, instant visibility in a world where religion had for so long simply not been NEWS, a way back into the world out of the privatized and suburban cul-de-sac, opportunities for busy witness and, as a bonus, a symbolic rejection of the old contamination with the cultural style of the squirearchy. It is, however, taking a long time for the clergy to notice how badly it has all backfired, leaving the Churches banal and cliquey and driving the transcendent, the ecstatic and the daemonic to lodge in the 'lunatic fringe'.

Part of the trouble, of course, is that the mainstream cleric is caught in a pincer movement. There are the radicals in direct descent from the counter-culture, busy heaping anathemas on moderation of all kinds and still being something of a religious *succès de scandale*, and there is the Charismatic Movement which offers many of the same attractions as the fringe cults but from within the conventional Churches. Until very recently the usual response to these challenges was to borrow ever more items of radical style to package a moderate or even puritan message. Just as we noted an insidious anti-intellectualism as the (partly) intentional product of radical style in education, so it is in religion. These developments have a natural affinity with those aspects of popular Protestantism which celebrate the simple and childlike at the expense of intellectual muscle and aesthetic complexity: as one popular evangelical poster has it (unconsciously echoing Richard Neville as much as Jesus Christ): 'It's child's play – the Mums an' Dads are learning fast.'

An articulate defence of tradition and complexity in the Churches has been slow to show itself though recently there are signs of what one might call a catholic as distinct from a protestant counter-blast, an unashamed advocacy of the objective against the subjective, the historical against the topical and above all the need for frames and boundaries around the sacred. This movement has for example focused on the liturgical issue.[33] It remains to be seen what the impact of this defence of Word and Ritual will be.

Nevertheless, up to the present, the main reply to the counter-culture in religion has been a Conservative Evangelical girding of the loins. As we have seen, however, these Puritan responses do partly subvert themselves by borrowing a radical style to package a message which comes right from the heart of the old culture of control. Backlash though they may be, they have also done their bit in assisting the popularization of the Expressive Revolution. They march, demonstrate in the streets and display the new imperatives of informality and diffuse mutual affection even while they are protesting against abortion, pornography, obscenity in the mass media, and so on. Christian rock festivals and the popular religious rock musicals are part of the old technique which the early Methodists understood so well (you must never let the Devil have all the good tunes). Even the Festival of Light, the best known defence movement of the traditional religious culture of control, has inadvertently colluded with the cultural revolution of which it so disapproves. As Wallis has pointed out, though its leaders present it as a moral crusade and urge their followers to bombard local newspapers and MPs with protests about moral pollution, the youthful demonstrators who make up most of the active movement prefer just to march and proclaim that Jesus lives: style is everything.

The least equivocal response from the culture of control has been Mrs Mary Whitehouse's crusade, conducted largely through her organization, the National Viewers' and Listeners' Association. The target of Mrs Whitehouse's righteous indignation is the propagation of the values of the 'permissive society' through the mass media. Mrs Whitehouse and many of her supporters are evangelical Christians for whom the changes in style, standards, and values in the past decade or so pose a major challenge and affront to the Puritan conscience. Being predominantly middle-class, this group is able to call on all the organizational skills and social resources necessary to make an articulate protest against what they experience as a morally and religiously shocking drift in society and culture. There are some indications that among those minority segments of the working class where the same shock is felt, social skills are not easily available, with the result that the inchoate sense of having been betrayed by Church, state and cultural leaders paves the way to conversion to the older group of morally fundamentalist sects like the Jehovah's Witnesses. My point here is simply that the symbolic significance of Mrs Whitehouse and her movement is far greater than might be suggested by simple head-counting of the active participants in a small protest lobby. *Par excellence* she is the mouthpiece of what remains of the strict culture of control in British society, and it would be a great mistake to treat her as a semi-comic anachronism, as much of the liberal press originally did. The cause for which she crusades has parallels in North America and in all the Protestant cultures of Europe.

I want therefore to take Mrs Whitehouse's crusade as the peg on which to hang my final remarks and the occasion for assessing the wider implications of the Expressive Revolution. The matter really has two cruces, sex, and 'culture' in its narrow sense. Until now I have deliberately avoided the popular cliché, the 'permissive society', precisely because its connotation is almost purely sexual, and I have wanted to emphasize the many other facets of expressive anti-structure which have no necessary sexual implication. Yet the important point about Mrs Whitehouse and the National Viewers' and Listeners' Association (NVALA) is so obvious that it could easily be ignored:

here, too, 'moral pollution' has an almost entirely sexual meaning and that (the crucial symbolic role of sexuality in the popularization of the Expressive Revolution) must be one of the main axes of the discussion in the final chapter. The second issue which Mrs Whitehouse and her movement serve to highlight is the role of 'culture' in its narrow sense and the role of the mass media in particular. Television especially, that intimate stranger which invades the privacy of all our homes, is the source of many problems. The special target of Mrs Whitehouse's attention is the BBC as the traditional guardian of modern cultural values, and her vision of its proper role is closely akin to that of Lord Reith himself. The NVALA represents the deep suspicion of the culture of control that the central organ of mass communication and opinion formation has already fallen to the culture of expressive permissiveness.

The role of mass media is peculiarly important if my case so far in this chapter is correct. I have argued that a brake is ultimately applied wherever the expressive imperative runs up against powerful and necessary elements of instrumentality in institutions such as education and welfare. The permissive revolution is therefore pushed back into the more purely expressive (and increasingly specialized) activities of leisure and the consumption of 'culture'. Hence the place where we would expect to find expressive anti-structure at its most naked would be popular (and elite) 'culture' and the mass media. These issues must then form a central part of the final assessment to which I now turn.

CHAPTER 11

A Cultural Revolution?

Ever since observation taught me temptation
Is a matter of timing, I've tried
To clothe my fiction in up-to-date diction,
The contemporary jargon of Pride.
> *I can recall when, to win the more*
> > *Obstinate round,*
> *The best bet was to say to them: 'Sin the more*
> > *That Grace may abound.'*

Since Social Psychology replaced Theology
The process goes twice as quick,
If a conscience is tender and loth to surrender
I have only to whisper: 'You're sick.'
> *Puritanical morality*
> > *Is madly non-U*
> *Enhance your personality*
> > *With a romance, with two.*

If you pass up a dame, you've yourslf to blame,
For shame is neurotic, so snatch!
All rules are too formal, in fact they're abnormal
For any desire is natch.
> *So take your proper share, man, of*
> > *Dope and drink:*
> *Aren't you the Chairman of*
> > *Ego, Inc.?*

Free-Will is a mystical myth as statistical
Methods have objectively shown,
A fad of the Churches: since the latest researches
Into Motivation it's known
> *That Honor is hypocrisy*
> > *Honesty a joke.*
> *You live in a Democracy:*
> > *Lie like other folk.*

Since men are like goods, what are shouldn'ts or shoulds
When you are the leading Brand?
Let them all drop dead, you're way ahead
Beat them up if they dare to demand
    What may your intention be,
        Or what might ensue:
There's a difference of dimension be-
        tween the rest and you.

If in the scrimmage of business your image
Should ever tarnish or stale,
Public Relations can take it and make it
Shine like a Knight of the Grail.
    You can mark up the price that you sell at, if
        Your package has glamour and show:
Values are relative
        Dough is dough.

So let each while you may think you're more O.K.
More yourself than anyone else,
Till you find that you're hooked, your goose is cooked,
And you're only a cipher of Hell's.
    Believe while you can that I'm proud of you,
        Enjoy your dream:
I'm so bored with the whole fucking crowd of you
    I could scream!

W. H. Auden: 'The Song of the Devil', in *Collected Poems*

How much of a cultural revolution is it, in the last analysis? Are we, as Auden's Devil boasts, left with a commercialized selfishness parading as the new free morality and dependent on the social sciences for its dubious legitimation? The survival of the fittest decked out in the trappings of equality and liberty, with a 'total fraternity' reserved for those who lack the stomach for the individual survival course? Is anything left of the solidities of landmark and boundary by which all but that tiny minority at the bohemian top and lumpen bottom of the social scale have traditionally measured their lives and found their places?

I think we must conclude that the romantic crusade was always an impossible Utopian dream: it mistook the nature of liminality. The essence of that liminal experience which the cultural radicals sought to universalize is that it cannot last, it is no recipe for a total way of life. That perfect moment when the opposites are poised and fused *is* only a moment and must always tip over into imbalance: ecstasy crumbles and we face the same old paradox. The internal logic of symbolic anti-structure and the opposed logic of communitas tear us apart and we find oursleves forced to make choices, to organize, to exercise and accept control *whichever half of the paradox we follow*. The cultivation of pure anti-structure, if unchecked by any element of classical form, turns into self-defeating silence or an incoherent babel, even when the aim of the exercise, as in the arts and popular culture, is entirely non-utilitarian: as Auden wrote in a review of Lewis Carroll, anarchy and incompetence are incompatible with play. Boundary violation turns the romantic impulse over on its back: it produces minimalism, camp, parody, irony and often no communication at all. Moreover, an overdose of anti-structure swiftly brings the drastic medicine of rigid communitarianism where the maladies of individualism are cured by the application of the pure group remedy – and nothing, not even the old culture of control, is as inexorably structured and rule bound as the cultural manifestations of total communitas.

Yet despite the dilemmas, the expressive imperative has undoubtedly gained ground in quite fundamental ways in all the cultural milieux which we have visited. As a cultural style it contains elements which are increasingly appropriate to a complex, mobile and privatized social system in which ego rather than any natural 'tribal' group forms the basic unit. As we have seen, the crucial mechanism by which the old culture of control was broken open to the possibilities of change was the counter-culture of the late 1960s, with its vision of permanent liminality, a boundary-and rule-free Utopia. Inevitably, that missionary generation suffered the worst casualties when the destructive logic both of pure anti-structure and of total communitas began to be applied to social arrangements as well as to cultural forms. In the first flush of creative euphoria, the existential communitas generated in the various movements loosely called the counter-culture served to offset the ultimately disintegrative and anomic effects of unrelieved anti-structure. But in the longer run the negative side-effects and inner contradictions began to be felt.

At this stage, there appeared a series of processes which, in effect, put the frames back around the liminal moments. In the arts themselves, the expressive media both popular and elite, this process took several guises. We have already examined the first in the relevant chapters. This is the paradoxical consequence of the wholesale application of the principle of boundary demolition: every crusade of artistic anti-structure whatever its particular logic (minimalism, surrealism, preoccupation with meta-structure, multimedia happenings or whatever) is turned into instant fashion. However hard the radicals tried to eliminate the distinction between life and art, their very success in removing the distinction between different classes of 'public' ensured that their various efforts have become styles, forms and fashions ready for imitation, marketing and consumption right down the line. The contemporary culture market muddles together elite and vulgar, yesterday's shock and today's joke, in one gloriously trivial *bricolage*. Style is everything and anything can become a style. Malcolm Bradbury offers a masterly summary of the most important dimensions of these developments.

> Today, evidently, we live in a stylistic melting pot, a world of transforming social, sexual and epistemological relationships, a world in which new stylistic negotiations have a significant social function. There are bohemians on every street corner, self-parodists in every boutique, neo-artists at every discotheque.
>
> The new narcissism of contemporary Western culture has been much analysed lately; part of that narcissism is that stylistic negotiation has a social function, become a way of intersecting with contemporary history and the conditions of the late technological world. The foregrounding of style has led in discussion of art and writing to much talk of meta-art, para-criticism, sur-fiction. But at the same time the emphasis on style has tended to acquire a certain character as irony. It is hard to distil any dominant characteristics from an artistic scene that has taken in abstract expressionism, pop, op and kinetic art, photo realism, minimalist and conceptual art, multi-media events and happenings, and which has taken its funds from an enormous variety of cultural milieux. But if there is a dominant feature, it is surely an element of inbuilt provisionality: an instinct indeed towards parody and self-parody.[1]

The anti-art crusade produces a set of fashions for mass consumption; the riotous market in styles in turn provides a vocabulary, a set of codes, through which we negotiate and display our professional and private identities and achieve a tentative relationship with a complex and impersonal world; the romantic impulse to spontaneity and unmediated experience ends up as irony and self-parody. The counter-cultural generation of the late 1960s took themselves and their mission very seriously. To do so today would be quaintly uncool: contemporary man can only bear his own seriousness or his romantic aspirations if he disguises them as self-parody and camp humour. As Auden wrote towards the end of his life: 'I suspect that without some undertone of the comic genuine serious verse cannot be written today.'[2] All these developments in the arts show that the liminal flood is under control: its natural inner logic was anyway a process of distancing. The frames are emphatically back in place, but with one significant difference. We are now able to tolerate a vastly expanded range of liminal pictures inside them; much that was only 'lurking irreality', or unspeakable in the 1950s is now the stuff of daily cultural consumption. This routinization of symbolic anti-structure as items of popular taste (Bradbury's bohemians on every street corner, etc.) has had two further consequences which we have already noted in the rock music world. Though a stylistic *mélange* based on *bricolage* might be expected to lack historical sensibility (and has even been known to boast of it), in fact in all cultural spheres there is a passion for tracing the history of the constituent elements in the currently popular packages. The London art galleries and the popular booksellers run highly successful retrospectives on expressionism, symbolism, surrealism, and so on. A similar process occurs in both popular and avant-garde film, in the cinema and crucially on television. So the media become preoccupied with the *history* of styles: it is all very classical and academic, this re-contextualization of all that had been deliberately *de*-contextualized in the cultural jumble sale of the sixties.

There is a further process too, akin to what we have seen in rock music's rediscovery of its own origins. In all the arts, since the late seventies, we are seeing revivals of neo-classicism and above all the rediscovery of simplicity (as distinct from minimalism). Public voices are heard with increasing frequency arguing a restrained and rational case for the indispensability of structure, form and ritual in the arts. One powerful voice making this case is Sir Ernst Gombrich.[3] He summarizes his basic position in these words:

I claim that the formal characteristics of most human products, from tools to buildings and from clothing to ornaments, can be seen as manifestations of that sense of order which is deeply rooted in man's biological heritage. Organic life is governed by hierarchical structures which not only secure the interaction of internal functions (e.g. heartbeat and breathing), but also assist adjustment to the environment. Here the role of the sense of order is complementary to the perception of meaning. Because the detection of food, of mates, or of danger first requires orientation in space and anticipation in time. Those ordered events in our environment which exhibit rhythmical or other regular features (the waves of the sea or the uniform texture of a cornfield) easily 'lock' in' with our tentative projections of order and thereby sink below the threshold of our attention while any change in these regularities leads to an arousal of attention. Hence the artificial environment man has created for himself satisfies his dual demand for easy adjustment and easy arousal.[4]

The rediscovery of 'order' as the prerequisite for 'arousal' – the symbiosis between structure and anti-structure – is an important element in the current cultural scene. Once the old, contingent 'order' of the pre-war culture of control had been effectively jostled into a new pattern by the counter-culture's onslaught on order *per se*, it slowly became possible for a defence of order and structure to be distinguished from a last ditch stand of the Old Order.

The history of the expressive professions outlined in the previous chapter was another facet of the process by which liminality was reframed and the necessity of order, even a a precondition of expressive enrichment, was reaffirmed. In all the cases we examined – education, the welfare professions and the Churches – the expressive imperative made a great deal of headway against earlier structures based on formality, hierarchy and ritual. To put it at its very lowest, the *style* of informality and the *manners* of egalitarian spontaneity became the preferred mode, and it was ever more widely assumed that the natural objective of these institutions was to enable ego to achieve self-realization. (You're more yourself than anyone else.) The basic premises of what has been called the New Narcissism ('Aren't you the Chairman of Ego, Inc.?') became deeply etched into the cultural and political base of these professional activities. Yet in the cases of education and welfare at least, the continued, if half-concealed imperatives of utility and instrumentality put a sharp brake on the more extreme developments of the expressive imperative particularly when it took the form of symbolic anti-structure. Governments, the bread-and-butter segment of the profession, and the representatives of the mainstream culture of control (often the consumers and always the taxpayers), all began to demand the reaffirmation of structure, limits and even hierarchy in these expensive branches of public policy. So the expressive imperative, (especially in the guise of symbolic boundary destruction) was curbed and controlled by the second half of the 1970s.

Central to this process were the awful lessons drawn from the self-defeating logic of anti-structure as a recipe for social living (as distinct from its use as rhetorical ploy of artistic style). Expressive narcissism as an axial principle of social life extorts a heavy price in competitiveness, isolation and rootlessness. This is a point of central agreement among the writers who have recently analysed the New Narcissism – Rieff,[5] Lasch,[6] Sennett,[7] Slater[8] and Carroll.[9] What they share is a preoccupation with the *pathology* of the phenomenon: they are pessimists when it comes to assessing the consequences of the cultural shifts which I have called the Expressive Revolution. For Slater it amounts to 'the pursuit of loneliness'. For Carroll the hedonist attempt to exorcize the Puritan demon, guilt, has an inbuilt tendency to backfire: egoistic pleasure orientation leads to a prevalent ennui bringing nihilism and depression in its wake. Lasch and Sennett both excoriate the new cultural imperatives. They see the promises of pleasure and liberation as false. To Sennett, the erosion of the old distinction between public and private has resulted in a retreat from the public and a simultaneous impoverishment in both spheres. The public sphere, the traditional arena for citizenship (that is brotherhood and mutual responsibility), has been abandoned and has turned into no-man's-territory, a veritable Waste Land, architecturally, socially, politically. The tyranny of mandatory intimacy has taken its place. The privileged, indeed the only legitimate, model for interaction becomes that of personal intimacy. All interaction assumes the shape of the private relationship, thus at a stroke we all forfeit our right to privacy. Our frantic attempts to secure a retreat for the truly private self drives us into defensive narcissism. The false 'intimacy' of relationships which should be public and formal constantly distorts our closest relationships in what would be a genuinely private sphere, family, friendship and the like. Narcissism thus becomes increasingly and uselessly frantic: Mick Jagger's classic hymn to the frustrations of *anomie* becomes our common anthem, 'I can't get no satisfaction'.

Lasch comes at the same phenomenon from the exactly opposite angle. The apparent individualism, expressiveness and privatization of narcissist culture is false. The public (quasi-economic) imperative of competition and performance invades the private world of the self and the face-to-face relationship. The frenetic search for an enhanced quality of life becomes instead an anxious quantification of successes and failures. We can no longer do anything unself-consciously but we must constantly rate and grade ourselves – as parents, lovers, gourmets, golfers or whatever. Manuals of sexual practice (you *must* get some satisfaction!) and child rearing show our twentieth century preoccupations as clearly as did the Victorians' handbooks of etiquette and household management: not class and status but expressive virtuosity are our goals. Woody Allen, Jules Feiffer and their ilk are the jesters holding up the mirror in which modern man sees his own neurotic face.

There is no space here to discuss in any detail the very subtle twists of argument in these various theorists of the New Narcissism. What matters about them for my purposes is that they make a powerful and relatively consistent, but most important a *critical* case: they see it as a deeply problematic cultural and social form riddled with *anomie* in all kinds of brightly coloured new guises. The effortless optimism of 1968 is nowhere in evidence and indeed that is true not just of social scientists but of many cultural commentators. The contemporary world of the novel, the commercial film, of comedy and journalism echoes exactly the same themes. Even the persistent tail-end of the counter-culture proper recognizes the problems: Ogilvie and Roszak,[10] for instance, both find the optimism harder to generate and the obstacles to Utopia more intractable than they seemed in 1969. Furthermore, my references to Woody Allen and Jules Feiffer were deliberately chosen: they are the equivalent in semi-popular culture of Auden's 'undertone of the comic' without which serious verse cannot be written, and Bradbury's 'irony' and 'self-parody'. In them, and in novelists of contemporary manners like John Fowles, or Kingsley Amis, the expressive middle classes trace their own dilemmas and chart the unintended malaise of the culture of self-development. And *that*, of course, is just another dimension of the narcissim: as Carroll says, we find nothing of interest apart from ourselves. Nevertheless, the very fact that both popular culture and serious scholarship are coding and commenting on the ills and the partial retreat of the Expressive Revolution is of some significance. It is a point to which I will return below, but first I want, at last, to take up the issue of sexuality which I left dangling in the air at the end of the last chapter. It is a topic which is just as pivotal to the theorists of the New Narcissism as it is to Mrs Whitehouse.

Because it is a potentially ecstatic *experience*, sexuality easily stands for the symbolism of anti-structure and, for the same reason, it tends to be hedged around by cultural prohibitions which harness it to the central institutions of order and continuity. Mrs Whitehouse, the NVALA, the Festival of Light, indeed the whole Puritan conscience, is engaged in a classic duel with the champions of the Expressive Revolution for control over that crucial symbolic resource: free sexuality as *the* focus of expressive egoism, or bounded sexuality as the basis of the monogamous family and the whole culture of control. Either way, sex is a sacred symbol. It is a shorthand code, as it were, for the whole range of conflicts between the two cultures and like all powerful symbols it says more than it speaks: controversies about pornography, obscenity, abortion are about much more than sexuality. In many ways, Mrs Whitehouse and her supporters have been invaluable to the proponents of the culture of expressive openness. As we have seen, the practice of sexual taboo breaking often snaps off the branch on which the taboo breakers are sitting. If a taboo is broken often enough it ceases to be a taboo and becomes a secular fashion. This was why cultural representations of sexuality eventually veered to the black and daemonic pole and beyond that into self-parody, because the more people accept sunny sexual hedonism as a legitimate goal, the less easy it is for the taboo breakers to make sex sufficiently 'dirty' to have any impact. So Mrs Whitehouse and the moral fundamentalists have acted as the underpinning 'sense of order' in Gombrich's terms while the disciples of permissiveness are free to pursue 'arousal': they are the structure without which anti-structure can find no meaning or anchor. Without the NVALA, sexual explicitness in the mass media might have had to be far more perverse and perverted in order to get any notice at all.

But there is more to it than this: there is no doubt that the direct and explicit portrayal of sexuality is the most obvious single feature of recent changes in the media of both a mass and elite culture. (Swearing is perhaps the other.) Nakedness is no longer a matter for much comment; indeed, stage nudity is now taken for granted. What this suggests is that the normalization of sexual explicitness is not merely a feature of cultural symbols but of popular norms and behaviour also: and that of course is precisely what worries Mrs Whitehouse. Certainly, the rate of marriage breakdown is increasing steadily at all class levels; unconventional households (both heterosexual and homosexual) are more visible; formal marriage is rejected by a significant minority for a longer stretch of the life cycle; voluntary childlessness is more common. In short, whether or not there has been a real increase in sexual promiscuity (and no one knows whether that is so or not), there has certainly been a change in the shape of the social institutions which are based on sexuality as well as a cultural shift towards sexual openness. While cultural popularization via taboo violation was certainly a part of the process, I should be far from wanting to claim that it was the only, or even the most important part. The sexual revolution of the late twentieth century also has hard social foundations in the chemical technology of contraception, the medical provision for safe early abortion, and the control of venereal diseases. All these have radically altered the social and personal meanings of sexual behaviour. They make it possible for sexuality to be *reduced* to the expressive dimension, denuded of all attendant physiological, social, and moral consequences, and thus *of all risk*. Since the advent of the contraceptive pill and the medical capability of safe termination of pregnancy, human beings (significantly the female half of that plural) can separate sexuality from reproduction, and both from marriage, with greater ease than has ever before been the case. The medical control of VD removes another set of risks: it is, for example, virtually impossible to imagine that, if he were writing *Doctor Faustus* today, Thomas Mann would use Esmeralda and her venereal infection as symbols of Faust's pact with the Devil. Sexuality, by these seemingly benevolent means, has been shrunk to the status of risk-free play. Like film, television, and the rest of popular culture, it has become above all else entertainment.

Yet it is still not a trouble-free amusement. We have already noted Christopher Lasch's view that the promises of private expressive release are subverted by the invasion of the criteria of the market-place into the home, and crucially the bedroom. It is therefore perhaps more accurate to say that sex-as-play is not risk-free, but rather that it has shifted the risks to a new dimension for narcissistic modern man. Instead of VD, pregnancy, or loss of respectability, we risk loss of face if our performance fails to reach virtuoso standard. That is what all the secular bibles of erotic practice are about: so, after all, sex remains a prime source of anxiety, neurosis, and a sense of rootless inedequacy. Woody Allen displays the symptoms of the disease perfectly, and quinine cannot cure it. Free sexuality stands for expressive richness and release: but sexuality is also the site of the most characteristic traumas of the narcissist and his identity crisis. As the locus of the sacred ego it is fragile and explosive. And once more, the characteristic contemporary response is to indulge in self-parody, to make sex and its psychic ills the object of wry laughter. So again the romantic impulse undermines itself and sex-as-ecstasy first gives way to sex-as-dirt and then sex-as-comedy. When we have come this far around the circle, it even becomes possible for some weary pilgrims to rediscover, in theory at least, a nostalgia for fixed systems and coercive forms like monagamous marriage or even arranged marriages, or making-the-best-of-what-happened-to-be-available.

The main difficulty about this whole analysis, however, is that it is a map of the psycho-social terrain of the expressive professionals, of bohemia and its social hinterland. Indeed it is truer to California and New York even than to London NW1. Neither Mrs Whitehouse's middle England nor the mainstream working class can seriously recognize itself in the picture of the New

Narcissism. Of course, it is all a matter of degree, and one of the problems is that we lack an anthropology of our own contemporary cultural milieux which would enable us to say definitively *what* degree. The assessment must therefore be speculative and impressionistic. So far as sexuality is concerned, there is clearly still a powerful representation of the middle class (Evangelical and commercial predominantly) prepared to abide by the old culture of control and to defend monogamy and reticence. The working class and the routine white-collar segments of the service class have been more hospitable to expressive openness, of which the attitude to sexual explicitness is one index. Tolerance of sexual peccadillos (though they do remain peccadillos) is probably more widespread among the respectable working class than it was a generation ago. This stratum has coped with the popularization of sexual explicitness without serious trauma, probably because bawdy sexuality always figured prominently in the culture of working class leisure time liminality. The nude on page three of the tabloid newspaper (and page three is of course a *frame*) is just the updated analogue of the seaside postcard or Frank Randall's music hall scatology.[11] The (probably) more relaxed sexual mores of the most recent generations do not seem to have caused the kind of cultural spasms which other aspects of the Expressive Revolution's assault on the landmarks of respectability (welfare and education policies, for instance) provoked. I think there may be two main reasons for this. First, in working-class culture, sexuality was always heavily framed: it does not interfere too much with the serious business of living. When leisure, affluence and comfort increase, it is not too difficult a task to accept an expansion of the frames within which sex-as-liminality can operate. After all, the great merit of culture based on boundary and control is that provided everything *has* its place within some frame or other, there is no nonsense about inner consistency: the latter worry is a problem for the rational intellectual but not for the folk *bricoleur*. A culture which can happily absorb a rash of Tudor doors on 1930s' council houses, 1880s' factory terraces and 1960s' neo-Georgian houses (as long as the colours match of course), has no difficulty with a mass produced picture of naked, young love – again, so long as it tones in with the sitting-room décor, and such pictures happily tend to come in several popular shades.

The second reason why the working classes seem able to absorb sexual explicitness without serious trouble is that working-class households have been far more heavily saturated by the cultural artifacts of youth culture and rock music in which explicit sexuality is such a central feature, than have most middle-class households. It is after all the staple fare of the mass radio and TV networks: housewives and adolescents get much the same menu. Moreover, this particular branch of the Expressive Revolution has mostly wedded sexual explicitness to the traditional sex role dichotomy which gives working-class culture no trouble at all.

It seems likely that when the research is done it will show some increase

A replacement for The Light of the World *on the working-class wall: every-day nudity available for £10 by mail order or £5 on the market stall.*

of privatization and mobility and some erosion of the communal bases of neighbourhood and kin among the working classes and the new white-collar zone, but nothing like as much of either as has occurred among the middle range of the bourgeoisie and particularly the expressive professionals. Amongst the latter, the groups most exposed – and, let it be said, self-exposed – to the negative kick-back of the Expressive Revolution there have been signs of a counter movement, especially since the mid-1970s, with the object of re-creating structures of belonging, 'life worlds' sufficiently small and integrated to offer an alternative to communitas or the tribal unit. These are something less total than the cults and sects described in chapter 9, but something more than the normal middle-class associational forms: not so much golf clubs as shared life-styles. Such initiatives range from suburban associations of young couples and their children, who share chores and leisure and even housing arrangements, to more formal communities like the house-churches of the Charismatic Movement.

There has certainly been an Expressive Revolution but it is less total than the cultural radicals of the late sixties hoped or intended. In the media of pure expressiveness the indispensable basis of order has been rediscovered, and the praxis of anti-structural symbolism has been sharply checked in those areas of activity where instrumental norms exist alongside expressive ones. Liminality has been firmly put back where it always properly belonged, in ritual, in the arts, and above all in popular culture, but it is again a framed liminality. Instead of becoming a truly all-pervasive life-style, the culture of expressive disorder has retreated to become a leisure time relaxation. Even there it sits alongside the equally powerful symbols of conservation and continuity in twentieth-century folk culture.

One example will suffice to illustrate the point. Film, of all the con-temporary media, is the perfect vehicle for expressive liminality: it can play with time and space; it is multi-media; it was one of the pioneer cases of avant-garde anti-structure. Yet consider the currently popular genres. There is the fashion for horror/science fiction/disaster/suspense movies where images of random unimaginable horror are played within the safety of the well-upholstered cinema seat: it is an old and tried formula for catharsis through fantasy, with an ancestry that goes back to Red Riding Hood's wolf and all the fairy tale dragons; in short, the folk narrative, the ordeal, the quest, tension and release. Another popular genre is of particular interest in that it combines exactly the liminal duality – anti-structure and communitas. Violence, explicit sexuality, sadism, degradation and all sorts of norm-violation characterize the liminal situation where GIs in Vietnam (*The Deer Hunter*), besieged cops and convicts (*Assault on Precinct Thirteen*) or teenage gangs (*The Warriors*), nevertheless find pure and purifiying com-munitas. The machismo of this genre is less a rude reply to Women's Lib than an instance of that 'utterly unbourgeois ordeal' which secularization has banished from religious culture.[12] It is the symbolic test through which manliness, moral worth and adulthood is won and vicarious participation in such banished rituals obviously assuages a deep social lack in our culture. This particular contemporary genre is entirely of a piece with the classic western and even the old adventure stories of boys' papers. The 'road' films of the counter-culture (*Easy Rider*, etc.) form an obvious link between apparently opposed genres and are currently still popular with the same clientele who conduct their vicarious initiation ceremonials via the spaghetti westerns.

Thus, even the media of leisure time expressiveness serves up its liminality neatly framed and placed in the context of a folk mythology which codes precisely such fundamental structures as age and sex roles and generalized social values. In other ways, too, popular culture plays its part in domesticating the culture of liminalty. We have already noted a tendency for the media to document the history of the various cultural ingredients in the expressive package and to comment on the dilemmas of the narcissistic life-style after the dream has faded. This includes not just highbrow humour like Woody Allen but importantly, the television situation comedy and soap opera which inures us to such facts (and casualties) of the new expressive culture as the separated wife (Rhoda). Even the hippie, the alternative culturnik, is no longer a folk devil but a clown, for whom a wry affection can be entertained. He appears on greetings cards ('Hippy Birthday') in popular cartoons, and television comedies. The counter-culture is thoroughly domesticated when it becomes an established ingredient in the great British joke.

What can be said in conclusion? Social life is difficult, complex and full of dilemmas, perhaps no more so today than it ever was, though wider awareness of choice and alternatives does underline problems which might have been ignored when there was no help for them. Rising expectations bring new frustrations. Utopia is not available via any simple formula: neither the Expressive Revolution nor some unrealistic nostalgia for an illusory golden age can guarantee the good life. In every age, the same two terrifying traps loom to engulf us — Auden called them the heaven (or hell) of 'Pure Self' and of the 'Truly General Case'. In the contemporary landscape they take very clear shape. The first, egoist narcissim, has been well dubbed the 'awareness trap'.[13] He who contemplates his own navel for long enough will forfeit the blessing of human companionship. The other extreme, the total sect, I would call the 'brotherhood (and sisterhood) trap'. He who accedes to the Divine Right of the sacred group forfeits a crucial part of his selfhood: as Auden warned, 'Alienation from the Collective is always a duty.' Neither extreme, on its own, will bring satisfaction. There is no infallible technique for getting the balance right, only a long vigilance, and occasionally, often through sheer grace and not repeatable at will, the perfect experience of *coincidentia oppositorum*. I leave the last words to Auden.

In the twentieth century, it is not the failure but the fantastic success of our techniques of production that is creating a society in which it is becoming increasingly difficult to live a human life. In our reactions to this, one can see many parallels to the third century. Instead of Gnostics we have existentialists and God-is-dead theologians; instead of Neoplatonists, 'humanist' professors; instead of desert eremites, heroin-addicts and Beats; instead of the cult of virginity, do-it-yourself sex manuals and sado-masochistic pornography. Now as then, a proper balance between detachment and commitment seems impossible to find or hold. Both lead to evil. The introvert, intent upon improving himself, is deaf to his neighbor when he cries for help; the extrovert, intent upon improving the world, pinches his neighbor (for his own good of course) until he cries for help. We are not, any of us, very nice.[14]

Notes

CHAPTER 1: *Of Infinity and Ambiguity*

1 P. L. Berger. *The Social Reality of Religion*, Faber & Faber, London, 1969, p. 24.
2 T. Mann, *The Magic Mountain*, trs. H. T. Lowe-Porter, Penguin Books in association with Secker & Warburg, Harmondsworth and London, 1960, pp. 283–4.
3 W. H. Auden, 'Ode to Terminus', in W. H. Auden, *Collected Poems*, ed. E. Mendelson, Faber & Faber, London, 1976, pp. 608–9.
4 W. H. Auden, 'The Sea and the Mirror', in Auden, *Collected Poems*, p. 329.
5 W. H. Auden, 'Lullaby', in Auden, *Collected Poems*, p. 131.
6 W. H. Auden, *Paul Bunyan: An Operetta and a Prologue Set to Music by Benjamin Britten*, Op. 17, Faber Music Ltd in association with Faber & Faber, London, 1976.
7 W. H. Auden, 'Autumn Song', in Auden, *Collected Poems*, p. 118.
8 Auden, 'The Sea and the Mirror', in Auden, *Collected Poems*, pp. 330–1.
9 *ibid.*, pp. 337–8.
10 W. H. Auden, 'Contra Blake', from 'Shorts II', in Auden, *Collected Poems*, p. 540.

CHAPTER 2: *The Expressive Revolution*

1 The quotation is from Auden's long poem 'New Year Letter (January 1 1940) to Elizabeth Mayer', in W. H. Auden, *Collected Poems*, ed. E. Mendelson, Faber & Faber, London, 1976, p. 178.
2 M. Bradbury, *The History Man*, Secker & Warburg, London, 1975.
3 D. Caute, *The Confrontation: a trilogy*, (3 vols), Deutsch, London, 1971.
4 T. Parsons, 'The Educational and Expressive Revolutions'. Two special University of London lectures given at the London School of Economics, Spring 1975.
5 D. Bell, *The Cultural Contradictions of Capitalism*, Heinemann, London, 1976.

6 S. N. Eisenstadt, 'The Tradition of Modernity'. Mimeo. Paper given at the
Centennial Symposium of the Hebrew Union College, Jewish Institute of Religion, Jerusalem, April 1976.

7 Marcuse's most influential books – paperback bibles for the campus counter-
culture – were *Eros and Civilization*, Vintage Books, New York, 1962, and
One-Dimensional Man, Routledge & Kegan Paul, London, 1964. (The Sphere
paperback version of *One-Dimensional Man* (London, 1968) advertises on its
front cover 'In France [Marcuse's] work has sold more copies than Mao's
Little Red Book'.)

8 F. Parkin, *Middle Class Radicalism*, Manchester University Press,
Manchester, 1968.

9 The bourgeois individualism sometimes snapped back at its counter-cultural
detractors. See e.g. A. Rand, *The New Left: the Anti-Industrial Revolution*,
Signet Books, New York, 1971.

10 E. Shils, 'Centre and Periphery: Selected Papers 2', *Essays in Macrosociology*,
Chicago University Press, Chicago, 1975.

11 L. Kolakowski, 'The Concept of a Counter-Reformation'. The 1976 Hobhouse
Memorial Lecture given at Bedford College, University of London, May 1976.

12 Mary Quant cosmetics *par excellence*. They are both expensive and packaged
with pictures and names redolent of wholesome, 'natural', rural life ('Country
Clay'), or additionally echoing the Flower Power era ('Middle Earth'). The
Smirnoff Vodka advertisements are probably the cleverest and most blatant
examples of the use of a jet-set version of counter-culture motifs to sell a
luxury product to middle- and lower-income customers.

CHAPTER 3: *Symbols, Codes and Culture*

1 J. L. Borges, 'Pierre Menard, Author of the Quixote', in *Labyrinths*, edited by
D. Yates and J. B. Irby, Penguin Books, Harmondsworth, 1970. Borges is a
fascinatingly enigmatic figure vis-à-vis some of the avant-garde developments
in literature and film which will be discussed in chapter 5. He is a specialist in
and master of ambiguity, who became an important influence on the *nouvelle
vague* films of the late 1960s and early 1970s, and who explains the origin of
his own style as deriving from film, especially from von Sternberg. His narrative method is based on 'images' and 'significative moments' (like film frames),
rather than on 'characters'. He calls his own stories 'ambiguous exercises'
which began as 'the irresponsible game of a shy young man who did not dare
write a story and amused himself falsifying and distorting (perhaps without
aesthetic justification) other people's tales'. (preface to *A Universal History of
Infamy*, 1954, quoted E. Cozarinsky, 'Borges On and In Film', in *Sight and
Sound*, Winter 1975/6). That ironic, amused inversion of an expected
'aesthetic' justification reads very like Mann's descriptions of the irreverent
Adrian Leverkühn mocking humanist/aesthetic presuppositions throughout
Doctor Faustus (trs. H. T. Lowe-Porter, Penguin Books in association with
Secker & Warburg, Harmondsworth and London, 1968).

2 See C. Rosen, 'The Ruins of Walter Benjamin', *New York Review of Books*,

vol. XXIV, no. 17, 27 Oct. 1977, and Rosen, 'The Origins of Walter Benjamin', *New York Review of Books*, vol. XXIV, no. 18, 10 Nov. 1977.

3   P. Ricoeur, 'The Problem of the Double Sense as Hermeneutic Problem and as Semantic Problem', in J. M. Kitagawa and C. H. Long (eds), *Myths and Symbols: studies in honour of Mircea Eliade*, University of Chicago Press, Chicago and London, 1969, p. 66.

4   W. H. Auden, 'I am not a Camera', in Auden *Collected Poems*, ed. E. Mendelson, Faber & Faber, London, 1976, p. 630.

5   D. Sperber, *Rethinking Symbolism*, trans. by A. L. Morton, Cambridge University Press, Cambridge, 1975.

6   P. Ricoeur, 'The Problem of the Double Sense', p. 66.

7   ibid., p. 68.

8   Sperber, *Rethinking Symbolism*, p. 145.

9   Sperber, *Rethinking Symbolism*, pp. 115–19, contains a particularly revealing discussion of the symbolic nature of smells. Sperber points out that whereas most cultures provide classifications of colours, smells are not classified per se but *evoked* through the contexts in which they have been experienced; they are described or conjured but never defined. In short, they are part of the *bricolage* which operates through context and association rather than through classification proper. This elusive and uncategorized quality of smells is also discussed by A. Gell, 'Magic, Perfume, Dream —', in I. M. Lewis (ed.), *Symbols and Sentiments: Cross-cultural studies in Symbolism*, Academic Press, London, New York and San Francisco, 1977. Paralleling Sperber's argument, Gell writes 'smell is always incomplete by itself, ... it acquires meaning not by contrast with other smells, but by association with a context within which it is *typical*'; Gell argues that the olfactory quality of perfume gives it a special magical efficacy because it 'evokes transcendence'. It is 'of the world but not in it', it is 'spirit, half way between thing and idea', it cannot be confined but escapes the contours of the object from which it emanates. In fact its essentially *ambiguous* quality is the source of its symbolic power. 'Perfume is symbolic not linguistic because it does what language could *not* do.'

10 Mann, *Doctor Faustus*, p. 61. The point which Leverkühn makes here about the civilization/barbarism dichotomy holding only within 'the order of thought which it gives us' is the circular mode of thought which, by seeing thought as both determined and determinative, must relativize thought and truth and/or produce the warring philosophic projects of hermaneutics. If all thought is situated and determined (a) by social conditions, (b) by linguistic code, then no thought can be other than ideological and tautological, i.e. an expression of its own situated self. 'Objective' or what I refer to as 'fully conceptual' thought is in this view impossible. I recognize the problem, but retain the humanistic aspiration to a rationality which can, however partially, transcend its immediate context: any other position seems to me to lead to sterility and to an inability to speak about substantive matters because of the prelude of philosophical difficulties over the possibility or impossibility of speaking about speaking. A perfect example of convolution reaching the proportions of near-meaninglessness when determinism and relativism are combined can be seen in the occasional magazine pub. by the Dept of Sociology, Goldsmiths' College,

University of London, called *Writing Sociology. Writing Sociology*, no. 1, Oct. 1976, edited by P. Filmer, M. Phillipson, M. Roche and B. Sandywell, Expression Printers Ltd., London, 1976. In this case the code of communication has become so esoteric and unsubstantive that its impenetrability acts as a vehicle of in-group consciousness. See below n. 26, Eliade's treatment of just such phenomena as 'myths of the elite'. See also in chapter 5 the discussion on Surrealism.

11 C. Geertz, 'Thick Description: Toward an Interpretive Theory of Culture', in Geertz, *The Interpretation of Cultures: Selected Essays*, Basic Books Inc., New York, 1973.

12 T. Luckmann, *The Invisible Religion: The Problem of Religion in Modern Society*, Macmillan, New York, 1976. Luckmann and A. Schutz, *The Structures of the Life World*, trans. R. M. Zaner and T. Engelhardt, Heinemann, London, 1974.

13 P. L. Berger, 'The Social Reality of Religion', Faber & Faber, London, 1969. Berger, *A Rumour of Angels: Modern Sociology and the Rediscovery of the Supernatural*, Allen Lane, London, 1970. Berger and T. Luckmann, *The Social Construction of Reality: a Treatise in the Sociology of Knowledge*, Penguin Books, Harmondsworth, 1967.

14 K. Burke, *Language as Symbolic Action: Essays on Life, Literature and Method*, University of California Press, Berkeley, Los Angeles and London, 1966. Burke, *The Rhetoric of Religion: Studies in Logology*, University of California Press, Berkeley and Los Angeles, 1970.

15 C. Geertz, 'Ethos, World View, and the Analysis of Sacred Symbols', in Geertz, *The Interpretation of Cultures*, pp. 140–1.

16 C. Geertz, 'Religion as a Cultural System', in Geertz, *The Interpretation of Cultures*, p. 94.

17 W. H. Auden, 'Progress', in Auden, *Collected Poems*, pp. 663/4.

18 G. Orwell, *Nineteen Eighty-Four*, Penguin Books in assoc. with Secker & Warburg, Harmondsworth and London, 1954, pp. 44–5.

19 See e.g. Burke, *The Rhetoric of Religion*. In the Epilogue Burke plays on that clause of his definition of Man which runs 'Inventor of the negative' or 'Moralized by the negative'. It is a conversation between God and Lucifer in which Lucifer, the negation, is represented as God's most favourite and necessary complement.

20 See e.g. M. Edelman, *Politics as Symbolic Action: Mass Arousal and Quiescence*, Markham Publishing Co., Chicago, 1971.

21 See e.g. the account of the group dynamics of student protest given by K. Maharaj in *My LSE*, edited by J. Abse, Robson Books, London, 1977. The students were in need of a grievance, he writes, and once they had adopted the expedient of occupying the senior common room they felt much better (more solidary); in short the collective action was itself the existential justification for the students' oppositional stance.

22 D. Bell, *The Cultural Contradictions of Capitalism*, Heinemann, London, 1976.

23 C. Geertz, 'Deep Play: Notes on the Balinese Cockfight', in Geertz, *The Interpretation of Cultures*.

24 See e.g. D. A. Martin, *The Breaking of the Image*, Blackwell, Oxford, 1980.

25   Burke, *Language as Symbolic Action*.

26   M. Eliade, *Myth and Reality*, Allen & Unwin, London, 1964, pp. 187–93.

27   ibid., p. 145.

28   ibid., pp. 181–2.

29   ibid., p. 189.

30   ibid., p. 190.

31   For Wilson's sub-categorization of sects see B. R. Wilson (ed.), *Patterns of Sectarianism: organization and ideology in social and religious movements*, Heinemann, London, 1967.

32   D. A. Martin, *Pacifism: An historical & sociological study*, Routledge & Kegan Paul, London, 1963.

33   D. A. Martin, *Tracts Against the Times*, Lutterworth Press, Guildford and London, 1973, especially chapters 1–5.

34   M. Douglas, *Purity and Danger*, Routledge & Kegan Paul, London, 1966. Douglas, *Natural Symbols*, Barrie & Rockliffe, London, 1970, contains a certain amount of direct and implied reference to the 1960s' counter-culture. For Turner, see especially V. W. Turner, *The Ritual Process: Structure and Anti-Structure*, Allen Lane, London, 1969. See also Turner, *Dramas, Fields and Metaphors*, Cornell University Press, Ithaca and London, 1974, in which he discusses the Haight-Ashbury hippies in part of chapter 6, 'Passages, Margins and Poverty: Religious Symbols of Communitas', pp. 261–6.

35   B. Bernstein, *Class, Codes and Control*, vol. I, *Theoretical Studies towards a Sociology of Language*, Routledge & Kegan Paul, London, 1971, especially chapters 2 and 8.

36   M. Bloch, 'Symbols, Song, Dance and Features of Articulation: Is Religion an extreme form of traditional authority?', *European Journal of Sociology*, vol. XV, 1974, pp. 55–81.

37   This argument is implicit rather than explicit in Bernstein's work. He may perhaps, have been hindered in developing a serious discussion of what is involved in the conceptual adequacy necessary for scientific and rational discourse by the ideological wrangles into which his models of class-related linguistic codes thrust him. The argument of the pure relativists who attack Bernstein's work on compensatory education on the grounds that all linguistic codes are equally complex and adequate (for what?), may have made it impossible for Bernstein himself to discuss coolly either (a) the adequacy *for various purposes* of different linguistic codes or (b) the communicative adequacy of different categories of *users* of the same language code.

38   Douglas, *Natural Symbols*, p. 157.

39   The suggestion comes from Rudolph Müller in an M.Phil. thesis in progress, Dept of Sociology, Bedford College, University of London. The context is a discussion of 'conceptual adequacy' and the strategies which come into play when imprecise conceptualization gives rise to unmanageable amounts of 'dirt', i.e. uncategorizable experience lying on the ambiguous margins of the current conceptualizations of a person or group.

40   Douglas, *Natural Symbols*, p. 74.

41   B. Bernstein, *Class, Codes and Control*, 3 vols, Routledge & Kegan Paul, London, 1971–5, see vol. 3, ch. 5.

42   ibid., vol. 3, chapter 6.

43   M. Pawley, *The Private Future: causes and consequences of community collapse in the West*, Thames & Hudson, London, 1973. The dust-cover reads: 'Alone in a centrally heated, air-conditioned capsule, drugged, fed with music and erotic imagery, the pasts of his consciousness separated into components that reach everywhere and nowhere, the private citizen of the future will have become one with the end of effort and the triumph of sensation divorced from action. When the barbarians arrive they will find him like some ancient Greek sage, lost in contemplation, terrified yet fearless, listening to himself....'

44   Turner, *The Ritual Process*.

45   Turner, *Dramas, Fields and Metaphors*. Note especially his interpretation of the martyrdom of St Thomas à Becket and of Hidalgo as, at one level, the assumption of a culturally ready-made role.

CHAPTER 4: *The Kingdom of Terminus*

1   M. Spark, 'You Should Have Seen the Mess', in Spark, *The Go-Away Bird and Other Stories*, Penguin Books, Harmondsworth, 1963, pp. 135–41.

2   M. Douglas, *Purity and Danger*, Routledge & Kegan Paul, London, 1966.

3   Bernstein uses the example of the lavatory to illustrate rigid and loose classification and framing. See the Appendix, 'A Note concerning the coding of objects and modalities of control', to chapter 5, 'Class Pedagogies: Visible and Invisible', in Bernstein, *Class, Codes and Control*, vol. 3, 1975, pp. 151–6.

4   M. Douglas, *Natural Symbols*, Barrie & Rockliffe, London, 1970, p. 158.

5   R. Roberts, *The Classic Slum: Salford life in the first quarter of the century*, Penguin Books, Harmondsworth, 1973. R. Roberts, *A Ragged Schooling: Growing up in the classic slum*, Fontana/Collins, London, 1978.

6   Apart from my own recollections I have interviewed (sometimes with a tape recorder) my own extended kin and a network of their immediate contacts over the past decade. I have also conducted informal discussions without tape recorder in two Retirement Clubs in Bury in 1977.

7   J. Seabrook, *City Close Up*, Allen Lane, London, 1971.

8   G. Pearson, ' "Paki-bashing" in a North East Lancashire Cotton Town: a case study and its history', in G. Mungham and G. Pearson (eds.), *Working Class Youth Culture*, Routledge & Kegan Paul, (*Direct Editions*), London, 1976.

9   M. Carter and P. Jephcott, *The Social Background of Delinquency*, edited by W. J. H. Sprott. Mimeo. 1952, available at the University of Nottingham. Quoted V. Klein, *Samples from English Cultures*, 2 vols, Routledge & Kegan Paul, London, 1965, vol. I, p. 200.

10   J. M. Mogey, *Family and Neighbourhood: two studies of Oxford*, Oxford University Press, Oxford, 1956.

11   cf. Roberts, *The Classic Slum*, p. 75.

12   ibid., p. 116.

13   Mogey, *Family and Neighbourhood*.

14   cf. N. Dennis, F. Henriques and C. Slaughter, *Coal is our Life*, Eyre & Spottiswood, London, 1965. B. Jackson, *Working Class Community*, Routledge & Kegan Paul, London 1968.

15   Roberts, *A Ragged Schooling*, p. 85.
16   A. Oakley, *Housewife*, Allen Lane, London, 1974(a). Oakley, *The Sociology of Housework*, M. Robertson, London, 1974(b), especially chapter 6.
17   N. Dennis et al., *Coal is our Life*.
18   cf. J. Burnett, *Plenty & Want: A social history of diet in England from 1815 to the present day*, Penguin Books, Harmondsworth, 1968.
19   Mogey, *Family and Neighbourhood*.
20   For 'Ship Street', see M. Kerr, *The People of Ship Street*, Routledge & Kegan Paul, London, 1958. For Bethnal Green, M. Young and P. Wilmott, *Family and Kinship in East London*, Routledge & Kegan Paul, London, 1957. For Huddersfield, Jackson, *Working Class Community*. For 'Ashton', Dennis et al., *Coal is our Life*.
21   Roberts, *A Ragged Schooling*, pp. 158–68.
22   Roberts, *The Classic Slum*, p. 177.
23   Roberts, *The Classic Slum*, pp. 55–8, 231–3. Roberts, *A Ragged Schooling*, pp. 48–51, 85–93.
24   B. Bernstein, *Class, Codes & Control*, vol. 1, revised edn., Routledge & Kegan Paul, London, 1973.
25   Seabrook, *City Close Up*, p. 129.
26   Dennis et al., *Coal is our Life*.
27   See also A. E. Green, 'Only Kidding: Joking among coal miners'. Paper presented at the 1978 Conference of the British Sociological Association, University of Sussex. Mimeo. available, A. E. Green, University of Leeds. This paper illustrates both the role-based nature of swearing and a tradition akin to that of the apprentice rituals outlined by Roberts of using highly ritualized 'clichéd' joking as a technique of the work-group solidarity and control.
28   Klein, *Samples from English Cultures*, vol. 1, p. 201.
29   Roberts, *The Classic Slum*, pp. 172–3. See also J. H. Robb, *Working Class Anti-Semite*, Tavistock, London, 1954.
30   There are already signs that some of the ethnic minorities in Britain, especially the Muslims, would prefer segregated schooling, particularly in order to insulate girls from the liberal ethos of sexual equality and informal manners. The tradition of child labour among many of these minority groups is another source of potential friction with the 'enlightened liberal' ethos.
31   Roberts, *A Ragged Schooling*, pp. 73–85.
32   M. Paneth, *Branch Street*, Allen & Unwin, London, 1944.
33   Kerr, *The People of Ship Street*.
34   Mogey, *Family and Neighbourhood*.
35   Klein, *Samples from English Cultures*.
36   R. Hoggart, *The Uses of Literacy*, Penguin Books, Harmondsworth, 1957.
37   Klein, *Samples from English Cultures*, vol. 1, p. 193.
38   Dennis et al., *Coal is our Life*.
39   D. Lockwood, 'Sources of Variation in Working Class Images of Society', in *Sociological Review*, vol. 14, no. 3, Nov. 1966.
40   See e.g. M. Bulmer (ed.), *Working Class Images of Society*, Routledge & Kegan Paul/Social Science Research Council, London, 1975. In a number of the papers in this symposium, the attempt to produce a measure of 'deference'

was unsatisfactory precisely because of the ease with which class *attitude* and class or category *classification* can be confused. See especially the paper on the textile workers, R. Martin and R. H. Fryer, 'The Deferential Worker?' What is important for my argument is the fact that indices of a culture of boundary and control are strongly marked both in the classic home of the deferential traditional worker, i.e. Lancashire textiles (Roberts, for example, refers to his district as solidly Tory), *and* in the classic case of the traditional proletarian, i.e. mining, especially the Ashton study (*Coal is our Life*). A major distinguishing feature may be the greater violence and excess in the liminal state among the traditional proletarian than among the traditional deferential. An issue insufficiently explored by sociologists (as distinct from historians) is the long term effect on voting habits *and social conceptualization* of the fact that the basic alliance in the textile areas of the early nineteenth century in the factory legislation movements was between the textile operatives and Tories against the Liberal mill owners. In mining, by contrast, the workers' movements, though also involving protective legislation, were mobilized against a predominantly Tory and landholding class who owned the mines.

41   J. H. Goldthorpe et al., *The Affluent Worker*, 3 vols, Cambridge University Press, Cambridge, 1968 and 1969.

42   R. Gosling, *Sum Total*, Faber & Faber, London, 1962. See also V. S. Pritchett, *A Cab at the Door*, Penguin Books, Harmondsworth, 1970.

43   R. Firth *et al., Families and their Relatives*, Routledge & Kegan Paul, London, 1969.

44   In Oct. 1978, BBC 2 screened a programme called 'The Living Room' in which all the examples shown were 'eccentric' middle-class rooms, such as an enormous converted church with the telephone in the pulpit (sculptor and writer), and a totally empty and undecorated room in an equally empty house containing the minimum of a mattress and two upright chairs (poets and artists). The emphasis was on the flexible or unstructured space.

45   R. Silverstone, *The Message of Television*, Heinemann, London, 1981.

CHAPTER 5: *The Arts*

1   'The Composer as Librettist: A Conversation between Sir Michael Tippett and Patrick Carnegy', *The Times Literary Supplement*, 8 July 1977, pp. 834–5.

2   A particularly clear account for the layman of the development of expressive ambiguity in music can be found in L. Bernstein, *The Unanswered Question: Six Talks at Harvard*, Harvard University Press, Cambridge (Massachusetts) and London, 1976.

3   E. Gombrich, *The Story of Art*, 13th edn., Phaidon Press, Oxford, 1972, p. 429.

4   M. Bradbury, 'A Dog Engulfed by Sand', in *Encounter*, vol. 52, no. 1, Jan. 1979, pp. 36–42.

5   e.g., J. L. Borges, 'The Circular Ruins', in Borges, *Labyrinths*, edited by D. Yates and J. B. Irby, Penguin Books, Harmondsworth, 1970.

6   See e.g. D. Silverman, 'The Blood of Dreams: Robbe-Grillet's Project'. Mimeo, Dept. of Sociology, Goldsmiths' College, University of London.

7   T. Wolfe, *The Painted Word*, Bantam Books, New York, 1975.

8   P. White, *The Vivisector*, Penguin Books, Harmondsworth, 1973.

9   Gombrich, *The Story of Art*, and Gombrich, *Reflections on a Hobby-Horse*, Phaidon Press, Oxford, 1963.

10 Gombrich, *Reflections on a Hobby-Horse*, especially 'Expression & Communication' and 'Expression and Still Life'.

11 Wolfe, *The Painted Word*, p. 4.

12 ibid., p. 6.

13 See e.g. R. Smith-Brindle, *The New Music: The Avant-Garde since 1945*, Oxford University Press, Oxford, 1975. H. Cole, *Sounds and Signs*, Oxford University Press, Oxford, 1976.

14 A. Koestler, 'Literature and the Law of Diminishing Returns', *Encounter* vol. 34, no. 5, May 1970, pp. 39–45.

15 G. Steiner, *Language and Silence*, Penguin Books, Harmondsworth, 1969, especially chapter 2, 'The Retreat from the Word'.

16 Steiner, *Language and Silence*, p. 56.

17 Steiner, *After Babel*, Oxford University Press, Oxford, 1971.

18 R. Silverstone, *The Message of Television*, Heinemann, London, 1981.

19 T. Tzara, quoted J. Pierre, *Futurism and Dada*, Heron Books, London 1967, p. 118.

20 M. Leiris, quoted D. Ades, *Dada and Surrealism Reviewed*, Arts Council of Great Britain, London, 1978, p. 235.

21 B. S. Johnson, *House Mother Normal*, Collins, London, 1971.

22 J. Fowles, *The French Lieutenant's Woman*, Jonathan Cape, London, 1969.

23 Particularly influential was the Peter Brook production of *Marat/Sade* in London in 1972.

24 T. Gunn, *Moly*, Faber & Faber, London, 1972.

25 H. Hesse, *The Glass Bead Game*, trans. R. Winston and C. Winston, Penguin Books, Harmondsworth, 1972.

26 Hesse, *Klingsor's Last Summer*, trans. R. Winston and C. Winston, Pan Books, London, 1973.

27 Steiner, *Language and Silence*.

28 ibid.

29 T. Stoppard on *Orghast* in *The Times Literary Supplement*, 1 Jan. 1971.

30 Produced by The Other Company at the Almost Free Theatre, London, Jan. 1972.

31 Programme from *Dance* by Dance Group presented at The Place, London, May 1972.

32 K. Stockhausen, quoted Smith-Brindle, *The New Music*, p. 96.

33 K. Emerson, sleeve note for the LP, *Five Bridges*, by the Nice.

34 *Musics* no. 16, Feb. 1978. A good summary of avant-garde innovations can be found also in W. Mellers, 'Turning in to the Natural Law', *The Times Literary Supplement*, Jan. 1971. (This clearly outlines the objectives in music which parallel *Orghast*.) See also a technical manual of avant-garde innovations in

musical notation, E. Karkoschka, 'Das Schriftbild der Neuen Musik', trans. by R. Koenig, Universal Editions, London, 1971. A simple textbook for schools (*sic*) is G. Self, *New Sounds in Class*, Universal Editions, London, 1967.

35   J. Cage, *Silence*, MIT Press, Cambridge (Massachusetts) and London, 1967. R. Kostelanetz (ed.), *John Cage*, Allen Lane, London, 1971.

36   Cage, *Silence*, p. 51.

37   D. Judd, 'Arts in Society', in *New Society*, 20 July 1970.

38   D. Southall interviewed in a BBC 2 television programme, 'Review', 19 May 1971.

39   A. Henri (ed.), *Environments and Happenings*, Thames & Hudson, London, 1975.

40   A. Warhol, quoted P. Gidal, *Andy Warhol: Films and Paintings*, Studio Vista/Dutton, London, 1971.

41   Gidal, *Andy Warhol*.

42   ibid.

43   N. Mailer's review, 'A Transit to Narcissus', is reprinted in B. Bertolucci, *Last Tango in Paris*, Plexus, London, 1976.

CHAPTER 6: *The Underground*

1   D. Ades, *Dada and Surrealism Reviewed*, Arts Council of Great Britain, London, 1978, p. 85.

2   P. Gidal, *Andy Warhol: Films and Paintings*, Studio Vista/Dutton, London, 1971, frontispiece.

3   R. Gosling, *Sum Total*, Faber & Faber, London, 1962.

4   J. Orton, quoted in R. Gosling's review of Orton, *Head to Toe*, Anthony Blond, London, 1972; in *The Times*, 25 Jan. 1972.

5   Gosling, *Sum Total*, pp. 66–7.

6   ibid., p. 94.

7   ibid., p. 73.

8   ibid., p. 73.

9   ibid., p. 72.

10   ibid., p. 72.

11   Nuttall, *Bomb Culture*, McGibbon & Kee, London, 1968, p. 249.

12   ibid., p. 73.

13   ibid., p. 74.

14   ibid., p. 77.

15   ibid., p. 236.

16   ibid., p. 137.

17   ibid., p. 135.

18   ibid., p. 223.

19   ibid., p. 205.

20   ibid., p. 245.

21   ibid., p. 246.

22   ibid., p. 204.

23   ibid., pp. 204–5.

24 ibid., p. 252.
25 R. Neville, *Play Power*, Paladin Books, London, 1971 (1st pub. in hardback, Jonathan Cape, London, 1970).
26 ibid., p. 51.
27 ibid., p. 53.
28 ibid., p. 63.
29 ibid., p. 68.
30 ibid., p. 65.
31 ibid., p. 161.
32 M. Farren and E. Barker, *Watch Out Kids*, Open Gate Books, London, 1972 (no page nos).

CHAPTER 7: *Youth Culture*

1   R. Roberts, *The Classic Slum: Salford Life in the first quarter of the century*, Penguin Books, Harmondsworth, 1973. R. Roberts, *A Ragged Schooling: Growing up in the classic slum*, Fontana/Collins, London, 1978.
2   R. Blythe, *Akenfield: Portrait of an English Village*, Penguin Books, Harmondsworth, 1972.
3   V. Klein, *Samples from English Cultures*, 2 vols, Routledge & Kegan Paul, London, 1965.
4   D. Matza, *Becoming Deviant*, Prentice-Hall: Englewood Cliffs, New Jersey, 1969.
5   P. Rock and S. Cohen, 'The Teddy Boys', in V. Bogdanor and R. Skidelsky (eds.), *The Age of Affluence 1951–64*, Macmillan, London, 1970. See also S. Cohen, *Folk Devils and Moral Panics*, Paladin, St Albans, 1972; T. Jefferson, 'The Cultural Responses of the Teds', in S. Hall and T. Jefferson (eds.), *Resistance through Rituals*, Hutchinson, London, 1976.
6   P. E. Willis, *Profane Culture*, Routledge & Kegan Paul, London, 1978.
7   S. Daniel and P. McGuire (eds.), *The Paint House*, Penguin Books, Harmondsworth, 1972. J. Clarke, 'The Skinheads and the Magical Recovery of Community', in Hall and Jefferson (eds.), *Resistance through Rituals*.
8   D. Hebdige, 'Reggae, Rastas and Rudies', in Hall and Jefferson (eds.), *Resistance through Rituals*. S. Davis & P. Simon 'Reggae Bloodlines' Macmillan, London, 1979.
9   P. E. Willis, *Learning to Labour*, Saxon House, Garnborough, 1977.
10 P. Marsh, E. Rosser and R. Harré, *The Rules of Disorder*, Routledge & Kegan Paul, London, 1978.
11 Clarke, 'The Skinheads and the Magical Recovery of Community'.
12 Daniel and McGuire (eds.), *The Paint House*.
13 P. Wilmott, *Adolescent Boys of East London*, Routledge & Kegan Paul, London, 1966.
14 Daniel and McGuire (eds.), *The Paint House*, p. 55.
15 ibid., p. 25.
16 ibid., p. 35.
17 ibid., p. 113.

18   ibid., p. 73.
19   Willis, *Profane Culture.*
20   ibid., p. 13.
21   P. Corrigan, 'Doing Nothing', in Hall and Jefferson (eds.), *Resistance through Rituals.*
22   T. Wolfe, *The Noonday Underground*, quoted Cohen, *Folk Devils and Moral Panics.*
23   D. Hebdige, 'The Meaning of Mod', in Hall & Jefferson (eds.), *Resistance through Rituals.*
24   Willis, *Profane Culture*, p. 85.
25   ibid., p. 168.
26   ibid., p. 169.
27   Clarke, 'The Skinheads and the Magical Recovery of Community'.

CHAPTER 8: *Rock Music*

1   R. Gosling, *Sum Total*, Faber & Faber, London, 1962.
2   S. Frith, *The Sociology of Rock*, Constable, London, 1978.
3   ibid.
4   T. W. Adorno, 'Jazz' in Adorno, *Prisms*, trans. by S. and S. Weber, Neville Spearman, London, 1967, p. 121.
5   Adorno, 'Jazz', in *Prisms*, p. 123.
6   Mick Jagger, interview in *The Rolling Stones' Story*, BBC Radio 1, March, 1973.
7   M. Zerwin, 'A Lethal Measurement', in R. Kostelanetz (ed.), *John Cage*, Allen Lane, London, 1971.
8   N. Cohn, *AwopBopalooBopalopBamBoom: Pop from the Beginning*, Paladin Books, St Albans, 1970. Cohn, incidentally, is author of the screenplay for the film, *Saturday Night Fever.*
9   Cohn, *Pop from the Beginning*, p. 242.
10   R. Meltzer, *The Aesthetics of Rock*, Something Else Press, New York, 1970, pp. 112–13.
11   ibid., p. 120.
12   Many rock journalists and critics have traced the social history of rock styles, notably C. Gillett, but this is not musicology: see e.g. Gillett, *The Sound of the City*, Sphere Books, London, 1971. One obvious exception, however, is W. Mellers, an academic musicologist, who has written a detailed analysis of the music of the Beatles: W. Mellers, *The Twilight of the Gods*, Faber & Faber, London, 1973.

       In the discussion of the musicology of rock in the text I am indebted to Rudolph Müller, a graduate student of sociology at Bedford College, University of London, and an experienced jazz/rock performer, for many conversations and for the opportunity to consult his unpublished essay, 'A provisional itinerary of musical devices in rock', mimeo, Dept. of Sociology, Bedford College, University of London.
13   Professor G. H. Bantock suggested to me in a private conversation that the sixties' rock festivals were a species of *pastoralia* parallel to the custom of the Versailles court of playing shepherds and shepherdesses.

14   W. Mellers, 'Pop as Ritual in Modern Culture', *The Times Literary Supplement*, 19 Nov. 1971.

15   G. Melly, *Revolt into Style: the pop arts in Britain*, Penguin Books, Harmondsworth, 1970.

16   P. and A. Fowler, 'Log of British Chart Hits 1955–'69', in C. Gillett (ed.), *Rock File*, Pictorial Presentations, London, 1972.

17   Cohn, *Pop from the Beginning*, p. 31.

18   It is easy to forget that the social world out of which the Beatles came is the working-class Kingdom of Terminus which we examined in chapter 4, and although they often make subversive use of them, the staple images in much of their work come out of that world, e.g. 'Penny Lane', 'She's leaving Home', 'When I'm sixty-four, even 'Day in the Life'.

19   Nuttall, *Bomb Culture*.

20   P. Fowler, 'Skins Rule', in Gillett (ed.), *Rock File*, p. 18.

21   A. Scaduto, *Bob Dylan*, Sphere Books, London, 1972, p. 178.

22   ibid., p. 180. See also F. Taylor, 'Dylan disowns his protest songs', in C. McGregor (ed.), *Bob Dylan: A Retrospective*, Picador (Pan Books), London, 1972.

23   Scaduto, *Bob Dylan*, p. 179.

24   ibid., p. 70.

25   G. Murdoch and R. McCron, 'Scoobies, skins and contemporary pop', in *New Society*, no. 547, 29 March 1973.

26   B. Sugarman, 'Involvement in youth culture, academic achievement and conformity in school', *British Journal of Sociology*, vol. 18, 1967.

27   P. Marsh, 'Dole Queue Rock', *New Society*, no. 746, 20 Jan. 1977. J. Gabiel, 'Chaos out of Order', *The Times Educational Supplement*, 24 Dec. 1976.

28   T. Cummings, 'The Northern Discos', in C. Gillett and S. Frith (eds.), *Rock File 3*, Panther Books, London, 1975.

29   S. Frith, 'The Punk Bohemians', *New Society*, no. 805, 9 March 1978.

30   Jagger's avant-garde film, *Performance*, was reissued in London in 1977. The advertisement for it in the London Tube stations ran: 'Ten years ago it was too far ahead of its time. Now you're just ready for it.'

31   T. Palmer, *All you need is Love*, edited by P. Medlicott, Weidenfeld & Nicolson (hardback) and Chappell (paperback), London, 1976.

32   Melly, *Revolt into Style*, p. 8.

33   A. McRobbie and J. Garber, 'Girls and sub-cultures', in Hall and Jefferson, (eds.), *Resistance through Rituals*. M. Meade, 'The degradation of women', in R. S. Denisoff and R. A. Peterson (eds.), *The Sounds of Social Change: studies in popular culture*, Rand McNally, Chicago, 1972.

34   R. Banham, 'Schlock Horror Sensation', *New Society*, no. 856, 1 March 1979.

35   ibid., p. 474.

36   The film wholly misrepresents, indeed completely inverts, the 'acid rock' message of the original *Sergeant Pepper* album: another piquant example of laundering the product for the teenybop market.

37   G. Marcus, *Mystery Train: Images of America in rock 'n' roll music*, Omnibus Press, New York, Sidney and London, 1977.

38   S. Frith and A. McRobbie. Unpublished paper presented at the Conference of

the British Sociological Association on 'Culture', University of Sussex, March 1978. S. Frith, 'Rock and Sexuality', mineo, dept. of Sociology, University of Warwick, Coventry, 1978.

CHAPTER 9: *The Expressive Professions I*

1   W. H. Auden, 'The Protestant Mystics', in Auden *Collected Works*, edited by E. Mendelson, Faber & Faber, London, 1976, p. 50.
2   See e.g. D. A. Martin, 'Revs and Revolution: Church Trends and Theological Fashions', in *Encounter*, vol. 52, no. 1, Jan. 1979.
3   See e.g. Martin, *A Sociology of English Religion*, SCM Press, London, 1967. Also B. Martin and R. Pluck, *Young People's Beliefs*, Board of Education, General Synod of the Church of England, Church House, Westminster, 1976.
4   P. Bourdieu, 'Cultural Reproduction and Social Reproduction', in R. Brown (ed.), *Knowledge, Education and Cultural Change*, Tavistock, London, 1973.
5   B. Martin, 'Progressive education versus the working classes', in *Critical Quarterly*, Winter 1971.
6   Central Advisory Council for Education (England), *Children and their Primary Schools* (Plowden Report), HMSO, 1967, vol. I, p. 87.

CHAPTER 10: *The Expressive Professions II*

1   B. Martin, 'The Mining of the Ivory Tower', in P. Seabury (ed.), *Universities in the western world*, The Free Press/Macmillan, New York and London, 1975; also printed in C. B. Cox and R. Boyson (eds.), *Black Paper 1975*, Dent, London, 1975.
2   See e.g. M. F. D. Young, 'An Approach to the Study of Curricula as Socially Organized Knowledge', in Young (ed.), *Knowledge and Control*, Collier Macmillan, London, 1971. This perspective is challenged on rational (objectivist) grounds by A. Flew, *Sociology, Equality and Education*, Macmillan, London, 1976.
3   T. Curry quoted in *Radio Times* for 15–21 Sept, 1979, p. 93.
4   See e.g. B. R. Wilson (ed.), *Rationality*, Blackwell, Oxford, 1970, particularly 'A Sociologist's Introduction'.
5   I. Illich, *Deschooling Society*, Harper & Row, New York, 1970.
6   Notoriously so in the research appendices of the Plowden Report.
7   See e.g. B. Bernstein, *Class, Codes and Control*, 3 vols, Routledge & Kegan Paul, London, 1971–5, vol 3 chapters 2 and 5.
8   The point seems to be taken as established for instance in J. Karabel and A. H. Halsey, 'Educational Research: A Review and an Interpretation', in Karabel and Halsey (eds.), *Power and Ideology in Education*, Oxford University Press, New York and Oxford, 1977, pp. 69–71.
9   B. Bernstein, 'Class Pedagogies: Visible and Invisible', in Bernstein, *Class, Codes and Control*, vol 3 chapter 6.
10   A. Hargreaves, 'Progressivism and Pupil Autonomy', Occasional Papers, no. 5, Dept. of Sociology, University of Leeds.

11   S. N. Bennett et al., *Teaching Styles and Pupil Progress*, Open Books, London, 1976. S. N. Bennett, 'Recent Research on Teaching: a dream, a belief and a model', in *British Journal of Educational Psychology*, vol. 48, pp. 127–47.

   A report of the School Inspectorate which is in sharp contrast to the assumptions and optimism of the Plowden Report is *Primary Education in England. A Survey of* HM *Inspectors of Schools*, HMSO, 1979. This is highly critical of the 'exploratory' style of teaching and argues that this used alone, without some admixture of 'didactic' teaching, produces lower test scores in basic skills such as reading and mathematics at any given age level.

   See also K. Postlethwaite and C. Denton, *Streams for the Future? The long term effects of early streaming and non-streaming – The Final Report of the Banbury Enquiry*, Pabansco Publications, Banbury, 1978. This finds the case for the pedagogic superiority of non-streamed teaching less than wholly convincing. Again the problem is to isolate the relevant variables in teaching style as they affect pupil success, and in my view the inconclusiveness of this comparison of streaming and non-streaming is in part attributable to the prevalence of *mixed* knowledge codes and pedagogic assumptions underlying apparently comparable classroom styles.

   There is evidence of some disillusion in the United States as well as Britain with 'open' pedagogies, e.g. the City of New York announced in October 1979 the intention to reinstate formal teaching styles, and an emphasis on basic skills in the city schools.

12   M. Rutter et al., *Fifteen Thousand Hours: Secondary Schools and their effects on children*, Open Books, London, 1979. The most significant finding of this research is that its various indices of the successful school (i.e. the one in which pupils are most educationally successful and least delinquent) add up to a profile of a school which is a personalized and integrated community.

13   C. B. Cox and A. E. Dyson (eds.), *Black Papers on Education*, nos 1 and 2, Critical Quarterly Society, London, 1969. C. B. Cox and R. Boyson (eds.), *Black Paper 1975*, Dent, London, 1975. Cox and Boyson (eds.), *Black Paper 1977*, M. T. Smith, London, 1977. The National Council for Educational Standards is the body set up, parallel to the Black papers, to conduct research and publicity.

14   T. S. Szasz, *The Manufacture of Madness*, Routledge & Kegan Paul, London, 1971; *Law, Liberty and Psychiatry: An Enquiry into the Social Uses of Mental Health Practices*, Routledge & Kegan Paul, London, 1974; *The Myth of Mental Illness* Paladin, London, 1972; *Ceremonial Chemistry: the Ritual Persecution of Drugs, Addicts and Pushers*, Routledge & Kegan Paul, London, 1975.

15   'Tailgunner Parkinson', in *New Society*, vol. 49, no. 883, 6 Sept. 1979, p. 524. The point is also well made by S. Rees, 'How misunderstanding occurs', in R. Bailey and M. Brake (eds.), *Radical Social Work*, Edward Arnold, London, 1975.

16   P. Heelas, 'Californian Self-Religions and Socializing the Subjective', mimeo, Dept. of Religious Studies, University of Lancaster, May 1979.

17   C. Campbell, 'The Cult, the Cultic Milieu and Secularization', in M. Hill (ed.),

A Sociological Yearbook of Religion in Britain, no. 5, SCM Press, London, 1972.

18 R. Wallis makes this point in his Inaugural Lecture. See Wallis, 'The Re-birth of the gods: Reflections on the New Religions in the West', The Queen's University, Belfast, May 1978. New Lecture Series, no. 108.

19 The most important source material on the new cults can be found in B. R. Wilson, *Contemporary Transformations of Religion*, Oxford University P ess, Oxford, 1976; C. Y. Glock and R. N. Bellah (eds.), *The New Religious Consciousness*, University of California Press, Berkeley, 1976; I. Zaretsky and M. P. Leone (eds.), *Religious Movements in Contemporary America*, Princeton University Press, Princeton (New Jersey), 1974; Wallis, 'The Re-birth of the Gods'; and *The Contemporary Metamorphoses of Religion*, Acts of the 12th International Conference on the Sociology of Religion (The Hague) 1973. Published CNRS/CISR, Lille, 1973.

20 Wallis, 'The Re-birth of the Gods'.

21 As always one must distinguish between the ideas of the founder/inspirer (Janov) and the movement based on them. Only a part of the Janov movement is developing a theology of reincarnation, and that in a sporadic, piecemeal fashion. (Private communication from P. Razzell, Dept. of Sociology, Bedford College, University of London.)

22 Wallis 'The Re-birth of the Gods'.

23 J. Rubin, *Growing (Up) At Thirty-Seven*, M. Evans & Co., New York, 1976.

24 Information about the development of a commune movement as an offshoot of primal therapy: private communication from P. Razzell, Dept. of Sociology, Bedford College, University of London. On the commune, 'Atlantis', located off the coast of Eire, see: J. James, *To The Limit, Caliban Books*, Firle, forthcoming 1981, and James, *They Call Us the Screamers*, Caliban Books, Firle, forthcoming 1981.

25 The point is particularly strongly made by E. Barker with reference to the Unification Church: Barker, 'Living the Divine Principle', in *Archives de Sciences Sociales des Religions*, vol. 45, no. 1, 1978. J. Beckford argues a similar case: Beckford, 'Cults and Cures', paper presented at the 9th World Congress of Sociology, Uppsala, Sweden, 1978. These writers both point out that most cultic converts from the drug scene have already given up drugs *before* joining the Unification Church, etc. Other commentators have noted (a) that a degree of disillusionment with the secular counter-cultural milieu normally precedes the attachment to a cult, and (b) that the most active political demonstrators in the secular counter-culture are not usually found among these converts. This seems to me to lend weight to a case for regarding these cults as consciously chosen plausibility structures as I argue in the text, rather than as evidence against the view that the cults have an 'integrative' function. See the discussion in Wallis, 'The Re-birth of the Gods', pp. 20–1.

26 See e.g. Barker, 'Living the Divine Principle', in *Archives de Sciences Sociales des Religions*, vol. 45, n. 1. Also, Barker, 'Whose Service is Perfect Freedom', in D. O. Moberg (ed.), *Spiritual Well-Being*, University Press of America, Washington DC 1978.

27 Wallis makes this point: Wallis, 'The Re-birth of the Gods'.

28   J. V. Thurman, 'New Wineskins: A Study of the House Church Movement', MA thesis, Birmingham University, 1979.

29   G. Moyser, 'The Political Organization of the Middle Class: the case of the Church of England'. Privately circulated in 'Papers in Religion and Politics', Manchester University, Summer 1977.

30   M. W. B. Moore, 'Progressive Anglican Clergymen: A Sociological Case Study', mimeo, Keynes College, The University of Kent at Canterbury, 1977. See also Moore, 'The Negotiation of Appropriate Occupational Role', PhD Thesis, University of Kent at Canterbury, 1972.

31   D. Birch, 'Sense and Word in Liturgical Language', in *New Blackfriars*, April 1978, pp. 178–9.

32   ibid., p. 181. The point is made with even more force by V. W. Turner, 'Ritual, Tribal and Catholic', in *Worship Jubilee*, 1977, pp. 504–26.

33   See particularly D. A. Martin (guest ed.), *Crisis for Cranmer and King James*, *P. N. Review*, no. 13, Carcanet Press, Manchester, 1979. This special issue of P. N. Review is an extended case for restoring the Book of Common Prayer and the Authorized Version of the Bible to the mainstream of Anglican practice. It was presented, along with three Petitions signed by leading figures in the arts, education, politics, the judiciary and the armed forces, to the General Synod of the Church of England on 5 Nov. 1979. Clerical response was defensively hostile while the laity and the press were markedly more sympathetic.
   See also B. Morris (ed.), *Ritual Murder*, Carcanet Press, Manchester, 1980.

CHAPTER 11: *A Cultural Revolution?*

1   M. Bradbury, 'A Dog Engulfed by Sand II: Abstraction and Irony', in *Encounter*, vol. 52, no. 1, Jan. 1979, pp. 39/40.

2   W. H. Auden from Shorts II, in Auden, *Collected Poems*, p. 643.

3   E. H. Gombrich, *The Sense of Order*, Phaidon Press, London, 1979.

4   E. H. Gombrich and H. Zerner, '*The Sense of Order*: An Exchange' in *New York Review of Books*, vol. 26, no. 14, 27 Sept. 1979, p. 60.

5   P. Rieff, *The Triumph of the Therapeutic: the Uses of Faith After Freud*, Chatto & Windus, London, 1966.

6   C. Lasch, *Haven in a Heartless World*, Basic Books, New York, 1977, and *The Culture of Narcissism*, Norton, New York, 1978.

7   R. Sennett, *The Fall of Public Man*, Cambridge University Press, Cambridge, 1974, and *The Uses of Disorder: Personal Identity and City Life*, Penguin Books, Harmondsworth, 1973.

8   P. E. Slater, *The Pursuit of Loneliness: American Culture at the breaking-point*, Allen Lane, London, 1970.

9   J. Carroll, *Puritan, Paranoid, Remissive: A Sociology of Modern Culture*, Routledge & Kegan Paul, London, 1977.

10   J. Ogilvy, *Many Dimensional Man: Decentralizing Self, Society and the Sacred*, Oxford University Press, New York, 1977; J. Roszak, *Unfinished Animal: the Aquarian Frontier and the Evolution of Consciousness*, Faber & Faber, London, 1976.

11   J. Nuttall's latest published work is a biography of Frank Randall, an inter-war Lancastrian comedian whose style of crude, vigorous vulgarity and incipient violence clearly appealed to Nuttall as well as to the working-class liminal taste for the gross and 'disgusting' – the belch and fart syndrome in humour. See J. Nuttall, *King Twist: A Biography of Frank Randall*, Routledge & Kegan Paul, London, 1978.

12   I am indebted to Jonathan Chandler for a detailed and convincing account of the mythic in the genre of commercial machismo film in his dissertation on this topic 'John Wayne Ain't No Faggott'. (Dept. of Sociology, Bedford College, University of London).

13   E. Schur, *The Awareness Trap*, Quadrangle, New York, 1976.

14   W. H. Auden, 'Heresies', in Auden, *Collected Works*, p. 48.

Name Index

Subject Index